BMP WORKS 4

13 Award Winning Case Histories from BMP DDB Ltd

Edited and introduced by

Paul Feldwick

Executive Director of Planning
BMP DDB Ltd

NTC PUBLICATIONS LIMITED

For Stanley Pollitt

First published in 1999 by
NTC Publications Limited
Farm Road
Henley-on-Thames
Oxfordshire RG9 1EJ
United Kingdom
Telephone: 01491 411000

A CIP catalogue record for this book is available
from the British Library

ISBN 1 84116 049 0

Produced by NTC Publications Ltd
Printed and bound in Great Britain by
Biddles Ltd, Guildford and King's Lynn

Contents

Welcome to *BMP Works 4*

The full canon of IPA Award winning papers produced by BMP DDB has long been too bulky for all of them to be contained in a single volume of manageable size. In making available for the first time the five winning papers from 1998, we have taken the opportunity to also include three papers from the previous contest in 1996, and a selection of cases from the earlier 1990s.

The choice of what to include and what to drop was not always easy, but we hope the present selection displays a wide range of work that we can justifiably take pride in, as well as illustrating a number of different approaches to the difficulties of quantifying advertising results. The other cases (listed in full after this introduction) can be found somewhere in the first three volumes of *BMP Works* – we believe we still have some back numbers if anyone would like to ask – and, of course, in the various volumes of *Advertising Works*, the books of winners published by the IPA and from which, with their kind permission, these cases are now reproduced.

BMP DDB continues to head the various league tables which collect results from the major creative advertising awards – as for instance, the following (reproduced from *Campaign*):

CAMPAIGN'S 30TH ANNIVERSARY CREATIVITY LEAGUE TABLE

	Agency	Total Points
1.	**BMP DDB**	**4715**
2.	Saatchi & Saatchi	4360
3.	Collett Dickenson Pearce	4280
4.	TBWA GGT Simons Palmer	2350
5.	Bartle Bogle Hegarty	2300
6.	Abbott Mead Vickers. BBDO	2185
7.	Lowe Howard-Spink	1915
8.	J. Walter Thompson	1225
9.	Leagas Delaney	970
10.	WCRS	770

We have always valued creative awards highly. But not more highly than we value the IPA Effectiveness Awards. The ultimate purpose for which we do whatever we do must be the benefit of our clients businesses. And our dominance of the effectiveness league table is, if anything, even clearer:

IPA ADVERTISING EFFECTIVENESS AWARDS 1980-1998

	Grand Prix	Gold/ 5*	Silver/ 4*	Bronze/ 3*	Total
BMP DDB	**4**	**17**	**14**	**7**	**42**
J. Walter Thompson	1	6	6	-	13
WCRS	1	3	1	7	12
Bartle Bogle Hegarty	–	2	5	–	7
Duckworth Finn Grubb	1	1	1	3	6
Saatchi & Saatchi	–	2	1	2	5
Abbott Mead Vickers. BBDO	1	1	1	1	4
Ogilvy & Mather	1	–	3	–	4
TBWA GGT Simons Palmer	–	1	3	1	4
FCB	1	1	–	1	3

One criticism that is sometimes levelled at the IPA Awards is that of all the hundreds of campaigns produced each year in the UK, only a relative few are able to produce a plausible entry – let alone a top award winner. The imputation is that advertising success is a relatively rare commodity.

What we know from experience is that producing a rigorous case for success is not easy. The campaign must have succeeded (not all do), there must be sufficient research data of a reliable kind to demonstrate this fact (which is, depressingly often, not the case) – finally, the client must be happy to disclose the results publicly (and some have particular reasons for not wanting to do this).

However, if we look at a list of our agency's fifteen largest clients (in terms of 1998 billings) – which between them represent over 80% of the agency's total turnover – no less than nine out of these fifteen have received at least one IPA Effectiveness Award in the past ten years, and some more than one:

Volkswagen	2
Meat and Livestock Commission	1
Barclaycard	2
Johnson and Johnson	1
Anheuser-Busch	1
Friskies Petcare	1
Alliance and Leicester	3
Van den Bergh Foods	1
Bestfoods	2

(NB Van den Bergh and Bestfoods also received awards in the earlier years.)

Of the other six of our top fifteen clients, three – ONdigital, National Savings, and Reuters – only appointed BMP DDB after the 1998 awards, and so clearly have had no opportunity as yet to enter. (And as for the other three – we'll keep working on it.)

In other words, our success in the IPA Effectiveness Awards is not peripheral or limited to a couple of atypical clients – it runs right through the heart of our business.

Other critics have pointed out – sometimes with glee – the number of occasions on which IPA Award winning brands have subsequently failed, or where the successful agency shortly afterwards lost the account. Certainly both these things have happened and each story is probably unique as to why. Two years after the Walker's campaign had won a Silver award in 1996 (p.105), the account was moved to another agency as a result of a decision taken in New York to align the brand with a single network worldwide – a decision that was widely criticised in the trade press. The new agency has continued with the Gary Lineker campaign that BMP DDB created. The Frizzell insurance brand, another 1996 Silver winner (not included here) was sold to the Liverpool Victoria for £180m – £80 more than it had been sold for four years previously. The new owners seem to have decided to abandon the Frizzell name, despite its considerable and distinctive consumer equity.

The fact is that no advertising campaign, no matter how successful, can guarantee a brand's success in perpetuity. The nearest we can find to an exception is the PG Tips campaign (p.209), already thirty-five years old when the case won the Grand Prix back in 1990. But the key facts here are that the client has remained committed to the central executional idea throughout that time without fundamentally changing it (nor, we are glad to say, the agency); while the campaign, and the brand as a whole, have also responded and adapted in numerous ways to changing circumstances, and in order to keep up to date.

Conversely, those IPA Award winners that subsequently 'fail' can nearly always be seen to do so for one or more of the following reasons:

1. Ownership or structure of the client management changed.

2. The successful advertising, or other aspects of the marketing were changed, either deliberately or as a result of external circumstances.

3. Competitive or environmental change made the existing strategy no longer adequate.

4. The brand was deemed to be no longer viable or at least, viable as an advertised brand (either as a result of (3) or, in the case of new brand launches, failure to achieve critical mass).

5. Advertising support was reduced or removed.

None of these invalidate the success chronicled in the original case study. It just goes to show that brands are continually facing changing situations and new challenges, and having to respond and adapt accordingly.

Consider, for example, **Volkswagen**. In an earlier paper (*BMP Works 2*) we reported on how advertising for the Golf between 1984 and 1990 had defended the brand's share and increased its profitability in the face of strong competition. But hardly was this paper completed before Volkswagen began to face new problems in the UK market – a combination of heavy advertising from continental competitors, and consumer perceptions (largely exaggerated) that the marque was outside their price range, led to three years of declining brand share. How we helped Volkswagen UK respond to this situation, and the resulting growth of share to unprecedented heights, you may read below (p 67). You will see that while remaining true to the brand's core values, we employed new thinking and a substantially new approach. This did not mean that the previous decade's campaign was wrong or ineffective – just that the world moves on, and there is no room for complacency just because you have won an IPA Award.

To be successful, it is not enough for a brand to have one great advertising campaign at one point in time. For long term profitable growth, there needs to be a long-term commitment to advertising support; the brand also needs to get the executional balance right between consistency over time, and the ability to change and adapt, sometimes radically, when it is right to do so. **Marmite** exemplifies all these points. Since 1975 the brand has enjoyed continued growth, fuelled by advertising support, while not being afraid to move in the 1980s from a 'mother and baby' approach to a much more hard-hitting, adult-directed set of messages in 'Soldiers' and more recently the 'Love-Hate' campaign.

And thinking of advertising as a response to changing environmental pressures, few brands can have had such a hostile environment in the last few years as red meat in general and beef in particular. Already dogged with negative imagery and a set of (mainly unfounded) health criticisms, the explosion of the BSE crisis in 1996 could have been disastrous. While some might have been tempted to keep quiet until things got better, the **Meat and Livestock Commission** case (p.351) demonstrates that a sensitive dramatisation of the product's benefits combined with a factual information campaign stopped the fall in red meat consumption and then even increased it.

It is sometimes questioned whether advertising can influence total category consumption as opposed to simply shifting brand shares. Our experience is that it certainly can, and the MLC case is not the only example we know of: the only reason it doesn't happen more often is that industry committees do not always succeed in collaborating and in making a long-term commitment to advertising support as the MLC have so effectively done.

In the case of Johnson and Johnson's **Clean and Clear**, we responded to evidence that the existing campaign, a direct adaptation of the US campaign, was underperforming in sales terms, and to research that explained the advertising was failing to achieve sufficient impact or credibility because it was not speaking to its target audience – teenage girls – in their own language. (And if there is one secret of success in all advertising, it must be 'Know your audience'). The new campaign for Clean and Clear continued to follow the basic strategic concept of the US execution – the idea of 'girls talking' – but was interpreted so that these were more clearly 'real girls' that the target group could relate to. As a result the brand enjoyed an immediate uplift in share and within two years has achieved its objective of taking brand leadership in the category from Procter and Gamble!

The last of our 1998 winners and of the new papers included here was another launch, which succeeded by understanding correctly the mood of its young target audience. **Bud Ice**, clearly positioned as 'the party beer', had within two years of its launch overtaken other established brands in the 'Ice beer' sector to vie for brand leadership. What is particularly interesting about this case is that, far from cannibalising the parent Budweiser brand, the advertising for Bud Ice can be shown to have strengthened the parent and increased its sales.

Each of these five new cases, like all the others in the book, has been honoured by an IPA Effectiveness Award because it shows, convincingly, how advertising made a real contribution to the advertiser's business. In the short term this contribution can generally be estimated with quite a high degree of accuracy. But these immediate effects also tend to understate the true benefit of advertising. Each of these brands (or categories) is in a far stronger position after the advertising than it was before – with an expectation of increased sales still to be realised in the future, and more resilient to future attack. It is this increased strength of position that is often called 'brand equity' and it is a real benefit of advertising – sometimes, a very important benefit. However, because this is to do with future potential performance, rather than actual accomplished performance, it is impossible to put a finite value on. As some past IPA cases suggest, events, either internally or externally generated, can easily threaten the most confident forecasts – it is for this reason that attempts to quantify the value of 'brand equity' are inevitably subjective, and must be based on certain assumptions that may or may not be borne out in practice.

Nevertheless, it is in these longer term and cumulative benefits of effective advertising that we must look for the full value of a return on advertising investment: a return that can sometimes be the difference between a brand that continues to grow and prosper, and a brand that has effectively ceased to exist.

We hope you find these papers interesting and a valuable reminder of the power of effective advertising. If you would like to discuss any of them further, or to find out how we might be able to help your own business, please don't hesitate to call Chris Cowpe on 020 7258 4301. He'd be delighted to hear from you.

BMP DDB
Prize Winners 1980-1998

1980 IPA ADVERTISING EFFECTIVENESS AWARDS

How advertising helped make Krona brand leader
Stephen Benson for *Van den Bergh Foods*
Category: New Products, Consumer Goods and Services *First Prize and Grand Prix*

The launch of Tjaereborg Rejser
Damian O'Malley for *Tjaereborg Rejser*
Category: Direct Response: Consumer Goods and Services *First Prize*

Swan Vesta Matches
Nigel Beard for *Bryant & May*
Category: Established Products: Consumer Goods and Services *Certificate of Commendation*

1982 IPA ADVERTISING EFFECTIVENESS AWARDS

The 'Big John' campaign: Advertising in the beer market
James Best and Tim Broadbent for *Courage*
Category: Established Consumer Goods *First Prize and Grand Prix*

Home protection: How advertising helps fight crime
Chris Cowpe for *Central Office of Information*
Category: Special *First Prize*

How advertising helped Frish refresh a market
Ian Crammond for *Lever Brothers*
Category: New Consumer Goods *Certificate of Commendation*

1984 IPA ADVERTISING EFFECTIVENESS AWARDS

Hofmeister: A study of advertising and brand imagery in the lager market
Peter Field and Adam Morgan for *Courage*
Category: Established Consumer Goods and Services *First Prize*

The repositioning of Hellmann's Mayonnaise
Paul Feldwick for *CPC (UK)*
Category: Established Consumer Goods and Services *Second Prize*

Chip pan fire prevention 1976-84
Chris Cowpe for *Central Office of Information*
Category: Special *Second Prize*

Home protection revisited: The national rollout of a regional test
Sandra Yarwood and Chris Cowpe for *Central Office of Information*
Category: Special *Certificate of Commendation*

1986 IPA ADVERTISING EFFECTIVENESS AWARDS

Kensington Palace
Giles Lury and Nigel Beard for *The Department of the Environment*
Category: Small Budgets *First Prize*

The GLC's anti-paving bill campaign: Advancing the science of political issue advertising
Dennis Robb for *The GLC*
Category: Special *Second Prize*

The repositioning of Mazola
Tony McGuinness for *CPC (UK) Ltd*
Category: Established Consumer Goods and Services *Certificate of Commendation*

1988 IPA ADVERTISING EFFECTIVENESS AWARDS

The launch of Miller Lite
Nigel Jones for *Courage*
Category: New Consumer Goods and Services *First Prize*

Going for the heart of a market: Kia-Ora orange squash 1983-86
Antony Buck for *Schweppes*
Category: Established Consumer Goods and Services *First Prize*

Clarks Desert Boots
Antony Buck for *Clarks*
Category: Small Budgets *First Prize*

Alliance and Leicester: Advertising for success in the financial market
Yvonne Maclean for *Alliance and Leicester*
Category: Special *Second Prize*

Quaker Harvest Chewy Bars: How advertising established the leading personality in an emerging market
Martin Deboo for *Quaker*
Category: New Consumer Goods and Services *Certificate of Commendation*

1990 IPA ADVERTISING EFFECTIVENESS AWARDS

How the chimps have kept PG Tips brand leader through 35 years of intense competition
Clive Cooper, Louise Cook and Nigel Jones for *Brooke Bond Foods*
Category: Longer and Broader Effects *First Prize and Grand Prix*

Marketing sleep: The relaunch of Karvol
Diana Redhouse and Les Binet for *Crookes Healthcare*
Category: Established Consumer Goods and Services *First Prize*

Alliance and Leicester: First time buyer mortgages
Antony Buck for *Alliance and Leicester*
Category: Special *First Prize*

Knorr Stock Cubes: How thinking local helped CPC develop advertising which toppled the brand leader
Sarah Carter and Louise Cook for *CPC*
Category: Established Consumer Goods and Services *Second Prize*

Value for money in charity advertising: Advertising for Amnesty International 1988-1990
John Grant and Les Binet for *Amnesty International*
Category: Small Budgets *Second Prize*

Hogshead revisited: How advertising helped accelerate the development of Aberlour Malt Whisky
Ian Forth for *Campbell Distillers*
Category: Small Budgets *Third Prize*

Vote Valley! Changing one agenda in a local government debate
Richard Hunt for *Charlton Athletic Supporters Club*
Category: Special *Chairman of Judges Prize*

1992 IPA ADVERTISING EFFECTIVENESS AWARDS

National Dairy Council: The Milkman relaunch
John Grant for *National Dairy Council*
Category: Established Consumer Goods and Services *First Prize and Grand Prix*

Scottish Amicable: How it paid to be Amicable
Richard Storey for *Scottish Amicable*
Category: Special *First Prize*

The Volkswagen Golf 1984-1990
Gavin Macdonald and Antony Buck for *VAG UK Ltd*
Category: Longer and Broader Effects *Second Prize*

The launch of Gini
Anneke Elwes for *Schweppes GB*
Category: New Consumer Goods and Services *Second Prize*

Alliance and Leicester Building Society: Advertising effectiveness 1987-1991
Will Collin and Les Binet for *Alliance and Leicester*
Category: Special *Second Prize*

An eye to the future: The role of advertising in raising Optrex's defences
Louise Cook, Anna Hutson and Diana Redhouse for *Crookes Healthcare*
Category: Longer and Broader Effects *Certificate of Commendation*

Barclaycard: How a bungling secret agent did more than you'd credit
Sarah Carter for *Barclaycard*
Category: Special *Certificate of Commendation*

1994 IPA ADVERTISING EFFECTIVENESS AWARDS

HEA AIDS Advertising: The effective use of mass media advertising to meet the challenge of AIDS
Louise Whittet for *The Health Education Authority*
Category: Advertising Over The Longer Term *Silver*

The Launch of CICA: How advertising helped Clarks gain entry into the premium trainer market
Colin Mitchell for *Clarks Shoes*
Category: New Brands or Advertisers *Bronze*

"A widget we have got": How advertising helped John Smith's Bitter to break into an established market
Dean Webb and Richard Butterworth for *Courage Limited*
Category: New Campaigns For Previously Advertised Brands *Bronze*

How advertising helped Strepsils to grab a market by the throat
Malcolm White and Les Binet for *Crookes Healthcare Limited*
Category: New Campaigns For Previously Advertised Brands *Bronze*

National Dairy Council: The riddle of twin peaks
Rachel Hatton for *The National Dairy Council*
Category: New Campaigns For Previously Advertised Brands *Bronze*

1996 IPA ADVERTISING EFFECTIVENESS AWARDS

Barclaycard: 'Put it away Bough!'
Paul Feldwick, Sarah Carter and Louise Cook for *Barclaycard*
Category: Long-Running Campaigns *Gold*

Garymania!
Gavin Macdonald and Jeff Lush for *Walkers Snack Foods*
Category: New Campaigns *Silver*

Felix: How the cat that crept got the cream
Richard Butterworth and Les Binet for *Spillers Petfoods*
Category: New Launches *Silver*

Frizzell Insurance: When the customer is not always right
Diana Redhouse and Les Binet for *Frizzell Financial Services*
Category: New Launches *Bronze*

'No use crying': How advertising prevented milk from getting spilt
Rachel Hatton for *The National Dairy Council*
Category: New Campaigns *Commended*

Frizzell Insurance: When the customer is not always right
Diana Redhouse and Les Binet for *Frizzell Financial Services*
Category: Special Prizes *Special Prize*

1998 IPA ADVERTISING EFFECTIVENESS AWARDS

Marmite
Lucy Jameson and Les Binet for *Bestfoods UK Ltd* *5 Star*

Volkswagen
Richard Butterworth, Cathy Reid and Les Binet for *Volkswagen (UK) Ltd* *5 Star*

Red Meat
Sarah Carter and Sam Dias for *Meat and Livestock Commission* *4 Star*

Johnson's Clean & Clear
Polly Evelegh and Sam Dias for *Johnson & Johnson* *3 Star*

Bud Ice
Matt Willifer and Les Binet for *Anheuser-Busch European Trade Ltd* *2 Star*

1

Johnson's Clean & Clear

Global advertising in a local market

ABOUT THE PAPER

This paper demonstrates that the global advertising idea can be more effective in a particular country if the advertising in that country is not simply adopted and translated, but instead, that the global advertising is re-interpreted for the local market, using insightful, local consumer understanding.

The Vision for Clean & Clear in the UK

Johnson's Clean & Clear was launched in the US in 1991 and then in the UK in 1992, using both the American positioning and advertising.

While the brand grew, it became alarmingly clear that the brand was not going to meet its objectives. The majority of the brand's growth was due to aggregate distribution gains, due to new product launches, rather than consumer demand. The brand was not establishing a positive relationship with teenage girls and J&J's objective of nurturing young consumers for the future of the Johnson's portfolio was not going to be met.

The problem lay with the translation of the American advertising into English, which UK girls found difficult to relate to. It was clear that we needed to make the promise come alive and become 'real' for UK teenage girls.

Results and Payback

Within just one year of new locally tailored advertising the brand fulfilled all of the objectives set: becoming the No. 1 brand in the medicated skincare market and becoming the most popular brand among female teenagers and forging an empathetic relationship with them.

An econometric model, which accounted for all the factors that could have driven growth, proved that the new advertising was the sole reason for success. The new advertising was far more effective at generating a return – in fact the return was 30 times bigger. Furthermore, Clean & Clear now enjoys over half a million female teenage buyers who are empathetic towards the brand and as such Johnson & Johnson has half a million potential adult Johnson's users.

INTRODUCTION

This paper attempts to show that a global advertising idea can be more effective in a particular country if the advertising in that country is not simply a 'translation' of the global idea, but instead a 'reinterpretation' of the idea based on insightful, local consumer understanding.

This particular story concerns a medicated skincare brand that began life in the USA and was then launched successfully in the UK using 'translations' of the American advertising. The brand's performance was however subsequently significantly improved in the UK, when this advertising was replaced by local 'reinterpretations' of the core American creative idea.

BACKGROUND

The Heritage

By 1990, Johnson & Johnson (J&J) was the proud parent of a healthy brand called Johnson's Baby in both the USA and the UK.[1] As a result, the 'Johnson's' name had a strong reputation for gentleness, care, trust and expertise in babies' skin.

J&J recognised that the name, Johnson's, known for expertise in babies' skin, might have credibility outside the baby market on the basis that the baby market is seen to be the most exacting skincare market.

They therefore decided to develop a series of sub-brands under the Johnson's name, with each sub-brand being specifically targeted at different lifestages.

The Teenage Brand Concept

Because they had a relevant technological lead, J&J first launched a medicated skincare range targeting female teenagers.[2] They launched this under the Clean & Clear name, which they bought from Revlon.[3] Prior to this, Clean & Clear had been a very small and unremarkable adult skincare range, but J&J believed the name was suitable for the medicated market, hence the decision to purchase it. The vision was to make Clean & Clear 'The global leader in female teen skincare'.[4]

Why did they target female teenagers?
Because they:

— have spots;

---

1. Johnson's Baby was launched in the USA at the end of the nineteenth century and in the UK in the 1920s.
2. The medicated skincare market consists of products that help to get rid of existing spots (treatment products) and to a lesser extent products that offer ways to prevent spots (preventive products). Both are used largely by teenagers.
3. Johnson's Consumer Products acquired the worldwide rights to the Clean & Clear name and products in 1991.
4. Clean & Clear Brand Footprint.

— use a lot of medicated products, and;

— more importantly, they would grow up to be potential adult buyers of other Johnson's sub-brands,[5] and by demonstrating understanding and skincare expertise to this audience now, there was the hope that they would carry this belief with them as they grow older.

J&J's Clean & Clear was launched in the UK in 1992, following its successful launch in the USA in 1991.

CLEAN & CLEAR IN THE UK FROM 1992 TO 1996

Despite Clean & Clear's previous existence, in 1992 it was virtually unknown among teenagers.[6] Hence, this was effectively a completely new launch to the female teenage medicated consumer.

The Market

Prior to Clean & Clear's relaunch, the medicated market was dominated by three brands (Table 1).[7]

TABLE 1: THE UK MEDICATED MARKET 1991

	Owned by	Value share	Adspend
Clearasil	P&G	38.2	£2.8m
Biactol	P&G	30.5	£2.0m
Oxy	Smithkline Beecham	12.2	£0.9m
Others	Various	19.1	£0.1m

Source: Nielsen/MEAL

P&G owned both Clearasil and Biactol; both were long-established brands, characterised by angst-ridden advertising: Oxy was launched in the 1980s and was known for its radical, humorous advertising, 'Blitz those zits with Oxy'.[8] All had been heavily supported since 1980 (Table 2).

5. J&J launched Johnson's pH5.5 in 1993, targeting adults, and as future mums they were potential buyers of Johnson's Kids, launched in July 1994, and of course, Johnson's Baby.
6. Clean & Clear had existed as an extremely basic skincare range targeted at adult women. It had had little support (MEAL registers only £117,000 between 1978 and 1991).
7. When looking at medicated skincare products in aggregate it is usual to talk in terms of value rather than volume, as some products are high value/low volume (for example, Invisible Treatment Gel) while for other products the reverse is true (for example, Facial Wash).
8. Clearasil and Biactol have historically been advertised and continue to be advertised in a way that plays on teenagers' anxiety about having spots. Oxy, however, broke the mould with a humourous advertising campaign which entered into the 'playground parlance' of teenagers.

TABLE 2: COMPETITIVE MEDICATED BRANDS PRIOR TO CLEAN & CLEAR

Brand	Launch	Target	Benefit	Character	Adpsend since 1980
Clearasil	Pre-1970s	a) Girls and b) boys	Gets rid of spots	Reassuring medical	£20m
Biactol	1970s	a) Boys and b) girls	Facial wash that gets rid of spots	Reassuring medical	£13m
Oxy	1980s	All against spots	Powerful humorous	Streetwise	£5m

Source: MEAL/J&J

Marketing Objectives

Against this tough market background the objectives for Clean & Clear were to:

1. Become the No. 1 medicated skincare brand by value.
2. Become the most popular medicated brand among female teenagers.
3. Establish a relationship with teenage girls that would lead to loyalty to Johnson's for the rest of their lives. This meant getting teenage girls to believe that Johnson's understood them and their needs.

J&J believed this was possible beacause there was a gap in the market. No other brand offered teenage girls their very own skincare range. Clean & Clear's global positioning uniquely filled this gap: a combination of medicated products with adult feminine, skincaring values.[9]

Getting Medicated

Part of the task of transforming Clean & Clear into a medicated brand was launching new products (Table 3).[10]

9. Teenage girls want to look after their skin like grown-up women but they need to use medicated products because they have spot-prone skin. They therefore fall between two stools: on the one side there are products offering feminine, caring values but no medicated efficacy, while on the other side there are medicated products that lack the feminine, caring values. Clean & Clear was positioned to fill this gap. Part of this was focusing on the benefits of clean and clear skin, rather than simply getting rid of spots which the competitors did at the time.
10. Includes products launched in 1997 to give the complete picture.

TABLE 3: CLEAN & CLEAR'S PRODUCT RANGE TO 1997

	Pre 1992 (Revlon)	1992	1993 (Johnson & Johnson)	1994	1995	1996	1997
Cleansing Gel 200ml	x D						
Cleansing Lotion 200ml	x D						
Moisturiser 100ml	x D						
Cleansing Bar 100g		x	x	x	x	D	
Facial Wash 150ml		x	x	x	x	x	D
Cleansing Milk 200ml		x	x	x	x	x	D
Cleansing Lotion 200ml		x	x	x	x	x	x
Sensitive Cleansing Lotion 200ml		x	x	x	x	x	x
Deep Cleansing Cream Wash 150ml	x	x	x	x	x	x	
Invisible Treatment Gel Regular 20ml				x	x	x *	
Invisible Treatment Gel Sensitive 20ml				x	x	x †	
Exfoliating Daily Wash 150ml						x	x
Skin Balancing Moisturiser 100ml					x	x	
Clear Skin daily Treatment 40ml						x	
2-in-1 Treatment Stick 4.6ml						x	

D = Discontinued
* Now in Boots only
† Now discontinued
Source: J&J

Advertising

In keeping with Johnson & Johnson's 'Best Practise' policy for global brands,[11] the UK adopted the US advertising. These were translated by BMP DDB into English, using English girls and their colloquialisms.[12]

The television advertising, 'Girls Talking', featured confident 'Girls Talking' about how they did not worry about spots because they used Clean & Clear. The idea had emerged from the observation that teenage girls spend a lot of time talking about spots among themselves. Press advertising also ran. The ads ran in the UK from 1993 to 1996, as shown in Table 4.

TABLE 4: CLEAN & CLEAR MEDIA PLAN 1993 TO 1996

	£000	Jan	Feb	Mar	Apr	May	Jun	Jul	Aug	Sep	Oct	Nov	Dec	Annual Total
1993	TV				438									438
	Press													
1994	TV			600										600
	Press									65	92	90	28	275
1995	TV								128					128
	Press	4	0	44	74	101	32	53	117	107	134	90	81	836
1996	TV		395								125			520
	Press	36					90							126

11. J&J's Best Practice policy results in something that is proven to work in one country being adopted, with minor adaptations, for another country, with the aim of creating a global identity.
12. There were a number of different films, edits and cutdowns.

US 'GIRLS TALKING AD'

Yeah, I use it as an ice-breaker – a conversation piece.

(FVO) Introducing Johnson's Clean & Clear – an oil-controlling astringent.

I'm not going to lose sleep, or not go out over this here today, gone tomorrow, I'm just going to ruin your life today, thing.

(FVO) Deep cleaning with a pharmaceutical ingredient no leading astringent has.

Zit – I mean what's that?

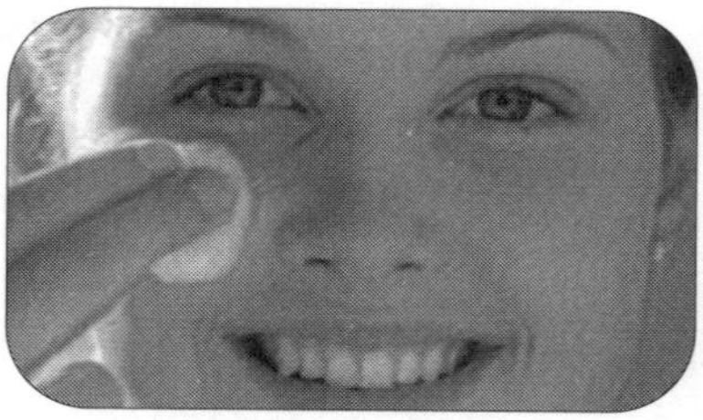

(FVO) It actually helps prevent pimples. Skin is clean, beautifully clear and under control.

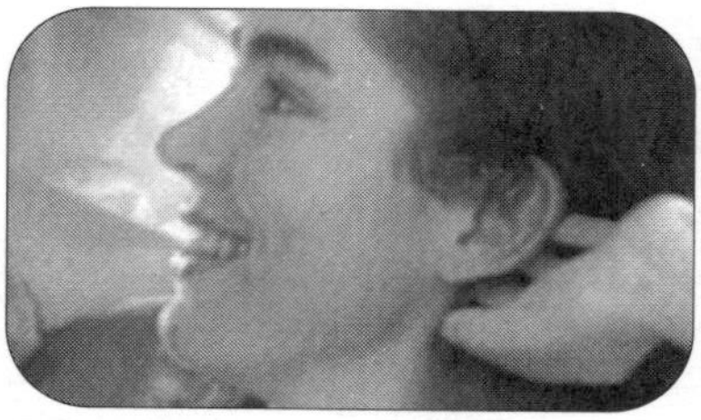

Can you handle it, I can handle it.

Clean & Clear and under control.

UK 'GIRLS TALKING AD'

As you get older you definitely feel more in control of your skin.

When your skin is clear and clean ...

... that tends to make you feel healthier.

(VO) Johnson's Clean & Clear is clinically tested to effectively remove everyday dirt and grease.

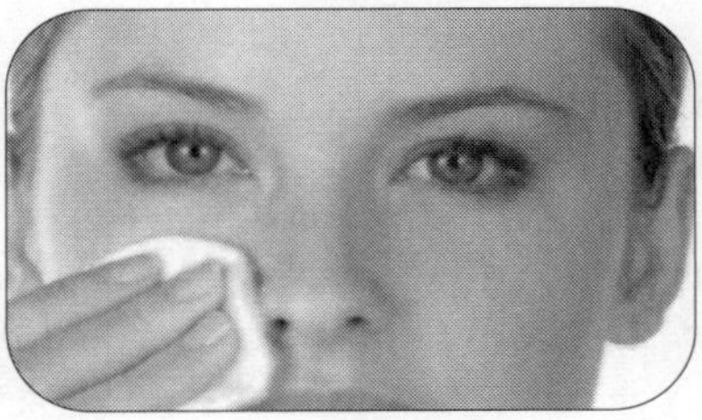

(VO) Clean skin is the secret of clear skin.

The thing is to get a boyfriend with glasses ...

... and then hide his glasses.

(VO) Johnson's Clean & Clear and under control.

UK PERFORMANCE 1992 TO 1996

Clean & Clear's value share increased significantly over the period of the 'Girls Talking' campaign (Figure 1).

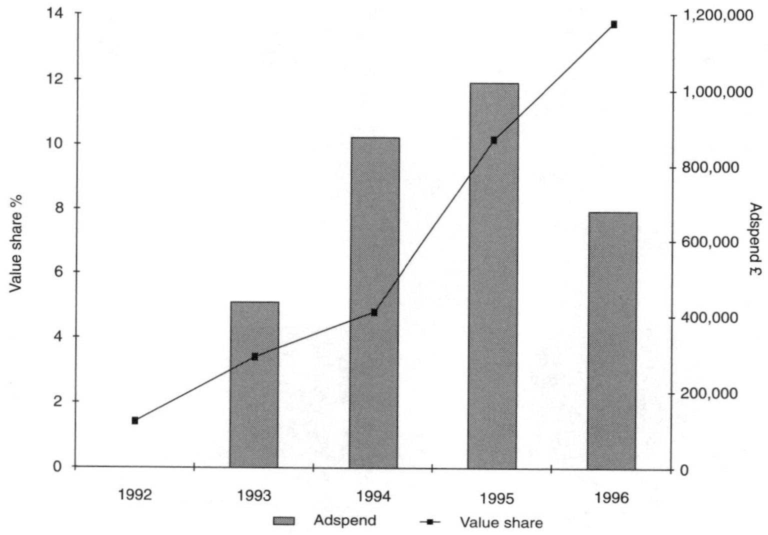

Figure 1: *Clean & Clear value share of the medicated market and adspend*
Source: IRI /MEAL

However, despite this growth there were worrying signals beneath the surface.

WARNING SIGNS

After five years, Clean & Clear had still not achieved its objectives: it was not the No. 1 medicated brand and it was not the most popular brand among teenage girls, which suggested that it was not establishing the depth of relationship that had been hoped for (Tables 5 and 6).

TABLE 5: BRAND VALUE SHARE OF MEDICATED MARKET %

Oxy	23
Clearasil	19
Clean & Clear	14
Biactol	12
Others	33

Source: IRI Infoscan four weeks ending December 1996

TABLE 6: BRAND VALUE SHARE AMONG TEENAGE GIRLS %

Oxy	46
Clearasil	21
Clean & Clear	20
Biactol	7
Others	6

Base: 13 to 18-year-old female buyers
Source: Taylor Nelson year ending 7 April 1996

In addition, there were indications that the future growth needed to meet its objectives would not be forthcoming with the current marketing and advertising strategy. Although sales were rising:

Warning sign 1: Growth was being generated by distribution gains rather than consumer demand

We have already seen that ten new products were launched between 1992 and 1996. The products were high quality and the J&J salesforce was good at selling them into the trade (Figure 2).[13]

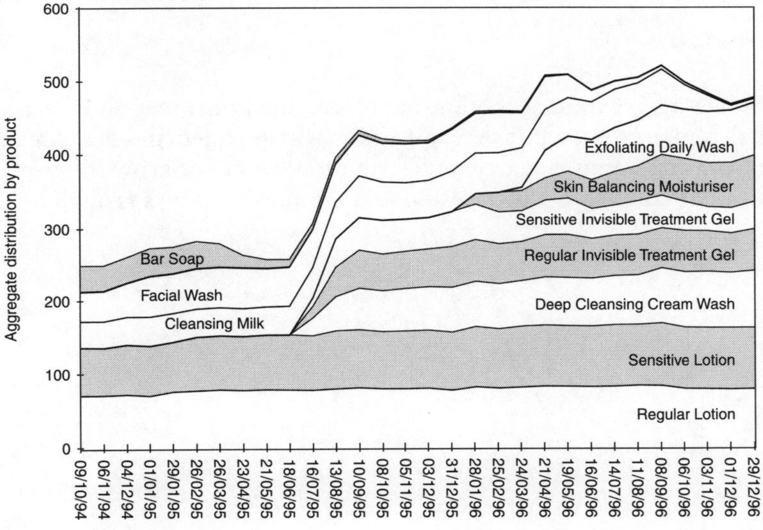

Figure 2: *Clean & Clear distribution by product*
Source: IRI

However, while new products were being launched the stockturn of the brand was slowing down (see Figure 3).[14] (The 1996 uplift is due to a new product promotion, where a free sachet of a new product was attached to a press ad.)

13. Figure 2 shows 'aggregate distribution' which is the sum of the distribution facings for each product. So if four products each have 100% distribution, 'aggregate distribution' is 400%. Aggregate distribution can be a more meaningful way of summarising a brand's distribution when it exists in many varieties.
14. Stockturn measures the rate at which the total brand's products are moving off the shelf. It is measured by dividing total value sales by aggregate distribution. It therefore takes into account the breadth (distribution in stores) and the depth (facings) of distribution.

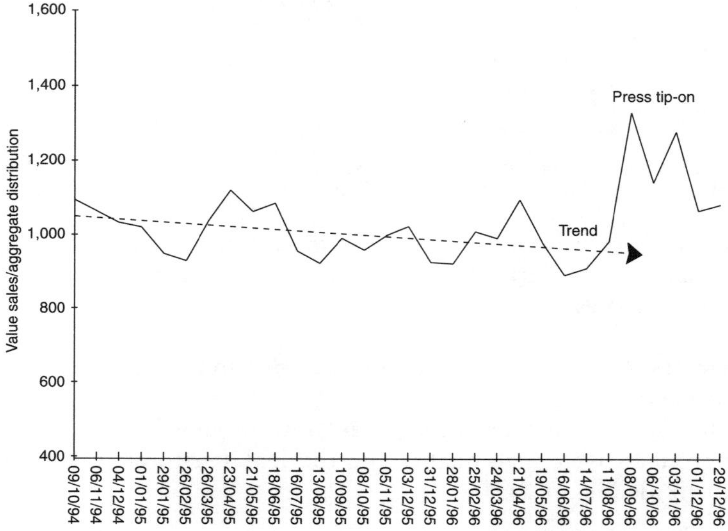

Figure 3: *Clean & Clear stockturn*
Source: IRI

Thus while aggregate distribution increased, stockturn was slowly declining. It appeared that the growth in sales and share was less demand-led than expected. This was worrying because aggregate distribution could not grow forever. Indeed, it had already started to slow down resulting in diminishing sales growth.

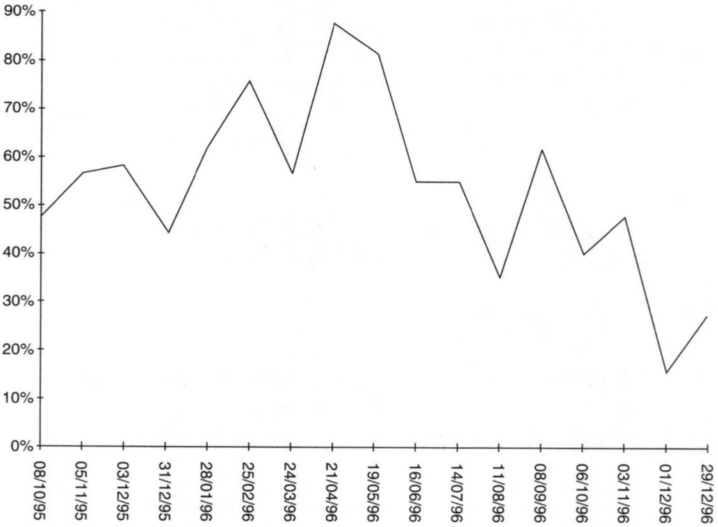

Figure 4: *Clean & Clear year on year growth*
Source: IRI

Furthermore, the rate of sale of the more established products was declining.[15] This suggested that the brand's growth was being driven by new products. This was worrying, because the more established products, particularly the lotion, were more profitable. The new products were more technologically sophisticated and hence less profitable.

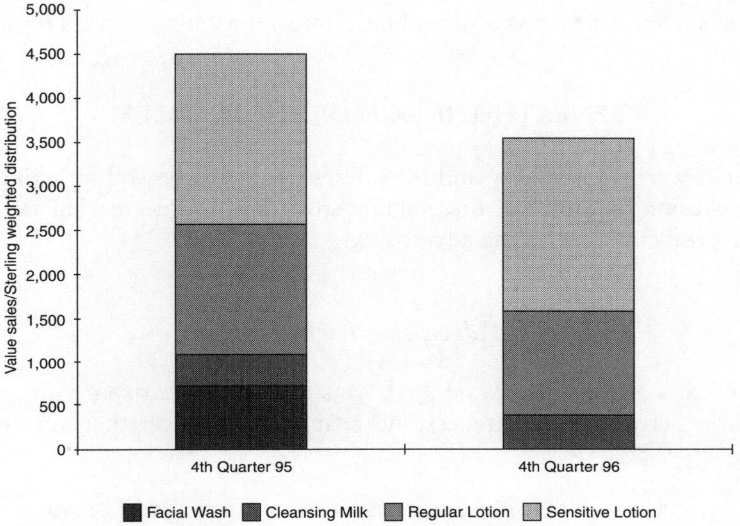

Figure 5: *Clean & Clear – average rate of sale of established products*
Source: IRI

Warning sign 2: Future growth was threatened by the competition becoming increasingly teen-girl targeted

Clean & Clear's unique positioning was increasingly under threat. Oxy launched an Oxy Sensitive range in 1996, offering effective yet gentle products, supported with a stylish new campaign, which would increase the brand's appeal to teenage girls.

There was also an increase in the launch of 'preventive' products, including own label, in direct competition with Clean & Clear.[16]

IMPLICATIONS FOR THE FUTURE OF CLEAN & CLEAR

1. Distribution-led growth, from new products, was unlikely to be sustainable or profitable for much longer.

15. Rate of sale can be thought of as how fast a product is selling in the average shop. It is calculated by dividing sales by sterling weighted distribution which, unlike aggregate distribution, can never exceed 100.
16. For example, both Clearasil and Oxy were increasingly offering preventive style products, and T-Zone was launched in 1995.

2. Without stockturn improvements it was unlikely that Clean & Clear would become No. 1 and in a lesser position the brand would become difficult to support and would be potentially untenable.
3. Clean & Clear was not the most popular brand among teenage girls and with the increasing competition it was unlikely that it would be. It looked decreasingly likely that it would generate significant future loyalty to the Johnson's name and act as a springboard into Johnson's products for adults.

BENEATH THE SKIN OF THE PROBLEM

The products were high quality and the salesforce was successful at selling them. So what was causing the problem of declining stockturn and decreasing sales growth? Part of the problem lay with the advertising.

The Advertising Lacked Impact

Clean & Clear's advertising awareness[17] was low in comparison with competitors and the ratio between ad awareness and adspend was lower than for competitors (Table 7).[18]

TABLE 7: ADVERTISING AWARENESS COMPARED TO ADSPEND IN 1996

	Total ad awareness end of 1996 %	Adspend during 1996 £m	Ratio of awareness adspend	Indexed ad awareness
Oxy	72	2.01	36	106
Clearasil	69	1.35	51	150
Biactol	66	0.51	129	379
Clean & Clear	23	0.68	34	100

Sample: Female spot product users
Source: Millward Brown U&A, December 1996
Source: MEAL

Qualitative Research Highlighted the Reasons for the Lack of Empathy Towards the Advertising

Teenagers can be very critical of advertising, especially of what they see as poor creativity, prosaic thinking, lack of style or inappropriate tone and poor production values. They want to see that the 'producers' have made an effort and they don't

17. Low advertising awareness had been indicated through qualitative research but was confirmed in a Millward Brown U&A study completed in December 1996.
18. The percentage awareness point per £million spent was lower than its competitors.

make allowances for the medicated advertising sector, judging Clean & Clear against their favourite advertising. As a result, 'Girls Talking' was viewed negatively:

— not realistic enough;

— too perfect;

— slightly patronising;

— not reflecting a picture of life that they could empathise with;

— not displaying enough understanding of them and what they want.

Sample: Females 11–18 years old
Source: Sally Page Qualitative Research/Caroline Oakes BMP Teen Panel, Autmn 1996

Brand Awareness was Relatively Low

Unsurprisingly therefore, brand awareness, particularly spontaneous brand awareness, was also relatively low compared to competitors and in relation to Clean & Clear's value share of the medicated market (Table 8). This suggested that the brand was not at the forefront of buyers' minds[19] and was perhaps a result of low advertising awareness.[20]

TABLE 8: BRAND AWARENESS COMPARED TO VALUE SHARE IN 1996

	Spontaneous brand awareness end 1996 %	Total brand awareness end 1996	Value share end 1996	Spontaneous awareness share %	Total awareness share %
Clearasil	53	98	19.0	2.8	6.2
Biactol	24	94	11.8	2.0	8.0
Oxy	43	93	22.8	1.9	4.1
Clean & Clear	8	51	13.7	0.6	3.7

Sample: Female spot product users
Source: Millward Brown U&A, December 1996
Source: IRI Infoscan value share four weeks ending December 1996

The combination of unimpactful advertising and relatively low brand awareness partially explained the disappointing shifts in stockturn in relation to advertising. Stockturn either decreased at the time of advertising or increased, only to fall shortly afterwards (see Figure 6 overleaf).[21]

19. The implication of this is that buyers were simply 'coming across' Clean & Clear in stores rather than making a conscious, pre-planned decision to examine and buy the brand.
20. By comparing the ratio between brand awareness and value share it was clear that Clean & Clear's brand awareness was relatively low in relation to its value share. This was particularly so for spontaneous brand awareness.
21. Figure 6 compares the value of stockturn three months before, during, and three months after bursts of 'Girls Talking'. The first burst refers to 'Girls Talking' in 1995, the second to 'Girls Talking' in early 1996 and the third to 'Girls Talking' later in 1996.

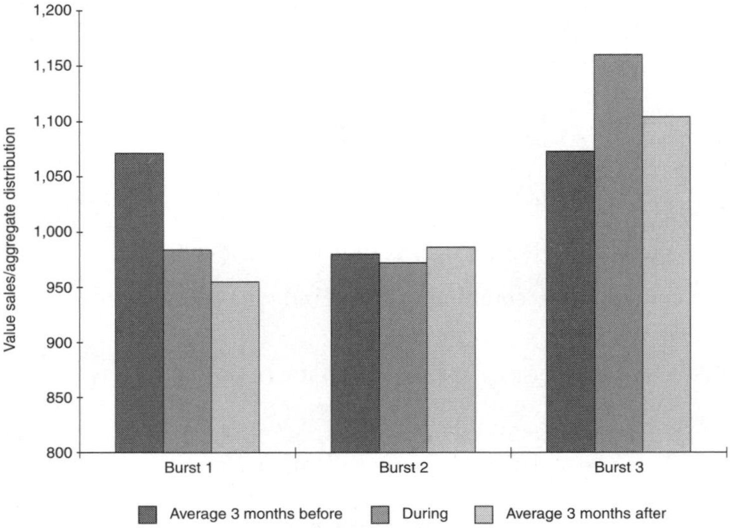

Figure 6: *Clean & Clear stockturn – before, during and after bursts of 'Girls Talking'*
Source: IRI

SUMMARY

It was clear that the translations of the US advertising were not working as well as intended. They lacked impact among teenagers, did not help to generate empathy and led to small or very short-term lifts in stockturn and sales. New advertising was clearly required.

THE NEED FOR NEW ADS

It was essential that the advertising worked harder to:

— Increase brand and advertising awareness among teenage girls.

— Make teenage girls feel that Johnson's understood them more.

— Generate a more sustained sales effect.

If advertising could achieve the above, Clean & Clear might still meet its objectives of:

— Becoming brand leader in the medicated skincare market.

— Becoming the most popular brand among teenage girls.

— Fuelling future loyalty to the Johnson's name.

WHAT NEEDED TO BE DONE

The global advertising idea intended to demonstrate that Clean & Clear had 'a unique understanding of teenage girls' skincare and emotional needs[22] and, because teenage girls talk about spots among themselves, the creative idea was based upon 'Girls Talking' about skincare. In its current form, 'Girls Talking' worked in the USA, but the UK girls found the execution of 'Girls Talking' to be artificial. As such, it was not helping to generate interest or empathy among teenage girls.

It was clear that the insight of 'Girls Talking' was relevant but that we needed to make it 'real' for UK girls. Instead of simply translating the American ads, we needed to understand UK girls and the way they talk about skincare in terms of the language and context of this type of conversation. We therefore developed a new creative brief that focused on 'getting real'.

ADVERTISING SOLUTION

With the help of video diaries, the result of giving video cameras to teenage girls over the Christmas period, we were able to develop new scripts that incorporated shrewd insights into real conversations between UK teenage girls. Two scripts, known as 'Big Bum' and 'Photos', worked best in qualitative research because:

1. Teenage girls recognised themselves in the scripts, which made them feel that Clean & Clear had bothered to find out about them, and therefore would have products they wanted.
2. The scripts were based on universal truths which meant that:

— teenage girls felt they were being treated like grown-up women;

— anyone could empathise with them, whether trendy or square.

Both scripts were made into TV ads, together known as 'Real Girls'. 'Big Bum' featured the long-established lotion product and 'Photos' featured a product to be launched in the Autumn of 1997, Clear Skin Daily Treatment. We also developed a press ad for the existing Deep Cleansing Cream Wash, which ran with an attached sachet.

22. Clean & Clear Brand Footprint.

'BIG BUM'

How do they look?
They make my bum look big don't they?

What bum?

Come on it sticks out a mile.

It's a good job you don't have spots to worry about as well – we'd be here all night.

(VO) Clean & Clear's lotion is clinically tested to effectively remove everyday dirt and grease.

(VO) So no matter what, you'll feel confident your skin is beautifully Clean & Clear.

So ... how does this look?
Great!

Are you sure?
Clean & Clear and under control.

'PHOTOS'

Oh no ...

Oh no ...

Oh no!

Well at least we didn't have any spots.

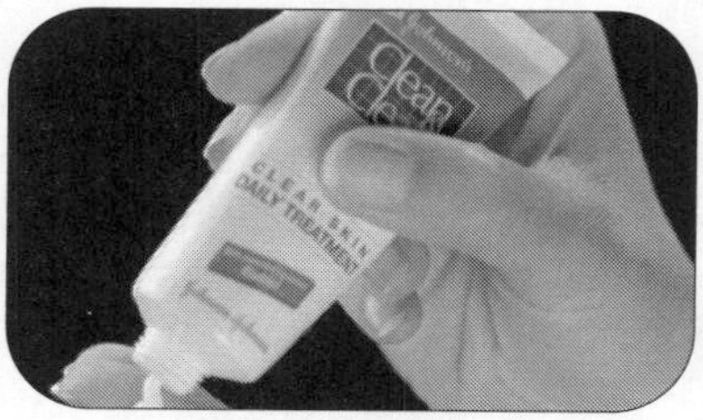

(VO) Clean & Clear New Clear Skin Daily Treatment fights the root cause of spots by controlling oil production.

(VO) So no matter what, you'll feel confident your skin is beautifully Clean & Clear.

Oh no.

Clean & Clear and under control.

MEDIA STRATEGY

BMP Optimum designed the media plan to be very tightly focused on teenage girls' favourite TV programmes such as *The Big Breakfast* (Table 9). In the past, media had been less focused on teenage girls, resulting in wastage and hence a shorter presence among this key target. This tight targeting enabled Clean & Clear to talk to teenage girls for longer.

In keeping with this targeting, we spotted an unusual opportunity: a Boyzone concert in July 1997, where 'Big Bum' appeared on a giant screen in front of screaming fans.

'Big Bum' was the first ad to be shown, aired nationally in two bursts. It was followed by a regional test in Scotland of 'Photos', in October and November of 1997 (Table 9).[23]

The press ad ran in May 1997.[24]

TABLE 9: CLEAN & CLEAR MEDIA PLAN 1997

	£000	Jan	Feb	Mar	Apr	May	Jun	Jul	Aug	Sep	Oct	Nov	Dec	Annual Total
1997	TV				525				227		35			787
	Press					85								85

WHAT HAPPENED?[25]

Increase in Sales

Clean & Clear experienced the largest single increase in value share *ever* in an eight-week period, immediately following the airing of 'Big Bum'; equivalent to two years of the previous distribution-led growth.[26]

The increase was maintained, without falling back to pre-advertising levels, despite a marked increase in competitive spend following 'Big Bum'. Sales increased 26% from year end 1996 to year end 1997, taking the brand to an all-time high.

By April 1998, Clean & Clear had met its objective of becoming the number 1 brand in sales terms only a year after the new advertising had broken (Table 10).

TABLE 10: VALUE SHARE OF MEDICATED SKINCARE MARKET, APRIL 1998 %

Clean & Clear	20
Oxy	17
Clearasil	16
Biactol	10

Source: IRI Infoscan four weeks ending 26 April 1998

23. 'Photos' was later aired nationally in March 1998.
24. This was for Deep Cleansing Cream Wash.
25. The majority of our analysis concentrates on the period from March to December 1997, but while writing this paper some data have become available for 1998. The additional data enabled us to carry the analysis forward with reference to some measures. This will be made clear where appropriate.
26. Value share increased 5%. IRI Infoscan.

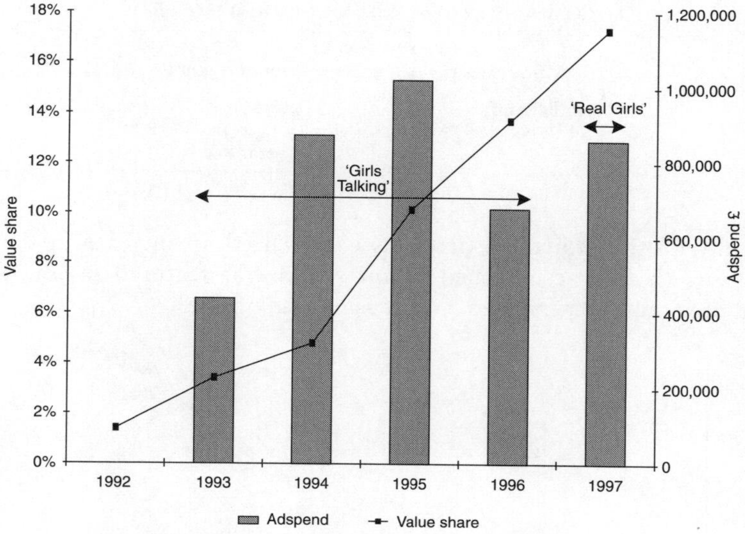

Figure 7: *Clean & Clear value share of medicated market and adspend*
Source: IRI, BARB

Increase in Stockturn and Rate of Sale

Stockturn increased dramatically at the time of the 'Real Girls' advertising (Table 11), demonstrating that growth was now demand-led rather than supply-led and the increase in stockturn was sustained (Figure 8).

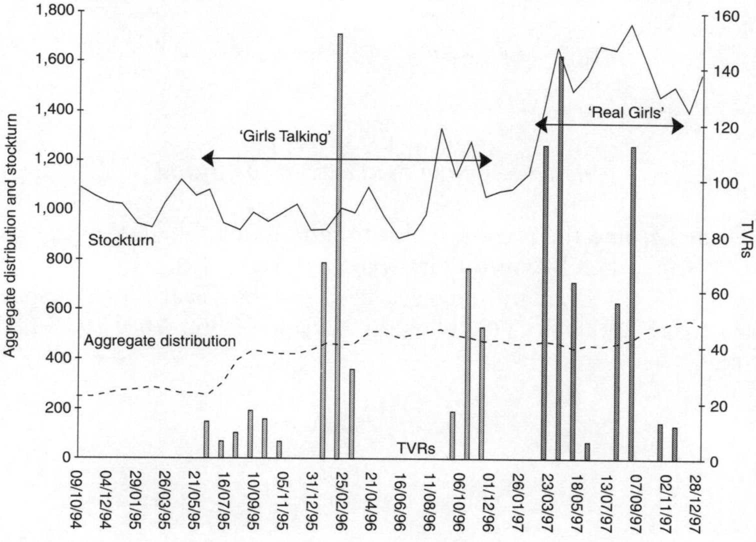

Figure 8: *Clean & Clear stockturn versus TVRs and aggregate distribution*
Source: IRI, BARB

TABLE 11: COMPARISON OF STOCKTURN 1994 TO 1996 VERSUS 1997

Average stockturn (Value sales per aggregate distribution point)	
'Girls Talking' (Oct 1994 to Feb 1997)	'Real Girls' (Mar 1997 to Jan 1998)
1,032	1,558

Source: IRI Infoscan

Practically all the individual products experienced an increase in their rate of sale, including the long-established lotion which was featured in 'Big Bum' and which had previously experienced a decreasing rate of sale.

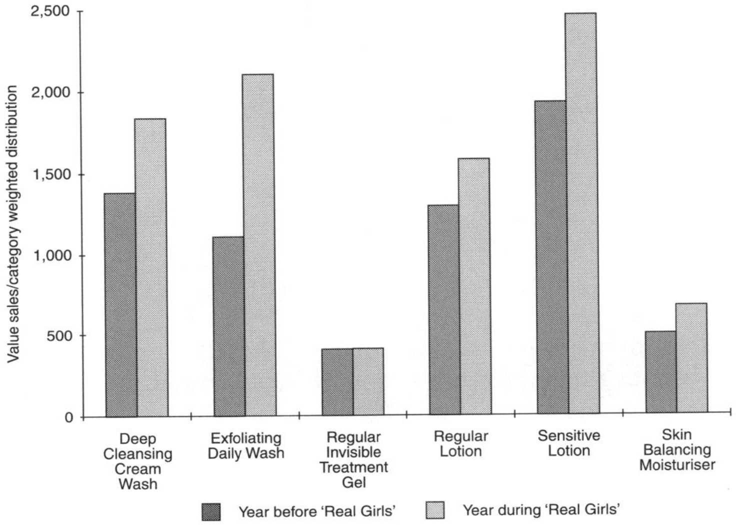

Figure 9: *Clean & Clear average rate of sale by product*
Source: IRI

Increase in the Popularity of the Brand

Clean & Clear became the most popular brand among female teenage buyers[27] of medicated skincare, thereby meeting its objective (Table 12).

This resulted in a dramatic increase in Clean & Clear's brand share among teenage girls (from 20.2% to 28% between April 1996 and April 1998).

27. Purchase data is significant because it represents teenagers who actually bought and used the products themselves.

TABLE 12: PENETRATION AMONG TEENAGE GIRLS[28]

	Year to April 1996 'Girls Talking' %	Year to April 1998 'Real Girls' %	% change 1996 to 1998
Clean & Clear	9.6	40.8	+325
Oxy	19.8	18.9	- 5
Clearasil	18.9	18.7	- 1
Biactol	9.4	7.0	- 26

Source: Taylor Nelson Year Ending April 1996/Year Ending April 1998
Sample: Female buyers, 13 to 18 years old

A Dramatic Shift in Teenage Empathy Towards the Brand

Girls now felt that Clean & Clear and Johnson's understood them and what they wanted from skincare.

'There's always something to worry about and one less thing the better – and that's exactly what they're saying.'

15-year-old

You try everything on and then at the last second you get your jeans out and change. That's just like me.'

14-year-old

Sample: Females 13 to 16 years old
Source: Qualitative Research, RDS, August 1997

In fact, teenagers empathised with the brand to the degree that if they could use only one brand, Clean & Clear would be their most preferred choice (Table 13).

TABLE 13: BRAND PREFERENCE

	'If you had to use only one of the following medicated brands over a 6 month period, which one would you use?'
Clean & Clear	35%
Clearasil	32%
Oxy	18%
Biactol	4%
None of these	11%

Sample: Females, 11 to 19 years old
Base: 317
Stimulus: Showcard: Clearasil, Oxy, Clean & Clear, Biactol, None of these
Source: BMP/SNAP Quantitative Survey, April 1998

28. We have shown Taylor Nelson data from 1996 and 1998 and not from 1997, because data do not distinguish between the 'Girls Talking' and the 'Real Girls' periods of advertising.

SUMMARY

In short, Clean & Clear had met all of its objectives within one year of the launch of the new advertising. It was now:

1. No. 1 medicated skincare brand.
2. Most popular medicated skincare brand among female teenagers.
3. A brand with which female teenagers could empathise and hence these girls were quite likely to become future adult users of Johnson's other products.

PROVING THE CONTRIBUTION MADE BY ADVERTISING

How do we know that the new advertising had been instrumental in Clean & Clear's accelerated growth? We will prove this by showing:

1. Direct evidence that the new advertising worked as planned.
2. Timing of sales shifts coinciding with advertising.
3. Sales results from a regional advertising upweight.
4. Econometric analysis.
5. Elimination of other variables.

Direct Evidence that the New Advertising Worked as Planned

Impactful advertising and the creation of a famous brand
Advertising awareness improved considerably in relation to competitive brands (Table 14).[29] This occurred even though adspend on Clean & Clear increased only slightly between 1996 and 1997, from £0.68 million in 1996 to £0.87 million in 1997, and share of voice remained stable at 12%. In comparison, Clearasil increased spend from £1.36 million to £3.59 million, accounting for a 50% share of voice in 1997 compared to 25% in 1996.

29. While two data sources are used, which could reduce the robustness of the absolute movement, the relative movement in comparison to competitors is meaningful.

TABLE 14: TOTAL ADVERTISING AWARENESS

	Total advertising awareness 1996 %	Total advertising awareness 1998 %	% Change 1996 to 1998
Clean & Clear	23	37	+61%
Clearasil	69	50	-28%
Oxy	72	39	-46%
Biactol	66	21	-68%

Sample: Females, 11 to 19 years old
Base: 317
Source: BMP/SNAP Quantitative Survey April 1998

Source: Millward Brown U&A Study December 1996
Sample: Female spot product user
Source: MEAL

The ratio between ad awareness and share of voice improved in relation to competitive brands (Table 15).

TABLE 15: THE RATIO OF ADVERTISING AWARENESS TO SHARE OF VOICE[30]

	Ratio ad awareness/share of voice		Index of ratio on Clean & Clear	
	1996	1998	1996	1998
Clean & Clear	1.89	3.06	100	100
Clearasil	2.81	0.99	149	32
Oxy	1.98	2.25	105	74

Sample: Females, 11 to 19 years old
Base: 317
Source: BMP/SNAP Quantitative Survey, April 1998

Source: Millward Brown U&A Study, December 1996
Sample: Female spot product users
Source: MEAL

In October 1997 the second execution, 'Photos', was aired exclusively in Scotland, with 275 TVRs, with no other Clean & Clear advertising aired in the rest of the UK at this time. As Table 16 shows, as a result, advertising awareness is higher in Scotland than elsewhere and considerably higher than competitive brands in both Scotland and the rest of the UK.

30. We have not included the share of voice of Biactol because it was consolidated under the Clearasil brand name in 1997.

TABLE 16: TOTAL ADVERTISING AWARENESS

	Scotland %	Rest of UK %
Clean& Clear	57	35
Clearasil	50	50
Oxy	47	39
Biactol	30	20

Sample: Females, 11to 19 years old
Base: 317
Source: BMP/SNAP Quantitative Survey, April 1998

Increase in Brand Awareness

As a result of the increase in advertising awareness, brand awareness also increased (Table 17).

TABLE 17: TOTAL BRAND AWARENESS

	Total brand awareness 1996 %	Total brand awareness 1998 %	% change
Clean & Clear	51	76	+49%
Clearasil	98	88	-10%
Oxy	93	78	-16%
Biactol	94	69	-27%

Sample: Females, 11 to 19 years old
Base: 317
Source: BMP/SNAP Quantitative Survey, April 1998
Sample: Female spot product users
Source: Millward Brown U&A, December 1996

Similarly in the Scottish test market, brand awareness was higher in Scotland than in the rest of the UK (Table 18).

TABLE 18: TOTAL BRAND AWARENESS

	Scotland %	Rest of UK %
Clean & Clear	83	76
Clearasil	80	89
Oxy	73	79
Biactol	63	69

Sample: Females, 11 to 19 years old
Base: 317
Source: BMP/SNAP Quantitative Survey

Increase in empathy towards the advertising and the brand

For the first time teenage girls enthused about Clean & Clear's advertising, even laughing about how true it was to their lives and attitudes towards skincare. This was completely different from earlier reactions and was unlike that produced by competitive advertising, which they felt was unnatural and contrived.

'That one's really good.'

13-year-old

'I really like those.'

14-year-old

'They're much better. I can't stand those Clearasil adverts. Really fake. They get on my nerves.'

14-year-old

The advertising depicts, 'A convincing scene which is a major breakthrough where other brands are contrived.' (RDS)

Sample: Females, 13 to16 years old
Source: Qualitative Research, RDS, August 1997

As a result, teenage girls were more likely to use Clean & Clear if they had been exposed to the 'Real Girls' campaign:[31]

TABLE 19: PROPENSITY TO USE CLEAN & CLEAR

	1996 'Girls Talking'	1997 'Real Girls'	% change
Big Breakfast Fans:	110	122	+10.9
Big Breakfast Rejectors:	67	58	-13.4

Question: Of spot creams, lotions and gels, which brand do you use most often?
Sample: Females, 11 to 19 years old
Source: Youth TGI 1996 and 1997

In fact, girls who were aware of the advertising were more likely to claim they would use Johnson's brands when they grew up as well (Table 20). This suggested that this advertising was now helping to establish a long-term relationship with teenage girls.[32]

31. Table 19 compares the likelihood of teenage girls aged 11 to 19 using Clean & Clear according to whether or not they were fans of the *Big Breakfast*, across 1996 and 1997.
32. While it is virtually impossible to gain an accurate measure of future propensity to purchase a product or brand, we asked teenage girls, both those who were aware and those who were unaware of Johnson's Clean & Clear advertising, 'How likely are you to use a Johnson's brand, such as Johnson's pH5.5 or Johnson's Baby when you are in your twenties?'. Given that we asked female teenagers, regardless of current brand usage, the results showed that teenagers who were aware of the advertising were more likely to say that they were using or were very likely to use Johnson's brand when they were in their twenties.

TABLE 20: LIKELIHOOD OF USING A JOHNSON'S BRAND AS AN ADULT

	Aware of Clean & Clear advertising	Unaware of Clean & Clear advertising	Index of aware/unaware
Very/quite likely	76	51	150
Neither/nor	11	28	39
Quite/very unlikely	13	21	62

Sample: Females, 11 to 19 years old
Base: 317
Source: BMP/SNAP Quantitative Survey, April 1998

Further evidence of the effect of the new advertising came from the J&J salesforce.

> ' "Big Bum" had a terrific impact on sales across the whole range. It demonstrated to our customers, the trade, both our commitment to support the brand and our ability to communicate to our target consumers.'
>
> Neil Dickenson, Group Controller, J&J Salesforce, May 1998

The feedback didn't stop there. J&J was inundated with letters from teenagers eulogising the advertising, the brand and the products, which had never happened before; plus the advertising was also featured in a television show and a teen magazine.

The Timing of the Sales Shifts in Relation to Advertising

Stockturn increased at precisely the time when 'Big Bum' was aired, a time when there were no increases in distribution and no new product launches (Figure 10).

This led to value share increasing dramatically at precisely the same time when 'Big Bum' was aired, again suggesting advertising's key role (Figure 11).

The Sales Results from a Regional Advertising Upweight

As already discussed 'Photos' was aired only in Scotland in October 1997. Scotland's performance, relative to the rest of the country, improved significantly exactly when these extra TVRs were screened (Figure 12).[33]

33. Figure 12 shows Clean & Clear's value share in Scotland versus the rest of the UK, which increased at the time of 'Photos'.

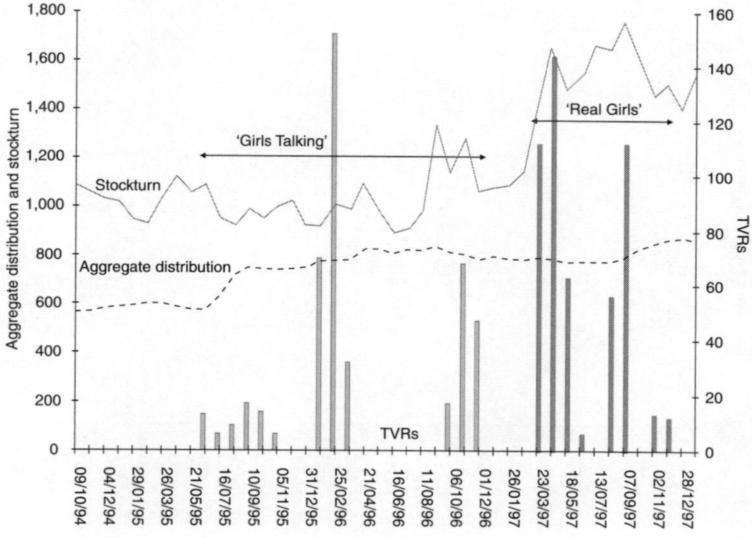

Figure 10: *Clean & Clear stockturn versus TVRs and aggregate distribution*
Source: IRI, BARB

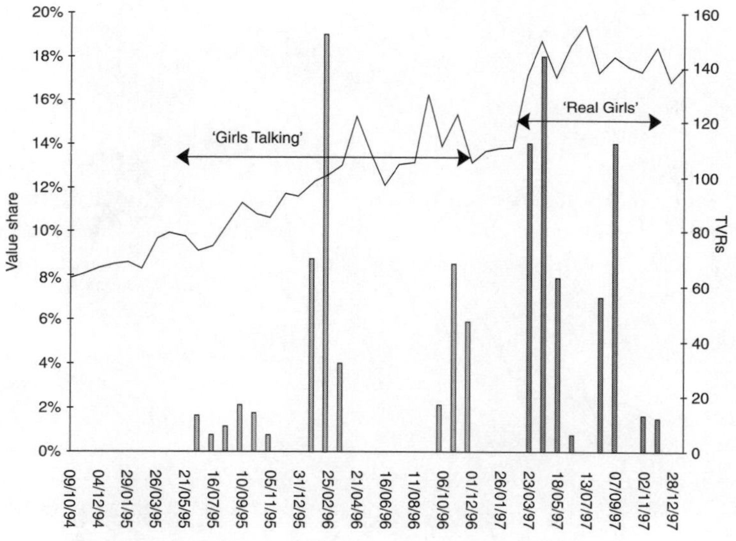

Figure 11: *Clean & Clear value share versus TVRs*
Source: IRI, BARB

Econometrics

An econometric model, which takes account of the different factors that might affect sales growth, provides further evidence of the effect of the 'Real Girls' campaign. The model shows that without 'Real Girls', value share would have been markedly lower and growth would indeed have petered out (Figure 13).[34]

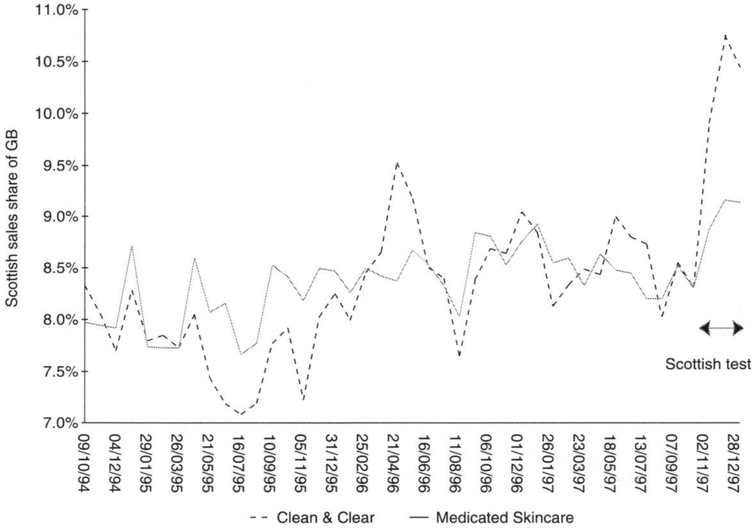

Figure 12: *Scottish share of GB sales*
Source: IRI

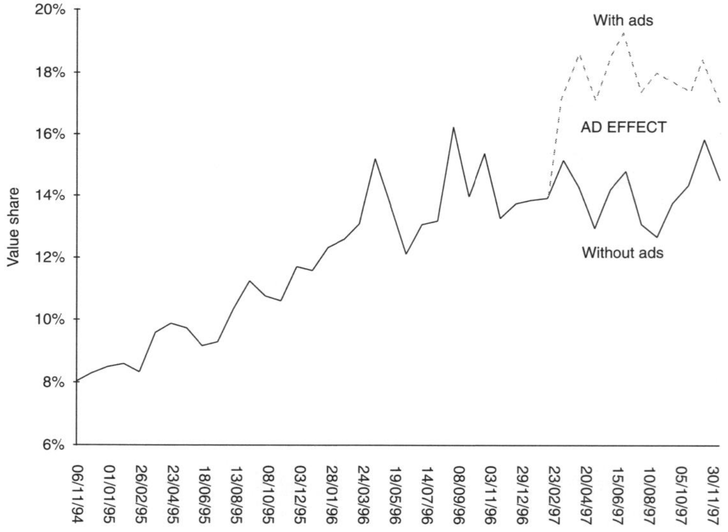

Figure 13: *Clean & Clear value share effect of 'Real Girls'*
Source: IRI, BMP Model

34. The exact revenue generated from 'Real Girls' is discussed in the Payback section.

Eliminating Other Factors

Although Clean & Clear's rapid and sustained increase in sales, share, stockturn, rate of sale and the positive movements in intermediary measures all reflect the campaign's effectiveness, we need to eliminate the possible effects of some other factors in order to be certain.

New products
New products cannot have caused the bulk of Clean & Clear's growth during 1997, because this occurred immediately after the start of the 'Real Girls' campaign and during this time no new products were launched

Furthermore, as we have already seen, rate of sale increased across practically all of the product range, so growth cannot be attributed only to new product launches. We have also shown that stockturn, which accounts for the number of facings, increased (Figure 10).[35]

Product improvements or reformulations
No products were reformulated or repackaged in 1997.

Distribution
The initial increase in sales could not have been driven by an increase in distribution, as Clean & Clear's distribution across all the products was static at the start of the 'Real Girls' campaign (Figure 14).

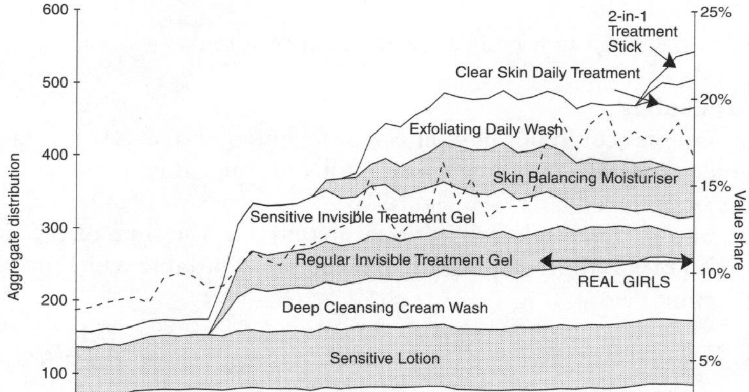

Figure 14: *Clean & Clear value share and aggregate distribution*
Source: IRI

35. Two new products were eventually launched in Autumn 1997 – Clear Skin Daily Treatment and 2-in-1 Treatment Stick – but this occurred six months after the initial increase in sales.

In addition, the market became tougher in terms of new launches and distribution. The aggregate distribution of Clearasil, Biactol and Oxy actually increased after the start of the 'Real Girls' campaign, both in the short term and in the long term, so Clean & Clear's relative distribution actually fell.

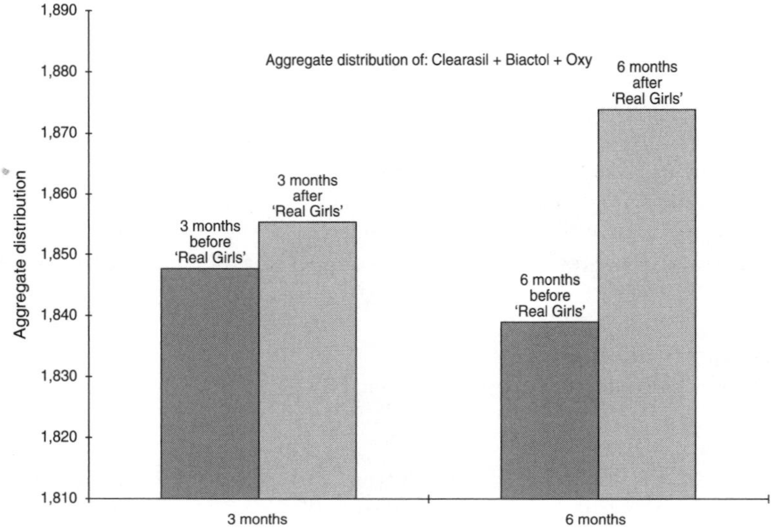

Figure 15: *Average aggregate distribution of competition – before and after start of 'Real Girls' campaign*
Source: IRI

There was no change in Clean & Clear's instore siting.

Promotions/sampling

Promotional samples could not have effected the initial and largest increases in sales because there were no sampling promotions during this period. A sampling promotion only occurred later (see Figure 16).

There was no point-of-sale promotional material at the time of the 'Real Girls' campaign. Price promotions are captured in the price variable which is discussed in the pricing section below.[36]

Pricing

Because we are concentrating on sales value, it might be argued that the uplift we have seen was an artefact of rising prices, or volume increases might be a result of price cutting. Neither is true. Prices did rise a little (absolutely and relative to competition). See Figures 17 and 18.

36. Price promotions are captured in the definition of price (value/volume).

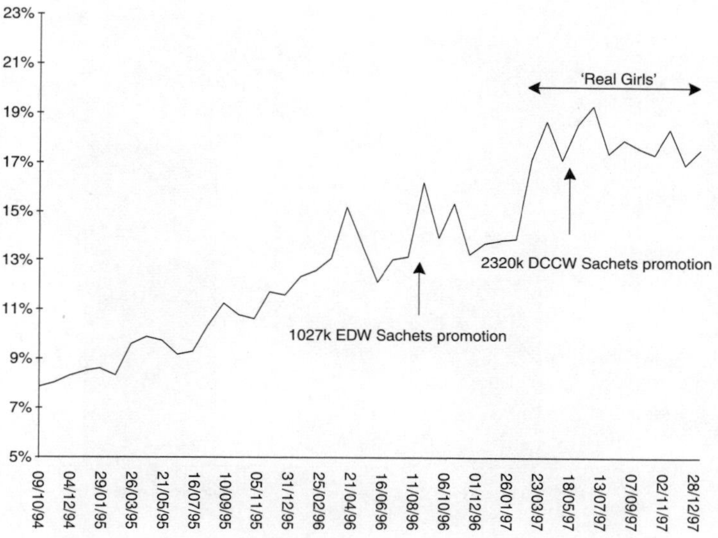

Figure 16: *Value share and promotions*
Source: IRI, J&J

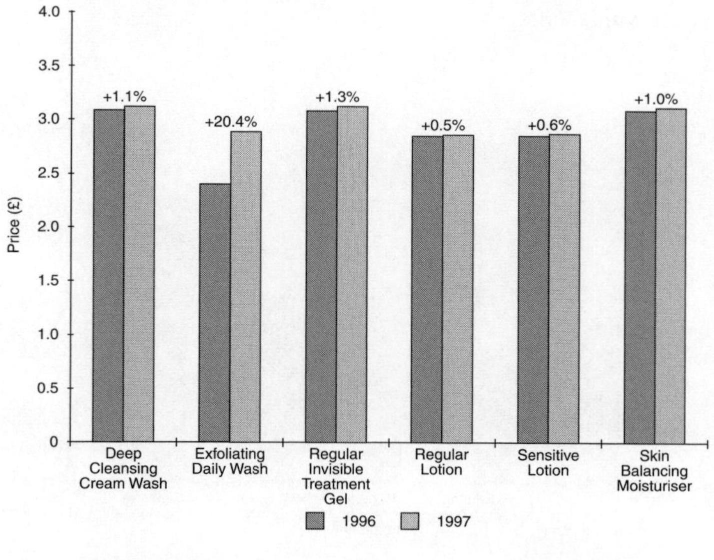

Figure 17: *Clean & Clear price by product*
Source: IRI

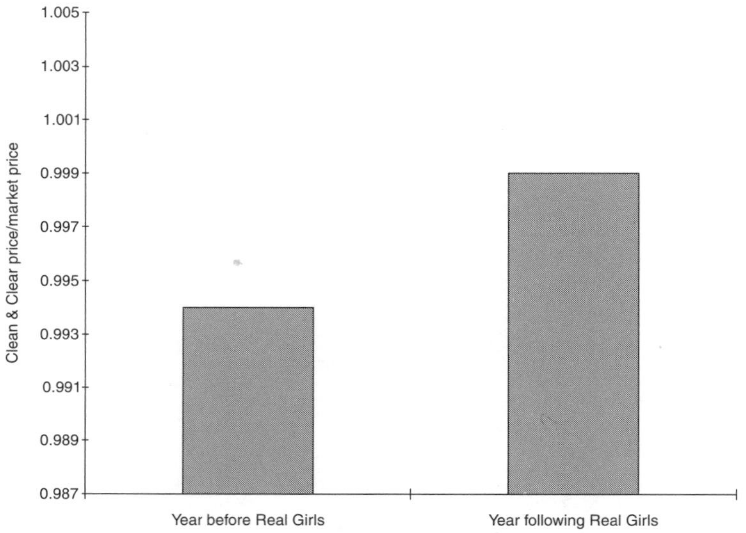

Figure 18: *Clean & Clear average price relative to medicated market average price*
Source: IRI

Thus price could not have driven volume. In addition, volume, not just value, grew substantially (see Figure 19). Hence price rises cannot account for the (much larger) growth in value sales.

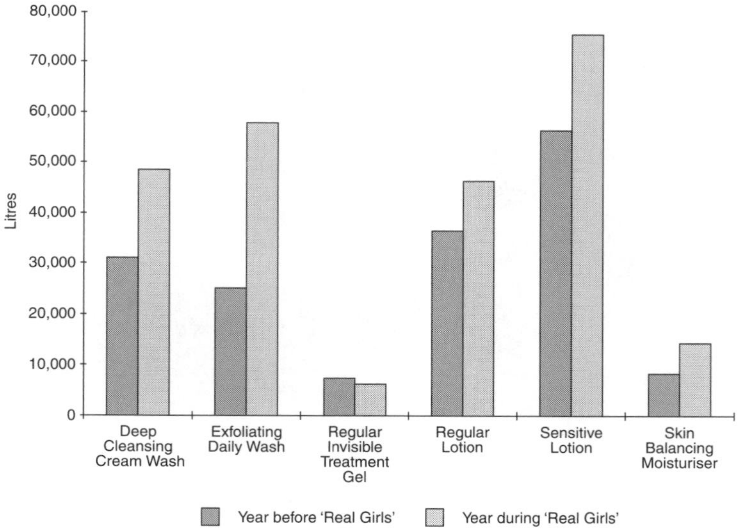

Figure 19: *Clean & Clear volume by product*
Source: IRI

Competitive adspend

Competitive adspend increased in 1997, especially for Clearasil, making Clean & Clear's performance more remarkable and proving that Clean & Clear did not benefit from any decrease in competitive adspend (Figure 20).

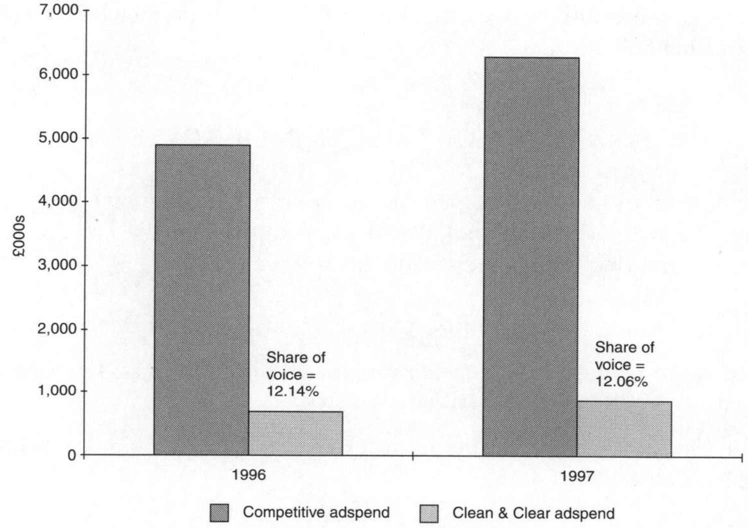

Figure 20: *Clean & Clear adspend versus competition*
Source: MEAL

Competitive product changes

The medicated market became more competitive in 1997. Clearasil launched a totally new product, Clearasil Complete, Boots relaunched their medicated range, giving it a more up-to-date image, and Clean & Clear's product positioning was further threatened by the introduction of similar products.

Despite the launch of competitive products, new brands and the blurring of Clean & Clear's unique positioning, Clean & Clear's value share grew.

Consumer factors

Other factors, such as an increase in the population of teenage girls, an increase in the number of teenage girls suffering from spots or an increase in teenage girls' disposable income, can be eliminated as factors affecting Clean & Clear's success because the brand's share increased. If the above factors had played a part they would have affected the total medicated market.

Momentum of previous advertising, 'Girls Talking'

It is possible that the previous four years of 'Girls Talking' advertising might have generated sufficient momentum to drive the initial increase in sales after 'Girls Talking' was taken off air. However, this cannot be the case because there was a gap of three months between the 'Girls Talking' advertising and the 'Real Girls' campaign. If 'Girls Talking' had generated a head of steam, sales would have increased before the airing of 'Real Girls'.

SUMMARY

It was clear that the new advertising had a momentous effect. Brand and advertising awareness was boosted and now on a par with competitive brands, sales and value share had increased, stockturn had increased and teenage girls could empathise with the advertising, the brand and with Johnson's, and no other factors could explain such improvements.

THE FINANCIAL CONTRIBUTION OF ADVERTISING

The econometric model has helped us to assess the financial contribution of advertising. We will show that the advertising running in 1997 (ie, the 'Real Girls' campaign) has had two financial consequences:

1. A profitable return within the first year, ie, from March to December 1997.
2. An even more profitable forecasted return within two years, from March 1997 to December 1998 based on estimated adstocks.

We will also provide the estimated returns had 'Girls Talking' continued to be aired instead (Tables 21 and 22).

TABLE 21: THE RETURN IN THE PERIOD MARCH TO DECEMBER 1997

THE RETURN FROM 'REAL GIRLS' Return within one year of airing 'Real Girls'	
Revenue from 'Real Girls'	£1.75m
Adspend on 'Real Girls'	£0.87m
Short-term return from 'Real Girls'	£0.88m
THE RETURN THAT WOULD HAVE BEEN GENERATED HAD 'GIRLS TALKING' BEEN AIRED INSTEAD OF 'REAL GIRLS' Return within one year of airing 'Girls Talking' (if it had been aired at the same weight)	
Revenue from 'Girls Talking'	£0.78m
Adspend	£0.87m
'Girls Talking' would not have covered adspend	-£0.09m

Note: Based on IRI Infoscan value

Had 'Girls Talking' been aired instead of 'Real Girls' there would have been a negative return from advertising within one year.

TABLE 22: FORECASTED RETURNS IN THE PERIOD FROM MARCH 1997 TO DECEMBER 1998

From the model we estimate that the adstock is 75%. This means that the direct effect of airing ads in 1997 will have reached almost zero by the end of 1998.

THE RETURN FROM 'REAL GIRLS'	
Return within two years of airing 'Real Girls'	
Revenue from 'Real Girls'	£2.04m
Adspend on 'Real Girls'	£0.87m
Short-to medium-term return from 'Real Girls'	£1.17m
THE RETURN THAT WOULD HAVE BEEN GENERATED IF 'GIRLS TALKING' HAD BEEN AIRED INSTEAD OF 'REAL GIRLS' (if it had been aired at the same weight)	
Revenue from 'Girls Talking'	£0.91m
Adspend during this period	£0.87m
Short + medium-term return from 'Girls Talking'	£0.04m

Note: Based on IRI Infoscan value

In summary, because 'Real Girls' was aired instead of 'Girls Talking', an extra £1.13 million return has been forecasted after adspend has been deducted.

Figure 21 shows the difference in sales generated by: (a) What actually happened; the airing of 'Real Girls'; (b) What would have happened if 'Girls Talking' had continued to be aired, and (c) What would have happened if no advertising had been aired at all.

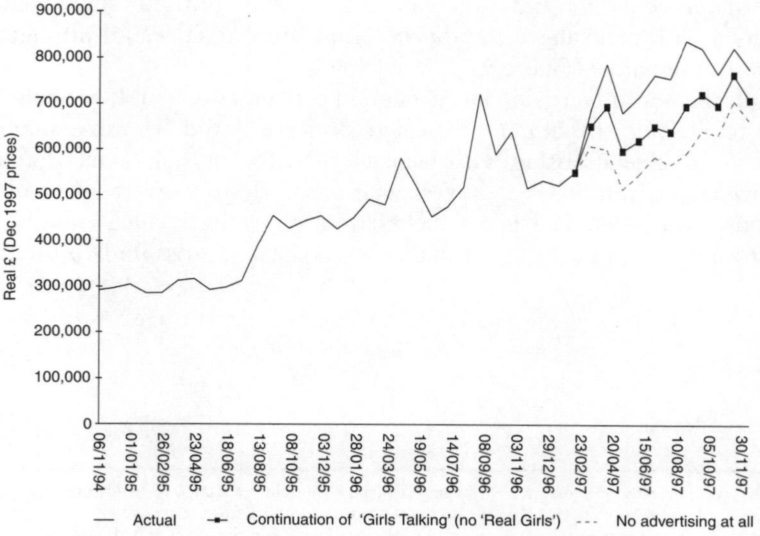

Figure 21: *Clean & Clear value sales: actual versus different advertising scenarios*
Source: IRI, BMP Model

Profit

In terms of profit in the short-to-medium term, 'Girls Talking' would require a break-even profit margin of at least 95.6% for the advertising to have been profitable.[37] By comparison, 'Real Girls', requires a break-even profit margin of 43% for the advertising to be profitable. The industry average profit margin lies between 50% and 70%.[38] Therefore it is not unreasonable to suggest that 'Real Girls' will be making a profit for J&J which would not have been the case if 'Girls Talking' had been aired in its place. Based on these margins we can calculate a return on investment (Table 23):

TABLE 23: RETURN ON INVESTMENT CALCULATION

	Profit generated from extra revenue due to advertising	Minus advertising expenditure of £0.87m	Return on investment %
50% profit margin	£1.02m	£0.15m	17.2
70% profit margin	£1.22m	£0.35m	40.2

Longer Term Payback

The new advertising has helped both Clean & Clear and the Johnson's brand portfolio for the future. Until the airing of the new advertising, Clean & Clear's growth was substantially driven by distribution and economic growth, together accounting for approximately 60% of the growth in the previous three years. Given that distribution growth is unsustainable and given that economic growth is forecasted to slow down in the future, Clean & Clear was on borrowed time.

The new advertising has addressed this problem, reducing Clean & Clear's reliance on the economy and aggregate distribution. Without such a change, the brand was at risk of losing a significant proportion of sales and ultimately would have become untenable (Figure 22).

Instead, the new advertising has generated consumer demand, has enabled Clean & Clear to become the No. 1 medicated skincare brand by value share and has helped to forge a relationship with teenage girls. J&J now has over half a million existing teenage Clean & Clear buyers who are likely to convert into half a million adult Johnson's buyers. This is not included in the payback calculation because it is difficult to quantify, but this must make the payback a gross underestimate of total return.

37. Break-even profit margins are measured by dividing adspend by revenue generated form advertising. Therefore to make a profit, the margin on the products needs to be above this percentage.
38. This includes the more sophisticated, technological products which are at the lower end of the profit margin.

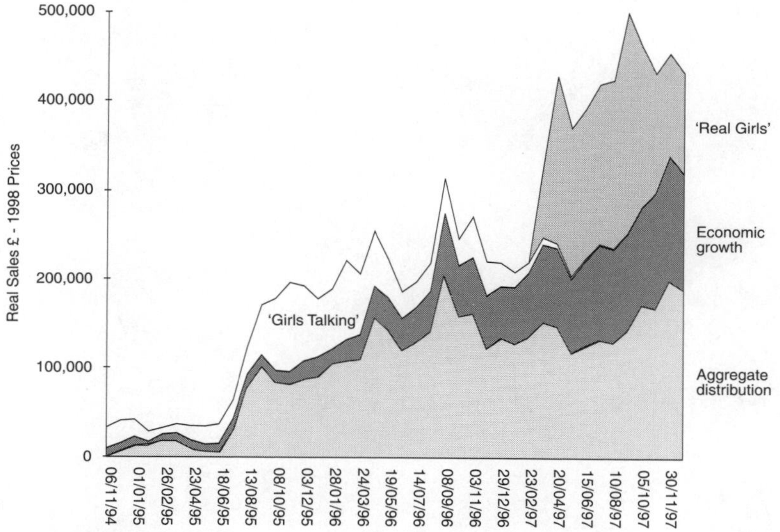

Figure 22: *Clean & Clear growth (November 1994 – December 1997) and main conributors to growth*
Source: IRI, BMP Model

CONCLUSION

Prior to the 'Real Girls' campaign, the brand was not on track to meet its objectives. By maintaining the theme of a global advertising idea but changing the UK advertising from translations of the US ads into ads based on genuine insights gained from local consumers, the situation was dramatically reversed. The brand's stockturn increased and the brand was able to become the No. 1 medicated skincare brand by value share. At the same time the advertising developed strong brand values which forged a relationship with teenage girls. This has increased Johnson's chances of building a lifelong relationship with them.

As a result of the new advertising, Clean & Clear became a star in J&J's portfolio. J&J was thrilled with the performance and became increasingly confident about rolling out the brand into 14 countries across Europe and the Middle East, doing so with advertising that suited each country's local needs.

2

Knorr Stock Cubes

How Thinking 'Local' Helped CPC Develop Advertising which Toppled the Brand Leader

INTRODUCTION

This paper sets out to demonstrate how, in a world of increasing focus on '1992', 'pan-European' strategies and 'global brands', thinking locally can still pay handsomely!

It shows how CPC exploited distinctive, local characteristics, ie home-made soup-making in Scotland, to develop a campaign that has become akin to popular Scottish folklore, and against all the odds, taken Knorr to brand leader in the Scottish cube market.

BACKGROUND

Knorr Stock Cubes were launched in the UK in 1954, as the first real alternative to Oxo. In many ways Knorr could hardly have been more different.

1. Whilst Oxo had its *own* distinctive flavour, Knorr cubes (available in beef or chicken) had a more authentic meaty taste, enhanced with herbs.
2. Oxo tended to mask other flavours with its own particular taste: Knorr more subtly *enhanced* other flavours.
3. Oxo was a 'dry' cube which could be crumbled into cooking. Knorr had a 'moist' format and required dissolving in boiling water before addition.
4. Knorr was launched at a significant price premium (+200%) relative to Oxo.

In effect, Oxo was a flavour and colour additive. Knorr was more akin to real stock.

Knorr's Position by Mid 1970s

Some 20 years after launch, Knorr had carved a small but profitable niche in the UK cube market.

TABLE 1: UK VOLUME SHARE 1975

	%
Knorr	7.8
Oxo	89.6
Others	2.6

Source: Nielsen

Usage

Whilst Knorr's characteristics of subtlety and lightness made it particularly appropriate for chicken dishes (casseroles and soups), the more robust flavour of Oxo was particularly suited to red meat (casseroles, minces and gravies). As a result, Knorr volume was biased towards its chicken cube, with Oxo volume biased towards its beef cube.

TABLE 2: UK CUBE MARKET PROFILE, 1975 (VOLUME)

	Total Market %	Knorr %	Oxo %
Beef	84	42	88
Chicken	16	58	12

Source: Nielsen

Attempts to Grow Knorr 1970 – 1977

Knorr was regularly supported by national TV advertising during the 1970s, with the proposition:

> 'Only Knorr stock cubes have a subtle enough flavour to truly complement the flavour of poultry and meat'.

TABLE 3: KNORR PENETRATION AND VOLUME SHARE 1970 – 1975

	1970 %	1974 %	1975 %
UK Penetration			
Total Knorr	*14.5*	*13.7*	*13.2*
Red Oxo	54.7	60.8	61.7
Chicken Oxo	18.9	17.6	19.2
UK volume share			
Total Knorr	*7.8*	*7.9*	*7.8*
Total Oxo	89.6	89.8	89.6

Source: Nielsen, TGI
Base: All UK housewifes

These attempts to grow the brand, however, met with little success.

Factors Holding Back Knorr Growth

In competing with Oxo, Knorr faced a challenging task!

1. It is difficult to overestimate the strength of the emotional bond between the British public and Oxo. Oxo was, and still is, one of the truly great food brands, enjoying both huge loyalty and unquestioning, almost ritual purchasing behaviour.
   The following comment was typical:

   'I don't know really why I use Oxo – I just do. Mum always used it I suppose, so I do too'.

2. People *liked* the strong, beefy taste of Oxo. Most people, therefore, saw no potential benefit from a more subtle tasting alternative.
3. Knorr's 'non-crumble' format was unfamiliar.
4. Knorr was much more expensive than Oxo.

In addition, even if Knorr *could* increase penetration, clearly its *nature* excluded it from the real volume of the market, which Oxo dominated – red meat casseroles and gravies.

Thus, whilst Knorr was left little choice but to play the same game as Oxo, the odds seemed heavily stacked in Oxo's favour.

KNORR'S POSITION IN SCOTLAND IN 1975

Although the cube market in Scotland as a whole behaved similarly to the UK, Knorr's position in Scotland was very different. As a result, Scotland accounted for over 25% of Knorr's total volume.

TABLE 4: CUBE VOLUME SHARE 1975

	UK %	Scotland %
Knorr	7.8	35.2
Oxo	89.6	62.2
Others	2.6	2.6

Source: Nielsen

Behind this difference lay an activity firmly entrenched in Scottish tradition, the making of home-made soup!

HOME-MADE SOUP IN SCOTLAND

In a region characterised by long, cold winters, and where family budgets were traditionally stretched, it is not difficult to see how home-made soup became so firmly rooted in Scottish heritage. As one respondent described her grandmother's lifestyle:

> 'It was economy cooking then; big families, pots of broth and potato stovies'.

In many ways, home-made soup seemed to form the backbone of the family – always there as a warm welcome, and a powerful expression of the 'provider' role which Scottish women strongly adhered to.

> 'The pot was always boiling on the stove'.

> 'I remember coming home from dances and having a bowl of soup'.

Quantitative data strikingly confirmed the role home-made soup continued to play in Scottish family life.

TABLE 5: HOME-MADE SOUP-MAKING, 1977

	Scotland	Rest of UK
% housewives claiming made any home-made soup in past 4 weeks	91	14

Source: Marplan, April 1977

How was Soup Made?

At the heart of a good soup, was good stock. Stock was made by simmering meaty bones in a large pot for a number of hours. After this, the liquid would be drained off to form the 'base' of the soup, to which vegetables or meat were then added.

Traditionally, women would obtain bones free from their local butcher for soup-making. Any left-overs, like chicken carcasses, would also find their way into the stock pot (the Scots were not ones for waste!).

How did Soup-Making Influence Knorr's Position in Scotland?

1. Stock making was a time-consuming business. Bones needed to be boiled for several hours and this process needed on-going attention. With Scottish women living more busy lives, they were less willing than their mums to 'spend all day over the stove'.
2. It was becoming increasingly difficult to obtain bones for soup-making. Many women complained that their butchers simply didn't seem to keep bones like they used to and bones certainly weren't easy to find in supermarkets!

Despite no previous soup-related promotional activity for Knorr cubes, 'discoverers' of Knorr felt they had found a genuine alternative to bone-boiled stock, which both looked and tasted like home-made. Oxo, with its distinctive taste and dark colour, did not.

This explained Knorr's strength in Scotland.

DEVELOPING A NEW STRATEGY FOR KNORR IN SCOTLAND

Research in 1977 in Scotland revealed both an untapped opportunity, and a cause for concern.

A Growth Opportunity for Knorr?

Many Scottish women, it seemed, had not yet discovered Knorr. When we talked to them, we found they were very interested in Knorr's benefits over home-made stock. However, they clearly felt somewhat guilty at the prospect of using a convenient alternative. If we could assure them that Knorr gave results as good as the real thing, it seemed we could exploit this potential. Quantitative research confirmed this opportunity.

Despite home-made soup accounting for half Knorr cube volume in Scotland, *only 25% of all home-made soups contained any cube at all* (Marplan 1977).

A Long-Term Threat to Knorr?

Younger women, in particular, seemed to be making home-made soup less often. It seemed very possible that these women were starting to adopt a more UK pattern of behaviour, only making soup when left-over carcasses were available, and otherwise using packet or canned soup.

Outside soup-making, Knorr's product characteristics clearly left it ill-equipped to challenge Oxo. If Knorr could not retain a soup-based 'foothold' in cupboards, there was a real danger of being squeezed out completely.

To sum up, we identified a real opportunity for Knorr to grow volume by actively exploiting Scottish soup-making. This potential growth, however, could only be realised if, in the long-term, Scottish women maintained their desire for home-made soup.

1977 – A NEW MARKETING STRATEGY FOR SCOTLAND

Knorr's most competitive positioning outside Scotland seemed to remain one of focusing on its more subtle flavour contribution in the context of casseroles. Soup-making was infrequent and a 'real stock' claim had little relevance – most women had never made real stock in their lives!

We decided to be bold, and to tailor a new strategy specifically to Scotland. Instead of playing the same game as Oxo – we were changing the rules.

MARKETING OBJECTIVES

We set out to exploit Knorr's unique competitive benefit in Scotland, to grow sales, share, and via maintaining our price premium over Oxo, to increase profit. We hoped to achieve this by:

Primarily
1. Increasing frequency of usage of Knorr in soups among existing Knorr users.
2. Encouraging trial of Knorr in home-made soups by non-Knorr users.

Secondly
3. Maintaining levels of home-made soup-making.
4. Increasing Knorr usage in other meals.
   (Qualitative research suggested that once Knorr was in cupboards, usage tended to spread to other dishes).

THE CREATIVE BRIEF

Advertising Objectives

1. To reinforce existing users' perceptions of Knorr as a genuine alternative to home-made stock and so encourage more frequent usage in soups.
2. To make more women aware of the benefits of Knorr cubes in home-made soup-making and so encourage them to try Knorr cubes in soups.
3. To maintain the frequency and appeal of home-made soup-making.

Proposition

Because stock made with Knorr stock cubes is as tasty as home-made stock, but more convenient, they are particularly suitable for making soup.

NB: Convenience in this sense meant more than just time-saving. It embraced the broader issues of no mess, no need to have key ingredients (eg a chicken carcass) etc.

Tone

This needed to reflect the cultural context of soup-making in Scotland, ie everyday, family cooking.

Target Market

All home-made soup-makers (over 90% of housewives in Scotland).

We knew that our target felt a degree of guilt at the idea of 'cheating' by using stock cubes – we therefore needed to assure them that Knorr produced stock that was as good and wholesome as the 'real thing'.

Executional Guidelines

We decided to feature Knorr Ham Cubes – a flavour introduced in 1974. Ham cubes were sold predominantly in Scotland, where they were particularly popular for making Pea and Ham soup.

THE CREATIVE SOLUTION

BMP produced a creative idea called 'Monday Night' – centred on two Highland friends, Hughie and Jamie.

The men were so naïvely innocent of the cooking process that they could only assume that chicken the night before inevitably meant chicken soup the night after.

They were left totally bewildered when Hughie's wife somehow managed to create a wonderful Pea and Ham soup the next day. Her little secret – Knorr Ham Stock Cubes.

PRE-TESTING THE CAMPAIGN

'Monday Night' was qualitatively tested – with extremely positive results. The campaign was felt to be perfectly in tune with Scottish values: the wry humour, the ignorance of the men about cooking, and the value attached to good home cooking. The message was felt to be relevant and appealing to both Knorr users and non-users. The campaign clearly showed the potential to meet our stated advertising objectives.

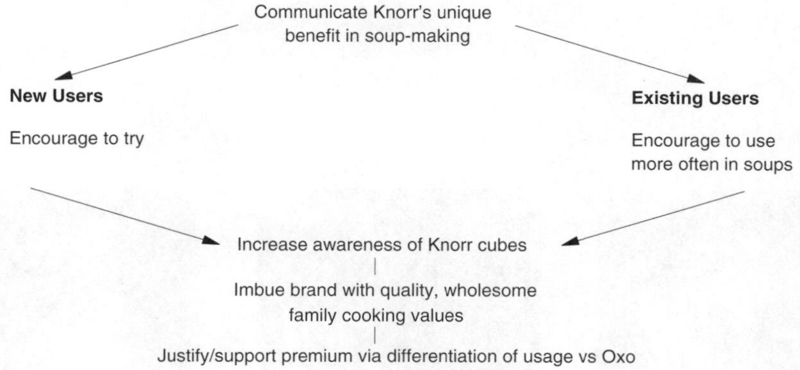

Figure 1. *How the campaign would work*

'MONDAY NIGHT'

'What d'you think the wife's cooking tonight Hughie?'
'Oh, I don't think at all – chicken soup. We had chicken soup yesterday.'

VO: Hughie doesn't know his wife uses Knorr Stock Cubes.

Boiling water over a Knorr Ham Stock Cube gives a delicious meaty tasting base for lentils and beans.

'This'll be the chicken soup then?'

'No Hughie, this'll be the pea and ham.'

'mmm. pea and ham...'

'How was your soup last night Hughie?'
'Oh delicious and the remarkable thing was it wasn't chicken, it was pea and ham.'

'Pea and ham from a chicken, now that's clever.'

VO: Knorr Stock Cubes – good soup and no bones about it.

From Small Beginnings...

Few people could have predicted, back in 1977, that we were embarking on a campaign which would still be running 13 years later! Few could have imagined the extent to which Hughie, Jamie and friends would touch Scottish hearts.

'Pea and Ham from a chicken' quickly became a national catchphrase. Phil McCol (the actor playing Jamie) became a 'celebrity' over-night. And even now, women in groups talk about 'Pea and Ham' cars (Morris Minors!) and 'Pea and Ham' roads (winding Highland roads!).

CAMPAIGN DEVELOPMENT HISTORY

1977 – 82

'Monday Night' ran annually from the winter of 1977/78 until 1980. The CPC account then moved agency, where it was recommended that given the strength of Knorr cubes in Scotland, all available monies be deployed behind more aggressively trying to grow Knorr cube volume in the rest of the UK – where sales remained static.

As a result, Scotland received no support after December 1980 until the winter of 1982, when BMP regained the account.

Analysis at this time revealed indications that Knorr's hold had begun to slip in Scotland.

TABLE 6

	1980 %	1981 %	1982 %
Knorr volume share	39.1	39.1	35.1
Knorr penetration	39.2	38.6	34.5

Source: 1980/81 Nielsen, 1982 NMRA, TGI

It was decided to re-air 'Monday Night' in December 1982, with a 'holding' objective.

In 1983, the strategy in Scotland was re-evaluated.

1983

Research concluded that whilst the soup-making strategy was still the optimum route for Knorr in Scotland, and whilst 'Monday Night' was as popular as ever, some younger women were beginning to feel it portrayed Scottish life in a somewhat negative way. The *appearance* of Hughie's wife was the main cause of this criticism.

'She really annoys me – she looks very old fashioned – a 'wee wifey' in her pinney'.

The wife's role as a 'provider' was clearly not contentious – Scottish women respected this. It was agreed to develop a new execution within the same campaign which updated the *look* of the wife, rather than her *role*. The objectives of the advertising remained the same.

A new creative idea, 'Moira', was developed. Jamie and Hamish were seen lamenting the apparent sad demise of their hen 'Moira', as they approvingly ate a fine Cock-a-Leekie soup – only to be interrupted by 'Moira' miraculously appearing in the door-way!

Pre-testing confirmed 'Moira' as tremendously appealing and clearly having the potential to refresh the campaign as intended. 'Moira' ran for the first time in December 1984.

1984 – 1989

One interesting finding from developing 'Moira' was that Hamish's more contemporary looking wife seemed to set 'Monday Night' back in context – to the extent that both executions ran in tandem until 1989.

'Monday Night' was then replaced by 'Hen Night', which brought the campaign raucously up to date. Hamish is seen proudly relating how his wife had gone all the way to Inverness for a hen night – such was her dedication to finding just the right hen for his soup. Instead we see her catching a stripper's sporran to the strains of 'What's New Pussycat?'!

This idea received a tremendous reception in research (with lots of cock-a-leekie jokes!). The idea of the wife using a stock cube for her *own* benefit (ie, so she could get out) while, importantly, the men still enjoyed a great tasting soup, was clearly a very modern expression of Knorr's 'real stock' benefit.

> 'Little do they know we're not at home slaving over their soup!'

> 'It's brilliant – even better than the Pea and Ham one'.

'Hen Night' ran with 'Moira' in November/December 1989.

MEDIA

The media strategy has been broadly similar since the beginning of our campaign: a burst of activity focusing on the key Knorr cube sales periods in Scotland (ie November, December and January) at an average weight of 1,000 housewife TVRs.

Some years have differed slightly. If additional advertising monies have become available at the end of the CPC fiscal year, it has been agreed to deploy them in Scotland to give the campaign an additional 'kick' at the beginning of the soup-making season.

'MOIRA'

'This is a great drop of Cock-a-Leekie Hamish'
'Aye, she was a fine wee bird was Moira'
'Best soup I've ever tasted'
'Aye, she never let us down, even to this day. I miss the eggs though.'

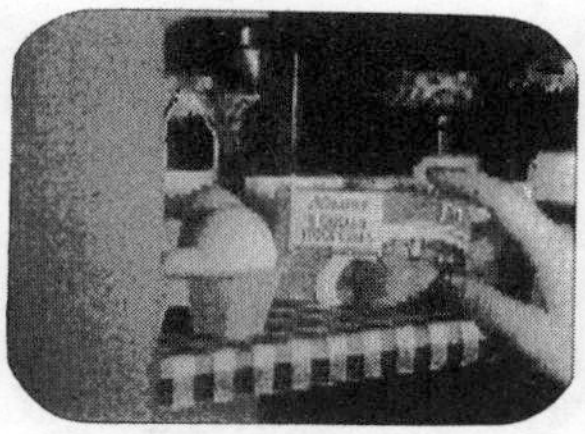

VO: What Hamish doesn't know is that his wife uses Knorr Stock Cubes.

Simply pour boiling water over a Chicken Stock Cube and you've a delicious meaty tasting base

for Cock-a-Leekie soup without the bones.

'Och, it's how she would have wanted it.'
'Aye, I suppose...'

SHOT OF CHICKEN AT DOOR

'Moira?'

'Moira...'

VO: Knorr Stock Cubes – good soup and no bones about it.

'HEN NIGHT'

'On your own tonight Hamish?'
'Aye, Elspeth has gone to Inverness for a hen night.'

'All that way just to pick up a chicken?!'
'Aye, she doesn't make the best soup in the Highlands for nothing'

VO: Hamish doesn't know his wife uses a Knorr Stock Cube to make a delicious meaty base

for Cock-a-Leekie soup

'Probably spent hours deciding on just the right hen for your soup'
'Aye well, that's devotion for you'

MUSIC STARTS: Tom Jones, 'What's new Pussycat'

MUSIC CONTINUES

MUSIC CONTINUES

MUSIC FADES OUT...

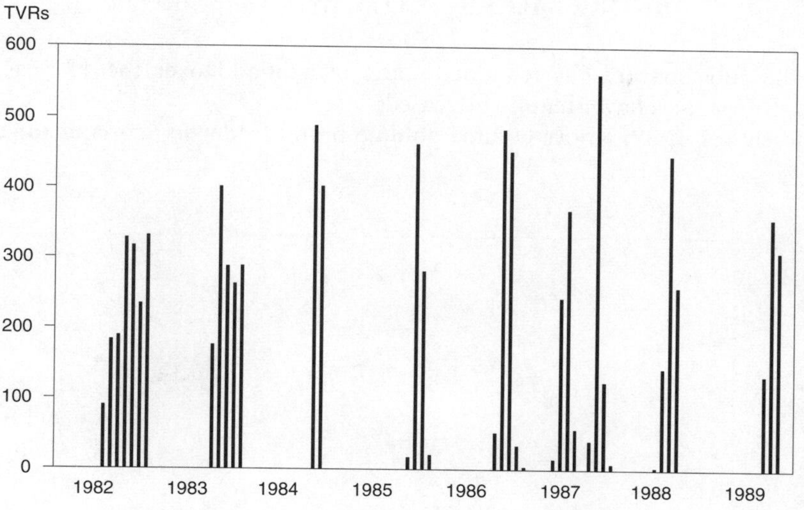

Figure 2. *Knorr housewife TVRs in Scotland*
Source: 1981–90 BARB

EVALUATING THE CAMPAIGN

We have faced a number of difficulties in evaluating this campaign.

1. Stock cubes sales are highly seasonal. Knorr sales in Scotland (due to the soup-making bias) are even more so. We have thus had to attempt to remove the effect of seasonality from our analysis.
2. Knorr has been supported every year in Scotland (as has Oxo), with the exception of 1981. As such, there is little inbuilt variability in the advertising data to help in isolating advertising effects.
3. In the year Knorr received no advertising, the retail audit company was changed – altering pick-up on both market and brand level. Our *sales* trend analysis has thus largely focused on the period since 1981.
4. Bovril cubes were launched nationally in 1978, which introduced a considerable change in the structure of the cubes market, at the same time as the start of the Knorr campaign in Scotland.
5. Research budgets only allowed ad hoc tracking of usage behaviour in Scotland.

In spite of these difficulties, we are able to demonstrate how:

— Sales and share increased steadily over the 13 years from introduction of our campaign, to the extent that Knorr is now *brand leader* in Scotland.
— Knorr's volume gains have resulted from long-term changes in soup-making behaviour which exactly match those set out in our advertising objectives.
— Behavioural changes and hence Knorr's growth, were a direct *result* of our Scottish campaign and would not have occurred in its absence.

KNORR SALES IN SCOTLAND, 1977 – 1990

While the cube market has remained static in Scotland over the 13 year period studied, Knorr sales have steadily increased.

At the end of 1989, Knorr became volume brand leader in Scotland for the first time.

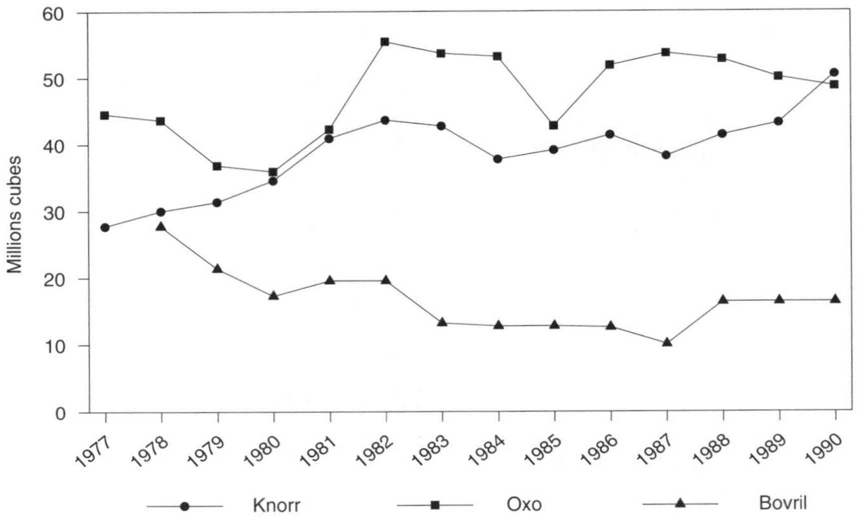

Figure 3. *Cubes volume Scotland*
Source: Nielsen 1977–81, NMRA 1982–90

TABLE 7: VOLUME BRAND SHARES

	1977 %	1981 %	1989 %
Oxo	60.6	40.5	43.7
Knorr	37.4	39.1	45.8
Bovril	—	18.8	5.5
Others	2.0	1.6	5.0

Source: 1977 & 1981 Nielsen, 1989 NMRA

Because of Knorr's continued price premium relative to the rest of the market, the volume share in 1989 equated to a value share of almost two thirds of total market value.

Knorr cubes are now a £4m brand in Scotland – more than twice the value of Oxo (NMRA, 1989).

Effect of New Varieties

Two new varieties of Knorr cubes were successfully introduced in 1984 (lamb and vegetable).

However, these varieties still account for less than 14% of annual volume in Scotland. The best selling varieties (chicken and ham) have both steadily grown in volume by more than 40% since 1984.

Therefore, overall brand growth is due to core variety growth, not just new introductions.

WHERE DID KNORR GROWTH COME FROM?

Bovril cube volume has been in long-term decline as its distribution has steadily been eroded. Bovril cubes are very similar to Oxo in both flavour (strong, beefy) and format ('dry', crumbly) – as such it seems highly probable that Bovril's volume is being picked up by Oxo. This has therefore 'buoyed up' Oxo sales and share.

What seems to be emerging in Scotland is not *one* cube market but two!

— A soup-making cube market (Knorr) which is increasing.
— A non soup-making cube market (Oxo/Bovril) which is declining.

Although we don't have quantitative data to validate this hypothesis, it seems the most probable scenario from both sales and qualitative data.

Thinking back to our objectives, this is exactly what we would expect to see if advertising was working as we planned.

We were not expecting Knorr volume to be gained primarily from other cubes at all – our 'competitors' were either bones or convenience soups. We would therefore expect additional Knorr cube volume to be largely incremental to the rest of the market.

This would also seem to explain why Scotland is increasing its share of all cubes sold in the UK, soup-making being the only major difference between the two markets.

SOUP-MAKING BEHAVIOUR IN SCOTLAND, 1977 – 1990

Long-term trends illustrate that the behavioural objectives of our advertising have been met.

Home-made soup has remained popular in Scotland

Home-made soup-making has not collapsed in Scotland as we feared.

TABLE 8: TOTAL HOME-MADE SOUP OCCASIONS IN SCOTLAND (MILLIONS OF OCCASIONS)

1981	1985	1986	1988	1989
57	53	61	56	59

Source: Family Food Panel, Winter/Spring

Neither has home-made soup lost out to more convenient versions.

TABLE 9: HOME-MADE SOUP IN SCOTLAND
PERCENTAGE OF ALL SOUP OCCASIONS

1981 %	1985 %	1986 %	1988 %	1989 %
47	47	45	45	48

Source: Family Food Panel, Winter/Spring

We had a particular fear that a new generation of women would reject making soup. This has not occurred.

TABLE 10: PERCENTAGE OF HOME-MADE SOUPS MADE BY YOUNGER WOMEN

Age	1981 %	1988 %
17–34	17	19

Source: Family Food Panel, Winter/Spring
Base: Home-made soup occasions

Therefore, the long-term platform on which Knorr depended, ie home-made soup-making, remained stable. We achieved our first objective.

With the home-made soup-making platform stable, cube usage in soups has increased.

There has been a dramatic increase in both the number of Scottish women who regularly use cubes in soups, and in the number of soups made with a stock cube.

The possible scenario whereby women only make soups when they have a left-over carcass available does not seem to have materialised.

TABLE 11: PENETRATION OF CUBES AMONG HOME-MADE SOUP-MAKERS IN SCOTLAND

	1977 %	1983 %	1986 %
Ever use cubes in soups	25	35	48
Always use cubes in soups	22	27	43

Source: Marplan 1977, Schlackman 1983 & 1986
Base: All housewives in Scotland

Our second objective of effecting a long-term increase in cube usage within home-made soups has been met.

TABLE 12: PENETRATION OF CUBES IN HOME-MADE SOUPS IN SCOTLAND

	1977 %	1986 %
Soups containing a cube	25	47

Source: Marplan 1977, Schlackman 1986
Base: All home-made soups in Scotland

Knorr usage within soups has increased

A growing proportion of soups contain a Knorr cube. Knorr is the dominant brand of cube used in soups – by 1986 accounting for nearly 75% of all 'cube soup occasions'. This has led to a dramatic increase in the penetration of Knorr in soups.

TABLE 13: PERCENTAGE OF ALL HOME-MADE SOUPS CONTAINING A KNORR CUBE IN SCOTLAND

1977 %	1986 %
24	35

Source: Marplan 1977, Schlackman 1986
Base: All home-made soups in Scotland

We have achieved another of our objectives.

Knorr usage in other dishes has increased

Having gained a presence in cupboards via soup-making, Knorr cubes are increasingly being used in other dishes.

TABLE 14: KNORR USAGE IN OTHER DISHES

Using in casseroles			Using in gravies			Using in mince		
1981 %	1983 %	1986 %	1981 %	1983 %	1986 %	1981 %	1983 %	1986 %
41	63	74	20	41	50	N/A	21	23

Source: SRA 1981, Schlackman 1983 & 1986
Base: Knorr buyers in Scotland

We have therefore met our final behavioural objective – that of increasing Knorr usage in meals other than soups.

In Summary

Long-term behaviour has changed exactly as we planned in our advertising objectives.

It appears that the home-made soup-making platform has been maintained, and Knorr has been able to capitalise on this, in a way which has increased both penetration among soup-makers (as shown earlier) and frequency of use (see Table 15).

TABLE 15: AVERAGE NUMBER OF KNORR CUBES USED PER YEAR PER USER IN SCOTLAND

1977	1981	1986	1989
41	58	63	78

Source: Nielsen 1977, NMRA 1981/86 & 1989, TGI

We hope by now to have demonstrated that we have met our sales and share objectives for Knorr and that these were achieved via behavioural changes exactly as planned.

It could well be argued that all this is completely unrelated to the advertising. We will now show that this is not the case.

EVALUATION OF 'INTERMEDIATE' DATA

Appeal

This campaign is hugely popular. It is always discussed spontaneously in groups and despite the high exposure, women never seem to tire of seeing it.

Hughie, Hamish and friends are perceived as charmingly naïve, but totally believable – people have taken them to their hearts.

> 'That ad's been out for years and we're still laughing at it'.

> 'I come from the West Highlands and I know these people. I know lots of people like that and I just relate to them'.

> 'It's a nice humour as well – very sort of dry – a Highland humour'.

This is supported by tracking data. 60% of women recalling the Knorr cubes advertising in Scotland in 1989 stated that they liked it (50% higher than the Millward Brown average).

Awareness

1. Knorr's 'Base Level' of advertising awareness, as measured by Millward Brown, has more than trebled over the monitored years. This is a rough measure of

awareness 'credit' – the higher the base level, the longer the campaign would be remembered after it stopped.

2. Spontaneous awareness of Knorr cubes has steadily increased over the period tracked, and in 1989 moved above that of Oxo.
   As media spend has remained relatively static, it seems that we are benefiting from an accumulating advertising effect; with each new burst building on the success of the former. (NB: As we will discuss later, econometric modelling supports this view).
3. Absolute levels of advertising awareness are also very high. Photoprompted awareness of Knorr advertising in Scotland stood last year at over 75%, with two thirds of those aware remembering the brand correctly.

Communication

The campaign clearly communicates the proposition of good, natural stock, ideal for soup-making.

TABLE 16: COMMUNICATION (SPONTANEOUS)

	%
Tastes as good as the real thing	30
Makes good soup without the bones	25
Quick and convenient	20

Source: Millward Brown, November 1989 – January 1990
Base: All recalling Knorr cubes advertised in Scotland

Knorr Imagery

The imagery of Knorr stock cubes in Scotland is one of goodness and wholesomeness – not a convenient cop-out!

TABLE 17: KNORR STOCK CUBE IMAGERY

	Scotland %	UK %
Makes a good stock	89	76
Suitable for home-made soup	94	80

Source: Millward Brown
Base: All Knorr users

In Summary

The advertising seems to have met all of its 'intermediary' objectives – generating awareness for Knorr cubes and communicating their benefit via a very popular, high profile campaign (and at much lower levels of TVRs than our largest competitor).

TABLE 18: SCOTLAND TVRs, 1982 – 1989

Total Oxo	Knorr
16,136	8,876

Source: BARB

PROVING THE CONTRIBUTION OF ADVERTISING

We have shown how Knorr sales and share have grown as a result of behavioural changes, in exactly the way we planned. We have also shown how we have met our advertising objectives, in terms of 'intermediate variables'. The question now is, did our advertising *cause* these changes?

There are two methods by which we will answer this question:

1. By eliminating other variables.
2. By validating our hypotheses through an econometric model.

ELIMINATING OTHER VARIABLES

Distribution

Sterling distribution has remained constant for both Knorr and Oxo at nearly 100% since our advertising began, thus it cannot have been a significant catalyst for change.

Packaging

There have been only very minor modifications to packaging.

Other Activity

There have been no significant PR or promotional campaigns over the period. CPC have intermittently developed press campaigns for Knorr to a 'rest of UK' strategy (ie, non soup-making). These have of course run in Scotland, but research has consistently suggested they have limited relevance to Scottish women.

Although Knorr markets other products in Scotland, any activity during the advertised period has been on a national level.

Meat Consumption

Meat consumption has remained constant in Scotland since 1979. There seems no indication therefore that a decline in 'left-overs' has resulted in an increased need for cubes in soup.

Pricing

Knorr has, in real terms, become better value relative to Oxo by about 10%, over the period analysed. We would hypothesise however than the influence of this is probably relatively small, for two reasons:

1. The absolute premium of Knorr is still very significant. Qualitative evidence suggests that for people for whom price is important, the reduction of a few pence per packet for Knorr would make minimal difference to purchase intention.
2. Knorr is not primarily competing with Oxo or any other cube – certainly not in the key usage area of soups.

As we show later, econometric modelling confirms that Knorr price has minimal influence on sales.

In Summary

We find it difficult to see what factor, other than our advertising, could have produced the behavioural and sales effects which we planned and have achieved in Scotland.

VALIDATING OUR HYPOTHESES THROUGH AN ECONOMETRIC MODEL

In order to validate our conclusions concerning other possible causal variables, and in turn *quantify* the sales contribution of advertising, we constructed an econometric model.

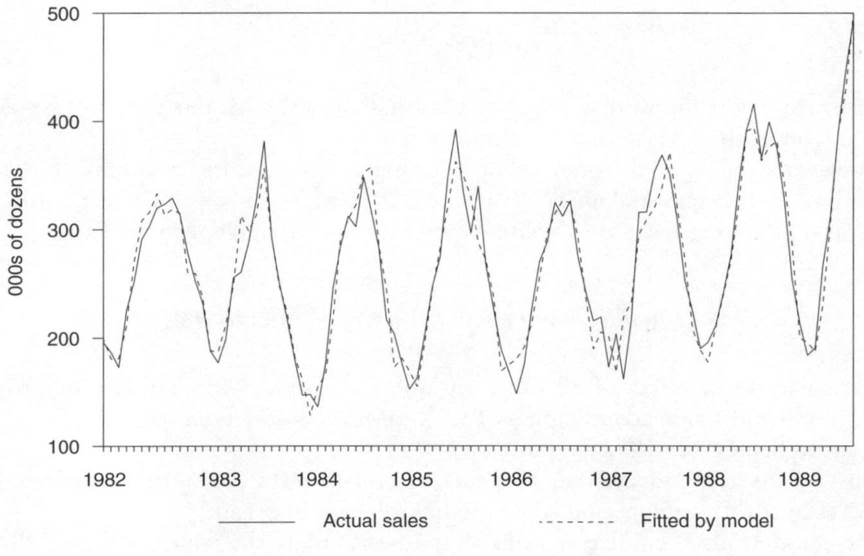

Figure 4. *Knorr Stock Cubes volume sales – actual vs fitted*
Source: NMRA

The technical details of the model are appended, together with appropriate tests to demonstrate its statistical validity.

Figure 4 shows Knorr's actual sales volume and the model's fit to it. The model explains 94% of the variation in Knorr sales from September 1982 to January 1990.

The model investigated the influences of the following factors on Knorr sales over the period 1982 to 1990:

1. Pricing and distribution for Knorr, Oxo, Bovril and own label.
2. New Knorr varieties.
3. Seasonality.
4. Knorr, Oxo and Bovril advertising.

Pricing

Knorr sales were found to be remarkably price insensitive. The decline in real price since 1982 would seem to have contributed only 1.6% of Knorr volume over the period studied.

No impact of competitive pricing was found.

Distribution

This had no significant effect on Knorr sales.

New Knorr Varieties

Introduction of new Knorr varieties was found to have minimal influence on sales.

Seasonality

Temperature was found to be the key seasonal variable. More cubes will be sold in a cold winter, the reverse in a hot summer.

However, the model found that although temperature accounts for slight variation in the seasonal peaks from year to year – it was not responsible for generating the long-term sales volume increases that we have seen for Knorr.

Quantifying the Contribution of Advertising

After isolating the effect of all other variables, the model was able to quantify the direct contribution of advertising as *12.5% of total Knorr volume* in Scotland, over the period September 1982 – January 1990.

This means that advertising alone is responsible for *90%* of Knorr's volume increase over this same period (the remainder is due to price).

The model also confirmed our hypothesis that the sales volume directly attributable to advertising was growing from year to year.

UNDERSTANDING HOW THE ADVERTISING WORKS

Shorter and Longer Term Effects

In our evaluation of this campaign, two 'levels' of effect have emerged.

1. *Short-term Effects:*
   These mirror the timing of the advertising bursts and produce discernible short-term uplifts in sales. This is a result of an immediate behavioural response, advertising increasing both immediate purchasing of Knorr cubes, and also usage of those cubes already in the cupboard at home (resulting in re-purchase a short time later).

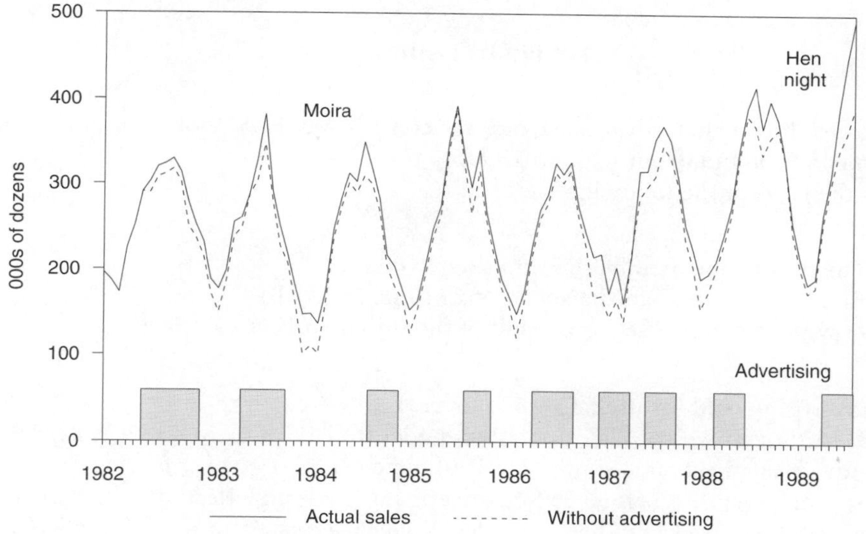

Figure 5. *Knorr stock cubes volume sales, actual versus without advertising*

   The introduction of new executions seems to have effected a particularly marked short-term uplift in sales over the advertised period.
   Awareness data mirrors this pattern of short-term response.
2. *Longer term Effects:*
   Even though the model was not specifically set up to measure a genuine, long-term accumulating effect of advertising on sales, the previous figure shows:

   — Each burst produces a sales effect with a very long 'tail' (to the extent that there is no point during any year when advertising is having no effect on sales).
   — Sales are always above the level preceding the last burst, when the subsequent burst of advertising takes place.

> As we have seen, this pattern is reflected in both brand and advertising awareness data. Awareness is steadily building over time, despite an almost constant level of media weight.

It seems, therefore, that advertising effects are by no means restricted to the short-term. Instead, there seems to be a 'building' effect over a longer period of time.

This longer-term effect has undoubtedly played a key role in the success of the campaign – enabling us to achieve a significantly higher level of return over the 13 year advertised period than we would perhaps otherwise expect to achieve from a low absolute level of media spend.

It is interesting to speculate whether Knorr could have realistically achieved long-term volume growth, without the benefit of these carry-over effects.

PROFITABILITY

We have shown that advertising directly contributed 12.5% of total Knorr cubes volume in Scotland, from 1982 to 1990.

On the basis of the following factors:

1. The profit generated by this additional volume
2. An average annual media spend of £110,000 (BARB)
3. Low production costs, as a result of the stability of the campaign

the advertising paid for itself 1.8 times over.

NB: Although we couldn't apply the model to data prior to 1982, it is probable that advertising generated similar levels of incremental profit *before* this date.

However, even if, before 1982, advertising had no effect at all, subsequent incremental pay-back has been at a level which *alone* ensures profitability of the overall campaign (from 1977 to 1990).

The Real Value of the Advertising

In estimating that advertising directly generated 12.5% of total Knorr volume (1982–1990) the model had to assume that had the campaign never run, there would have been no adverse market trends working to reduce Knorr's sales.

However, as we have seen, we believe this assumption to be highly optimistic.

Our research in 1977 clearly highlighted the likelihood that home-made soup-making and cube usage within it would gradually decline. A decline in Knorr volume would inevitably follow.

The *real* contribution of our advertising to CPC profit is therefore likely to be considerably higher.

THE IMPLICATIONS OF ADOPTING A 'LOCAL' STRATEGY

We have proved that our advertising successfully generated incremental profit for CPC in Scotland.

Fundamental to this success was our decision to adopt a 'local' strategy.

Only by doing so could we effectively exploit a unique competitive benefit, ie Knorr's suitability for making home-made soup.

Only by thinking 'local' were we able to 'change the rules' and consequently topple Oxo to become brand leader.

A comparison with the performance of Knorr cubes in the rest of the UK confirms this view.

Continued support (on a 'more subtle flavour' platform) has encouraged some volume growth for Knorr, but this growth has largely been flavour and distribution-led.

Oxo still massively dominates the market.

TABLE 19: VOLUME BRAND SHARES

	Scotland %	Rest of UK %
Knorr	45.8	10.3
Oxo	43.7	74.6
Bovril	5.5	10.8
Others	5.0	4.3

Source: NMRA, year to January 1990

SUMMARY

CPC adopted a bold, new strategy when they agreed to develop advertising for Knorr cubes which specifically targeted Scotland, in order to exploit and defend a unique competitive advantage.

We have shown that these objectives have been very successfully achieved.

Since its inception in 1977, a famous, long-running campaign has developed – the effects of which have built year on year, with the result that Knorr now outsells all other cubes in Scotland.

The advertising worked exactly as we planned:

— By helping to maintain Scottish women's commitment to making soup.
— By encouraging more Scottish women to use Knorr cubes more often in their home-made soups.
— And by fuelling increased use of Knorr cubes in other meals in Scotland.

Most importantly, not only has the advertising *worked*, it has also demonstrably contributed to overall CPC profit.

CONCLUSIONS

We acknowledge that we have set ourselves a difficult task – that of proving that *only* by developing advertising to meet the specific needs of Scotland, were CPC able to defend and grow a vital proportion of their total business.

We feel convinced however that this is so and it is only thanks to Hughie, Hamish and friends, that Knorr is now brand leader in Scotland.

Maybe sometimes *only* thinking and acting 'local' can pay.

TECHNICAL APPENDIX

An explanation and validation of the econometric model

For reasons of space and confidentiality, this is an abbreviated version of the technical appendix submitted to the judges.

Stock cubes are essentially a store-cupboard item of which consumers tend to hold several weeks supply. Advertising may not therefore necessarily prompt any immediate purchase but simply encourage faster use of existing stores.

This led us to develop the hypothesis that any Knorr advertising potentially had two effects, one reducing the existing level of stores in consumers' cupboards, the other prompting actual purchase at, or close to, the time of advertising.

We developed the following theoretical model which relates the quantity purchased in any four-weekly period to a range of marketing factors, both Knorr and competitive, to consumers' *usage* and expected usage in that period and to the *change in household stores* between any one period and that prior to it.

The Theoretical Model

(1) $Q_t = a_0 + a_1S_t + a_2E(U)_t + a_3T + a_4P + a_5A$

Q = quantity purchased, S = consumers' stores at the beginning of the period, E(U) = expected usage, T = temperature, P = price, A = advertising, for both Knorr and competitors.

(2) $S_t = S_{t-1} + Q_t - U_t$
(3) $U_t = b_0 + b_1T + b_2A$
(4) $E(U) = f(T)$ proxied by $c + c_1T_t + c_2T_{t-1}$
ie expected usage in period t is a function of temperature.

By rearranging equation (2), substituting for household stores in equation (1) and taking first differences, we obtained a theoretical equation linking Knorr sales in any four-weekly period to usage, store levels and marketing activity. In order to estimate the model, the empirical specification necessarily differed from this theoretical one in two minor respects.

We used the model to test the following hypotheses:

1. That the model specification is appropriate.
2. That as stores increase, quantity purchased will decrease, all else remaining equal.
3. As temperature increases, stores will be depleted less quickly and less will be bought.
4. As advertising increases, stores will be depleted.
5. As temperature rises, purchases fall.
6. An increase in price leads to a drop in sales.
7. An increase in advertising leads to an uplift in sales.

The final empirical model was estimated by non-linear least squares using four weekly NMRA retail audit data over the period July 1982 to January 1990 – 99 data points. The advertising data was in TVRs, the source of which was BARB. The model includes an additional advertising term for the recently introduced 'Hen Night' film which appears to be working harder than previous films and a dummy variable for a most unusual data period in February/March 1984.

The coefficients of the model all had signs consistent with the above hypotheses, demonstrating the appropriateness of the model. Apart from the 'Hen Night' campaign which was significant at the 90% level, all of the variables were significant at the 95% level. The model passes a range of diagnostic tests indicating that the data supports the theory. The reported statistical tests were: R^2, $\overline{R}^2$ standard error of regression, sum of squared residuals, Durbin's h-test, Lagrange multiplier tests (portmanteau tests for higher order autocorrelation) with up to 1, 4 and 13 lags, ARCH tests for auto-regressive heteroscedasticity (up to 1, 4 and 13 lags), the variance ratio test for homoscedasticity, Chow (parameter stability), Chow (post sample pred. failure), Q test (Box-Cox) 13 lags.

3

Volkswagen

How advertising helped Volkswagen and its dealers recover their profitability

ABOUT THE PAPER

This case highlights the broad benefits to a business of keeping demand ahead of supply and the power of advertising as a tool to achieve this.

Results and Payback

Since autumn 1995, Volkswagen and its dealers have enjoyed unprecedented success. They have sold 61 per cent more cars and achieved their highest ever share of the UK car market.

The evidence for advertising's part in this success is considerable. First, the paper demonstrates a statistical relationship between advertising communication and short listing of Volkswagen cars. Second, the paper demonstrates a correspondence between advertising and short-term growth in the UK. Third, it demonstrates that the different performance between the UK and other European markets can be related to different levels of advertising investment. Finally, the paper shows that other non-advertising factors, although vital to growth, can explain neither the pattern or the magnitude of this growth.

Advertising has enabled Volkswagen to keep demand for its products consistently ahead of supply. Short-term revenue gains are dramatic and the high lifetime value of a customer in the car market means that these benefits extend significantly into the long term.

Furthermore, the costs of doing business have decreased. In a market typified by surplus stock, Volkswagen has been selling cars as soon as they have left the factory. This has reduced storage costs and enabled Volkswagen to sell cars without the need for costly give-aways. It has also enabled Volkswagen to meet specific customer demands and therefore sell a richer mix of product. Economies of scale have further reduced unit costs.

Consumers too have benefited. In becoming more demand driven in the way it does business, Volkswagen is now more able to meet consumers' specific requirements. Moreover, by fuelling demand for its product in the new car market, resale values have increased, enabling customers to retain a higher proportion of their initial outlay when they come to sell their car.

INTRODUCTION

Since autumn 1995, Volkswagen UK and its dealers have enjoyed unprecedented business success. Making excellent products available at the right price was a necessary precondition for this success, but advertising – in bringing these developments to the notice of prospective car buyers – unlocked their full market potential and fuelled extraordinary levels of demand. In so doing, advertising has benefited three interested parties: Volkswagen UK (as an importer and wholesaler of cars), the Volkswagen dealer network, and Volkswagen's customers.[1]

MARKET BACKGROUND

Most of the UK car market falls into three volume sectors dominated by the three domestic marques: Ford, Vauxhall and Rover (Figures 1 and 2).

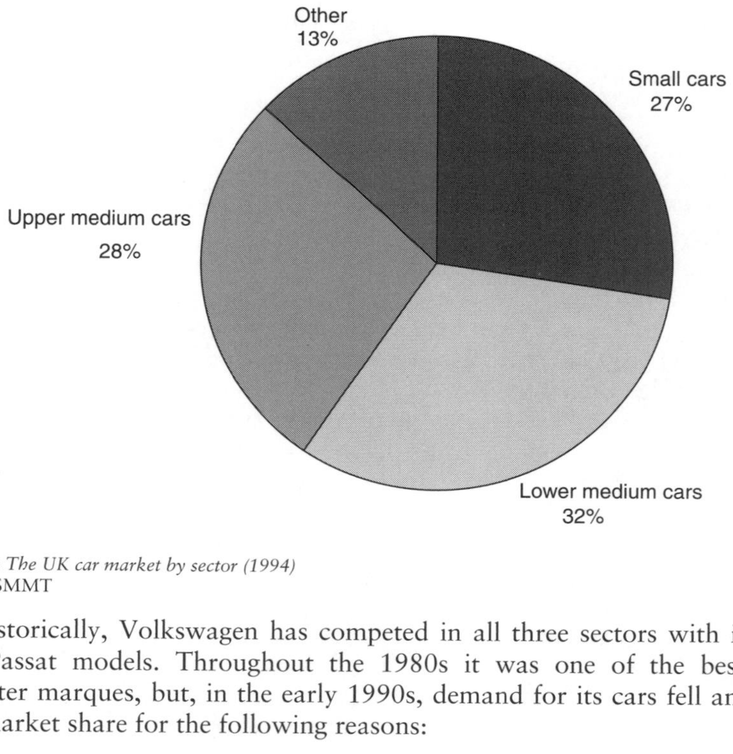

Figure 1: *The UK car market by sector (1994)*
Source: SMMT

Historically, Volkswagen has competed in all three sectors with its Polo, Golf and Passat models. Throughout the 1980s it was one of the best performing importer marques, but, in the early 1990s, demand for its cars fell and it began to lose market share for the following reasons:

1. Throughout this paper the following terminology will be used: Volkswagen = 'marque', Polo/Golf/Passat = 'model', Polo L/Golf GTi = 'variant'.

Price
Following Britain's withdrawl from the ERM, the value of sterling fell relative to the deutschmark, making Volkswagen's price position less competitive. Indeed, for a short period in Spring 1993, people had to pay an 18% premium for Volkswagens.

Competitive growth offensives
The French marques, Peugeot, Citroen and Renault, began to market themselves aggressively, advertising at a share of voice disproportionate to their market size, and (as the recession began to bite) offering more and more tactical sales incentives. For example, 0% finance deals or free insurance in the first year of ownership.

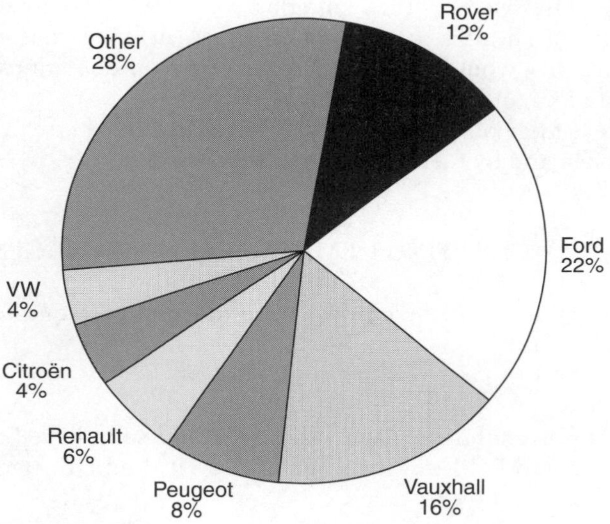

Figure 2: *The UK car market by manufacturer (1994)*
Source: SMMT

This had serious consequences for Volkswagen and its dealers. Costs increased as unsold cars languished in storage areas and showrooms. In addition, margins were sacrificed as Volkswagen offered more tactical incentives at both importer level and discounts at dealer level[2] in order to reverse declining share. Although decline was arrested in 1994, the long-term profitability of this 'holding strategy' was questionable.

2. The tactical sales incentives budget increased by a massive 350% between 1991 and 1994.

A STRATEGY FOR PROFITABLE GROWTH

In 1994 Volkswagen set itself two objectives:

— To increase its volume share in the UK not just to the point where the previous years' losses had been recovered, but beyond that, to achieve an unprecedented share level of 5.4% by 1996 and to continue to grow at a similar rate until the year 2000.

— To reduce the cost of doing business both as an importer and for its dealers, thereby increasing profitability at both levels.

Achieving improvements in both importer and dealer profitability was vital because their fates were mutually interlinked; without a significant improvement in profitability the dealers could not reinvest in their business. Without such reinvestment, they would not be able to gear up their operations to support a higher market share for Volkswagen in the long term.

To achieve these objectives Volkswagen needed to reverse the mismatch between supply and demand by fuelling demand for its cars.

CREATING DEMAND FOR VOLKSWAGENS

Good products at competitive prices were essential prerequisites for Volkswagen's subsequent growth:

Good products
Volkswagen was confident that it had, or would soon have, excellent products: a new and improved Polo was launched in late 1994 and a new Passat was expected in 1997.

Competitive pricing
Prices had been progressively realigned since their high point of early 1993. The last phase of realignment was completed in Autumn 1994, making Volkswagens competitive.

However, Volkswagen's market performance in late 1994 and early 1995 made it clear that product and pricing alone were not sufficient to fuel the demand necessary for profitable growth. Volkswagen therefore worked closely with BMP DDB to identify how demand could best be stimulated.

Key to subsequent strategy was a revised understanding of the car-buying process and the point at which marketing resources could be used most efficiently within it.

HOW PEOPLE MAKE DECISIONS IN THE CAR MARKET

Research indicated that the car-buying process typically divided into two phases: the passive phase and the active phase.

The 'Passive' Phase of the New Car-Buying Process

During the first phase, typically lasting two-and-a-half years, people were not consciously deciding which new car to buy but, by the end of it, most had actually formed a shortlist of the one or two models that most interested them. This shortlist was arrived at as a result of a continual – almost unconscious – review process, influenced by seeing cars around, or hearing good things about them via colleagues, friends, relations, or mass media (usually TV) advertising. To achieve a position on it, a car had to be deemed desirable and, just as crucially, affordable: if a car was assumed to be 'beyond my pocket' it would be rejected during this phase, no matter how desirable it was thought to be.[3]

> 'You know what you've got to spend so you don't bother going about looking at cars that are beyond your limits.'
>
> 'You've got a price range so you only look at what you think will fall within it.'
>
> 'I wouldn't go back to one of their dealers now unless I was really sure that I had enough money to buy the car I wanted, otherwise you feel so embarrassed.'
>
> Source: BMP DDB, Price and Price Communication Research

However, these all-important price perceptions were rarely based on any real knowledge about what a car would cost. In research, people who openly claimed to have no idea about car prices explained that they did not think about buying certain cars because they simply felt them to be beyond their budget. These feelings about price were based on various factors which often bore little relation to current pricing realities:

— A person's last active experience of the car market – probably two or three years previously.

— Word of mouth, usually based on other peoples' last active experience of the car market, again probably out of date.

— A car's image; more desirable, 'classy' car marques were assumed to cost more.

The 'Active' Phase of the New-Car-Buying Process

The second phase, lasting anything from one week to six months, was when people consciously looked to buy a new car by investigating the two or three models which had been shortlisted during the passive phase.[4] Most people started this process

3. The reasons for this were partly practical and partly emotional. On a practical level, people were far too busy to bother spending precious Saturday mornings traipsing round dealerships for cars they were not going to be able to buy. On an emotional level, they did not want to suffer the indignity of having to tell a dealer that they could not afford what was on offer.
4. The terminology here might be somewhat misleading because, for many prospective car buyers, even this phase is not terribly active. It often simply involves paying more attention than usual to car ads in national

with a clear idea of the car they wanted, and few changed their minds as a result of their investigation – they almost never bought a car which had not been on their original shortlist.

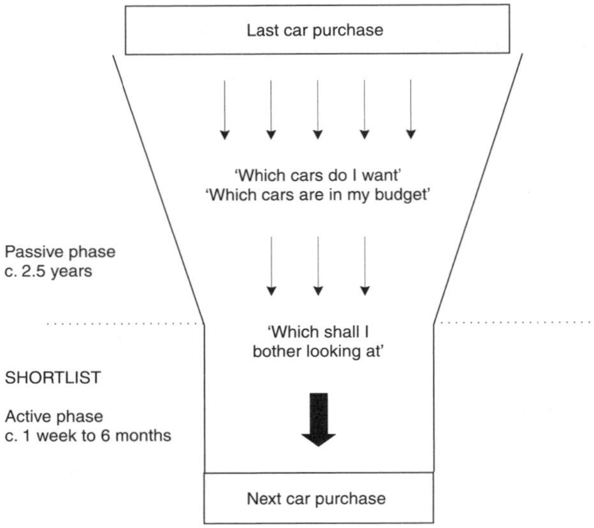

Figure 3: *The new-car-buying process*

VOLKSWAGEN'S PROBLEMS AND THEIR SOLUTIONS

This analysis of the buying process made it clear why demand for Volkswagens had declined:

— Not enough people wanted a Volkswagen car. Compared with heavily marketed 'stylish' French marques, Volkswagens were seen as much less desirable than they were in the heady boom-days of the 1980s. This was particularly true for Polo and Passat which, unlike Golf, had never really established identities in their respective market sectors.

— Not enough people realised that they could afford a Volkswagen car. People seriously overestimated the price differences between Volkswagen models and competitors. As a result, many people who clearly desired the cars were simply not bothering to shortlist them:

> 'I have thought about buying one, maybe a Golf, but they always come across as being more expensive, so I've always assumed that it wouldn't be a new car that I could afford.'

> 'I've thought about buying a Golf, but I've always associated them with being more pricey.'

---

newspapers, flicking through car magazines, picking up brochures from dealers, scanning list prices, and (perhaps) seeing what additional incentives might be on offer.

'The Polo's a nice little car ... but I wouldn't really look at one because it would be a bit more pricey.'

'The one thing that has always stopped me from looking at a Volkswagen is the cost.'

Source: BMP DDB Price and Price Communication Qualitative Research

These problems in the passive phase were exacerbated by a further problem in the active phase. Volkswagen and its dealers were spending a large amount of money on tactical purchase incentives to convert those people who had shortlisted Volkswagens. However, research into the impact of such incentives suggested that if people had got to the point of actually visiting a dealer, they were usually so committed to the idea of acquiring a Volkswagen that they were likely to buy one with or without any added incentive.[5]

Essentially, Volkswagen was spending a high proportion of its marketing budget on persuading the relatively small number of people who had shortlisted their cars to buy a car which they would probably have bought without such an incentive.

The solution was straightforward: Volkswagen needed to redirect its marketing budget if it wanted to fuel demand for its cars. Instead of offering unnecessary inducements to people in the active phase of the purchase process, it needed to focus on people when they were in the passive phase. These people needed to be persuaded that the marque and its models were both desirable and affordable; only then would Volkswagens get onto more shortlists.

IMPLICATIONS FOR ADVERTISING

The strategic implications for advertising were clear:

— We needed to move from a unified marque campaign to three model-focused campaigns.

— We needed to develop a campaign to tackle price misperceptions.

— We needed to increase the advertising budget.

Model-focused Campaigns

To ensure that all three volume models developed their own distinct and motivating identities – and, by doing so, to reinvigorate the overall marque – we needed to replace a common brand campaign, which had primarily benefited Golf, with three separate campaigns for Golf, Polo and Passat. Each campaign was designed to communicate the desirability of these models in the most appropriate way for the sector of the market in which they had to compete.[6]

---

5. BJM prices and incentives trade-off research, 1995.
6. Until 1995, Volkswagen's brand advertising had typically featured Golf GTi. The 'If only everything in life was as reliable as a Volkswagen' campaign was so strongly associated with Golf that even when other models were featured, consumers tended to assume that it was Golf being advertised.

— Polo advertising emphasised that Polo shared many of the benefits of a bigger car, most notably strength and safety. Two new television films ran between 1995 and 1997 which focused on this theme: 'Surprise' and 'Protection'. Press work also supported this theme.

— Passat advertising focused on the car's German design qualities. The 'Obsession' campaign ran on television, press and posters from the car's relaunch in April 1997.

— Golf advertising focused on product stories which still demonstrated class-leading qualities: direct injection diesel engineering and VR6 engine technology. 'UFO' and 'Beetle' ran on television throughout 1996 and early 1997.

A Campaign to Tackle Misperceptions about Volkswagen Prices

We needed to adopt an unconventional media and creative strategy to convince people that Volkswagens were not 'beyond their pockets' before they had finalised their new car shortlists.

Traditionally, advertising talking about car prices had appeared in the media used by people during the active phase of the new-car-buying process (such as local newspapers). However, research indicated that the ads which ran in such media were used selectively; prospective car buyers only attended to the prices of cars they had already shortlisted. We needed to talk to people while they were still in the passive phase. The implication was clear: we had to use relatively intrusive media channels.

Although people were genuinely surprised when confronted with Volkswagen's actual price levels in a research context, we found that communicating them in advertising was likely to be more tricky. People were so cynical about price points quoted in car ads that mere exposure to Volkswagen's prices would not be enough to address their misperceptions.[7] We needed to deliver that price point accompanied by some kind of overt challenge to their expectations. By doing so, we hoped that even if people had suspicions about the actual price points in the campaign, the challenging stance of the surrounding 'story' would be enough to leave people thinking 'Maybe Volkswagen's aren't beyond my pocket after all'.

A heavyweight television, poster, radio and press campaign aimed at sowing a seed of doubt in people's minds was developed called 'Letters'. This ran throughout 1996, featuring Polo and Golf models, and was refined in 1997 (evolving into 'Surprises').

7. There were two reasons for this cynicism: such prices tended to be surrounded by caveats and provisos (for example, 'excluding number plates and delivery'); or prices for bottom-of-the-range model variants were accompanied, somewhat misleadingly, by pictures of variants from the top of the range.

'AFFORDABILITY' ADS

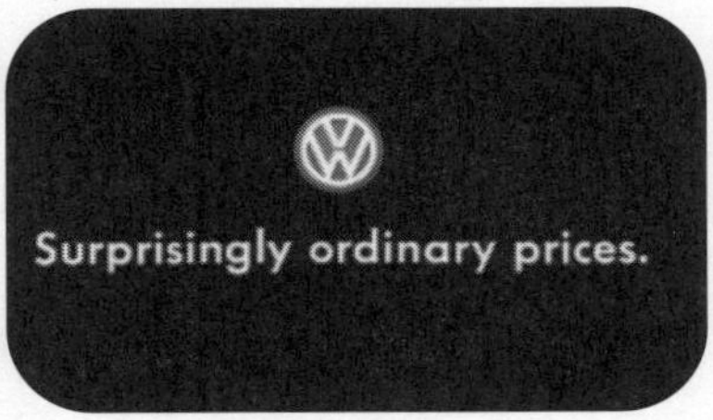

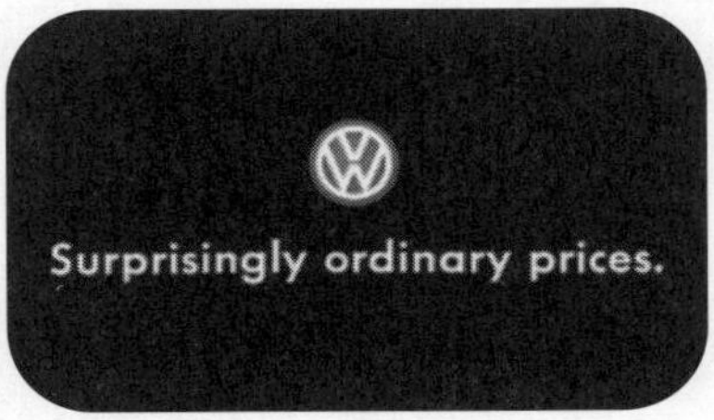

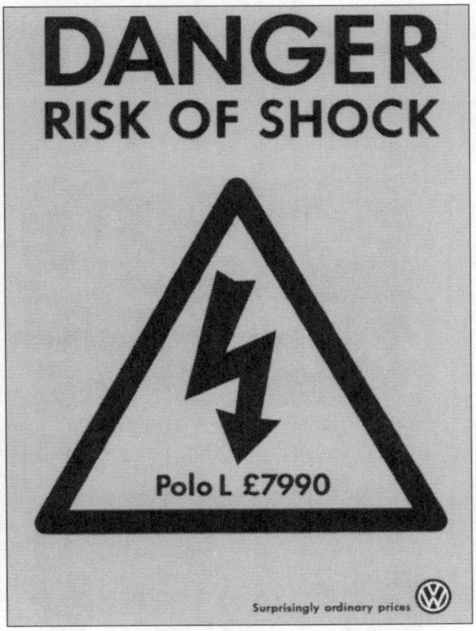

POLO 'PROTECTION'

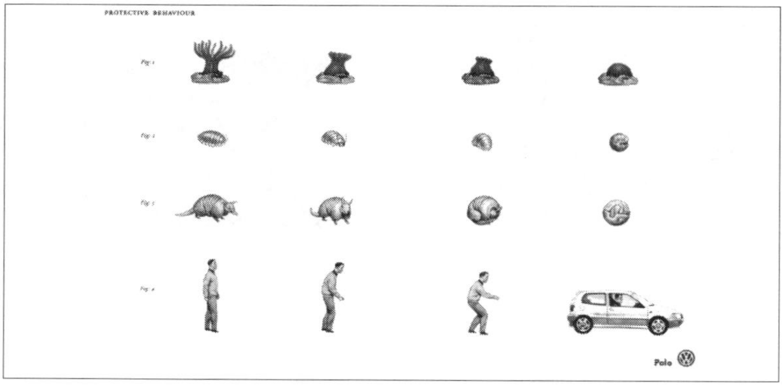

PASSAT 'OBSESSION'

GOLF 'BEETLE'

GOLF 'UFO'

Higher Level of Advertising Spend

Volkswagen could not support so many campaigns without spending more money on advertising. In 1995, following a detailed analysis of the optimum relationship between market share and share of voice in the UK car market, spend levels were increased.[8] This change took effect from September 1995.

This increase did not require a high increase in overall marketing spend. As outlined above, the strategy to boost demand for Volkswagens involved redirecting marketing resources which had previously been focused on people in the active phase of the purchase process to people who were in the passive phase. In practice, this meant that the money saved by reducing tactical incentives was spent on advertising instead.

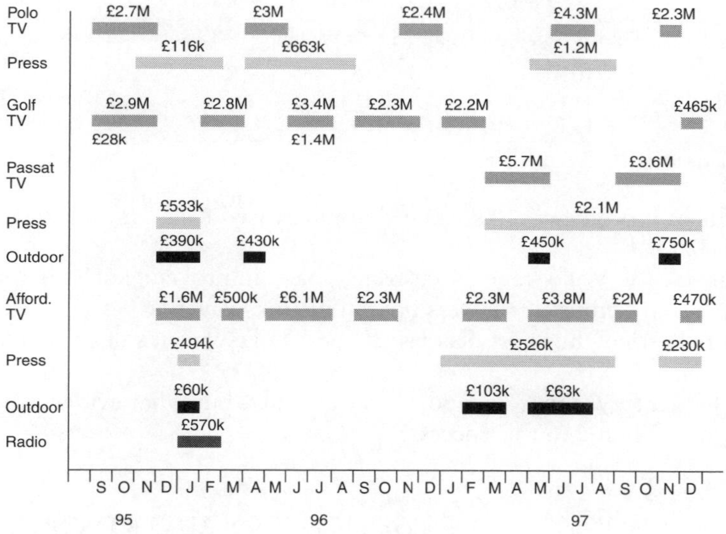

Figure 4: *Media schedule*

WHAT HAPPENED?

Between autumn 1995 and autumn 1997 Volkswagen met all its objectives. Overall sales grew by 61%, from 74,548 units in 1994 to 119,767 units in 1997.

Volume share increased. Indeed, in 1996 Volkswagen's share grew by 36%, the fastest rate of growth experienced by a top-ten car manufacturer for ten years, and far exceeding the original objectives set.[9]

8. Share of voice increased from 4.1% in 1994 to 5.2% in 1996 and to 5.9% in 1997.
9. In 1997 came the 'run out' year for the Mark 3 version of Golf. From September supplies were severely restricted as the factory prepared for mass production of the new (Mark 4) Golf.

The mismatch between supply and demand was addressed: demand moved ahead of supply to the point where the average time taken to sell a Volkswagen in the UK more than halved.

The amount of incentives offered to prospective Volkswagen buyers was reduced.

As sales became demand driven, Volkswagen increased its ability to predict – and then order from the factory – the model variants and specification levels which UK car buyers wanted. Since car buyers with precise needs (such as air-conditioning or blue metallic paint) were happy to pay for their needs to be met, the average price paid for Volkswagens increased between 1995 and 1997 relative to their sector averages.[10]

TABLE 1: ACTUAL PRICE PAID FOR VOLKSWAGENS INDEXED AGAINST SECTOR AVERAGE

	Polo vs. small	Golf vs. lower medium	Passat vs. upper medium
1995	101	110	103
1996	114	111	102
1997	114	114	109

Source: NCBS

Consequently, Volkswagen's value share increased even more dramatically than its volume share.[11]

The profile of Volkswagen's customer base improved; fewer bargain-driven, potentially 'promiscuous' car buyers bought a Volkswagen.

The costs of doing business decreased[12] and Volkswagen's dealers' margins were recovered.

Thus, the strategy was tremendously successful – but what evidence is there that advertising contributed to this success?

DEMONSTRATING THE EFFECT OF ADVERTISING

It is traditional in car market IPA effectiveness case studies to observe how hard it is to demonstrate an advertising effect in this market.[13] The most convincing cases tend to evaluate relatively 'discrete' advertising tasks such as campaigns to launch new models (for example, Nissan Micra) or coherent marque advertising campaigns which concentrate on promoting values common to all its models (for example, BMW).

10. This was not because people were paying less for other new cars within the respective market sectors: the absolute average amount spent increased in each successive year.
11. There is no standard industry-wide measure of value share available for the UK market. We calculated value share figures by using car volume data (from SMMT) and data on the average price paid for a new Volkswagen versus the average price paid for all new cars (from NCBS).
12. For example, car storage costs were reduced and the increased 'throughput' of cars meant that cashflow could be managed more astutely – see the section on 'Business Returns Due To Advertising'
13. The most commonly cited reasons are that it is a market where purchase is infrequent and 'high investment'; and where, because of the long purchase cycle, there are opportunities for many non-advertising variables to influence the ultimate purchase decision.

Volkswagen's move from one marque campaign to three model-specific and one price-related campaign made our evaluation task even harder than usual.

Nonetheless, we can show that the advertising has been extremely effective. Our evidence for this is as follows:

— Consumers responded to all the new advertising exactly as planned.

— There was a strong correspondence between Volkswagen's market performance and its advertising activity.

— Other factors cannot explain the pattern or the extent of Volkswagen's growth.

1. CONSUMERS RESPONDED TO THE ADVERTISING EXACTLY AS PLANNED

There is strong evidence that the advertising worked exactly as planned:

— It communicated the desirable qualities of the cars and, in so doing, improved their image.

— It communicated that the cars were not beyond people's pockets and therefore persuaded more people that the cars were affordable.

— This positioned Volkswagen as a better make to own.

— This translated into greater consideration and shortlisting of Volkswagens.

a) Advertising Communicated the Desirability of the Cars

As outlined above, the model campaigns were designed to communicate those aspects of the cars that were most desirable in the sectors of the market in which they had to compete. Each of the campaigns achieved this objective.

Polo advertising communicated that it had all the benefits of a bigger car, especially in the area of safety (see Figure 5).[14]

Quotes from Polo research:

'Surprise'

'Don't be deceived by its looks – it's a lot more than you'd expect from a small car.'

'It's got all the qualities of a big car, even though it's just a tiny little Polo.'

'With your eyes closed you would believe you were in a Ferrari.'

4. All the quotes in this section of the paper are from research conducted after work had appeared on air.

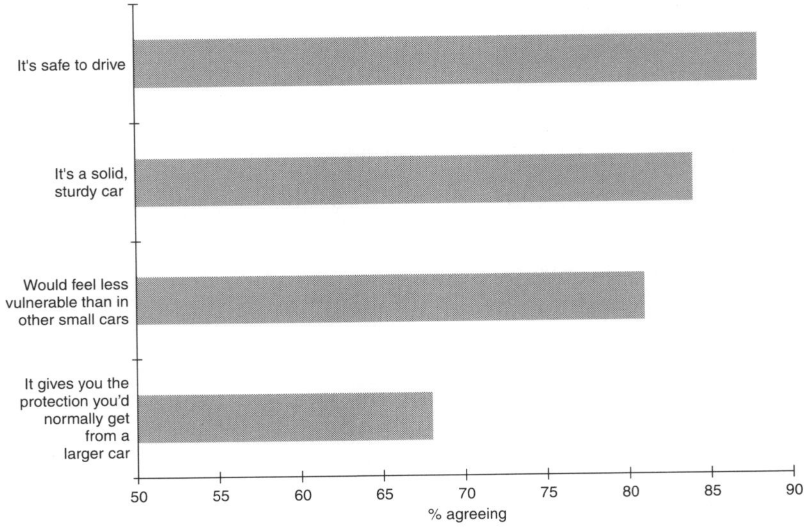

Figure 5: *Prompted impressions from the Polo 'Protection' TV ad*
Source: Millward Brown 22 September 1997 – 22 March 1998

'Protection'

'I got the impression that you feel safe when you're small.'

'Even though it's a small car, it's a safe car.'

'I think it was emphasising the compactness and safety of the car.'

'They're just trying to tell you that it's a safe car.'

Sources: Millward Brown tracking study verbatims, BMP DDB qualitative research

Golf advertising demonstrated its class-leading engineering credentials.

Quotes from Golf research:

'UFO' (TDi engine)

'It goes further on a tank of fuel than any other car.'

'It tells you that it can go so far without needing to be filled up which to someone like me who drives a long way to work is very important.'

'It's saying "look at this car, it's something out of the ordinary – it's unbelievable" '.

'Beetle' (VR6 engine)

'They've got amazing engines.'

'It's stronger, it's better, and it's super!'

'It's saying it's stronger and better and faster.'

'The difference is what's under the bonnet.'

Source: BMP DDB qualitative research

Passat advertising communicated its embodiment of the design standards and distinctive styling associated with German cars.

TABLE 2: PROMPTED IMPRESSIONS FROM PASSAT 'OBSESSION' CAMPAIGN[15]

	Designed with attention to detail %	Built to German design standards %	Technically advanced for its class %	It has distinctive distinctive styling %
'Karl Schneider'	80	63	30	77
'Video Diaries'	87	72	57	53
'Wind Tunnel'	61	63	55	49
'Doors'	91	75	61	47

Base: Definite recallers
Source: Millward Brown, June 1997, December 1997

Quotes from Passat research ('Obsession' campaign):

'It's trying to tell us it's a well thought out design.'

'It was trying to give the impression it's as good as other cars in its range such as Audi and BMW.'

'It was built and designed with precision.'

'They strive for perfection, even little details are important.'

Base: Non-owners of Volkswagens
Source: Millward Brown Passat Launch Monitor Tracking, June 1997

b) Advertising Improved the Image of Volkswagen Models

Polo's reputation was established as the best made, safest and most reliable small car.[16]

15. Each execution was intended to highlight different things; for example, 'Karl Schneider' emphasised the new Passat's distinctive styling, 'Doors' emphasised quality of construction.
16. Tables 3, 4 and 5 are based on the total sample and so, strictly speaking, do not control for ownership of the requisite Volkswagen model. However, because owners of Polos, Golfs, and Passats only constituted 5%, 8%, and 2% of the respective samples, we don't think that the pattern of these results can be wholly explained by owner's relatively high awareness of ads for their particular car.

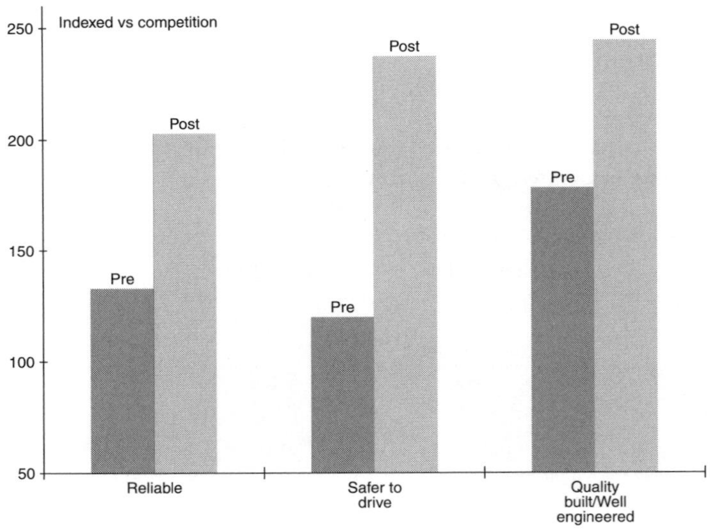

Figure 6: *Polo model image*
Base: Total sample (pre), excluding Volkswagen owners (post). Competitive set: Corsa, Peugeot 106, Clio, Micra, Punto
Source: Hall & Partners dipstick (June 1995), Millward Brown 22 September 1997 – 22 March 1998

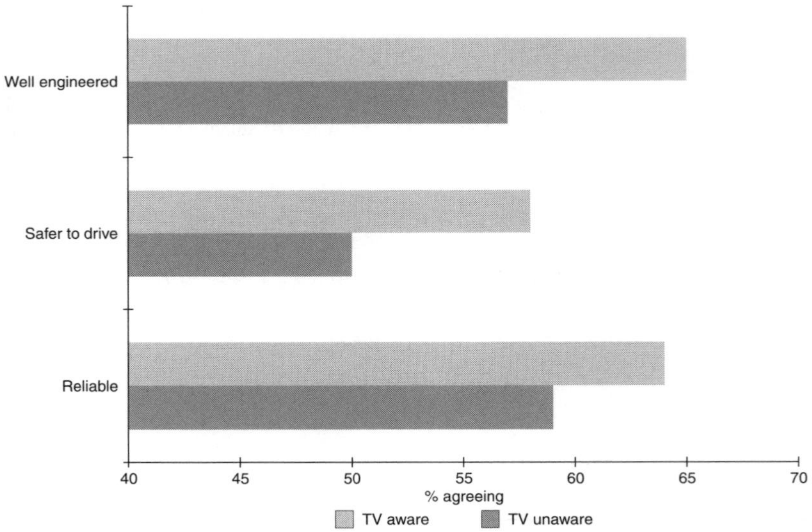

Figure 7: *Polo model image: TV ad aware versus unaware*
Base: Total sample (pre), excluding Volkswagen owners (post). Competitive set: Corsa, Peugeot 106, Clio, Micra, Punto
Source: Hall & Partners dipstick (June 1995), Millward Brown 22 September 1997 – 22 March 1998

TABLE 3: POLO'S IMAGE VS. OTHER SMALL CARS

	Well engineered %	Sturdy & solid %	Safer to drive %	Reliable %
Polo	64	62	56	61
(rank vs. comp.)	(1st)	(1st)	(1st)	(1st)
Fiesta	31	30	34	42
Peugeot 106	33	23	26	34
Corsa	28	25	27	34
Clio	26	19	24	27
Micra	28	15	24	37
Rover 100	29	25	24	29
Punto	16	13	27	18
Saxo	22	12	19	20

Base: Small car drivers who do not own a car from that marque
Source: Millward Brown 22 September 1997 to 22 March 1998

Golf's reputation for reliability, build quality and excitement was reinforced, leaving it well ahead of its competitors.

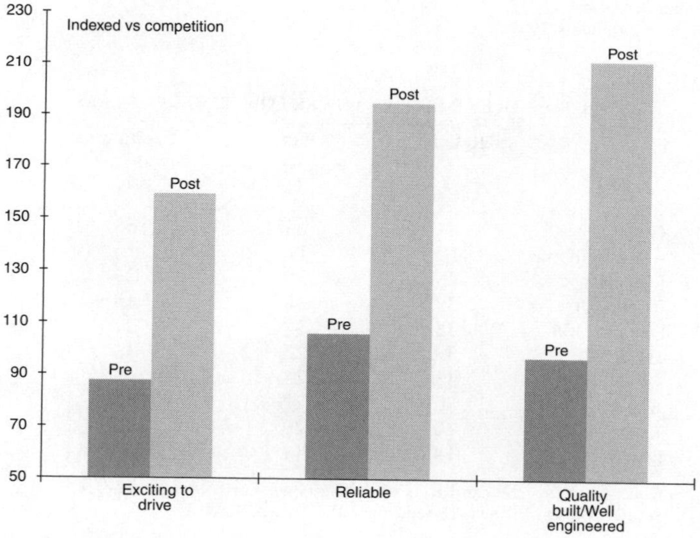

Figure 8: *Golf model image*
Base: Total sample (pre), excluding Volkswagen owners (post). Competitive set: Astra, Peugeot 306, Renault 19/Megane
Source: Hall & Partners dipstick (June 1995), Millward Brown 22 September 1997 – 22 March 1998

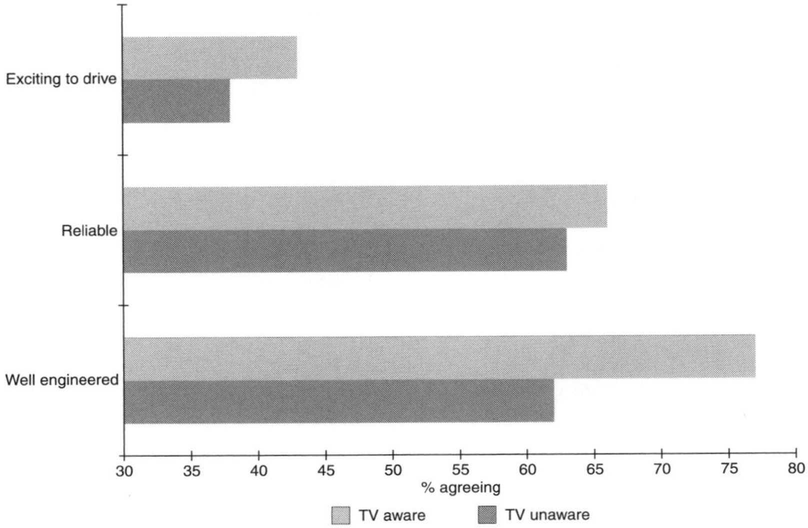

Figure 9: *Golf model image – TV ad aware versus unaware*
Base: Lower medium car drivers
Source: Millward Brown, January 1998

TABLE 4: GOLF'S IMAGE VS. OTHER LOWER MEDIUM CARS

	Reliable %	Well engineered %	Exciting to drive %
Golf	63	65	35
(rank vs. comp.)	(1st)	(1st)	(1st)
Megane	26	30	26
Rover 200	39	38	18
Peugeot 306	38	37	27
Escort	36	22	12
Astra	33	25	13
Almera	30	27	11
Xsara	20	20	13
Bravo	14	14	11

Base: Lower medium car drivers who do not own a car from that marque
Source: Millward Brown 22 September 1997 to 22 March 1998

Likewise, Passat's image was improved to the point where it was seen as the best engineered, best designed, most reliable, and least 'run of the mill' car in its sector.

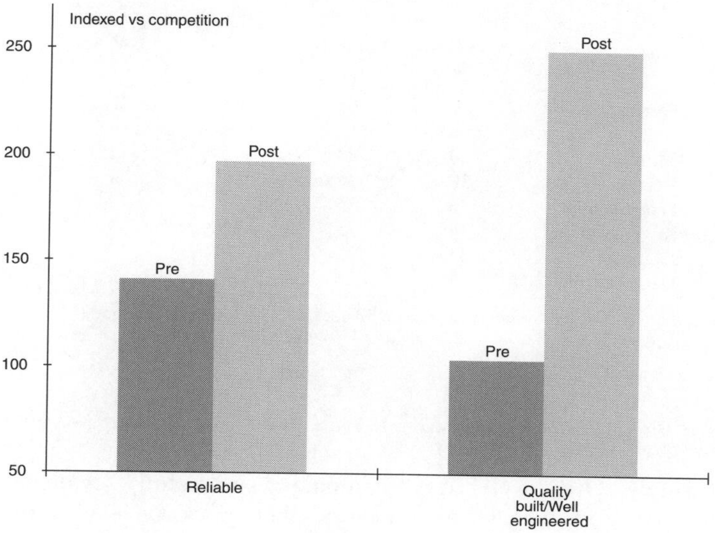

Figure 10: *Passat model image*
Base: Total sample (pre), excluding Volkswagen owner (post). Competitive set: Mondeo, Laguna
Source: Hall & Partners dipstick (June 1995), Millward Brown 22 September 1997 – 22 March 1998

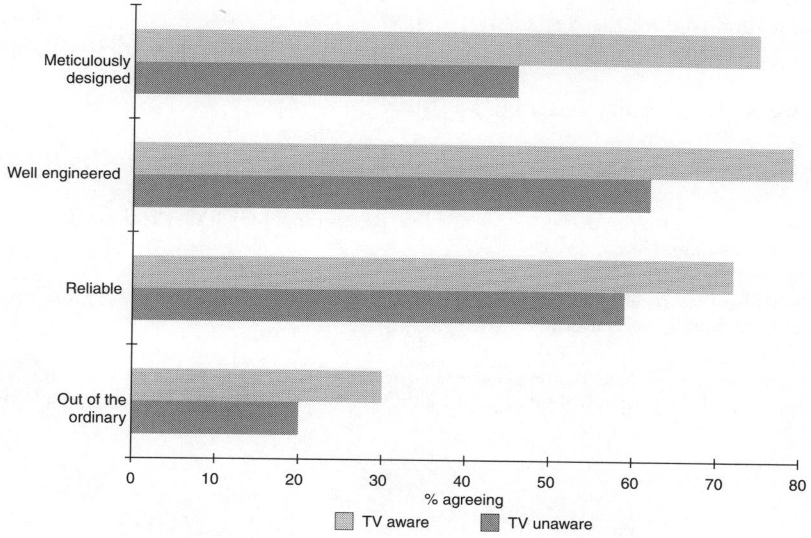

Figure 11: *Passat model image – TV ad aware versus unaware*
Base: Upper medium car drivers
Source: Millward Brown, January 1998

TABLE 5: PASSAT'S MODEL IMAGE VS. OTHER UPPER MEDIUM CARS[17]

	Meticulously designed %	Well engineered %	Reliable %	Out of the ordinary %
Passat	52	65	61	22
(rank vs. comp.)	(1st)	(1st)	(1st)	(1st)
Mondeo	26	24	32	2
Vectra	28	28	34	4
Peugeot 406	36	35	35	8
Rover 600	34	35	33	5
Laguna	31	28	30	13
Primera	26	30	37	4

Base: Upper medium car drivers who do not own a car from that marque
Source: Millward Brown 22 September 1997 to 22 March 1998

c) Advertising Communicated Volkswagens were not Beyond People's Pockets

The 'Surprisingly Ordinary Prices' campaign successfully challenged people's expectations that Volkswagens were beyond their pockets, leaving them eager to look more closely into buying one.

— Eighty-six per cent of people who recalled having seen the campaign spontaneously described the advertising message in (at least) one of the following ways: low prices, cheaper than people think, affordable, value for money, reasonable price.

— Ninety-three per cent agreed with the prompted impression 'It's saying Volkswagen make affordable cars.'

Source: Millward Brown, April 1998

Quotes from affordability research

'When you saw the advert you thought, "that's a reasonable price for a car".'

'I was surprised that they're that price because I've always thought that they're about fifteen hundred dearer than something like a ZX or 306.'

'They're telling you to get off your bum and go and have a look because you can get something that you didn't think you could afford.'

'They're saying you can have that expensive feel for not as much money as you think. I think it will work because I think people will think "But I didn't think I could afford a Golf, I think I'll just pop in and have a look." '

17. Other German cars such as BMW and Audi were not considered by Volkswagen to be direct competitors to Passat. The relevant competitive set in tracking terms therefore consists of mainstream marques.

'You think "Hang on, this car is supposed to be like a quality car and yet it's really cheap, so I am getting value for money, so I'll include it when I look". '

Base: Non-owners of Volkswagens
Sources: BMP DDB ongoing qualitative research. Verbatim from Millward Brown tracking study

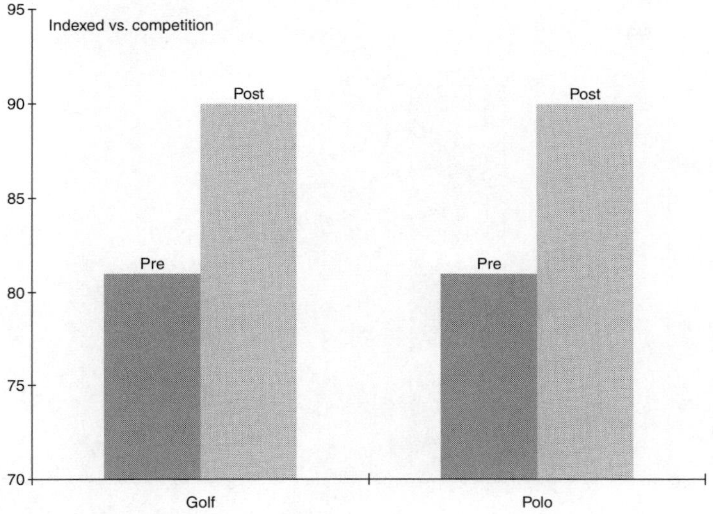

Figure 12: *Perceptions of Volkswagen model 'affordability'*
Base: Total sample (pre), excluding Volkswagen owner (post).
Competitive sets: Corsa, Peugeot 306, Clio, Micra, Punto, Astra, Renault 19/Megane
Source: Hall & Partners dipstick (June 1995), Millward Brown 22 September 1997 – 22 March 1998

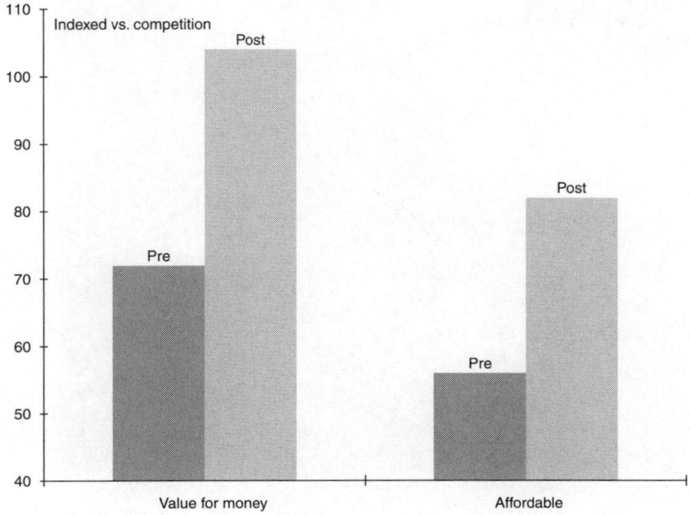

Figure 13: *Volkswagen marque image*
Base: Total sample
Competitive set: Vauxhall, Renault, Rover
Source: Hall & Partners dipstick (June 1995), Millward Brown 22 September 1997 – 22 March 1998

The perceived affordability of Polo and Golf improved dramatically. (By contrast, the perceived affordability of Passat, which was not included in the 'Surprisingly Ordinary Prices' campaign, fell.) The overall marque was also seen as more affordable and offering better value for money.

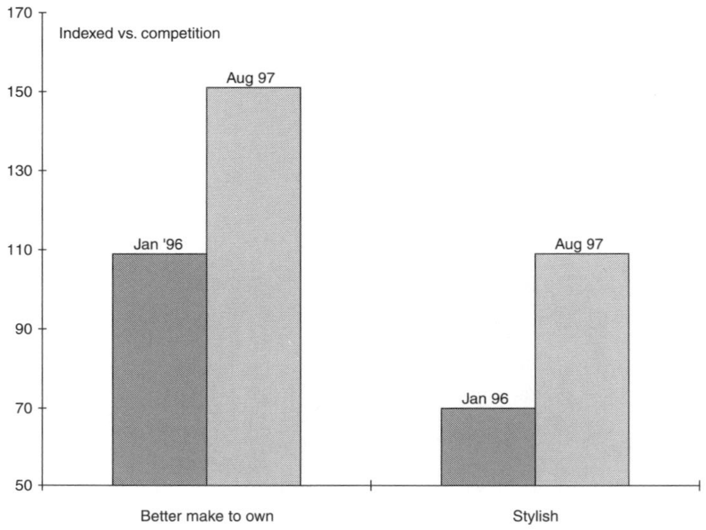

Figure 14: *Volkswagen marque image*
Base: Total sample. Competitive set: Vauxhall, Renault, Rover
Source: Hall & Partners continuous tracking (4w/e ending January 1996 versus August 1997)

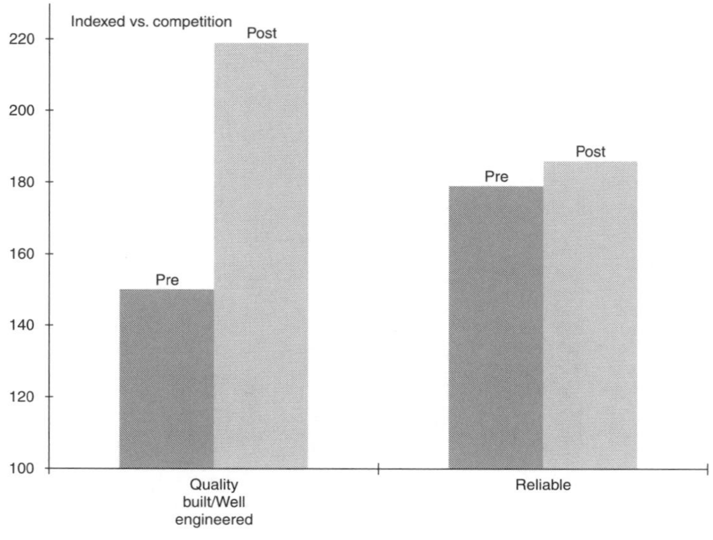

Figure 15: *Volkswagen marque image*
Base: Total sample. Competitive set: Vauxhall, Renault, Rover
Source: Hall & Partners dipstick June 1995, Millward Brown 1998

In combination, these developments fuelled the brand's reputation as a better make to own, positioned it as stylish, and reinforced its key image strengths of reliability and build quality.

TABLE 6: VOLKSWAGEN MARQUE IMAGE VS. COMPETITION

	Well engineered %	Reliable %
Volkswagen	65	62
(rank vs. comp.)	(1st)	(1st)
Ford	33	47
Vauxhall	27	38
Rover	37	35
Peugeot	29	33
Renault	25	27

Base: Total sample
Source: Millward Brown, January 1998

Not only did consideration increase by almost 100% between June 1995 and January 1998, but Volkswagen was established as the make of car that people would most want to have on their drive:

	June 95	Jan 98
'I would/might consider buying' indexed versus competition	57	110

TABLE 7: VOLKSWAGEN CONSIDERATION VS. COMPETITION

	Proud to have on my drive	Might consider buying
Volkswagen	53	47
(rank vs. comp.)	(1st)	(1st)
Ford	43	46
Vauxhall	38	47
Rover	51	45
Peugeot	38	41
Renault	33	34

Base: Total sample
Source: Millward Brown, January 1998

At both a model and marque level, the objective of getting Volkswagens on to more new car shortlists in the passive phase of the car-buying process was achieved. Within their respective market sectors Polo became the model most likely to be shortlisted, and Golf and Passat the second most likely. This was no mean achievement for the Golf, which was in the last few months of its model life cycle.

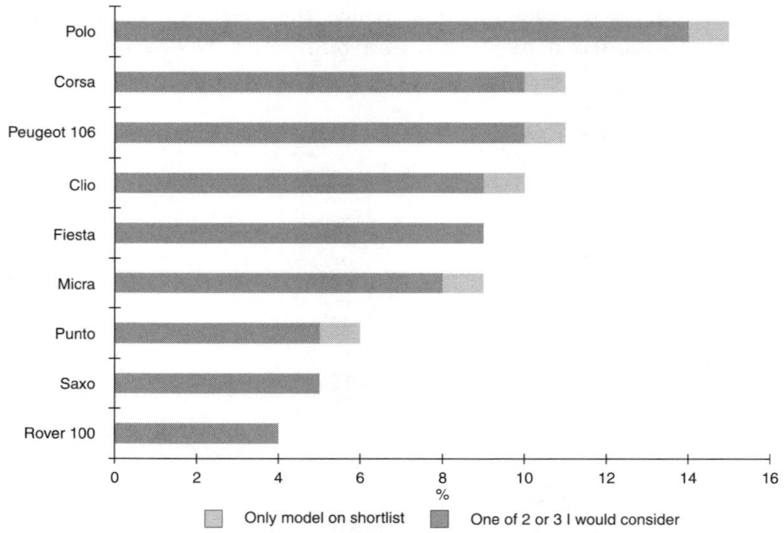

Figure 16: *Shortlisting of small cars*
Base: Drivers of small cars who do not own a car from that marque
Source: Millward Brown December 1998

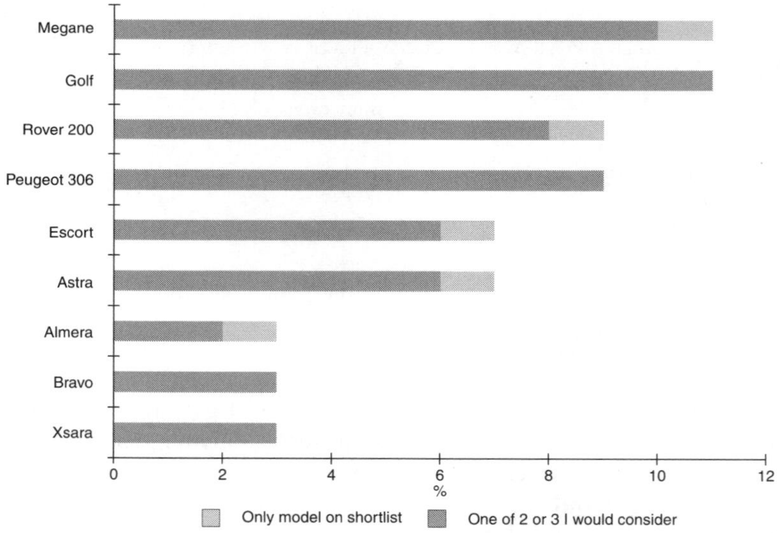

Figure 17: *Shortlisting of lower medium cars*
Base: Drivers of lower medium cars who do not own a car from that marque
Source: Millward Brown December 1998

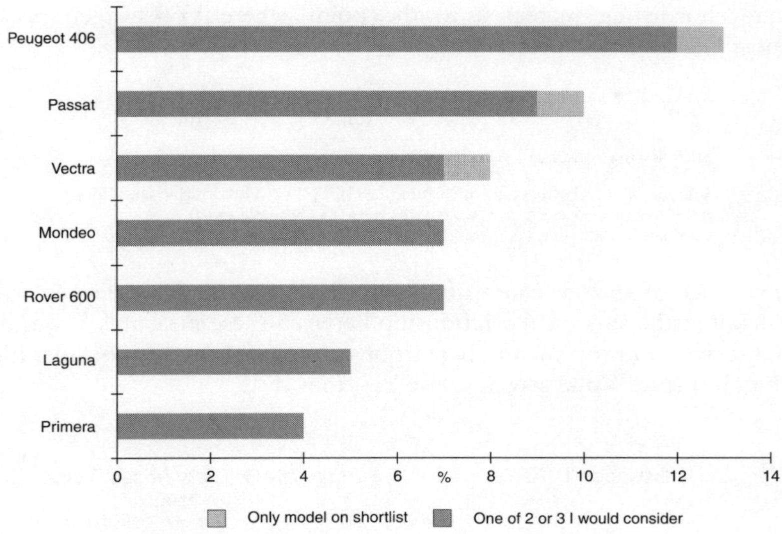

Figure 18: *Shortlisting of upper medium cars*
Base: Drivers of upper medium cars who do not own a car from that marque
Source: Millward Brown December 1998

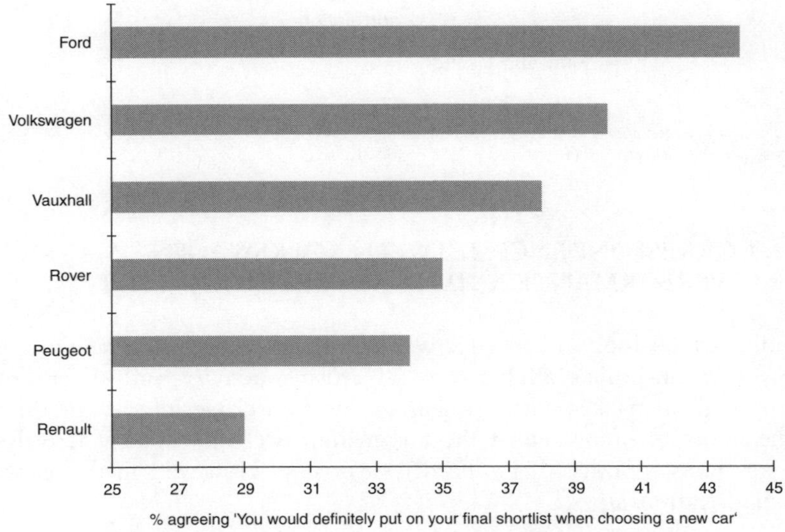

Figure 19: *Marque shortlisting – percentage agreeing 'You would definitely put on your final shortlist when choosing a new car'*
Base: Total sample
Source: Millward Brown January 1998

Marque shortlisting increased to the point where Volkswagen became the second most likely to be shortlisted.

	Jun 95	Jun 98
Shortlisting indexed vs. competition	29	112

Sources: Hall & Partners dip-stick (June 1995), Millward Brown (January 1998)
Base: Bought new car in last six months (pre), total sample (post)
Competitive: Renault, Peugeot, Vauxhall, Ford

The existence of such a 'chain of effectiveness' was confirmed when we looked in more detail at the statistical relationship between these measures.[18] But did these advertising-driven improvements in marque and model image, consideration, and shortlisting, influence Volkswagen sales? Yes, they did.

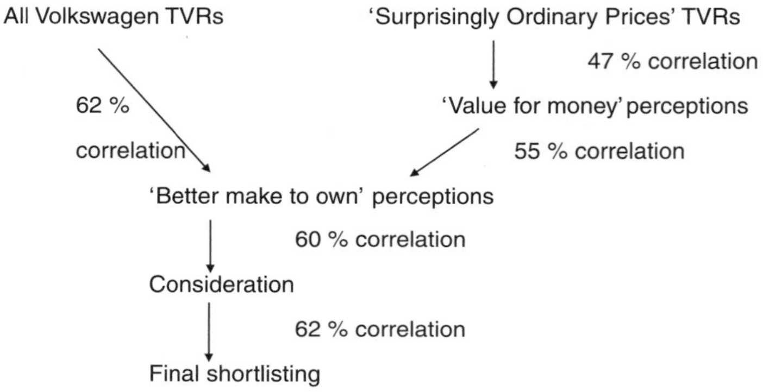

Figure 20: *The link between advertising and shortlisting*
Note: all these correlations were significant at the 95% confidence level

2. CORRESPONDENCE BETWEEN VOLKSWAGEN'S MARKET PERFORMANCE AND ITS ADVERTISING ACTIVITY

Case studies which look at the effectiveness of car advertising usually struggle to show any relationship at all between advertising activity and short-term share performance. In a market with an average inter-purchase interval of three years, where the majority of people in the target audience may not be actively 'in the market' for many months, this is hardly surprising. However, in this case we can show such a relationship.

18. There was a 62% correlation between Volkswagen TVRs and perceptions that the brand was 'a better make to own', there was a 60% correlation between these perceptions and consideration levels, and so on.

UK

The timing of Volkswagen's share growth, beginning in September 1995, exactly matches the time when the advertising spend increased. For many months thereafter, the two measures follow each other closely.

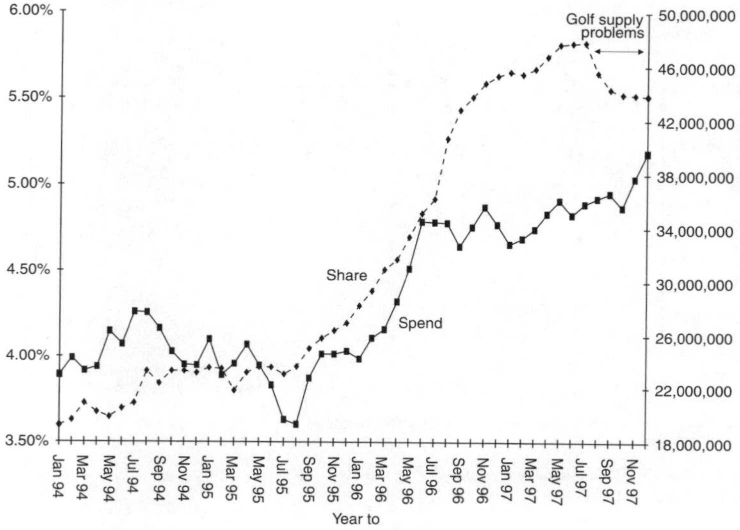

Figure 21: *Volkswagen's UK market share versus advertising*
Source: SMMT, Register-MEAL, Advertising Association

In fact, there was a statistically significant correlation between advertising spend and market share.

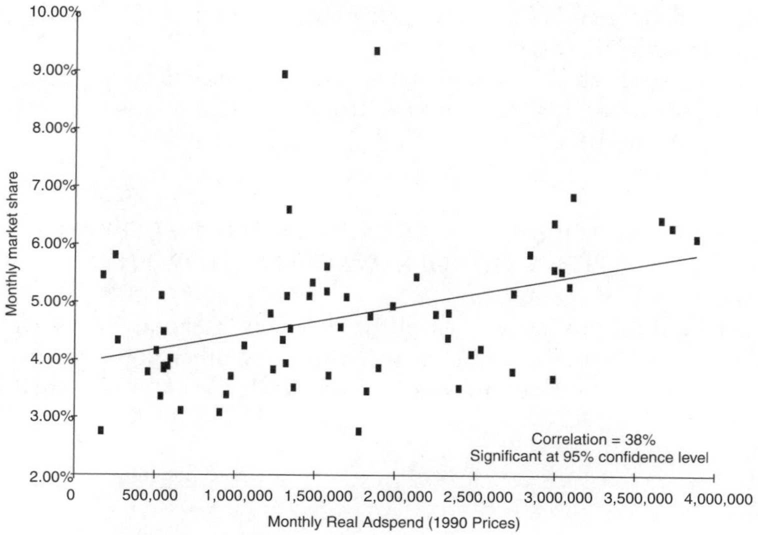

Figure 22: *Volkswagen's UK market share versus advertising*
Source: SMMT, Register-MEAL

Furthermore, there was a statistically significant correlation between advertising spend and share *gains* from month to month.

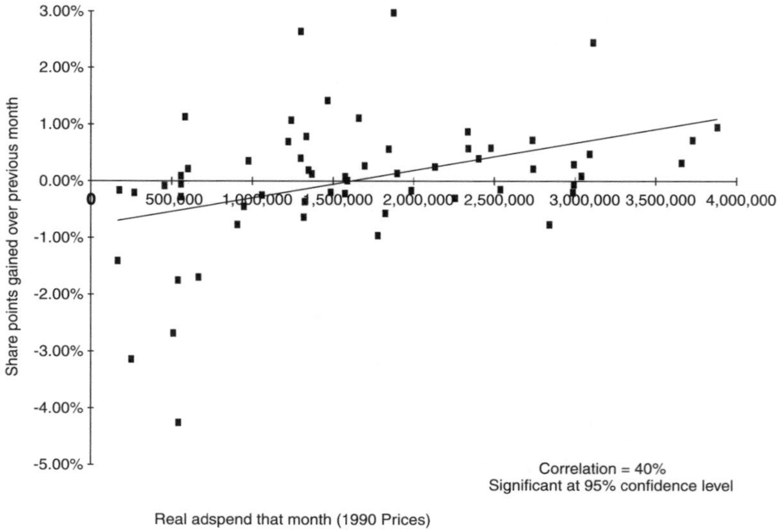

Figure 23: *Volkswagen's UK market share gains versus advertising*
Source: SMMT, Register-MEAL

Europe

There were two key differences between Volkswagen's advertising strategy in the UK and in the other major European markets: different copy was run and advertising share of voice increased more in the UK. Likewise, Volkswagen's UK share of market also saw the greatest increase (Figures 24 to 27).

Indeed, Volkswagen UK's share performance relative to Europe correlated almost directly with UK adspend levels.

Looking at annual share and advertising share-of-voice growth on a country-by-country basis, we found that there was a strong correlation between changes in the two across all the markets.

3. OTHER FACTORS CANNOT EXPLAIN THE PATTERN OR THE EXTENT OF VOLKSWAGEN'S GROWTH

As outlined in the introduction, excellent products at good prices were a vital precondition for growth. However, neither these nor other non-advertising factors can explain either the pattern or the magnitude of that growth. We shall now look at each in turn.

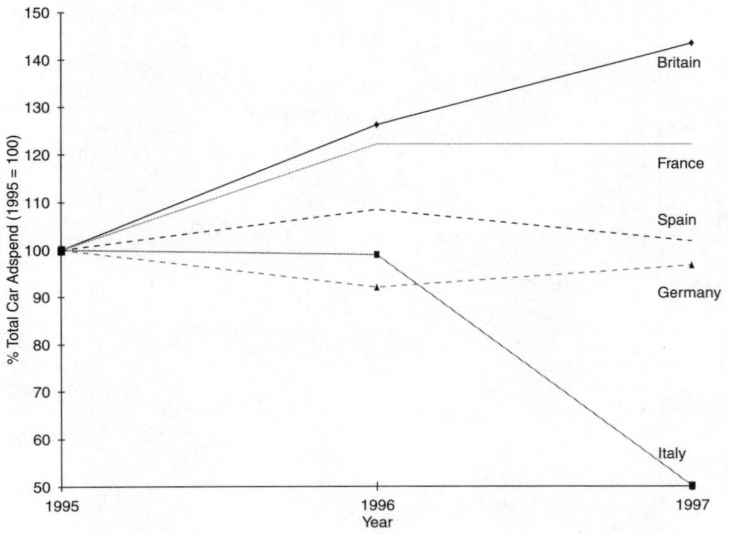

Figure 24: *Volkswagen's share of voice across Europe*
Source: BBJ

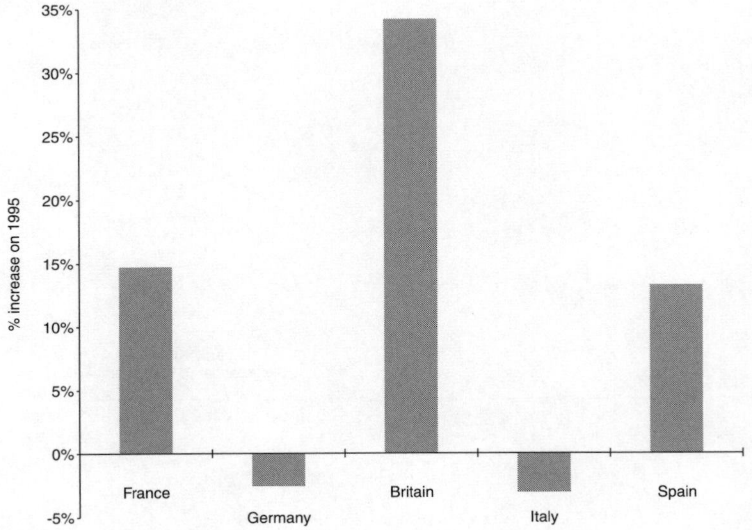

Figure 25: *Volkswagen share growth across Europe, 1996*
Source: SMMT

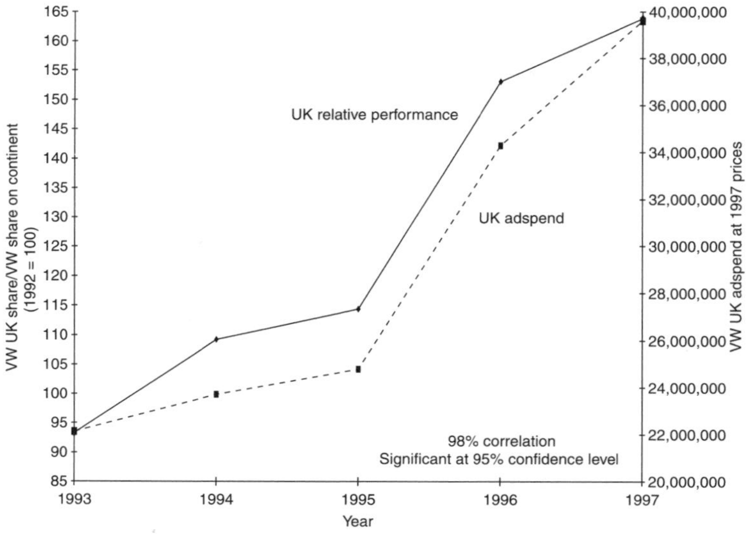

Figure 26: *Volkswagen UK performance relative to continent versus advertising*
Source: SMMT, BBJ

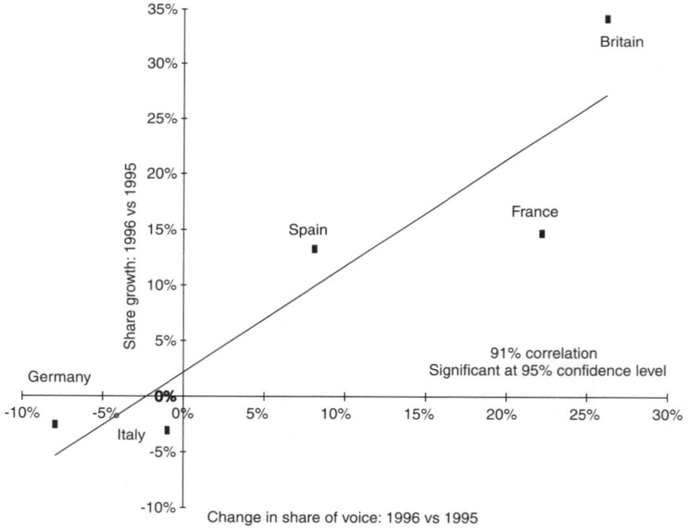

Figure 27: *Volkswagen European share growth versus advertising support*
Source: SMMT, BBJ

Better Product

The Volkswagen factory has always made excellent cars. However, excellent as these products were, the scale of Volkswagen's growth in the UK cannot be explained by the launch of upgraded models. Volkswagen Europe offered the same models in the four largest continental markets: Germany, France, Italy and Spain. Yet share growth in the UK far exceeded growth in those markets at both a marque level and at the level of individual models.

TABLE 8: % CHANGES IN VOLKSWAGEN MARKET SHARE ACROSS EUROPE 1996 VS. 1995

	Golf %	Polo %	Passat %	Total VW %
Britain	14	84	3	34
France	-4	43	0	15
Spain	-6	57	-17	13
Germany	-14	10	-6	-3
Italy	-18	21	-50	-3
Continental average	-13	22	-11	0

Source: SMMT, Volkswagen

Furthermore, the timing of Volkswagen model upgrades did not correspond with the timing of the share growth:

— The Golf was last upgraded in March 1992, over three-and-a-half years before share began to grow.

— A new version of the Passat was launched during the time period we are looking at. However, this launch was not until April 1997, over 18 months after market share began to grow.[19]

— There was a gap of nearly a year between the launch of the much improved Polo (in December 1994) and the time when Volkswagen's share began to grow.

Better Supply

Volkswagen's UK share performance cannot be explained by supply-related factors:

— Supplies became progressively tighter as Volkswagen's share grew (Figure 28).

— Lack of availability was cited as a greater barrier to purchase during the period when Volkswagen's share was growing than before that period.

19. Thus, during 20 out of the 29 months covered by this paper Volkswagen was selling the old Passat, a car at the end of its product life cycle.

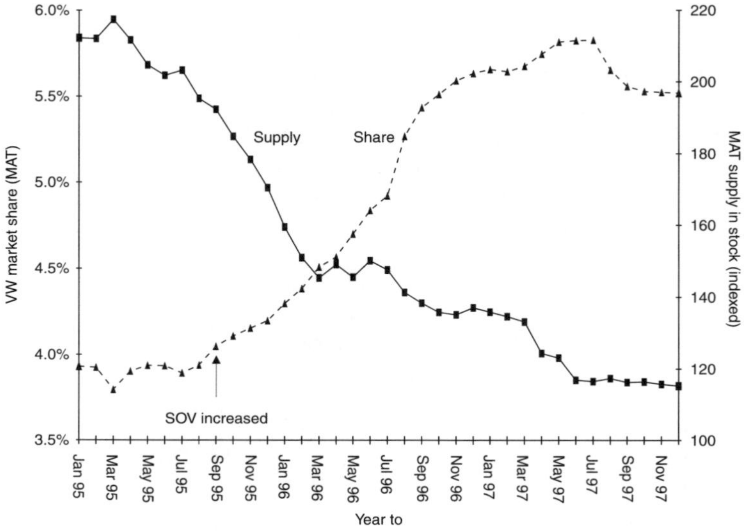

Figure 28: *Volkswagen UK market share versus supply of cars*
Source: SMMT, Volkswagen

TABLE 9: LACK OF IMMEDIATE AVAILABILITY WAS INCREASINGLY CITED AS A REASON FOR NOT BUYING A VOLKSWAGEN[20]

	Pre-growth 1993–95	During growth 1996–97
Percentage citing 'Lack of availability' as reason for rejection of shortlisted VW	7.7%	13.2%
Index vs. market average	192	241

Base: People who shortlisted a Volkswagen but did not actually buy one
Source: NCBS[21]

More Attractive Price

The pattern and extent of Volkswagen's share growth cannot be attributed to price cutting. List prices were cut significantly between April 1993 and September 1994 but there was only a relatively small uplift in market share. By contrast, there was a much smaller price cut between September 1995 and September 1997, yet this was the period when the most dramatic share growth occurred (Figures 29 and 30).

Furthermore, because Volkswagen and its dealers cut back on incentives its 'all in' price position relative to its incentive-offering competitors became less attractive to prospective new car buyers.

20. This pattern is almost certainly due to the supply restrictions in 1996–97.
21. NCBS data is annual, covering – conveniently – the period from September through to the following August. For example, data from 1995 actually covers the last four months of 1994.

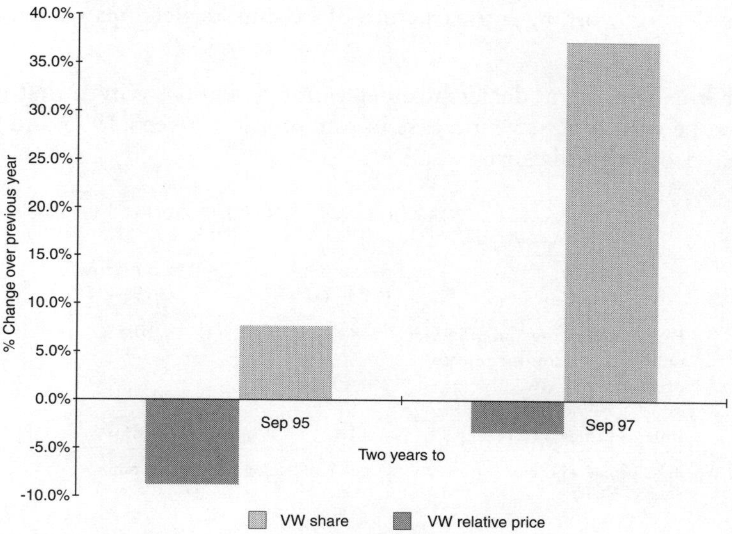

Figure 29: *Volkswagen UK share gains versus price changes*
Source: SMMT, Volkswagen

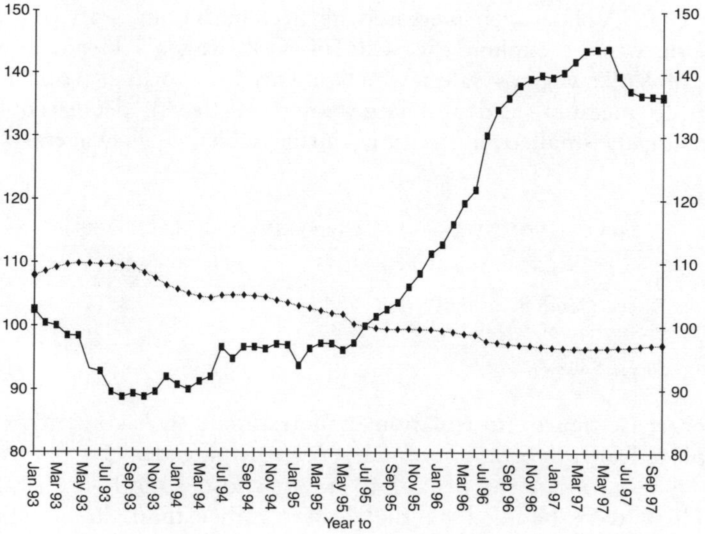

Figure 30: *Volkswagen UK share versus relative price*
Source: SMMT, Volkswagen

Better Distribution

Volkswagen's share growth was not driven by improvements in its distribution network:

— The number of dealerships decreased.

— There was no big programme to replace underperforming dealers with ones who had a greater talent for selling cars.

— The physical or working infrastructure of existing dealerships was not radically altered.

— Customer experience of dealerships deteriorated slightly. (Given that the dealers had to cope with a massive increase in rate of sale between 1995 and 1997, this marginal drop is hardly surprising.)

TABLE 10: UNSATISFACTORY SALES AND SERVICE QUALITY LEVELS CITED AS A REASON FOR NOT BUYING A VOLKSWAGEN.

	Pre-growth (1993–95)	During-growth (1996–97)
Percentage citing 'Sales/Service' quality as reason for rejection of shortlisted VW	6.8%	10.5%
Index vs. market average	110	260

Base: people who shortlisted a Volkswagen but did not actually buy one
Source: NCBS

Better Fleet Marketing

In autumn 1995, Volkswagen increased its fleet marketing staff levels. However, this expansion cannot explain the scale of Volkswagen's business success. The proportion of Volkswagen's sales, which it was their primary role to deal with (direct sales to medium-sized and large company fleets), decreased slightly and remained relatively small over the time during which Volkswagen's overall sales grew.

TABLE 11: VOLKSWAGEN DIRECT SALES TO CAR FLEETS 1995–97

	1995	1996	1997
Direct sales to fleet (units)	7245	9526	8514
Proportion of overall VW sales	8.8%	8.4%	7.1%

Source: Volkswagen

However, these figures (in isolation) underestimate their contribution. The new staff also played an important secondary role: helping dealers to prepare for the launch of the new Passat, and helping to service those demand-driven, smaller fleet accounts which were handled by the dealers rather than directly through fleet marketing.

Direct Marketing

Volkswagen's direct marketing strategy changed in early 1996 and this new strategy was demonstrably successful.[22] However, the absolute scale of this success accounted for less than 5% of total sales. This cannot explain either the pattern or the extent of Volkswagen's share growth.[23]

Better PR

Finally, it is unlikely that Volkswagen's growth was due to the coverage it received in motoring magazines or on the motoring pages of national newspapers. We have no reason to believe that Volkswagen had any more coverage, relative to its competitors, during the last three years than in the period before share began to grow.[24]

Summary

Although it would be wholly unrealistic to suggest that these factors played no part in Volkswagen's recent business performance, none can explain either its pattern or magnitude. By contrast, the fact that the advertising worked exactly as planned, and that it corresponded with Volkswagen's market performance, suggests that it made a vital contribution to success.

But how can this contribution be disentangled from the other factors which were necessary for growth?

QUANTIFYING THE CONTRIBUTION OF ADVERTISING

There is no wholly satisfactory technique for isolating and quantifying the contribution made by advertising. Such a task is both methodologically complex and philosophically intractable – how, for example, can the effect of a particular advertising campaign be separated from the quality and attractiveness of the stories being advertised?

Nevertheless, we have employed two different methods (neither ideal) to try to assess the magnitude of the advertising effect:

— We compared the extent of Volkswagen's growth in the UK with the extent of its growth in the major continental markets during the same time period. Such a comparison led to the conclusion that 78% of UK growth was related to advertising.

---

22. Source: Barraclough Hall Woolston Gray's records of the number of Volkswagen sales attributable to their direct marketing activity.
23. The strategy changed from offering incentives to encouraging test drives at the time of model launches to targeting people who were in the active phase of the new car-buying process. Such a change makes isolating the relative effects of advertising and direct marketing a somewhat artificial exercise, as the two were intended to work synergistically: advertising increased the number of people who shortlisted Volkswagens as they entered the active phase of the new car-buying process, and then direct marketing converted a greater proportion of those shortlisters into actual buyers.
24. Unfortunately, there was no formal 'share of press' audit data to confirm this. However, we could make an inference based upon an interesting cross-cultural phenomenon: drivers on the continent are generally keener to read about cars than drivers in the UK. Accordingly, in the major European markets there are many more motoring magazines, with greater readership levels relative to population size. Thus, given that UK and continental car magazines are likely to have covered the same Volkswagen-related stories, it seems fair to assume that Volkswagen received more 'coverage per driver' in these markets than in the UK. Yet, as we have seen, share growth in the UK far exceeded share growth in these markets.

— We constructed an econometric model looking at Volkswagen's UK sales performance. This model suggested that 70% of growth was related to advertising.[25]

ESTIMATING THE BUSINESS RETURN OF THAT ADVERTISING

Taking the more conservative of these estimates, we have tried to gauge both the direct and 'wider' business returns due to advertising, returns which have benefited three key parties: Volkswagen UK, its dealer network, and its customers.

Benefits for Volkswagen UK

Assuming that 70% of Volkswagen UK's growth between September 1995 and September 1997 can be related to its additional advertising investment, this equates to 52,000 extra cars sold. Using NCBS data on the average price paid for a Volkswagen over this period, this in turn equates to a revenue increase of £650 million.[26]

Volkswagen cannot publish details of its profit margins but we can assert with the utmost confidence that it has already more than recouped the £29-million increase in advertising investment which the strategy required.[27]

Bearing in mind that the advertising has already been profitable, it is worth stressing that this £29-million investment will continue to generate returns for many years to come. It is generally accepted that advertising can influence more than short-term sales; this is certainly true in the car market where the average purchase cycle is three years. It is therefore reasonable to assume the sales effects of much of the advertising that ran in 1996 and 1997 won't become evident until, on average, three years after it ran.[28]

But Volkswagen UK hasn't just benefited from extra sales; keeping demand ahead of supply has enormous implications for the cost of doing business in the car market:

— Storage costs have been substantially reduced.

— Additional revenue has been generated by astutely managing cash flow.

— More profitable 'up range' model variants have been sold.[29]

---

25. The similarity of the European comparison estimate to the estimate based on econometrics provides a degree of cross-validation for the latter.
26. Estimate based on the average price paid for a new Volkswagen during this period according to NCBS multiplied by 52,000.
27. This figure of £29 million overstates the investment made: it is based on Register-MEAL data and so does not take account of the substantial discounts obtained by Volkswagen's media-buying agency.
28. For example, someone who last bought a new car in August 1995 might have shortlisted Polo as a potential replacement for that car, having seen advertising which has run since then. However, because they will not be actively 'in the market' for a new car until Summer 1998, the effect of this advertising will not yet have had a chance to 'translate' into a sale.
29. Dealers have less financial necessity to sell existing surplus stock and therefore can order and sell cars

— Economies of scale have reduced unit costs.

— By attracting fewer incentive-hunting and potentially 'promiscuous' car buyers, it has improved the potential life-time value of its customer base.

And it has achieved much of this by re-investing, rather than simply increasing, its marketing budget.

Benefits for Volkswagen Dealers

The advertising benefits for dealers have been considerable. It has helped them to sell 52,000 more cars in the short term, and is likely to contribute to future sales. More significantly, because the increase in demand for Volkswagens allowed dealers to recover their profit margins, they have made more money on all the new Volkswagens they have sold since September 1995.

They have also benefited in two further ways:

— Many people who bought new Volkswagens did so having first traded in their old car; thus secondhand car sales have increased in value as a source of dealer income.

— After-sales and servicing revenues have increased because there are more Volkswagens on the road.

Perhaps most importantly from a long-term perspective, in helping to make the business of being a Volkswagen dealer more remunerative, advertising has helped to increase dealers' long-term enthusiasm and commitment to being holders of the Volkswagen franchise.

TABLE 12: OVERALL DEALER RATING OF THE VOLKSWAGEN FRANCHISE (SCORE OUT OF TEN)

	Winter 1995–6	Winter 1997–8
Volkswagen	6.1	8
(rank vs. comp.)	(6th)	(1st)
Competition Average	6.2	6.6

Base: Dealers who operate a franchise from that manufacturer
Competitive set: Ford, Vauxhall, Rover, Renault, Peugeot, Nissan
Source: RMI Dealer Attitude Survey

Consequently, these dealers are now willing to invest in future infrastructure changes which will be necessary to sustain Volkswagen's higher share position. Volkswagen will then be able to offer better service levels to its much expanded customer base. This is likely to translate into increased loyalty rates and, consequently, increased marketing efficiency. Thus, wholesaler gains, dealer gains and consumer gains are inextricably interlinked.

which are not already in stock.

Customer Gains

Volkswagen's customers have also benefited from advertising's contribution to demand levels for Volkswagen:

— People who bought new Volkswagens now retain a higher proportion of the money they paid when they come to sell them a few years later. This is because increased demand for new Volkswagens has reinforced (already high) resale values in the Volkswagen secondhand car market.[30]

— People are more likely to be able to obtain the exact model they want (in terms of variant and specification levels) because Volkswagen and its dealers can better predict exactly what they are likely to want.

CONCLUSION

Many marketing morals could be drawn from this case study:

— It adds weight to the view that advertising creativity and advertising effectiveness are mutually supportive objectives as the campaigns covered by this paper have, between them in the last two years, won every major creative award.

— It emphasises the importance of understanding not just purchase motivations but also purchase behaviour, and of isolating at what point in the consumer decision-making process marketing can have most effect.

— It demonstrates the wider benefits of advertising not just for the advertiser but for all its stakeholders.

However, two morals are key. First, this case highlights the wide-ranging benefits to a business of keeping demand ahead of supply and the power of advertising to do this. Second, and just as importantly, it emphasises that advertising is most effective when it has something good to say. It is only because Volkswagen had such a strong story to tell that its advertising was so effective.

30. For example, in November 1995 six-month-old three-door, one-litre Polos sold for 84% of their original purchase price. By March 1998 this figure, for the identical six-month-old variant, had increased to 91%. Such an increase in resale values leaves the average Volkswagen customer hundreds of pounds better off.

4

Walkers Crisps

Garymania! – how an already successful brand benefited from famous advertising

INTRODUCTION

This paper examines the effectiveness of BMP's advertising for Walkers Crisps since its appointment in August 1994, a period which has seen Walkers transformed into, arguably, the most famous and successful branded property in UK advertising.

THE HISTORY OF WALKERS CRISPS

Henry Walker's butchery business had flourished in Leicester in the 1930s. However, with the advent of rationing, the Second World War brought severe consequences to the whole food industry. Diversification was vital, and Henry's range of choices was finally narrowed to one option – potato crisps.

By 1960, distribution was still confined to the Midlands, but sales nonetheless trebled over the next decade.

The 1970s saw the start of a programme of regional expansion from Walkers' Midlands base into Yorkshire, Anglia, Lancashire, Wales, London and the South.

In 1989, Walkers and Smiths Crisps moved under the umbrella of PepsiCo Foods International. In 1993, the two brands were merged. With a turnover in the region of £300 million, Walkers Crisps had become the biggest single food brand in the UK.

THE SITUATION IN AUGUST 1994

By August 1994, Walkers had experienced two years of double-digit growth,[1] and the brand's share had reached 22%, over three times that of its nearest branded rival.

1. 11.2% year to August 1993, 17.5% year to August 1994. (All retail audit figures are derived from IRI Infoscan data, with all share figures based on the total market of crisps and other salty snacks, such as Hula Hoops, Quavers, etc.)

However, there were a number of clouds looming on the horizon.

Plateauing Distribution

A very significant proportion of the brand's growth over the last few years had been the result of distribution growth, particularly through regional roll-out. This was already coming to an end in the much larger Grocery channel, and was expected to do likewise in the Impulse channel soon after.[2]

March 1994 had seen the last (mainland) UK region succumb to the Walkers' bandwagon, with the launch into Scotland. This took national distribution to 95% in Grocery and over 60% in Impulse, in both cases nearing what appeared to be the 'natural' limit for the brand.

Growth through distribution gain as a result was unlikely to be as significant a contributor to the brand's success in the future.

Success of Promotions

However, beginning in March 1993, Walkers had embarked on a series of 'Instant Win' promotions which were dramatically successful, producing large and immediate uplifts in volume and ROS.

The scale of the immediate volume gains was beyond anything previously seen in this market and surprised even Walkers.[3]

So, even though growth through distribution gains might have been about to plateau, Walkers felt that in 'Instant Win' promotions it had discovered another engine for dynamic growth. However, even here there were two concerns. First of all, it was unclear how important the novelty factor of these promotions was to their success, and hence whether repetition would result in declining effectiveness over time.[4] Second, it seemed inevitable that the competition would try to copy such a successful idea.

---

2. 'Grocery', as defined by the retail audit, comprises the large supermarket chains, minor multiples (such as Budgen's) and Co-op. 'Impulse' comprises independent grocers, CTNs, garages, off-licences, etc. In the Impulse channel, strong regional brands and the sheer variety of smaller outlets severely restricts the distribution of national brands.
3. The reasons for its dramatic success can be found in the nature of the promotions themselves, which in a number of ways represented something entirely new in the market. The prize fund was beyond anything previously offered. The promotional mechanic, which was varied slightly each time to maintain consumer interest, was unique – on discovering a blue sachet in your packet of crisps, you knew instantly that you had won. In addition, each of the promotions was supported by national TV advertising.
4. In fact, of the three Instant Win promotions run between March 1993 and August 1994, the first had been very clearly more successful than the second, which was in turn more successful than the third.

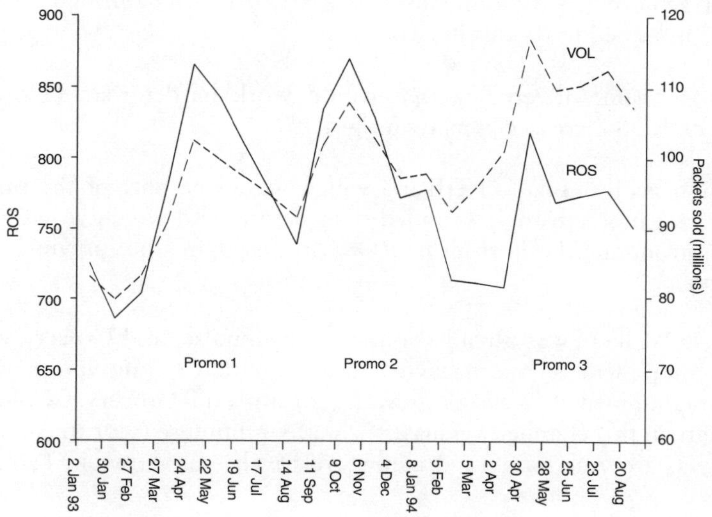

Figure 1: *Walkers volume and ROS pre-BMP*
Source: IRI Infoscan

Advertising

There was little doubt that the promotional advertising had been successful in boosting the sales effect of each promotion. However, in order to protect the salience of Walkers' own promotions in the face of almost inevitable copying by competitors, stronger branding of the 'Instant Win' promotions through advertising was felt to be desirable. It was felt that this could best be achieved by bringing the promotional and theme advertising together under a single brand umbrella.

There had been Walkers brand advertising on television at substantial weights both in the pre-promotional period and during 1994. Unfortunately, it had failed to increase brand awareness significantly. The feeling within the company at this time was that the brand was 'universal in size but not in perception' and that the advertising had to shoulder a large part of the blame. In addition, it appeared to have had little effect on sales.[5]

So, when Walkers put the advertising account out to pitch in mid-1994, it was with the intention of developing an integrated brand campaign incorporating new theme and promotional advertising.

THE PITCH BRIEFING

The brief recognised that distribution-derived growth was coming to an end, but asked for an advertising campaign that would maintain volume growth on a par

5. In fact, recent econometric modelling (see Appendix) has confirmed these suspicions. The pre-BMP advertising was indeed ineffective on sales performance.

with that achieved in the previous two years, primarily through ROS growth. In particular it needed to do this in two ways:

- Through theme advertising that would work harder than before and would generate ROS increases in its own right.

- Through promotional advertising which would be part of the same campaign and hence more strongly branded than before, and which would generate even more pronounced short-term ROS uplifts than the previous promotional advertising.

Because Walkers was already dominant in Impulse, and Grocery was becoming a larger component of the market, it was clear that strong volume growth could only be maintained if Walkers grew significantly in Grocery. Walkers had 22% brand share in this channel, versus 29% share in Impulse (year to August 1994) and Grocery was growing, Impulse declining, relatively – as shown in Table 1.

TABLE 1: WALKERS' SHARE OF MARKET

Share of market	Year to August 1992 %	Year to August 1993 %	Year to August 1994 %
Grocery	57	60	63
Impulse	43	40	37

So these objectives really implied the need to ensure strong rate of sale and volume growth in Grocery, while we could expect less of a volume increase from our already high share in Impulse.

With these aims in mind, BMP was appointed to handle the Walkers' business in August 1994.

DEVELOPING AN ADVERTISING STRATEGY

We knew that any advertising for the brand would have to appeal to children, who were heavy consumers of snacks, as well as purchasers in their own right in the Impulse channel. Much of the snack volume that they ate, however, was being purchased for them by their parents in the burgeoning Grocery channel. Here, 80% of purchases were made by adults. Adults were also becoming increasingly important as *consumers* of snacks – having grown up eating them they failed to desist from the habit in adulthood. It was clear that both children and adults were important to us.

We thus set out to create advertising that would genuinely and powerfully appeal to a mass audience of adults as well as children – no small task when the category advertising at this time was typified by short-term tactical approaches, irrelevant product claims, self-consciously zany imagery – and very few famous or talked-about campaigns.

From qualitative research conducted among crisp-lovers of all ages, we identified 'irresistibility' as the quality that embodied everything they most enjoyed about snacking. It followed that, whichever crisp could lay claim to being the most irresistible would, inevitably, also be the freshest, the tastiest, and so on: it was shorthand for the perfect crisp.

However, they also saw crisps as part of everyday life. As a result, it became clear that people were unlikely to empathise with any brand that took itself too seriously, and that any grandiose claims about irresistibility had to be treated with tongue firmly in cheek.

THE CREATIVE BRIEF

The creative brief thus called for advertising that would appeal to a mass audience, by owning the category high ground of irresistibility. The brief can be summarised as follows:

Target audience:	Adults and children
Proposition:	No one can resist Walkers Crisps
Support:	Product quality or Instant Win promotions
Tonal values:	Fun, unpretentious, informal, classless, social

THE WALKERS DUCK

The occasion for the launch of the new advertising was, in fact, a promotion, 'Moneybags II', which was to be launched in September 1994. The first advertising we produced featured the 'Walkers Duck', a talking duck from Leicester who was lucky enough to win £20 in his packet of Walkers. The endline 'There's Only One Walkers, Duck' worked both as a way of asserting the primacy of Walkers and as a colloquial nod to the brand's East-Midland roots. This execution proved to be very successful in supporting the promotion.

A subsequent series of 'Duck' executions, celebrating the irresistibility of Walkers crisps, had researched well in rough and the duck showed potential as a long-term spokesman for the brand. However, despite its success in boosting sales during the promotion, Walkers remained unsure about whether the subsequent executions really would have the necessary stature to make the Walkers brand famous. In October the difficult decision was made not to progress with the 'Duck' campaign, and to create another brand campaign for both theme and promotional advertising.

THE NEW CREATIVE BRIEFING

We wanted a creative vehicle that would generate PR and media coverage, but the revised creative brief was identical on all other critical dimensions. Given the importance of fame and the fact that we were aiming at a mass audience, we chose TV as the main medium.

In addition, this time the event that would occasion the new advertising was not a promotion, but the launch of an improved Cheese & Onion variety. It was felt that this much simpler piece of product news was a more appropriate place to start to establish a brand vehicle than a promotion, as had been the case with the duck.

THE CAMPAIGN IDEA

The idea for the campaign can be summarised as 'Walkers are so irresistible they make even nice guys turn nasty when it comes to crisps'.

What set the idea apart was the thought of casting ex-England and Leicester footballer Gary Lineker[6] as the nice guy turned nasty. Gary had appeared in Walkers advertising ten years earlier, and in the intervening period had gone from local hero to national institution.

While of the world of football, he was not confined to it; as the ambassador and genuine 'nice guy' of the game, Gary was as attractive to mums as to kids. His well-publicised return from playing in Japan offered us unique PR opportunities. Most important of all, his down-to-earth personality and roots in Walkers' Leicester heartland provided a seamless fit with our desired brand personality and the unpretentious values we wished to establish.

To date, five TV executions have been produced in the series, including two for further 'Instant Win' promotions (see Table 2).

TABLE 2: GARY LINEKER EXECUTIONS

Execution	Airdate	Objective
'Welcome Home'	Jan 95	Launch improved Cheese & Onion flavour
'Nun'	Mar 95	Support 'Instant Cheque' promotion
'Garymania'	May 95	Launch new Crinkles range
'Dial-a-Prize'	Sep 95	Support 'Dial-a-Prize' promotion
'Salt 'n Lineker'	Jan 96	Launch improved Salt & Vinegar flavour

MEDIA PLAN

The timing of the campaign and weights have been as shown in Figure 2:[7]

6. Whose great uncle, incidentally, used to supply potatoes to Walkers.
7. In addition to the main TV campaign, which was weighted towards mums and children, with special emphasis on programmes they might view together, a small portion of the budget (less than 9%) was allocated for tactical tasks and other media.

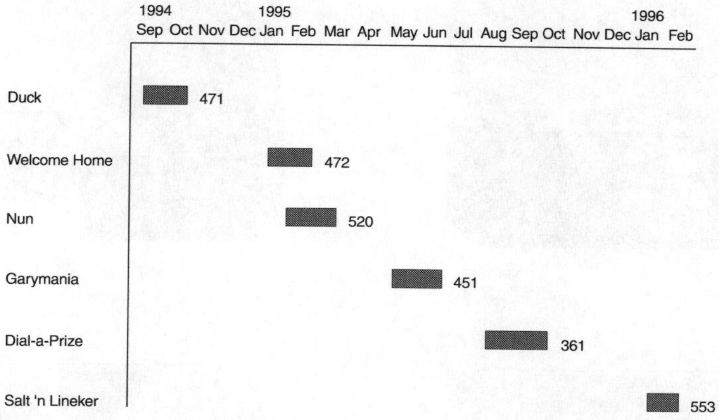

Figure 2: *Media plan (all figures in GRPs)*
Source: BARB

WALKERS' PERFORMANCE SINCE AUGUST 1994

Overall Volume Growth

Walkers' volume has risen strikingly since BMP's appointment in August 1994 and the rate of growth has actually improved upon that of the previous two years.

TABLE 3: WALKERS VOLUME AND RATE OF GROWTH

	Walkers volume (millions of packs)	Annual growth %
MAT to Aug 1993	1152	+ 11.2
MAT to Aug 1994	1354	+17.5
MAT to Aug 1995	1659	+22.5

Source: IRI Infoscan

This growth has also been maintained since August 1995: volume to February 1996 (the last period of available data) is 19.3% up on the same period 12 months earlier.

Since Walkers has continued to grow faster than the market over this period, its share has also risen (Figure 3).

In addition, the peaks in Figure 3 equate to promotions and it can be seen that the BMP-advertised promotions generated greater uplift (per TVR) compared with those that came before. We can also see that, in contrast to the past, share between the promotional periods settles to higher 'base levels', leading to higher sustained growth levels.

'WELCOME HOME' 60 SECONDS

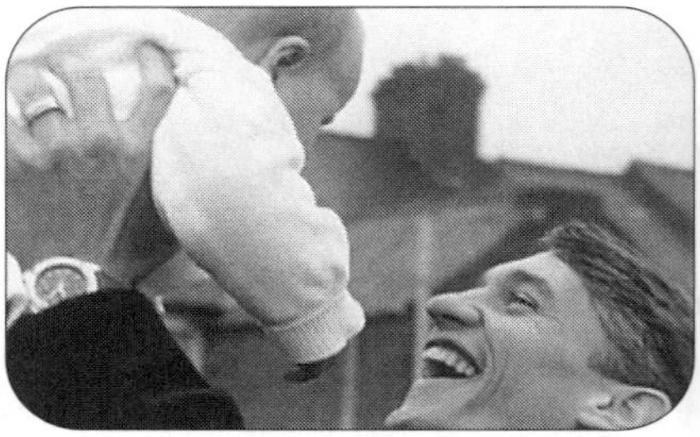

MVO: When a crisp as irresistible as Walkers introduces a new Cheese & Onion flavour...

...there's no more Mr Nice Guy.

'STAND' 30 SECONDS

MVO: To introduce Walkers new, tastier Salt & Vinegar flavour...

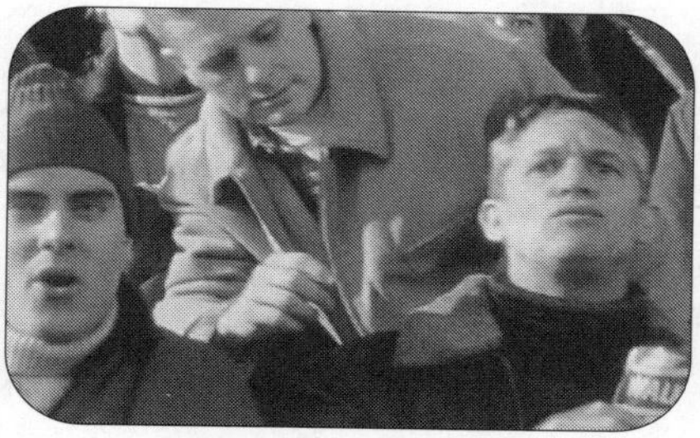

...they're calling them Salt 'n Lineker

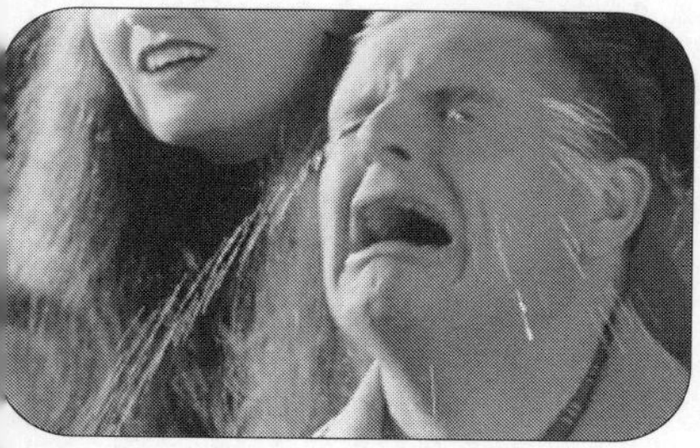

(Music plays: 'Nessun Dorma')

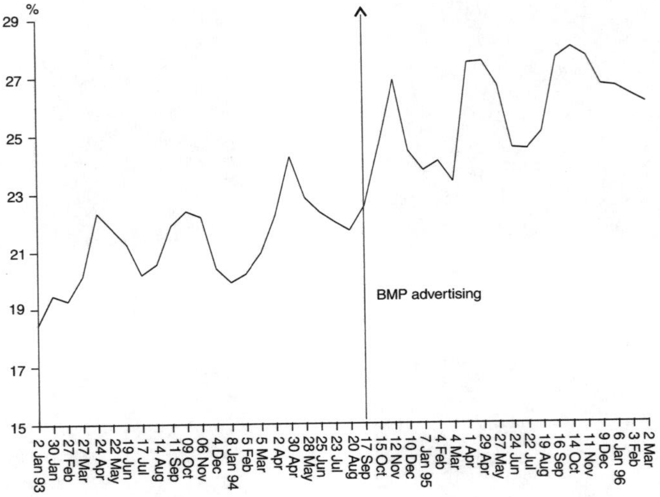

Figure 3: *Walkers' share of total salty snacks market*
Source: IRI Infoscan

Performance in Grocery

Walkers volume in Grocery grew by 44% between September 1994 and February 1996 (MATs), resulting in a growth in brand share which continues to trend upwards (Figure 4).

In addition this growth is, unlike that prior to September 1994, almost entirely the result of rate-of-sale growth rather than distribution gain.

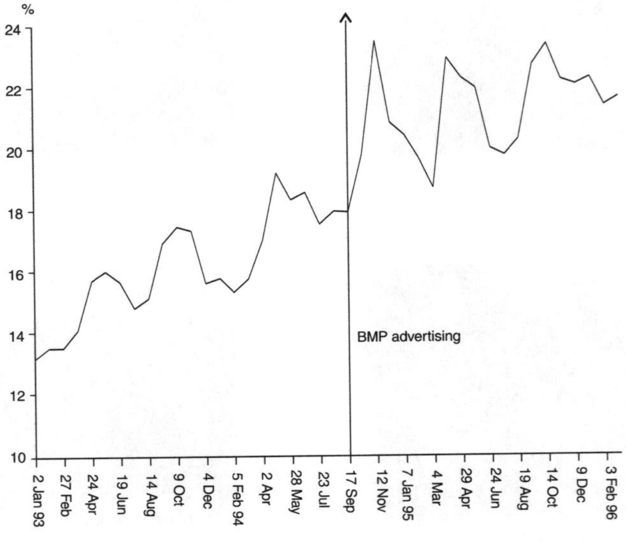

Figure 4: *Volume share of Walkers in Grocery*
Source: IRI Infoscan

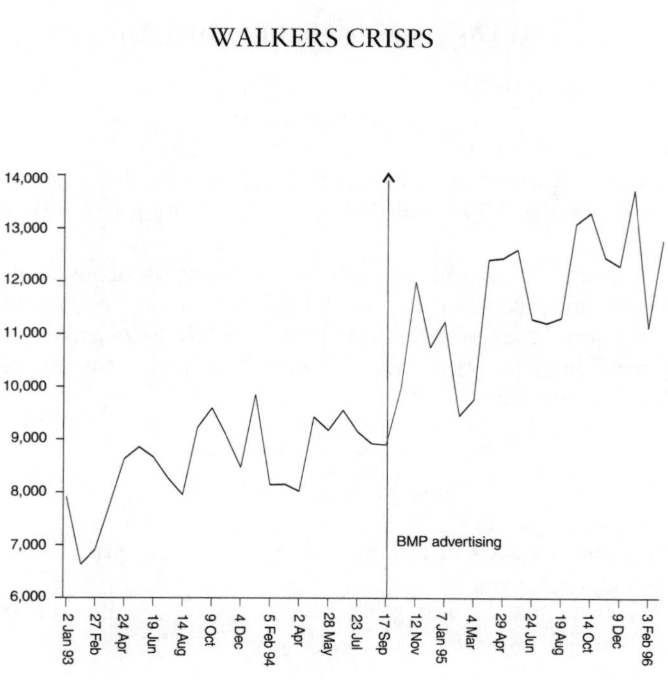

Figure 5: *£ weighted ROS of Walkers in Grocery*
Source: IRI Infoscan

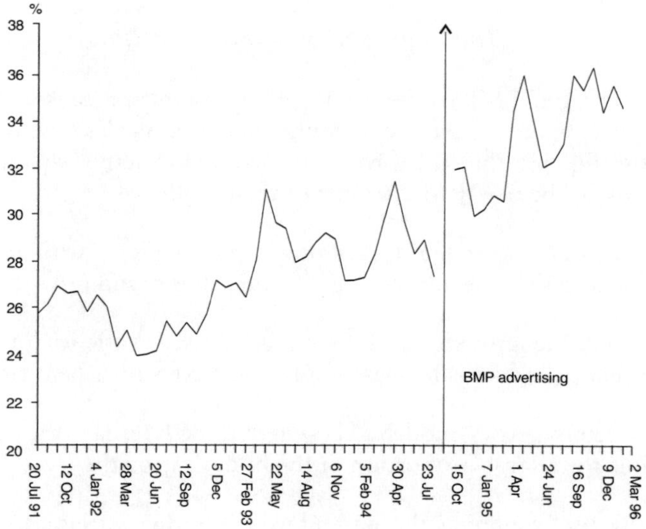

Figure 6: *Volume share of Walkers in Impulse*
Source: IRI Infoscan

Average rate of sale in Grocery over the first 12 months of BMP advertising was 23% higher than that during the previous year.

The pattern of peaks and troughs occasioned by promotional activity is still evident, as we would expect. But from January, following the peak coinciding with the 'Duck' promotion, a significant change to the pattern commences. In each case following a promotion, rate of sale settles to a new, and higher, base level.

Performance in Impulse

Walkers has also performed fantastically well within Impulse. Here volume grew by 21% between September 1994 and February 1996, taking MAT share from 28.6% to 34.2%.

This meant that the brand actually grew more vigorously in Impulse than expected. These increases were largely caused by an unexpected growth in distribution over the Lineker advertising period, while ROS grew only slightly. The econometric modelling has been able to directly link this unexpected distribution growth with the advertising.

Performance: Conclusions

The marketing objectives of sustaining volume and share growth were successfully exceeded. This was achieved by:

— dramatically increasing rate of sale in Grocery;

— increasing volume in Impulse through advertising-fuelled distribution growth.

The Contribution of the Advertising

We believe that the BMP advertising was a significant cause of this continued success and that, without it, growth would have been far less significant. We aim to prove this by showing that the advertising worked exactly as planned, and can be related directly to the newly found fame of the brand:

— by an analysis of share-gain variation across regions with different levels of TVRs, showing that the advertising was causal in brand growth;

— by analysing the growth in different advertised varieties of Walkers crisps, showing that the advertising clearly influences consumer behaviour;

— by two econometric models showing directly that the advertising was responsible for a large proportion of the brand's growth;

— and finally by examining the part played by other variables, showing that no other activity could have been responsible for the effect we claim for our advertising.

HOW THE ADVERTISING WORKED

We have said that we set out to make advertising that would make the brand famous by appealing powerfully and equally to adults and children. The evidence suggests that, with the Lineker campaign, we succeeded beyond expectation.

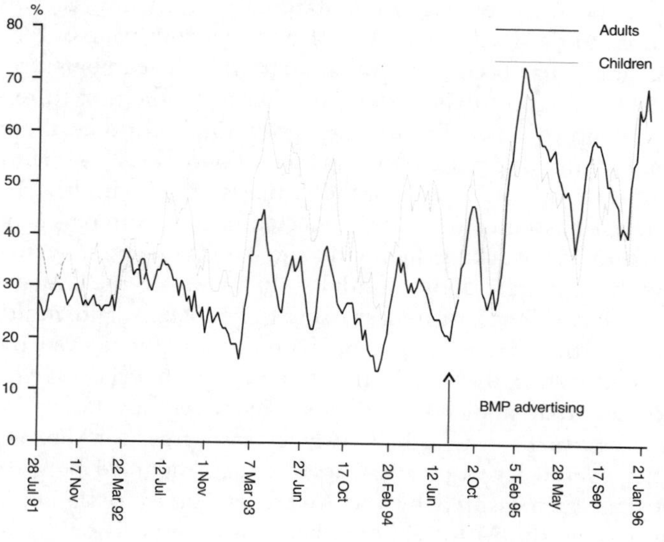

Figure 7: *Walkers – 'seen on TV recently'*
Source: Millward Brown

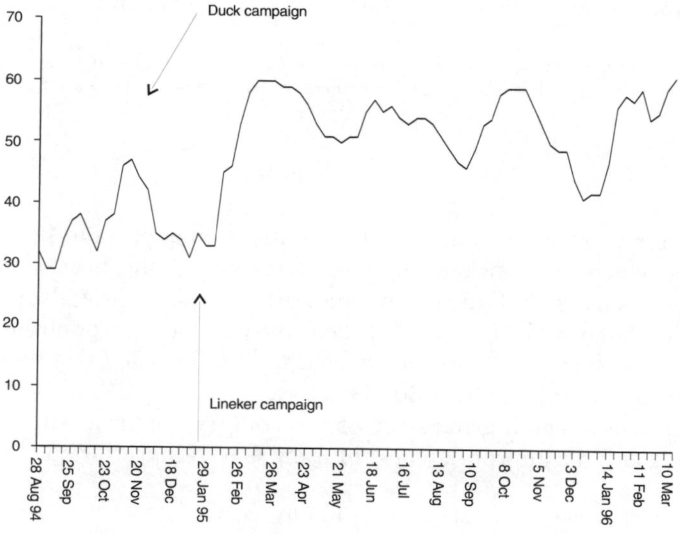

Figure 8: *'Have really good advertising' (Adult sample)*
Source: Millward Brown

Fame

From the outset, the Lineker campaign has generated an amount of TV and press coverage wildly in excess of anything previously seen in this market.

TV coverage has ranged from *News at Ten* to *Fantasy Football League*, *The Big Breakfast* and *How Do They Do That?*

It has also included coverage in *all* national press, from the *Times*, *Independent* and *Telegraph*, to the *Daily Mail*, *Mirror* and the front page of the *Sun* twice. Over time, as the public has become more familiar with the campaign theme, the tabloid newspapers have begun to vie with each other to be the first to release the news of 'What Gary is up to now'. Even in the 'grown-up' world of the business press, it has become standard practice for financial journalists to mention the Lineker campaign, and to link the success of the Walkers brand with it.

Such interest has, of course, been reflected in the awareness scores picked up by the Millward Brown tracking survey. In the past, Walkers' advertising was noticed much more by children than by adults. In contrast, the Lineker campaign has resulted in both *children's* awareness rising to new highs, and adult awareness being transformed, so that it has caught up with, and at times even overtaken, that of children. It is therefore the first Walkers campaign that has managed to attract the attention of the broad audience of all crisp eaters *and* buyers.

This appears to be true, albeit to a lesser degree, for the 'Duck' advertising. These higher overall levels of awareness are accompanied by greater *efficiency* of the advertising, as measured by the Awareness Index (AI). Immediately prior to BMP's advertising, the AI for children had fallen away to only 6 (category average 10), but over the course of the campaign it has risen to 15. Among adults the rise is much more remarkable, leaping first from 8 to 14, then to 16 for 'Nun', and 24 for Dial-a-Prize (category average 8).

Millward Brown's view of the Lineker campaign is that it:

> 'has generated the highest AI of any Walkers Crisps campaign (in the current survey) well above the market average, indeed, it is amongst the highest we have tracked across all markets'.

Appeal

Such awareness measures and such media attention appears to be a reflection of the extent to which the Lineker campaign has entered the hearts of the public.[8] In *Campaign*'s survey to find 'the nation's best-loved ads', Walkers took joint first place with Safeway's 'Harry'. Independently, a survey published in Marketing found Gary to be equal 'best-remembered face' in British TV advertising, with 77% branded recall, alongside BT's Bob Hoskins.[9]

Qualitative research groups across the country confirmed the popularity of the advertising and the appropriateness of using Gary Lineker as our 'crisp thief':

> 'I'd been told all about that ad before I saw it. Very funny.'
>
> 22-year-old lad

8. Indeed, the public outcry surrounding the story of the banning of 'Welcome Home', led to the unusual step of the ITC reversing its decision.
9. The latter campaign supported by approximately 20 times the spend of the Walkers advertising.

'There's not many people who could appeal across the board like him.'

Mum

'He's an idol, but because Walkers are so good, he pinches them.'

Mum

'He can steal my crisps anytime!'

13-year-old girl.

Source: Qualitative Research Groups

The Millward Brown attitudinal measures concerning the advertising are unfortunately not consistent pre and post the BMP advertising; however, the 'Have good advertising' statement clearly confirms that the duck to some extent, and Lineker to a great extent, not only cut through to, but were also highly appreciated by, our audience.

Millward Brown assessed the Lineker campaign as:

'extraordinarily successful, it has, in our view, contributed significantly to Walkers' ambition to become the definitive crisp brand – part of the fabric of British life'.

THE ADVERTISING CONTRIBUTION TO SALES

Regional Analysis

If, as we claim, the advertising was the major stimulant to the brand's recent growth, then we would expect growth to be more significant in areas exposed to heavier weights of the advertising. This is indeed the case.

It is best seen in the Grocery channel, where distribution growth was relatively small over the BMP-advertised period – distribution was already over 90% before BMP's appointment – and so correlation between growth and TVR levels might be expected to be seen fairly easily.

To illustrate this, we have compared Walkers' brand-share performance regionally across two periods:

Period 1 – the last 12 weeks immediately prior to BMP's first advertising for Walkers (June to August 1994)

Period 2 – the most recent 12 weeks of data available (approximately the first three months of 1996).

The country (excluding the Midlands)[10] breaks down naturally into three areas, defined by the amount of TV support over the whole BMP-advertised period – the time between our two test periods.

Area 1 – Scotland

Scotland received heavyweight support with 5,965 TVRs, as it was the area into which Walkers had most recently rolled out. The roll-out period, however, can fairly be said to have finished by the time we start our analysis in Period 1, given that the brand had already achieved 91% distribution in Grocery.

Area 2 – the rest of England and Wales (Excluding Anglia and Midlands)

These regions received very similar, higher levels of support – averaging 2,709 TVRs.

Area 3 – Anglia

This region received less advertising support than the rest of the country, with only 1,704 TVRs. This was because the price deal inherited by the new media agency in summer 1994 was considered too expensive, and the region was downweighted accordingly.

TABLE 4: CHANGES IN WALKERS' SHARE BETWEEN PERIODS 1 AND 2

Region	TVRs	Share Period 1	Share Period 2	% change
Scotland – high	5,965	8.18	15.95	95.0
Mid-weight areas	2,709	15.55	20.92	34.6
Anglia – low	1,704	23.80	27.58	15.9

We can see that higher levels of advertising support do indeed correlate with higher brand share growth rates. We do, however, need to eliminate the effects of (slightly) fluctuating distribution levels over the period, as in the following table:

10. We have not included the Midlands, Walkers' heartland, because there the brand is a well-loved local institution with nearly 50 years of history behind it. In the Midlands, Walkers dominates with a share of approximately 30% of the total crisps and snacks market, and the advertising was expected to, and did, work differently. The task was the more defensive one of holding onto existing loyal consumers, and maintaining the already high levels of share and rate of sale. Though even in the Midlands share increased by 8.6% between the two periods.

TABLE 5: EFFECTS OF DISTRIBUTION LEVELS

	Period 1		Period 2		Share divided by £dist		
	% share	£dist	% share	£dist	P1	P2	% change
Scotland	8.18	90.7	15.95	99.3	9.02	16.06	78.1
Mid-weight	15.55	96.4	20.92	97.6	16.13	21.44	32.9
Anglia	23.80	100.0	27.58	100.0	23.80	27.58	15.9

Source: BARB, IRI Infoscan

It is clear from this that share growth is still higher in regions with more advertising, and this is not the result of distribution.

This fairly 'blunt' kind of analysis is less appropriate in the Impulse channel, because distribution over the BMP-advertised period actually continued to grow quite significantly and rather unexpectedly, thereby making the correlation between share growth and advertising more difficult to isolate. Trying to eliminate the distribution effect by looking at rate of sale is not sufficient because it appears that the BMP advertising drives distribution gains in Impulse as well as rate of sale.

In order to be able to determine what was really happening to the brand in the Impulse channel as a result of our advertising (as well as to produce a more detailed quantification of the advertising contribution in Grocery), we needed to construct a series of econometric models, on which we will focus shortly. Before that, however, there is another piece of evidence that clearly links sales performance with our advertising.

Variety Analysis

Each of the 'theme' advertising executions focused on a particular variety of Walkers crisps – Cheese & Onion flavour for 'Welcome Home', Crinkles for 'Garymania', and Salt & Vinegar flavour for 'Salt 'n Lineker'. In each case the performance of the advertised variety is boosted substantially at the time of the advertising.

Cheese & Onion share of the Walkers brand rose from 22.9% prior to the 'Welcome Home' advertising, to a peak of 25.7% immediately following it; Salt & Vinegar share shot up from 14.5% to 17.8%; and Crinkles nearly doubled its contribution to total Walkers crisps volume from 3.6% to 6.2% during the advertised month.

Hence it is clear that our adverts are powerful at driving consumer behaviour. While this does not prove that it has caused brand growth, it is highly indicative of the power of the campaign to influence consumer behaviour. We suggest that this is indicative of the effects it has on consumer purchasing of the brand.

Evidence from Econometric Analysis

We have constructed two econometric models – one for each trade channel. This has enabled us to quantify the contribution of advertising directly to sales increases in each channel, and has also revealed that, in line with our objectives, this contribution is a combination of more effective promotional *and,* for the first time in many years, effective theme advertising.

Grocery

As the insertion rate of winning coupons remained constant throughout all of the promotions, their scale naturally increased over time as overall brand volume grew. Yet despite this, prior to BMP involvement, each successive promotion had been generating less volume per TVR, as perhaps the novelty of the mechanic wore off. The model shows that the drop in effect per TVR between the first and second promotions, pre-BMP, was of the order of 50%, and between the second and third promotions of the order of 30%. 'Duck', the first BMP promotional ad, managed to reverse this trend, and achieved 10% more effect per TVR than the previous promotion, whilst the two Lineker-supported promotions have improved upon even this achievement (Table 6).

TABLE 6: EFFECT OF THE PROMOTIONS

	Millions of packs generated	TVRs	Millions of packs per 100 TVRs	% change versus previous promotion
Promo1	93.4	309	30.2	
Promo2	47.8	316	15.1	-50%
Promo3	76.7	734	10.5	-31%
'Duck'	54.0	471	11.5	+10%
'Nun'	66.4	520	12.8	+11%
'Dial-a-Prize'	65.1	361	18.0	+41%

Source: BARB, Econometric model

In addition to this, the Lineker promotional advertising has worked in a way in which the previous ones had not, generating not only a short-term effect on share, but also a longer-term step-change increase in share. 'Nun' seems to have generated a long-term (ie well beyond the end of the promotion) increase in share of 0.5% points, and 'Dial-a-Prize' a gain of 1% point. By integrating the promotional and theme advertising into one very successful vehicle, we have been able to create promotional advertising which has not only increased the success of the promotions themselves, but has also continued to work hard as brand advertising after the promotion has finished.

The theme advertising itself is also having a strong effect on share, which was not the case prior to the development of the Lineker campaign. The model shows that 'Welcome Home' generated an uplift of over 6 million bags of crisps in Grocery. The very first effects of 'Salt 'n Lineker' are just coming through in our data sample and it appears to be generating a similar effect per TVR, whilst the 'Garymania' ad for Crinkles generated extra sales for Walkers in Grocery of 3.5 million packets.

Impulse

The model has, surprisingly, revealed that the decline in the effectiveness of advertising each subsequent promotion pre-BMP was not so apparent in the Impulse channel.[11] It is not clear why this is the case, although it is possible that there was less of a wear-out effect for the novelty of the 'Instant Win' idea among children (who dominate purchase in the Impulse channel), than among adults (who dominate in Grocery). Whatever the reason, the model shows clearly that the promotion advertised by the duck reversed this decline and that the two Lineker-supported promotions have been much more successful at generating sales per TVR than any previous promotions.

TABLE 7: SALES GENERATED PER TVR

	Millions of packs generated	TVRs	Millions of packs per TVRs
Promo1	15.8	309	5.11
Promo2	16.2	316	5.13
Promo3	22.4	734	3.05
'Duck'	20.9	471	4.44
'Nun'	33.4	520	6.43
'Dial-a-Prize'	25.4	361	7.04

Source: BARB, Econometric model

Again, the model confirms that the Lineker theme advertising has worked, and has had a positive and significant effect on sales, unlike pre-Lineker theme advertising. In Impulse alone, 'Garymania' generated extra sales of 0.8 million packets of Crinkles, while 'Welcome Home' and 'Salt 'n Lineker' have produced sales of an extra million packs each so far – and the effect of 'Salt 'n Lineker' continues.

ELIMINATION OF OTHER VARIABLES

We have exhaustively examined the effect of other variables, both independently and in the econometric modelling. None of these other variables can explain the tremendous growth of Walkers since August 1994.

WALKERS – OVERALL PROFITABILITY OF THE CAMPAIGN

The econometric models show a very substantial sales gain resulting from advertising, as the advertising has not only driven share directly but has helped to increase share of front stocks in Grocery and overall distribution levels in Impulse.

In Impulse the contribution has been 67 million packs (5.1% of Impulse sales between the four weeks ending 15 October 1994 (Duck) and 2 March 1996).

11. Given the relative size of Impulse to Grocery, in the overall market this trend is still true.

In Grocery, if we take the whole period, and simply add the individual effect of all the pieces of advertising activity, then the total advertising effect has been 169 million packs, equivalent to approximately 13% of all sales over that period. However, in terms of looking at overall payback, the models show that their total effect is actually multiplicative rather than additive, in which case the total contribution becomes 276 million packs or 20% of total sales.

For every 1p profit margin per bag, the additional bags sold generate £3.4 million. BMP's total advertising spend over the whole period was £8.94 million. The exact margin is confidential but is in excess of 2p. Table 8 shows examples of how only small levels of profit margin provide substantial advertising 'profits'.

TABLE 8: EFFECT OF INCREASED PROFIT MARGIN

Profit margin per bag (pence)	Extra profit (£m)	Advertising cost (£m)	Profit net of ads (£m)
1	3.4	8.94	-5.54
2	6.8	8.94	-2.14
5	17.0	8.94	8.06
10	34.0	8.94	25.06

Source: Register Meal, Econometric modelling

Importantly though, this does not take into account the value for future sales of having appropriated in Grocery such a large share of front stocks, or in Impulse, of having ousted the competition. It is almost impossible to put a meaningful figure on this. However, there is no doubt that in their respective sectors, front stocks and distribution are key determinants of overall volume.

In addition, Hill & Knowlton, Walkers' PR company, believes that, to date, the campaign has generated over £1.6 million (advertising equivalent spend) in additional unpaid-for editorial coverage.

CONCLUSION

When Walkers Crisps came to BMP in 1994 the brand was undeniably successful already. But success generates its own problems, chief among them for Walkers being how to sustain the growth of the brand into the future.

We believe we have shown that it was advertising that played the critical role in stimulating Walkers' amazing success since appointment. But it is remarkable in two other ways which lend the case a wider application.

— As an example of genuinely effective targeting of a mass market. The Walkers advertising was aimed squarely at a mass audience, yet appealed as powerfully and effectually to each sector of that audience as could any advertising aimed at a particular niche within it.

— As an example of how advertising can provide a focus for other forms of consumer communication. The Walkers advertising was used to powerfully enhance other forms of marketing activity (particularly promotions, PR and product innovation), which had previously operated independently and with less success.

Thus the advertising dealt with the problems of success by transforming Walkers from a big brand into a genuinely strong one for the first time.

APPENDIX

Elimination of Variables

Product Quality
Walker's consistent ability to innovate has enabled it to maintain significant levels of unbranded preference throughout the 1990s.

However, this has been true throughout the BMP period, and before and hence cannot explain the increased rise in ROS since BMP's advertising started.

It is possible that our variety analysis could be explained by increases in product qualities of the specified flavour featured in the analysis. However, this is not the case for Crinkles/'Garymania', where the variant remained the same in terms of quality/taste appeal. It is possible that the Salt 'n Lineker name change had an effect but, if so, this could not have happened without the Lineker advertising.

Finally, if flavour improvements were the primary factor affecting sales then we would expect to see a sizeable *step change* in share at their introduction. There is no evidence from the models that this occurred, instead, a short-term *'spike'* in share coinciding only with the timing of the advertising is visible.

Price Reductions and Advertising Effects
Walkers' price has actually been fractionally reduced in real terms over the last few years. This has helped to boost Walkers' sales in both Grocery and Impulse. However, the econometric models present the advertising effects which we have previously claimed for the advertising net of the impacts from all other variables, including price and distribution, so this has no effect on our conclusions.

Tactical Promotion
Regional tactical activity supported by advertising has taken place for Walkers. For four weeks in February and March 1995, the 'Walkerman' promotion ran in the Tyne Tees area only. This involved a 'Walkerman' walking around the towns of the area. Spotting him and answering a question correctly resulted in winning a small cash prize. This was supported by a 10-second TV ad, produced by BMP.

While this promotion was believed to be successful, it only ran in Tyne Tees during the period discussed in this paper (it subsequently rolled out into Scotland and Lancashire in April 1996).

Hence it can only have affected sales in Tyne Tees. Given the enormous effects we claim for the advertising, and the fact that they occur nationally, we can see that 'Walkerman' can only have affected national sales over the BMP period slightly.

Effects of Walkers Increased Size

It is possible that Walkers' growth and hence increased volume at the start of each promotion, has in some way determined the size of success of the subsequent promotion. This is actually not the case.[12]

Nature of Instant Win Promotions

The nature of each promotion was similar although, as mentioned earlier, the number of (smaller) prizes increased as the brand grew – but the top prize did not. Hence the increasing success of the promotions cannot be attributed to increases in the top prize.

Competitive Expenditure

Levels of competitive spend actually increased significantly over the advertised period.

TABLE 9: COMPETITIVE SPEND

	£m	Index
1993	20.5	96
1994	23.1	108
1995	28.0	131

Thus, Walkers' success cannot be explained by reduction in competitive activity.

PR and Media Coverage

We would suggest that the PR coverage that Walkers has achieved since the advent of the Lineker campaign (and hence any related sales), ultimately resulted from the advertising. This was the main reason we dispensed with the otherwise promising Walkers 'Duck' campaign. In addition, practically all the coverage features the campaign itself, suggesting strongly that it would not have occurred without Lineker.

Hence, rather than eliminating effects of PR, we see them as effects of the advertising.

Point Of Sale

It is true that, since the Lineker campaign started, Walkers has been able to increase its POS presence. However, the vast majority of this is Lineker-related material – from 'Gary' shelf-wobblers to life-size cut-outs – and it is clear that willing acceptance of this material by the trade is in fact a result of the popularity and

12. We would contend that a) if this were true, then advertising, as we have shown, has played its part in growing the brand and hence creating these effects, and b) these effects can be eliminated by looking at percentage increase in share per TVR rather than just volume increase per TVR for each promotion. If we do this, we see similar trends to those illustrated earlier with the percentage increase in share per TVR actually increasing with each promotion, not decreasing. In fact, in Grocery 'Duck' produced 2.23% uplift in share per 100 TVRs, 'Nun' 2.25% and 'Dial-A-Prize' 3.05%.

success of the Lineker advertising. So rather than *eliminate* its effect, we claim it is another *consequence* of the campaign.

ECONOMETRIC MODELLING

Walker's Econometric Analysis: Explaining and Validating the Models

The models for both channels, particularly Grocery, are actually fairly complex, both having two equations. In Grocery these equations form a simultaneous system where share of volume and share of front stocks are jointly determined. In Impulse the equations explain the performance of Walkers' total volume and of its aggregate pack distribution. (Aggregate distribution is the sum of the sterling distribution across all available pack sizes and is a way of taking account of both the 'width' and 'depth' of distribution.)

Grocery – Theoretical Background

If a brand achieved an increased share of shelf space and thus greater in-store visibility, all else remaining equal, then one would expect this to lead to a higher level of share.

However, in today's hard-nosed Grocery environment the only way a brand can ever get a permanent increase in shelf space (front stocks) is to permanently raise the level of its share through some other mechanism. This will be rewarded with a greater share of shelf space, which could then generate some further share gains. If the effort to raise share is relatively short term then the brand will fairly quickly settle at a newer higher share/front stocks equilibrium. However, if the share building momentum can be maintained, a virtuous circle can be set up where share increases merit front stocks increases, which generate further share increases then further front stocks increases etc.

Modelling this type of process requires a simultaneous equation model with two equations, one for share of volume and one for share of front stocks (shelf space). These equations then capture the feedback mechanism whereby a rise in advertising pushes up share then front stocks, then share again (though less than initially) then front stocks again, then share, with the increments in share and front stocks reducing at each iteration until the overall levels are in equilibrium once again.

This type of structure is not simply imposed on the data, the data has to support it and the Walkers' grocery data had all the classic signs.

Firstly, the volume share and share of front stocks series are highly correlated (as in Figure 9). The correlation between the two is 97%, making it impossible to meaningfully build an ordinary least-squares model of share which could include any factors other than front stocks.

It is clear from studying the various data series at a graphical level that movements in front stocks are not independent of movements in those other series (like price relative to competitors), which theoretically should be included in a volume share model. The explanatory variables in a single equation model must be independent of one another, otherwise biased estimates of their individual contributions will result.

The modelling results show that the data does indeed support the hypothesis that the brand works as described above and that there is feedback between volume share and front stock share.

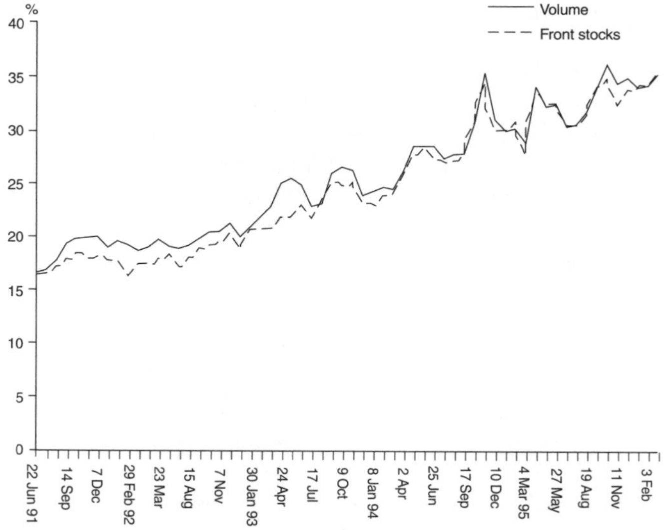

Figure 9: *Walkers' share in Grocery volume versus front stocks*
Source: IRI Infoscan

Grocery Simulation Results

It is interesting to see some of the results of the model simulations in order to appreciate the overall effect of the advertising. Figures 10 and 11 show the effects in Grocery of advertising on both volume share and share of front stocks.

Other results are:

— Pre-BMP brand advertising. There is no evidence from the econometric models that this was having a statistically significant effect on share.

— The step-change resulting from 'Nun' and 'Dial-A-Prize'. This resulted from a particularly strong increase in front stocks.

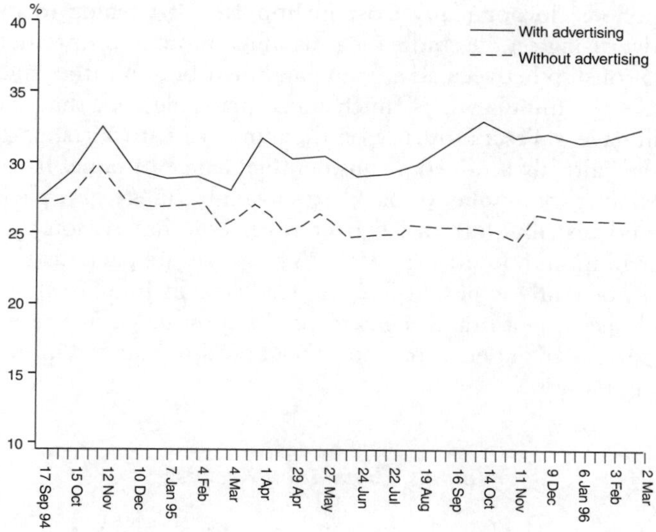

Figure 10: *Walkers volume share of crisps in Grocery, with and without advertising*

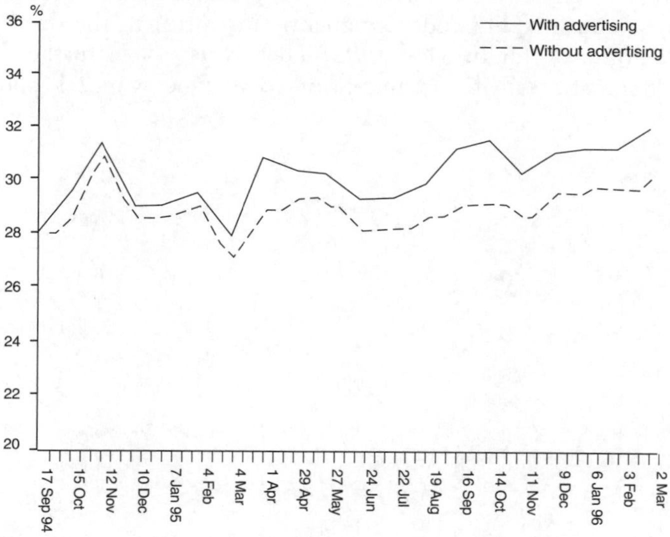

Figure 11: *Walkers volume share front stocks in Grocery, the effect of advertising*

Impulse – Theoretical Background

The environment in Impulse is clearly very different from that in Grocery. For a start, the Impulse sector has a tendency to stock only one brand of crisps with a smaller range of pack sizes. Changes in share of front stocks in Impulse are thus actually much more likely to be the result of distribution growth rather than increased visibility within any one store. (Things like gondola ends during promotional periods do not really exist in Impulse.) If wishing to investigate the influence of advertising on the trade it is thus much more appropriate in Impulse to look at the relationship between advertising and distribution rather than advertising and front stocks. In Impulse, it is much more plausible too, that the promise of advertising will have a direct influence on the number of stockists, particularly once the campaign has already attained a considerable degree of fame. It was also found that the implied average number of pack sizes available (aggregate pack distribution divided by brand distribution) varied over time. For that reason the most useful measure of distribution in Impulse appears to be aggregate pack distribution.

One would not really expect to see the feedback in Impulse that is evident in Grocery, mainly because a brand tends to be listed on its own. So, even if its sales improve in a particular outlet, it has no other brand to squeeze in order to set the virtuous circle in motion.

Impulse Simulation Results

Figures 12 and 13 show the total effects of advertising on sales and distribution in Impulse. The sales simulation includes the distribution effect.

Other results specifically mentioned are the promise of advertising. In Impulse, distribution rose considerably and permanently just prior to the third Lineker film ('Garymania') going on air in May 1995. There was also a further effect during airtime. The t-statistic on advertising prior to airtime was 2.1 and 4.8 during airtime.

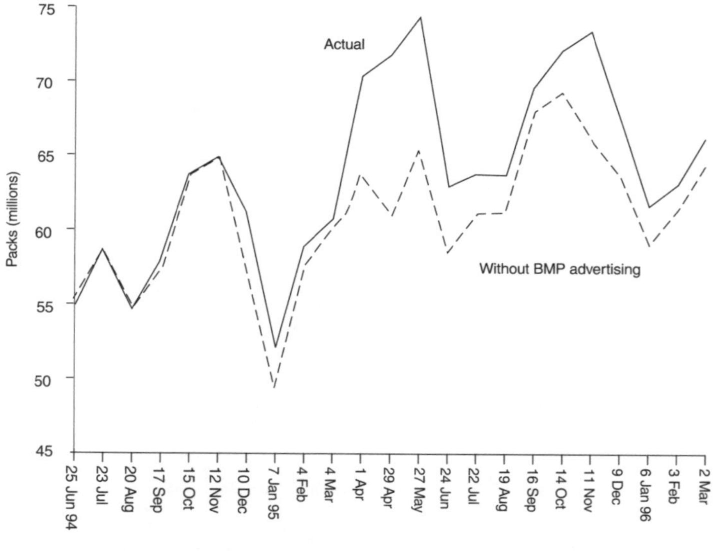

Figure 12: *Effect of BMP advertising on Walkers sales volume*

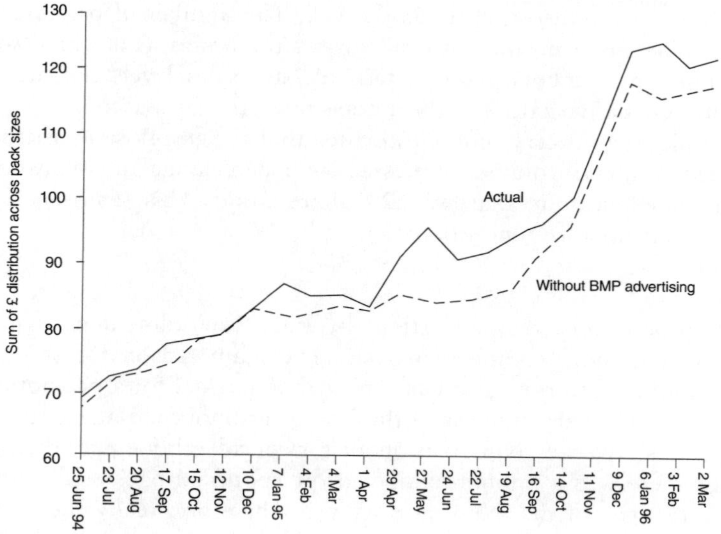

Figure 13: *Effect of BMP advertising on aggregate pack distribution*

Other Considerations

There are a number of features of the models which merit further explanation, most important of which is the treatment of promotions.

Promotions

In a market like this where the promotions and the advertising are so inextricably linked, it is a non-trivial task to separate the effect that the promotions themselves generate from that of the advertising. However, we are helped a great deal by the fact that different promotions have had different weights of advertising and that all the promotions in our sample have been relatively similar in terms of mechanic.

The model incorporates promotional uplifts in terms of two variables:

1. a promotional on-off switch which runs for the length of the production run (six weeks) but is lagged in the models to allow for the product to get from production line to shelf (the models are multiplicative in structure so they allow a larger promotional volume to occur as a result of promotion (rather than advertising) as the brand grows);

2. an advertising effect proportional to the weight of TVRs behind the promotion.

In addition, two promotions have a third component (an additional advertising variable specific to that promotion), as they experienced particularly strong responses proportional to the pattern of advertising activity behind them. One of these, 'Duck' ('Moneybags II') was a repeat of one of the earlier promotions, the other was 'Dial-A-Prize'.

There is no pre-determined production run for a promotion. The factory produces promotional packs for a period of six weeks and will produce more if a promotion seems to be doing particularly well. The number of promotional packs produced has increased in line with the size of the brand as a whole so that it is always roughly the same as a proportion of base sales levels but, as mentioned above, the multiplicative nature of the models takes this into account.

For example, the grocery model estimates that the promotions themselves add approximately 12% to volume (expressed as a percentage of four-weekly sales). Their initial contribution to share was 2.8 share points. This has risen as the brand has grown to 4.1 (on a four-weekly basis).

'Nun'

One of the promotions, that advertised by the 'Nun' film, does require special consideration and more complex analysis. The main reason for this is that the advertising continued to run for much longer than normal for a promotion in order to capitalise on the media interest in the brand. Promotional advertising normally runs for four to six weeks. 'Nun' was on air for considerably longer than this.

Although there was a limited number of promotional packs still lurking in the trade, the latter part of the 'Nun' activity was, therefore, really theme advertising and was not doing a genuine promotional job. The econometrics shows us that, after discounting the effects of the promotion itself, promotional advertising during Lineker generated approximately four times the volume per 100 TVRs that theme generates. In order to properly evaluate the effects of 'Nun', therefore, we must take this into account.

In order to realistically estimate what the 'Nun' promotional activity has contributed, we need to assume that the 520 TVRs originally allocated to the promotion were promotional and the rest were theme. The results presented earlier have taken this into account.

New Regions, Variants and Pack Sizes

Dummy variables were constructed for all these events, included in the analysis and tested for statistical significance.

Crisps Versus Salty Snacks

All the share data is expressed as share of salty snacks, as that is the market in which Walkers' considers it competes and thus the one whose trends are of most interest to it. Crisps are however the largest sector within this market and most of the competitive interaction is with them.

The econometric models all analyse Walkers' sales in the context of the crisp rather than the total salty snacks market. Obviously, from time to time, there are some effects on crisps from other products (eg Hula Hoops). However, evidence from the Grocery share model indicates that Walkers is only affected by these in line with its share of the market and therefore that it is unnecessary to include them in a share model. Although the Impulse model is of volume rather than share, there is no evidence that any systematic component is missing from the model and thus the concentration on crisps does seem to be valid.

5

Barclaycard

'Put it away Bough'

THE ARGUMENT

In 1990, important changes were taking place in the UK credit card market, threatening the position of the two dominant brands. This story is of how Barclaycard survived, and profited from, these upheavals – unlike Access which, without decisive management and effective advertising support, significantly declined.

Barclaycard reversed a declining share trend, achieved brand leadership, enhanced profitability, and established itself as a premium brand in an increasingly commoditised market. While a number of marketing activities together contributed to this success, the new advertising campaign, started in 1991, has been crucial in strengthening the brand's position. Also, a model shows that the advertising has already paid for itself in revenue from increased card turnover.

CREDIT CARDS IN THE UK BEFORE 1990

To understand how the market was changing by 1990, we first review briefly some earlier history.

Barclaycard was launched in 1966, the UK's first credit card. It was followed seven years later by Access, managed by a consortium of four other banks. For many years, these two brands dominated the market[1] between them.

Originally, Barclaycard and Access created their own retailer networks. After a few years, however, in order to extend their coverage abroad, each became part of a global network: Barclaycard with VISA, Access with MasterCard.

While this was a necessary move, it also helped open the market to competition. Now retailers would accept any VISA or MasterCard, new entrants to the market did not have to create their own networks; they simply made an agreement with VISA or MasterCard. Other VISA cards, like TSB Trustcard, began to appear.

---

1. An alternative product, the charge card, was available from American Express and Diner's Club. Charge cards were targeted at high earners who would pay off all charges each month, as well as a significant annual fee. Credit cards offered extended credit, and were free (before 1990); credit card issuers made their money primarily from the interest on outstanding balances.

Nevertheless, Barclaycard and Access continued to dominate the market during the 1970s and 1980s, supported by famous, heavyweight advertising campaigns.[2]

Meanwhile, the total UK credit card market continued to grow:[3]

TABLE 1: CREDIT CARD GROWTH 1974–88

Index 1974 = 100	1974	1977	1980	1983	1986	1989
Number of cards	100	110	200	260	370	410
Real turnover	100	120	210	430	920	1,520

Source: Barclaycard

THE SITUATION IN 1990

By 1990, elements of this picture were changing in ways which threatened both Barclaycard and Access.

Market Growth Plateaued

Card penetration levelled at around 32% – most of those whom card issuers regarded as sound credit risks had now got a card (or had decided they did not want one).

The Number of Visa Cards Available in the UK Increased

By 1989 there were more than 30 cards available. Meanwhile, a potential threat to the whole credit card category emerged in 1987 – the debit card.[4] And, despite the talk of a 'cashless society', ATMs (cash machines) mean cash is now easier to get hold of than ever – it still accounts for 90% of transactions.

The Beginning of the Recession

Not only was money tight, but people were conscious of financial difficulties associated with 'credit'.

2. Barclaycard used Dudley Moore and then, for nine years, Alan Whicker, who demonstrated the card's global acceptability. Access created the animated card, the well known 'flexible friend'.
3. Market growth was driven by increasing overall card penetration, and later by increasing retailer acceptability, which stimulated greater usage.
4. With a debit card, funds are immediately transferred electronically to the payee's bank account. While this has the disadvantage, relative to credit cards, of no interest-free period before payment is required, it appeals to people who prefer to make payments immediately in order to feel more in control of their finances. So, although debit cards have positioned themselves as a replacement for cheques, the fact that it is a plastic card, and works in a similar way to a credit card at the point of sale, makes it attractive to those customers who are reluctant to use credit cards because of the temptation of taking extended credit.

Profitability Became Harder to Achieve

— More credit card holders were 'full payers' (ie paying their account in full each month). This meant that they paid no interest to the card issuer, who effectively managed their account for nothing.

— Credit card fraud increased steadily – the costs of this are largely borne by card issuers.

— Meanwhile, the cost of funds (interest rates) was increasing, without a corresponding increase in the rates charged to customers, thus squeezing margins.

As a result, Barclaycard's card issuing operation made a loss in 1990.

THE BARCLAYCARD RELAUNCH 1990

In response to the profitability problem, by 1990, all the major card issuers were preparing to introduce an annual fee, to create a profit stream independent of the amount of extended credit and fluctuations in interest rates. Although the sums proposed were not large (around £10 a year), there was considerable customer resistance to paying anything for a service they traditionally regarded as free.

Given the increased competition and the onset of recession, card issuers were extremely apprehensive about being the first to move, fearing a large number of defections to 'free' cards.

At Barclaycard a great deal of thought and research went into managing this process. The fee was introduced as one element in a major product relaunch, code-named K2. The package finally chosen was as follows:

— an annual fee of £8;

— a small reduction in interest rate (from 29.8% to 27.8%);

— new cardholder benefits – Purchase Cover (100-day insurance on any item over £50 bought with a Barclaycard), and International Rescue (assistance and advice when travelling abroad). These were benefits that had previously only been available from exclusive, high-fee charge cards such as American Express;

— the opportunity for Barclaycard VISA holders to apply for a new Barclaycard MasterCard (included in the same annual fee).

As it turned out, Barclaycard was not the first: in January 1990 Lloyd's introduced a £12 fee on its Access card.[5] In May 1990, Barclaycard wrote to all customers with a brochure explaining the new package, supported by extensive telephone contact to answer queries and persuade immediate 'rejecters' to reconsider.

Customers were also assured that, if they decided to cancel their card within the next 12 months, their fee would be refunded.

As a result, Barclaycard lost about a million 'dormant' customers and a much smaller number of active customers – fewer, in fact, than anticipated.[6]

The relaunch was, effectively, handled without advertising support. Since 1981, the advertising had featured Alan Whicker in a variety of exotic locations, demonstrating that Barclaycard was accepted in many more places worldwide than 'certain other cards'.[7] This campaign was under review at the time of the relaunch for two reasons:

1. All the market changes described above, together with the enhanced product benefits, meant that 'international acceptability' on its own was no longer an adequate competitive positioning.[8]

2. Whicker himself, though still popular and closely associated with Barclaycard, was getting older, with declining appeal to younger consumers. The campaign itself was running out of steam after nine years and looking a little tired.

BMP DDB was appointed as Barclaycard's new advertising agency in May 1990, with the following brief.

ADVERTISING OBJECTIVES POST-RELAUNCH – GETTING, KEEPING, AND USING BARCLAYCARD

The relaunch had successfully negotiated the introduction of a fee and upgraded the product relative to competitors. This was a necessary step towards addressing the brand's longer-term objectives, but not enough on its own to achieve them. The advertising goals set in 1990 were as follows:

---

5. As a result Lloyd's lost some 30% of its Access customers.
6. Historically, Barclaycards had been issued to Barclays Bank current account customers for use as a cheque guarantee card. A proportion of users had therefore never wanted a credit card and in many cases never used it as such. Barclaycard were happy to convert these 'dormant' users to a simple cheque guarantee card – dormant cards are a source of cost, not revenue. So although the total user base went down from 8 million to 6.5 million, about a million of these were dormant users who represented no loss to the brand's income. 485,000 active users had been lost by December 1990, which was within the confidence limits of research predictions but towards the lower end of this range.
7. This was meant as a comparison with American Express, but frequently interpreted as a comparison with Access – a misunderstanding Barclaycard was happy to live with.
8. International acceptability was, in reality, a VISA property rather than a Barclaycard property.

Customer Retention

Although attrition at the relaunch had been minimised, we could not assume there would be no delayed reaction – customers had an increasing choice of cards with no fee. In particular, it was important to hold on to customers who, at least sometimes, took advantage of extended credit; customers with existing credit outstanding might only be waiting to repay this before moving.

Increasing Turnover

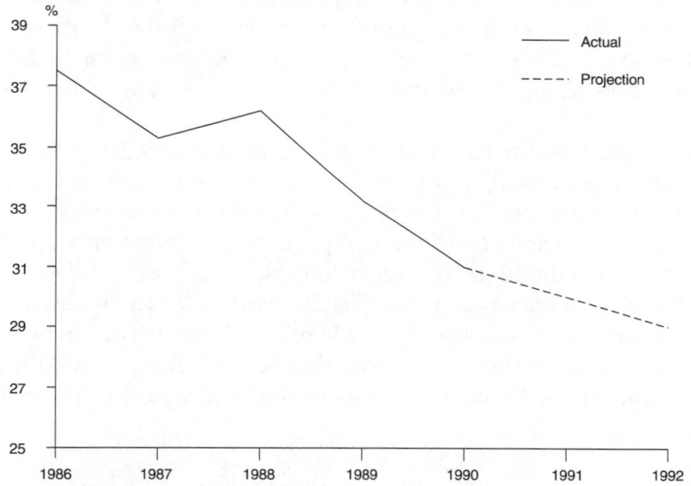

Figure 1: *Barclaycard share of turnover 1986–92 (including projection)*
Source: BBA

Barclaycard's share of turnover had been in decline during the late '80s as more competitors came into the market (Figure 1). Projections, if this continued, were a turnover share of 30% in 1991 and 29% by the end of 1992.[9] The target was to reverse this trend and be at 31% by the end of 1992.

Increasing Share of New Cardholders

While total penetration of credit cards was no longer expected to grow, there is always a need to attract new market entrants, primarily younger people (18–35). Barclaycard's share of new cardholders had declined as competitors such as TSB

9. This may not sound much, but 1% turnover share was worth about £280 million in 1990, and turnover is the main short-term determinant of extended credit which remained the main source of income.

Trustcard targeted younger audiences; in 1990 it was 15%, well below share of existing users. The task of reversing this decline would be addressed through direct response as well as media advertising;[10] the role of advertising was supportive, to increase the brand's attractiveness, especially to younger people.

In short, we wanted people to *get* the card, *keep* the card and *use* the card. These are linked: research shows that the more often people use a credit card, the more likely they are to keep it.

ADVERTISING STRATEGY

Research showed that, in 1990, most people saw all credit cards as very similar, with hardly any measurable image differences between Barclaycard and Access. The enhanced services offered by the card were potential differentiators. They also offered incentives to *get, keep,* and – especially in the case of Purchase Cover – *use* the card.

The new card benefits had already been communicated at relaunch via a mailed brochure (and a good deal of editorial coverage). As a result, research showed fairly high prompted awareness that Barclaycard offered these services.

However, there seemed to be an important difference between being aware of the benefits and valuing them, regarding them as personally relevant, or even believing them to be differentiating. Negative attitudes to credit cards generally led many customers to be suspicious – 'where's the catch?' or to find other ways of denying their significance – 'I expect they all do that, don't they?'. So neither general perceptions of Barclaycard nor turnover increased in the months following the relaunch.

TABLE 2: PROMPTED AWARENESS OF PRODUCT CHANGES

	October 1990 %
Annual fee	93
Purchase Cover	58
International Rescue	55
Free MasterCard	53

Base: Barclaycard holders
Source: Barclaycard Internal Research

10. The main mechanisms for recruiting new Barclaycard users are leaflets in Barclays branches (primarily targeted at Barclays customers); inserts in magazines; and direct mail, targeted at young people and others.

TABLE 3: ATTITUDES AND TURNOVER NOT IMPROVED BY AWARENESS OF PRODUCT CHANGES

(a) % agreeing that Barclaycard	Pre-April 1990	Post-October 1990
Provides special benefits and services for cardholders	40	39
Provides a high quality customer service	44	45
cares for its customers' needs	40	36
(b) Share of credit card turnover	31.8	31.6

(a) Base: Barclaycard holders
Source: Millward Brown
(b) Source: BBA

The role for advertising was to make these product benefits real, believable, relevant, and closely associated to Barclaycard, and so use them to develop a new overall positioning for the brand as a premium quality card, differentiated from the plethora of 'ordinary' credit cards available.

As a secondary communication, we wanted to continue to associate Barclaycard with worldwide acceptability, its one existing image difference from Access.[11]

The primary target audience was existing Barclaycard holders, and an important secondary audience was considered to be potential new entrants to the market, with the emphasis on younger people aged 18 to 34.

The creative challenge was to follow the Alan Whicker campaign. Although it was beginning to tire, it was still well liked by many, and almost synonymous with Barclaycard. Its scores for branded awareness and enjoyment were expected to be hard to match. Another 'personality' was only one way of replacing Whicker and this was the route eventually chosen. It had to be someone who appealed across a wide range of target groups, from the wealthy older users to 20-year-olds choosing their first credit card. We were fortunate to get Rowan Atkinson.

THE CAMPAIGN 1991–95

Although featuring a well known actor, the new campaign moved from Whicker's 'presenter' format to a dramatic mode. Rowan Atkinson appears as a bungling secret agent called Richard Latham. Although equipped with a Barclaycard, Latham is always dismissive about its usefulness and as a result is repeatedly without support or protection when things go wrong. In contrast his assistant, Bough, demonstrates the benefits of Barclaycard usage and provides a mouthpiece for information about it.

This formula has proved extremely effective. It is flexible enough to communicate a number of different messages and its intelligent humour, where the

11. Access, existing only in the UK and weakly associated in consumers' minds with MasterCard, was not believed to be as internationally acceptable as Barclaycard. This worked to Barclaycard's advantage, there were many cases of Access consumers applying for a Barclaycard when they had to make a trip abroad. In the long term, however, we realised that this was not necessarily a sustainable advantage.

cynical Latham always ends up a figure of fun, wins people over in a way that a more rational, straight approach would not.

Between 1991 and the end of 1995, 14 films were made featuring eight different benefits.

Media planning has focused advertising at peak times of user activity in order to stimulate usage:

January/February: sales, holiday booking;

June/July: holiday spending;

November/December: pre-Christmas.

From 1991 to 1995 £41.8 million was spent on the TV campaign, a total of 15,410 TVRs.[12]

THE RESULTS 1991–95

We can look at the results of the campaign at three levels.

First, responses to the advertising itself. The campaign has become extremely famous and well liked, exceeding the high standards set by Whicker. Besides being well branded and entertaining, it is also highly efficient in communicating specific product messages.

Second, we look at consumers' perceptions of the brand. Barclaycard has distanced itself from Access, and has got closer to (even overtaken) American Express. These changes in image are directly related to the themes of the advertising. The attractiveness of the brand to younger people has been improved.

Third, and most importantly, we estimate the contribution of the advertising to meeting Barclaycard's business objectives:

— Getting the card – increasing share of new acquirers.

— Keeping the card – ownership has held up in the face of ever-increasing competition. In particular the GM Card, despite a successful launch, took relatively little business from Barclaycard.

— Using the card – share of turnover and of outstandings[13] has increased, and an econometric model relates the increase in Barclaycard turnover to advertising.

---

12. Other media have been used at very low levels: posters on Purchase Cover in 1993 (£688,000), press in 1992 (£486,000) and radio in 1993 (£49,000). The TV films have also been shown in cinemas with a total spend of £822,000 between 1992 and 1995.
13. Outstandings = the total amount of extended credit outstanding at any point in time. In terms of business performance, share of outstandings is even more important than share of turnover.

'TEAPOT' 60 SECONDS

Latham: Excuse me, Sir Brian.

Bough: Got the present, sir?
Latham: Of course Bough.

Bough: Enough in the whip round then?
Latham: 75 pounds and 14p.
Bough: 14p! Who put that in? I don't suppose you bought it with your...

Latham: With my Barclaycard. Oh yes obviously Bough. I had a manilla envelope stuffed with cash so naturally I used Barclaycard.
Bough: It would have been insured against loss or damage.

Latham: Bough! This is the wedding of the daughter of the head of MI7. There are four men on the roof, two in the choir and the vicar has no previous convictions. I think that's ample insurance for a china teapot.

Sound: Breaking teapot.

'MOLE' 60 SECONDS

Latham: Thank you ladies and gentlemen, a very impressive turnout. In fact the only person I can't see here is the ambassador.

Latham: Ah, that's better.
Sir Wilfred: What the devil do you think you're playing at, Latham?
Latham: I was about to ask you the same question.

Latham: Yesterday you collected rather a lot of money from this man and today we hear you are to meet a courier in this very Embassy.

Latham: That ambassador has the behaviour pattern of a mole!
Bough: That is the behaviour pattern of a man who has lost his Barclaycard. First they send cash then a replacement card.

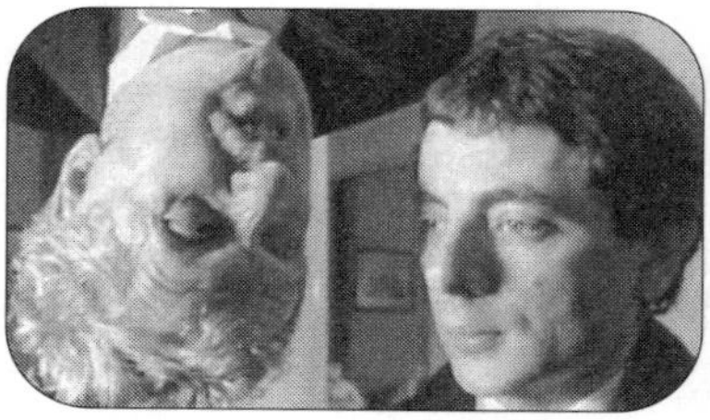

Latham: Oh come on Mr Moley. Yes Bough let him in, the more the merrier. A Barclaycard? To Moscow? And how do they do that, pray? By motorcycle messen... ger?

Latham: Thank you Sir Wilfred for taking part in our training exercise. Realism is obviously of paramount importance.

Latham: Come on Bough, untie Sir Wilfred.

'SNAKEBITE' 60 SECONDS

Bough: There's still no answer sir.
Latham: Right Bough, we're going in.

Latham: Wendy! Right Bough, you loosen his clothing, I'll get the local doctor.

Latham: Blast!
Bough: What is it sir?
Latham: Apparently he is the local doctor.

Latham: That's enough loosening for now Bough.
Bough: I'm looking for his Barclaycard sir.
Latham: His Barclaycard! This man's in no state to go shopping.

Bough: I'm going to phone them up for medical advice sir.
Latham: You're going to phone Barclaycard for medical advice?
Bough: Barclaycard International Rescue sir, they can send doctors…

Latham: We're wasting our time here Bough. This man has a serious case of snakebite and there's only one thing that's going to save him. I'm going to have to locate the wound and suck out the poison. Yes, I actually think perhaps you should phone Barclaycard Bough, I'm not sure I've got the… you know, my lips are a little…

Latham: Well, I thought I had a solution but then…

RESULTS: RESPONSE TO THE ADVERTISING ITSELF

Awareness of Barclaycard TV advertising grew steadily from 28% at the beginning of 1991 throughout 1992 and 1993 and, since then, has remained very high at around 50%, well above American Express and Access. The Millward Brown model of this trend calculates an Awareness Index of between 4 and 8 for the various executions; more significantly, it also shows a base level of ad awareness rising from 14% at the start of the campaign to 21% by 1994.[14]

Barclaycard anticipated that it might take two or three years before memories of the new campaign supplanted Alan Whicker. In fact, this happened much more quickly. By the end of the first year, identified recall of Atkinson was far higher than that of Whicker and, within two years, mentions of Whicker had virtually disappeared from the research.

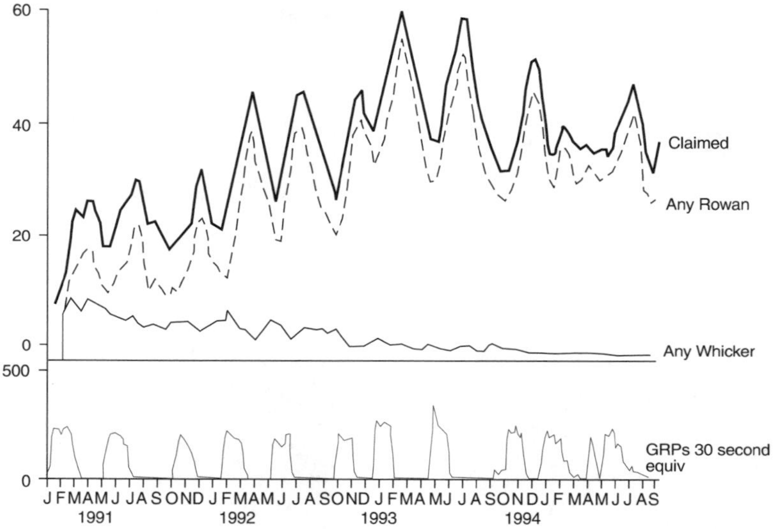

Figure 2: *Identified recall – Barclaycard (first recall only), rolling four-weekly data*

Opinions of the advertising are also strongly positive, both absolutely and relative to other credit card advertising. From the start, around 60% of those recalling the campaign claimed to enjoy watching it. The figures shown in Table 4 are totals for 1995:

14. Millward Brown's 'Awareness Index' indicates the amount of extra advertising recall generated by 100 TVRs. The base level is what advertising recall declines to when all short-term advertising memories have decayed. As the base can move over time it can be regarded as an indication of longer-term advertising effect. The all-category average is 4.

TABLE 4: OPINIONS OF THE ADVERTISING

1995	Barclaycard %	Amex %	Access %	GM Card %
Any positive	89	55	55	59
I like the people in it	63	11	28	9
I enjoy watching it	59	11	28	9
Any negative	12	29	26	32
I'm getting fed up with seeing it	9	20	15	18

Base: Definite recallers
Source: Millward Brown

Although some of the more popular films have now had very high ratings, viewers are not getting tired of them.[15] The Latham campaign has now had more than twice as many ratings in five years as Whicker had in nine, but enjoyment scores are far higher and wear-out much lower than they were for the last burst of Whicker.

TABLE 5: COMPARISON OF WHICKER AND LATHAM CAMPAIGNS

	Last burst of Whicker (May 1990) %	Latham burst (December 1995) %
I enjoy watching it	25	59
I'm getting fed up with seeing it	20	6
Total campaign TVRs to date	c 7,000	15,410

Respondents also agree that the advertising gives *positive impressions* of the brand.

TABLE 6: IMPRESSIONS GIVEN BY ADVERTISING: HOW STRONGLY DO YOU AGREE THAT THIS AD GIVES THE IMPRESSION THAT [BRAND]...?

% agree strongly	Barclaycard	Access	Amex
Is continuously looking at ways to update/improve service	23	12	8
Is in touch with the general public	22	9	12
Is offering you something different	19	5	12
Is the sort of card for you	12	4	6
Can always be relied on	28	17	32

Base: Definite recallers, 1994 total
NB: More recent data cannot be used for confidentiality reasons
Source: Millward Brown

15. 'Cairo' has had 2,262 TVRs, which means that, on average, everyone in the country has seen it 20 times! The most successful films therefore continue to be shown in the repertoire. We believe this contributes to the interest and variety of the campaign when on air.

Also:

— In a Campaign poll in 1996 among the general public, Barclaycard was voted the third best-liked advertising campaign in the UK.

— Of 1,200 ads tested using the Millward Brown Link Test, 'Teapot' and 'Cairo' have the fourth and sixth highest 'enjoyment' scores.

— In a survey conducted for Marketing magazine into personality advertising, 60% correctly associated Rowan Atkinson with Barclaycard (the third highest result).

Enjoyment and memorability do not themselves prove effectiveness, but given the traditional suspicion and even hostility with which many consumers regard credit cards, we believe that these positive responses to the advertising have been a crucial mechanism in increasing the positive perceptions and increased usage of Barclaycard.

Moreover, the ads clearly do more than entertain – the tracking study shows that they communicate specific product messages in an impactful way.

Table 7, for example, shows the percentage of definite recallers mentioning purchase insurance cover spontaneously when recalling each of four ads about that benefit.

TABLE 7: MESSAGE COMMUNICATION

	Cairo %	Dinghy %	Shopping %	Teapot %
Mentioning purchase insurance	81	91	78	89

Base: Definite recallers 1991–95[16]
Source: Millward Brown

These responses to the advertising have also influenced beliefs and feelings about the brand itself.

RESULTS: BRAND PERCEPTIONS

Before the current campaign, perceptions of Access and Barclaycard were virtually identical on all the quantitative measures taken, Barclaycard only having a higher score than Access on 'international acceptability'. Amex, on the other hand, had a more distinct image than either, and was found desirable and aspirational by many more consumers than were likely to own one.

16. The fact that Access scores also increase (though by much less) is best explained as a halo effect from Barclaycard, a legacy of the traditional belief that 'all credit cards are the same'. In fact Access (unlike some competitors) did not introduce any similar services.

Since 1991, Barclaycard has moved away from Access on a number of dimensions, and closer to Amex (though Amex remains a strong brand).

TABLE 8: CHANGES IN BRAND PERCEPTIONS 1990–94

	1990			1994		
	Barclaycard %	Access %	Amex %	Barclaycard %	Access %	Amex %
Provides special benefits and services for cardholders	22	22	38	45	34	37
Provides special emergency assistance anywhere in the world	17	17	45	59	29	47
Provides insurance cover on goods bought with the card	15	14	37	65	38	32
Provides high-quality customer service	21	23	33	45	38	33

Base: All adults
Source: Millward Brown

There is a clear relationship between the content of the commercials shown and movements on specific attributes such as 'insurance cover'; this can be shown by modelling trends in these attributes in a very similar way to modelling awareness (Figure 3).

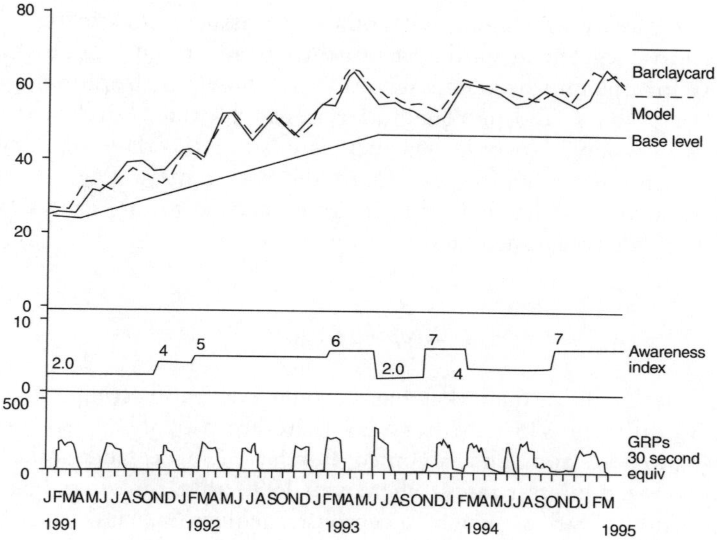

Figure 3: *Image – provides insurance cover on goods with the card. Rolling eight-weekly data*

Other image attributes show clearly that Barclaycard has established itself as the perceived leader and innovator in the market.

TABLE 9: BRAND PERCEPTIONS

	Barclaycard %	Access %	Amex %
Ahead of competition	40	21	21
Doing well these days	53	36	32
Among first to introduce new ideas	33	15	8
Is market leader	50	36	40
Wealth of experience	61	46	45

Base: All adults 1994
Source: Millward Brown

RESULTS: BUSINESS

Getting Cards

Since 1990 Barclaycard's share of new cardholders has risen substantially:

TABLE 10: SHARE OF NEW CARDHOLDERS

6 m/e September	1990 %	1991 %	1992 %	1993 %	1994 %	1995 %
Barclaycard VISA share	15	15	19	23	24	25

Source: FRS

Since 1993 Barclaycard (along with other card issuers), has increased its direct marketing effort targeted at card recruitment, so advertising alone cannot claim responsibility for this improvement. We do know, however, from many indications in the tracking study and in qualitative research, that Barclaycard's relative attractiveness to younger people has increased since the days of Whicker, even among those who have not responded to the direct marketing. It seems likely therefore that advertising has helped to make Barclaycard more generally attractive and has hence made recruitment activity more effective.

Keeping Cards

Since 1990, the credit card market has become ever more competitive. In 1990, there were 30 different VISA cards; today there are probably over 500. Many of these charge no fee. Some have copied Purchase Cover, and some now offer significantly reduced interest rates (whereas in 1990 all cards offered similar rates). Many are affinity cards, which incentivise acquisition and use by making contributions to charities or clubs.

Under these circumstances, it is a considerable achievement for Barclaycard to have increased its share of cards from 29% just after the relaunch to 32%, and then maintained this share in the face of competition – including the GM launch. In contrast, Access has declined from 37% to 25%, so that for some time now Barclaycard has overtaken Access (Figure 4).

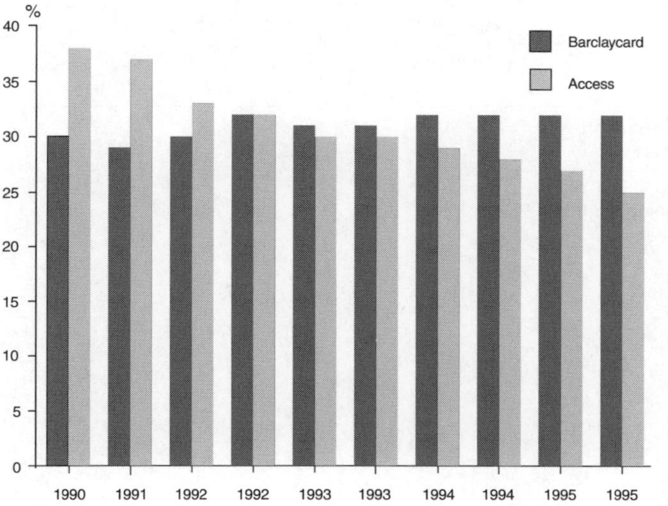

Figure 4: *Share of credit cards*
Source: FRS

While the numbers of cards are to some extent inflated by the issue of Barclaycard MasterCards, the same pattern holds if we look at the number of cardholders (Figure 5).

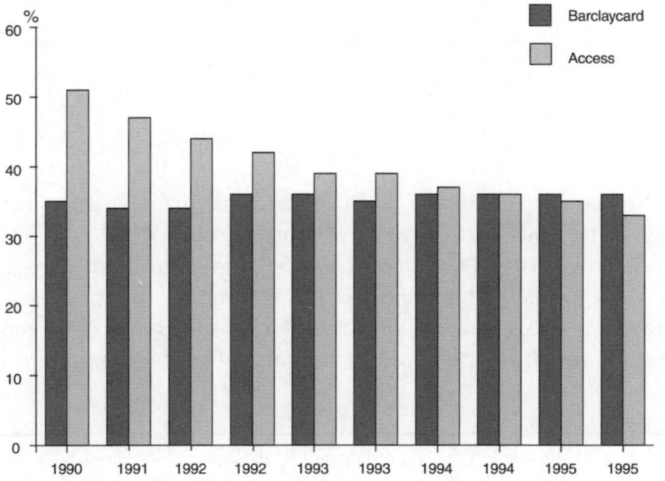

Figure 5: *Share of cardholders*
Source: FRS

A further indication of loyalty is given by the question (see Table 11), asked of dual brand users until 1993. This shows a marked increase for Barclaycard, against a static picture for Access.

TABLE 11: DUAL USERS' PREFERENCE – WHICH PAYMENT CARD WOULD YOU KEEP IF YOU COULD ONLY KEEP ONE?

	Dec 1990 (pre ads) %	1991 %	1992 %	1993 %
Barclaycard	40	44	49	51
Access	26	25	27	27

Base: Dual holders
Source: Millward Brown

Using Cards

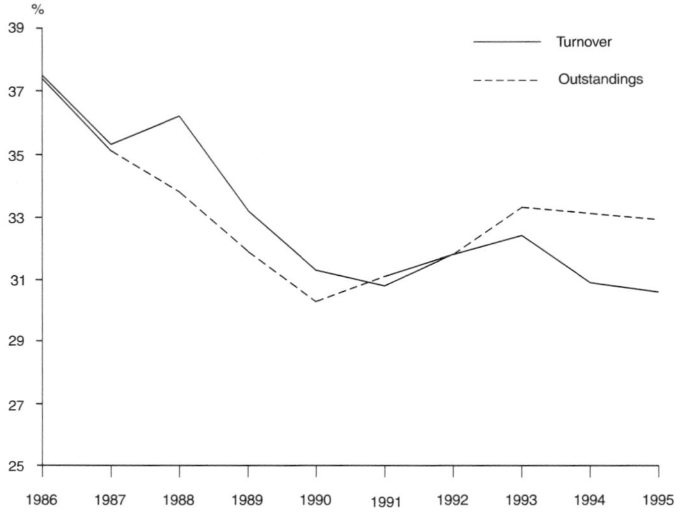

Figure 6: *Barclaycard share*
Source: BBA

Figure 6 shows how the decline in both share of turnover and share of outstandings was reversed after the start of the new campaign in 1991.[17]

The most conclusive evidence of advertising's effect on card usage comes from an econometric model. This measures the effects of advertising on average turnover per Barclaycard VISA card. (Any effects of MasterCard are therefore excluded.) Unfortunately, much of the detail of this model must remain confidential but, since

17. The dip in share of turnover in 1994 is caused mainly by the launch of the GM card. This was a new credit card offering holders collector points which could be redeemed for a discount against any new GM (Vauxhall) car. This launch increased total market turnover as GM cardholders began to use their cards whenever they could in order to save points towards their new Vauxhall. Most of this extra turnover did not translate into extended credit, which explains why Barclaycard's share of outstandings held up. Both turnover and outstandings for Barclaycard, however, increased strongly in 1994 and 1995 in absolute terms (in fact growth rates were higher than in the previous three years), despite the loss in share. Despite heavy TV advertising, the GM card has taken less than 3% of the market. In fact Barclaycard lost far fewer cardholders to the GM card than would be predicted from its market share.

1991, it shows that advertising increased total turnover per Barclaycard VISA by approximately 3% each year.[18]

OTHER POSSIBLE FACTORS THAT MIGHT HAVE EXPLAINED BARCLAYCARD'S PERFORMANCE

We believe that advertising for Barclaycard works in synergy with other parts of the marketing programme. But no other initiative taken since 1990 is enough to explain away the brand's improved position. Some other possibilities, however, deserve discussion.

The Launch of Barclaycard MasterCard

This has added to the number of Barclaycards issued, provided a useful additional service to some cardholders, and encouraged dual users to drop their Access cards.

However, total penetration of Barclaycard MasterCard has never been more than 10% of all Barclaycard cardholders and, as all MasterCards have been issued to existing Barclaycard VISA holders, it has had no effect on penetration. MasterCard has not been featured in media advertising. The model shows that advertising affects VISA turnover quite independently of MasterCard.

The Decline of Access

It seems, though we have no privileged information, that throughout this period there were differences between the Access banks on credit card policy.[19] As a result Access did not improve its product, and its advertising was inconsistent and lightweight. So is Barclaycard's success simply a reflection of the weakness of its major competitor?

The answer is no. Access declined partly because the Access banks were promoting their own VISA cards; the natural action for Access customers to take would be to stay with their own bank[20] or to defect to one of the other *free* cards on offer. So Barclaycard would not automatically benefit from the decline of Access.

Instead, it could be argued that the decline of Access was not particularly helpful to Barclaycard. It reinforced perceptions of the market as fragmented and commoditised, where cards were chosen on price or as a service provided by a

18. Bear in mind that total market turnover is now over £30 billion a year.
19. The strength of the Access brand was also seen as a barrier by the MasterCard network. In April 1996, the Access brand was sold to MasterCard by the four Access banks. It is believed that MasterCard will cease to use the name in the UK and replace it with the MasterCard brand.
20. Access customers nearly all banked with one of the Access banks. It is worth mentioning that the relative fortunes of Barclaycard and Access over this period were not influenced by any shift in patterns of current account holding.

current account bank. And the lack of effective Access advertising meant that the task of supporting credit card usage fell largely onto Barclaycard.

We suggest that Access is best seen as an indicator of what might have happened to Barclaycard. Access was originally, if anything, a larger and stronger brand but, without effective support, succumbed to competitive pressure.

Other Parts of the Marketing Mix

There is no point in trying to 'eliminate' the effects of other marketing activities since 1990 in the traditional 'effectiveness awards' style. The one thing that we can claim is that, despite price-led competition, Barclaycard's success is not due to reduction in price. In fact, the £8 fee was increased two years later to £10, with no adverse effects.

Barclaycard's success is a result of an *integrated* marketing programme:

— A successful points collection scheme, Profiles, has existed to encourage card use since 1988.

— In response to the GM Card, Barclaycard moved swiftly to tie up a parallel deal with Ford.

— Barclaycard makes extensive use of direct mail, both included in monthly statements and separately; a magazine is also mailed to cardholders.

— Telephone contact staff have been extensively trained in customer care.

It would therefore be meaningless to claim that advertising is responsible for any particular 'share' of the brand's success, which is due to the efforts of an extensive marketing programme. We can, however, point to some evidence that advertising has made a distinctive contribution: the modelling that relates awareness of product benefits to advertising, and the model that links advertising expenditure to turnover, as well as the extremely high profile and popularity the campaign has enjoyed. What we can also do, based on research evidence, is build a picture of how the advertising works, and why it is complementary to other marketing activities, doing specific things that they do not.

HOW DO WE BELIEVE THE ADVERTISING WORKS?

What are the particular mechanisms by which Barclaycard TV advertising assists the overall objectives of getting, keeping, and using the card?

Empathy/Involvement

Many consumers have traditionally regarded credit card issuers with some suspicion or even dislike – partly a fear of getting into debt, partly an understandable feeling about a company whose primary contact with the customer consists of a bill at the end of the month (and an occasional phone call, which may well only happen because some problem has occurred). The advertising provides Barclaycard with a continuous presence, a human face, and an effective way of communicating with an initially unsympathetic audience. We know from tracking and qualitative research that it also positions the brand as younger, more friendly and having a sense of humour. It therefore creates a more receptive atmosphere for other types of communication such as direct mail or telephone contact.

Relevance

The unique ability of television to 'dramatise' product claims makes these more interesting and relevant to the consumer – the lost binoculars, the burning rug, the police cell all create powerful visual demonstrations of what can go wrong. By doing this, advertising stimulates usage and gives rational reasons for choosing to get, or keep, the card.

Leadership

Having the most famous and best-liked advertising in the sector helps to position Barclaycard as perceived market leader (as does the use of 60-second time lengths and high production values). People want to be with 'the leader' – it offers both reassurance and a positive self image.

Positioning

Both the content of the advertising, and its sophisticated style, differentiate the brand from rival credit cards, particularly Access, and have moved it much closer in perceptual terms to American Express. In 1990, Amex was the only brand in the payment card area with a strongly distinguished brand image. For most credit card customers it was aspirational, but out of reach. Barclaycard now shares this position, while its humour also differentiates it from Amex's much more serious persona.

PUTTING A VALUE ON THE ADVERTISING

Looking purely at the short-term effects of Barclaycard advertising on turnover, the model shows that £40 million of advertising from 1991 to 1995 stimulated turnover per Barclaycard VISA card by an average of around 3% each year. We are unable to reveal precise turnover figures or financial calculations but, if this extra turnover is assumed in turn to create extra extended credit (and this is fair because in this market the two are closely correlated), it is not difficult to produce figures, even on conservative estimates, suggesting that this extra card usage has been sufficient in itself to pay for the cost of the advertising.

The real object of the advertising, however, was to help defend and strengthen the brand's competitive position. We have argued that it did this successfully. The financial benefits of this are far harder to quantify, but also considerably greater. If Barclaycard's share decline had continued, or if it had followed the pattern of Access, many more billions of turnover would have been progressively lost, as well as the fee income from lost cardholders, to say nothing of the future profit streams which the brand may now expect to earn in the future.

The market continues to become ever more competitive, with new American contenders now offering extremely low introductory rates in order to attract custom. (Low rates are not necessarily in the long-term interest of the consumer, as there are often hidden costs or reductions in service level involved.) With no signs of wear-out yet in the Latham campaign, we and Barclaycard feel confident that the brand will continue to withstand these pressures and to satisfy its six million customers.

6

Marmite

How 'The growing up spread' just carried on growing

ABOUT THE PAPER

By looking at the benefits of advertising investment over a 23-year period (1975–1998) this paper demonstrates the importance of thinking long term in a world where demand for instant results is becoming increasingly prevalent.

Marmite's Early History

From 1903 to 1975, Marmite consumption had its roots in the sampling and recommendation of Marmite by health professionals. This created a mother-and-baby life cycle, where mothers were persuaded to feed their babies Marmite and in turn these Marmite babies became Marmite mothers.

However, by 1975, where our paper starts, the future was looking bleak: the endorsement of health professionals had been lost, the declining birth rate threatened the mother-and-baby life cycle, the threat from Own Label was increasing and finally, increasing levels of concern about salt in the diet threatened Marmite's health position.

Results and Payback

Advertising (and in particular two campaigns – Ogilvy & Mather's 'Soldiers' and BMP's 'I Hate Marmite') successfully created higher levels of adult consumption of Marmite, meanwhile maintaining the core mother and baby life cycle.

Volume sales increased by over 50% over the period, which is remarkable given that Marmite was a mature brand.

As a consequence of their exposure to lower levels of advertising (nearly three time less over 23 years), the paper shows that the northern regions' share of sales has significantly declined since 1975 while those in the south grew. Penetration, consumption and levels of competition also responded to these regional patterns in advertising. Marmite advertising has also created extremely high financial rates of return. Without disclosing sensitive information, we can reveal that the average annual return on investing in Marmite advertising is 27%.

INTRODUCTION

This story begins in 1902, when a strange black substance, called Marmite, was launched on the unsuspecting British public. As the brand matured, it was supported by the endorsement of health professionals and became a firm family favourite.

By the 1970s, however, the brand was facing a mid-life crisis. This paper will show how Marmite coped with the crisis and has flourished as a result, experiencing two particularly sharp periods of growth from 1987 to 1989 and 1995 to 1998.

We will look at the contribution of advertising from 1975 onwards, and focus particularly on the two campaigns which drove those two periods of sharp growth: the Ogilvy & Mather 'Soldiers' campaign, and BMP's recent 'I Hate Marmite'/'My Mate Marmite' campaign.

WHAT IS MARMITE?

Origins

The first records of yeast show that it was used in the production of an acid beer called 'boozah' in Egypt in 6000 BC. People have enjoyed the effects of beer ever since and by the eighteenth century breweries in England were producing roughly 200,000 barrels of yeast a year as a by-product of brewing. As a result, new uses for yeast were sought, and during the late nineteenth century the German chemist Liebig discovered how to produce a yeast extract suitable for human consumption. In 1902, yeast extract was first manufactured in England under the name of Marmite, which refers to the French cooking pot which gave its shape to the Marmite jar.

Health Properties

Marmite received instant acclaim as a healthy and delicious product. Interest in Marmite, however, increased further early in the century, when the function of vitamins was discovered, as Marmite contains all five B-complex vitamins.[1] It is also 100% vegetarian, and contains virtually no fat and no sugar.

1. The B-complex vitamins are Thiamin (B1), Riboflavin (B2), Niacin, Folic acid and B12. These are crucial for the healthy growth and functioning of blood, as well as helping the body convert sugar and starches into energy.

Usage

Marmite is very versatile and can be used as a spread, a drink and a cooking ingredient. Marmite is, however, used almost exclusively as a spread (96%), and generally at breakfast time (52%). It therefore competes most directly against other spreads, and other breakfast foods such as cereals.

INTRODUCING PEOPLE TO MARMITE

The Barriers to Creating Adult Usage

Marmite is a unique product which looks quite unlike most foodstuffs. Non-users tend to find its smell, appearance and ingredients rather off-putting.

> 'Looks like tar', 'horrible black sticky stuff', 'smells disgusting'.
>
> 'It doesn't sound very nice', 'it looks like a brown stain on toast'.

Source: BMP Qualitative Research

Indeed, unfortunately for Marmite, it is often active prejudice against the brand, rather than apathy or lack of awareness, which stops many non-users trying Marmite (Figure 1).

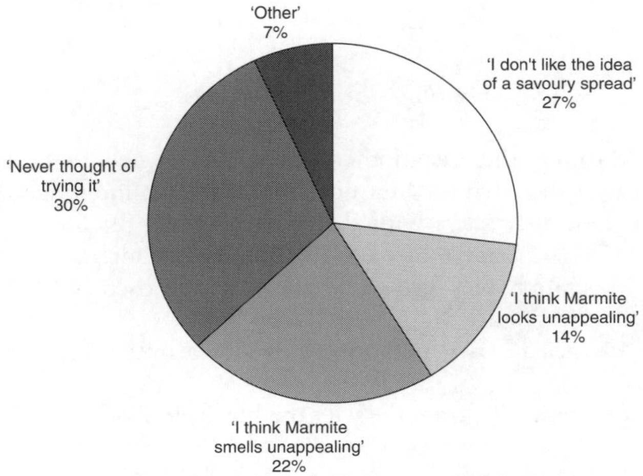

Figure 1: *Reasons for not trying Marmite*
Base: All adults who gave reasons why they had not tried Marmite
Source: Audience Selection Omnibus 1997

Marmite also has a very polarising taste and, compared to most foods, it evinces strong views (Figure 2).

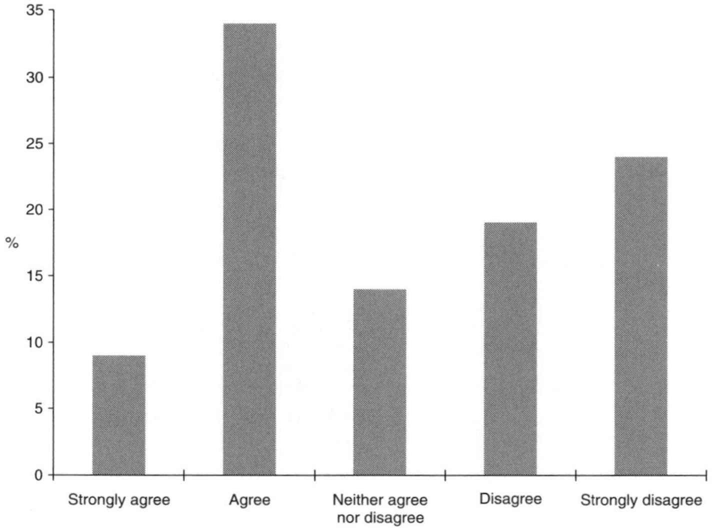

Figure 2: *'Marmite has a delicious savoury taste'*
Source: PPCR Non-User Taste Tests 1998

Gaining growth for the brand by targeting adult non-users is therefore exceptionally difficult. This consumer comment illustrates the point:

'If you don't like it by the time you're an adult, it's no good.'

Source: BMP Qualitative Research

Feeding Marmite to Babies

Fortunately for Marmite, there is another way to recruit new users. If mothers can be persuaded to feed their babies Marmite, then these children acquire a taste for Marmite, which frequently stays with them, on and off, for life. In fact, the vast majority of users (78%) are introduced to the brand as children.

When these 'Marmite babies' grow up and have their own children, they tend to feed them Marmite too (Figure 3).

This, in turn, creates a new generation of loyal Marmite users, and the life cycle is perpetuated.

Consumers' comments illustrate the way the life cycle works:

'I was always given it as a youngster, and if we have kids it will always be there.'

'Having the children myself, I'd go around the supermarket, and back to all the things I used to have as a kid. Marmite is probably the one that has stuck again.'

'I used to have it a lot when I was little, now I just have it when I give it to the children.'

Source: Leading Edge Qualitative Research, KGB Research

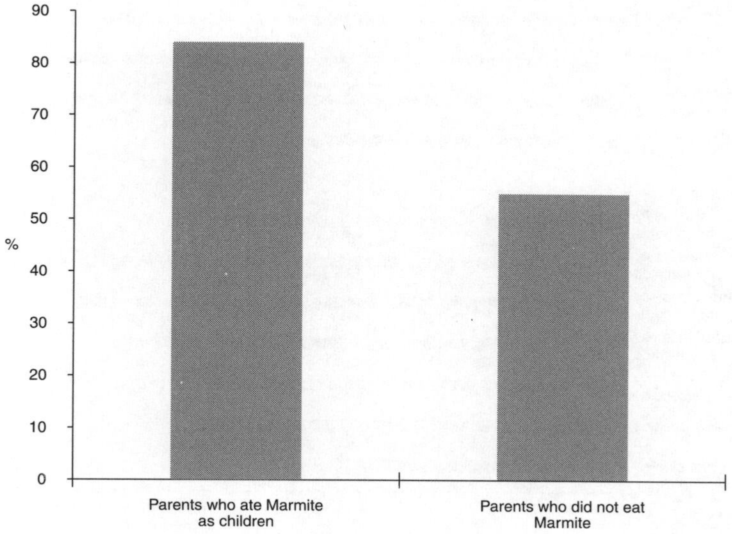

Figure 3: *The percentage of adults who feed their children Marmite*
Source: Audience Selection Omnibus 1998.

Finally, looking at the household penetration of Marmite by life stage, we can see exactly how the life cycle works. Marmite is much more likely to be present in households with young children, demonstrating that the mother-and-baby life cycle is key to penetration (Figure 4).[2]

THE MARMITE LIFE CYCLE, 1903 TO 1975

From 1903 to 1975, Marmite was highly recommended for children by numerous articles in newspapers and medical journals. It was distributed through the school meals programme and through traditional 'village hall' health clinics and child health clinics, which had shops attached selling Marmite. Up until the 1960s, there was even a dedicated Marmite medical sales force which called exclusively on clinics and health visitors. The Marmite cycle of consumption therefore had its roots in the authoritative sampling and recommendation of Marmite by health professionals.

Maintaining Broader Adult Usage

The medical profession also recommended Marmite as a dietary supplement for adults in order to combat various illnesses, which were seen as relating to vitamin B deficiency. (Constipation and consequent colitis, chronic appendicitis and innumerable other digestive troubles were all prevalent among the adult British

2. The earliest year in which Nielsen analysed penetration by life stage was 1993.

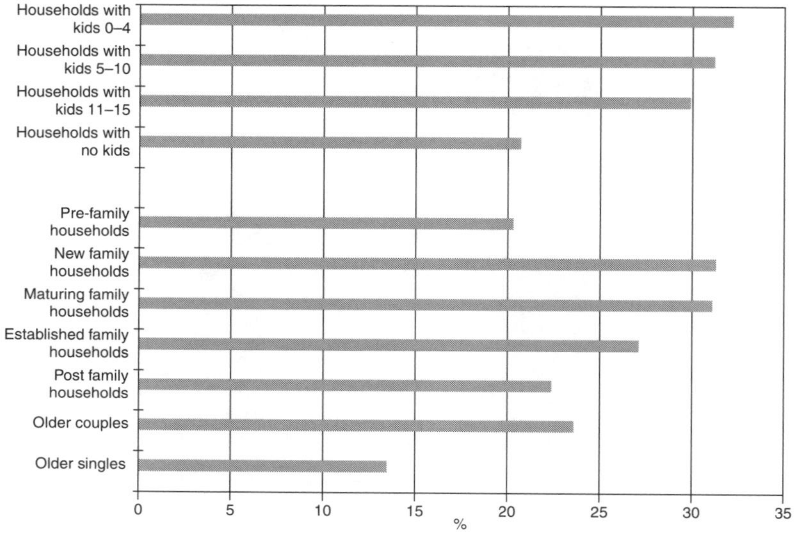

Figure 4: *Household penetration by lifestage*
Source: Nielsen Homescan 1993

population, and at the time were seen as directly related to lack of vitamin B in the diet.) Marmite was therefore also distributed to adults through health clinics and welfare associations. It was given to pregnant mothers and featured in hospital meals. Marmite was even used in the First World War to prevent outbreaks of beri-beri among English soldiers in Gallipoli, and it was sent to prisoners of the Second World War in Germany in Red Cross parcels.

MARMITE'S MID-LIFE CRISIS – THE SITUATION IN 1975

Marmite entered the 1970s, with a future that looked less clear.

Losing Endorsement/Distribution via NHS

First and most significantly, the reorganisation of the National Health Service in 1974, meant that traditional 'village hall' clinics were replaced by custom-built welfare centres where retail sales were forbidden. This meant that a vital prompt, which had encouraged Marmite usage among adults and children, had been removed.

The Falling Birth Rate

By the 1970s, demographics were also turning against Marmite. Birth rates were dropping, as women both had their children later and had fewer children. The larger gap between childhood and parenthood which women experienced and the increase in adult-only households were extremely worrying for Marmite, given its dependence on a mother-and-baby life cycle.

Own Label/Competition

With the growth of grocery multiples, all products, including Marmite, were facing increasing threats from own label brands.

Increasing Levels of Concern about Salt in the Diet

Finally, during the 1970s, people became increasingly concerned about salt and its link with heart disease. Although a serving of Marmite actually contains less salt than the bread it is served on, Marmite does contain salt. It was therefore prey to sensationalist articles in the media which, while unfounded, could have dented its position as a healthy product.

MARKETING OBJECTIVES – 1975 ONWARDS

Given the threatening situation, the marketing of Marmite was crucial, and focused on the following issues:

— Compensating for the loss of the NHS prompt to childhood usage, by maintaining Marmite's position as a healthy, vitamin-rich spread for children.

— Combating concerns over salt by focusing on Marmite's positive aspects; that is, Marmite's overall healthy image.

— Combatting the demographic trends against Marmite and the loss of the NHS prompt to adult usage, by broadening Marmite's positioning to support adult usage.

— Defending its territory against competition, by consistently supporting the brand.

THE IMPLICATIONS

Looking back at these objectives, one might question whether Marmite had been over-ambitious, attempting to increase adult usage and maintain the core mother-and-baby life cycle.

Figure 5, however, demonstrates that this was not the case. It shows that children whose parents continue to eat Marmite are more likely to eat Marmite than children whose parents are lapsed users. Hence increasing adult usage actually reinforces the mother-and-baby life cycle.

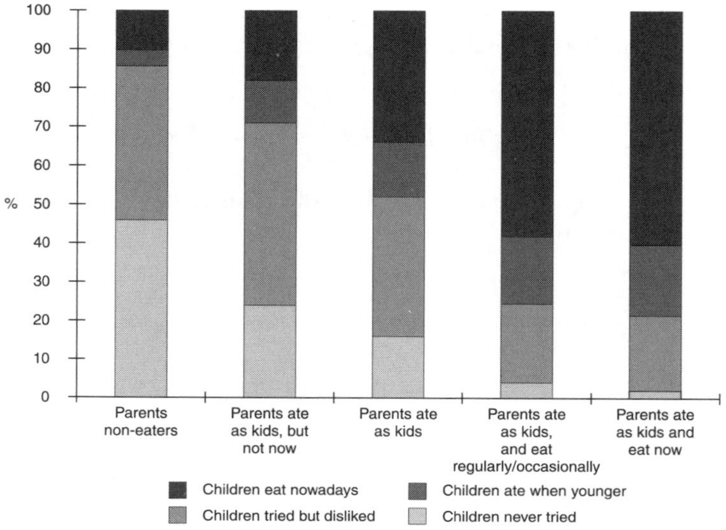

Figure 5: *The Marmite life cycle* – the likelihood of children eating Marmite according to their parents' Marmite habits
Source: Audience Selection Omnibus 1998

Intuitively this makes sense. Women are not likely to forget Marmite prior to parenthood if it remains relevant to them as adults. Furthermore, given the way children mimic adults, they are more likely to eat something that their parents enjoy rather than something which is forced upon them as 'good for children'.

The decision to encourage adult usage was therefore not only brave, but astute.

ADVERTISING OBJECTIVES – 1975 ONWARDS

The brand had always been advertised, but advertising now became critical. In 1975 the advertising spend was doubled, and it has remained at higher levels ever since (Figure 6).[3]

New advertising also needed to answer the new marketing objectives. In advertising terms, these can be summarised as follows:

1. Maintaining the mother-and-baby life cycle.
2. Making Marmite more relevant to adults.

3. Marmite advertising has primarily been on TV, and has consisted of at least one heavyweight burst per year, usually in wintertime.

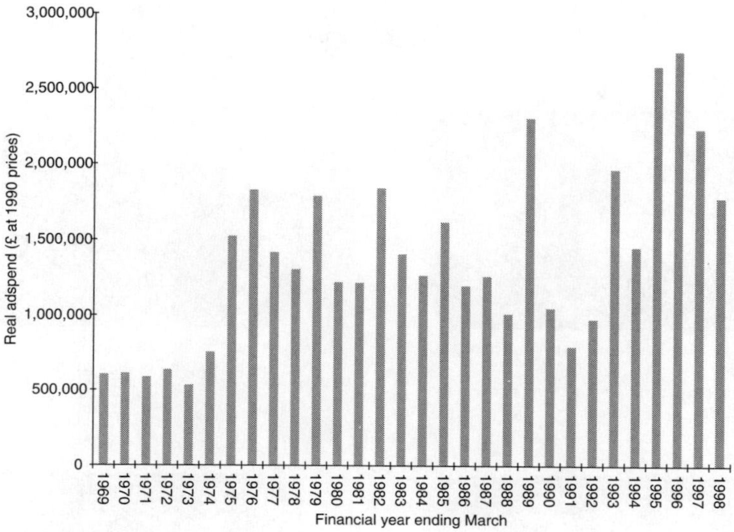

Figure 6: *Total Marmite adspend*
Source: MEAL

THE ADVERTISING: 1975 TO 1997

Theme 1: Maintaining the Mother-and-Baby Life Cycle

In the 1970s, advertising focused on Marmite's role at the heart of the family. Out of this emerged the famous and long-running 'The Growing Up Spread' campaign.[4] As the campaign continued, it gradually became less formal and didactic, and humour was introduced to ensure that the brand remained appealing.

By the 1980s, the mother-and-baby life cycle was supported by using more tightly targeted mother-and-baby executions and media selection.[5]

Theme 2: Making Marmite More Relevant to Adults

During the mid-1980s, there was concern that Marmite was being pushed too far into a mother and baby niche. As a result, Ogilvy & Mather launched the famous 'Soldiers' campaign in December 1987 and with it the enduring slogan, 'My Mate Marmite'.[6]

4. The campaign positioned Marmite as a spread which would help your children grow up healthy and strong, and featured various happy and healthy Marmite families.
5. The mother and baby TV executions usually ran on daytime and breakfast TV. Press campaigns also ran in specialist mother and baby magazines, and highlighted Marmite's health position as a savoury spread, rich in vitamin B.
6. The campaign was intended to update Marmite's image and raise its profile among adults in general by showing the product used by men and with a healthy outdoor appeal.

'SOLDIERS'

Sergeant: 1 2, 1 2. Move your feet, we're nearly there.
Men: Ten more miles and we don't care.

Sergeant: Feeling great and that's no lie.
Men: I'm so hungry I could die.

Sergeant: Let's get back to my mate.
Men: Whose mate?
Sergeant: Your mate.
Men: My mate.

Sergeant: Marmite.
Men: Marmite.
Sergeant: Want some?
Men: Want some?

Sergeant: Feed me.
Men: Feed me.

Sergeant: Good stuff.
Men: Good stuff.

Sergeant: My mate.
Men: Marmite.

'I HATE MARMITE'

Low Rider music throughout.

Singer: I hate Marmite.

Singer: I hate Marmite.

'MY MATE MARMITE'

Low Rider music throughout.

My mate, Marmite.

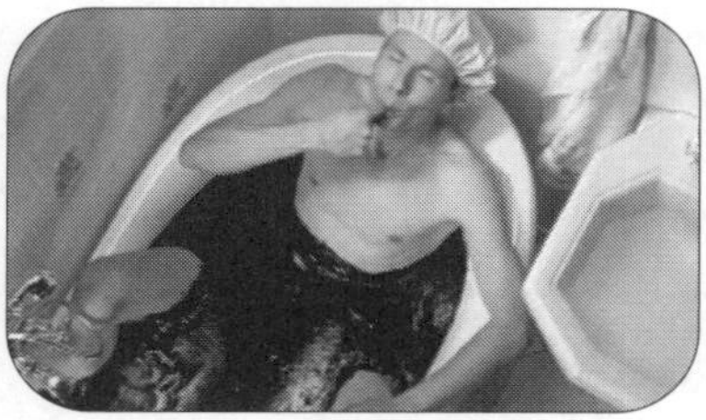

My mate, Marmite.

In 1996, BMP DDB and Best Foods again felt the need to focus on adult usage. This time, the response was to reinterpret the 'My Mate' theme in a more radical way, to target a younger adult audience who had become far more cynical and advertising literate.[7]

WHAT HAS HAPPENED TO MARMITE SINCE 1975?

Sales

Since 1975 sales have increased by 51%, with particularly strong growth between 1987 and 1989, and 1995 and 1998 (Figure 7).

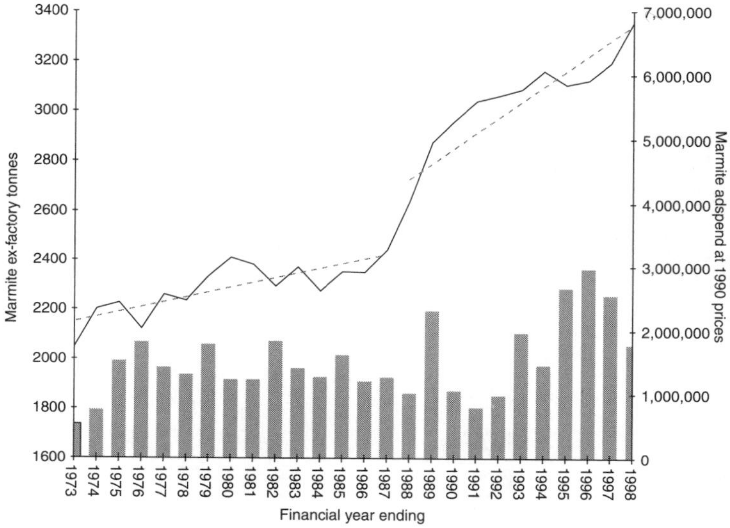

Figure 7: *Marmite sales versus advertising 1973 to 1998*
Sources: CPC, Register-MEAL

Moreover, since 1995, price has moved slightly ahead of inflation and therefore value growth has outstripped volume growth. In fact, between 1995 and 1998, Marmite has experienced its fastest value growth rate in a decade.

7. BMP's current 'I Hate Marmite/My Mate Marmite' campaign forced adult lapsed users to reappraise the brand. It also forced current users to reconsider Marmite as a modern and personal choice, rather than something which was merely a hangover from childhood.

Penetration

Household penetration has not, however, grown as much as sales. Unfortunately, household penetration can only tell us half the story, as it does not tell us who was eating Marmite within households.[8]

	1985	1997	
Household penetration	29.5	32.9	(+11.5%)

Source: TGI

Scrutinising household penetration further did, however, give us a clue about what had actually happened to produce the sales uplifts.

While household penetration had increased among all household types, the biggest increases had been among adult-only households and households with older children. This suggested that, in line with the marketing objectives, more adult usage was responsible for the extra sales growth, while the mother-and-baby life cycle had been maintained (and, in fact, had grown slightly).

Consumption

However, a breakthrough in understanding came when we examined a Usage & Attitude study from 1982.[9] This showed definitively that household penetration figures were masking increased levels of adult consumption within households. The marketing objectives of broadening out the life cycle had been successful.

	1982	1997
Housewives eating Marmite themselves (indexed against 1982)	100	124

Source: U&A 1982, Audience Selection Omnibus 1997

A Famous Brand

Marmite had also become something of a household icon and is now extremely well known and well loved.

8. NB. We are considering TGI household penetration figures from 1985 onwards as, prior to that, the question about Marmite was located at a different place within the questionnaire. This affected the levels of response to questions about Marmite, and thus prevents comparisons with earlier years.
9. Ideally, we would have liked to have looked at consumption data from the 1970s rather than from the 1980s. Since the 1970s, however, Marmite had changed hands twice, first from the Cavenham group to Beechams in 1980, and then more recently to Best Foods (formerly known as CPC UK Ltd). During this period, much data has inevitably been lost.

Brand awareness and image	
Prompted brand awareness	100%
Spontaneous brand awareness	70%
One of the nation's favourite brands	63% agreed with this statement

Base: Adults 20–60
Source: Research International Tracking, January 1998

Consumer Comments:

'I don't know of anyone who doesn't know what it is, it's like cornflakes.'

'Everybody has a jar of Marmite.'

'It's a classic', 'It's like an old friend.'

Source: Quotes from RDS Research and BMP Qualitative Research

Obsessive Marmite Users

Marmite has also created a peculiarly loyal following. Many users religiously take their Marmite on holiday and the Internet is clogged with messages from expats searching for Marmite abroad. Others even create websites to declare their love of Marmite. Even more extreme are those, such as Daniel Parkes, who exist on a diet of almost pure Marmite.

THE CONTRIBUTION OF ADVERTISING SINCE 1975

So far we have shown that Marmite has emerged from its mid-life crisis, not only intact but actually stronger. Sales have grown, the mother and baby life cycle has been maintained, and adult usage of the brand, as desired, has increased. Next, we intend to show that advertising has been crucial to this success.

It is immediately obvious that the two periods of particular growth between 1987 and 1989 and 1995 and 1998, coincided with two particularly famous advertising campaigns which were intended to increase adult usage. Putting these campaigns under the microscope was therefore our focus.

FAMOUS, IMPACTFUL ADVERTISING

'Soldiers'

During our search through the archives at Best Foods, we found the Millward Brown documents from the period of the 'Soldiers' campaign. These demonstrated that it was clearly impactful, communicative advertising.

OBSESSIVE MARMITE USE

Boy's Marmite diet 'perfectly healthy'

BY A CORRESPONDENT

AN 11-year-old boy who has eaten only Marmite sandwiches since he was weaned has been given a clean bill of health by a nutritionist.

Daniel Parkes said: "I've tried chips and burgers and pizzas. Maybe I will eat other things when I get older but I don't think so. I just don't like anything else." His mother Lynne said: "We thought he'd grow out of it, but he never has. Then we worried about his health but a nutritionist says he's perfectly healthy. So now we just let him get on with it."

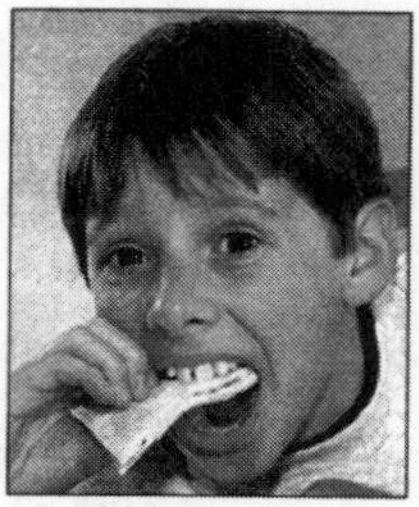

Daniel Parkes: "I don't like anything else"

Daniel, of Newton Abbot, Devon, takes Marmite sandwiches when he eats out with his family. They also take jars of the yeast and vegetable extract spread on holiday. Mrs Parkes said: "It comes as second nature to us now — just like checking we've got our passports."

Daniel eats at least one loaf a day and supplements his diet with milk, orange juice — and Marmite on toast.

Lyndel Costain of the British Dietetic Association said: "This isn't a diet I'd recommend for all kids but as long as he drinks plenty of milk and orange juice, he should be fine."

MARMY BARMY

	1988/1989 %
Claimed TV advertising awareness	50
Communication (unprompted)	
'Good for you/healthy/wholesome/nourishing'	35
'Makes you strong/keeps you fit, etc.'	14
Image **of Marmite (prompted)**	
Suitable for children	83
Suitable for women	84
Suitable for men	81
Up-to-date product	57

NB. All figures are averages taken from the period of 'Soldiers' advertising, 1988–1989.

Example verbatims
'Lots of hunky soldiers eating Marmite.'

'Men love Marmite too – anyone can eat it.'

'It's for tough people and it helps to build you up.'

'The one with soldiers, and they were on a run shouting and chanting about Marmite. It's so good everyone wants to come home to it.'

Source: Millward Brown International

'I Hate Marmite'/'My Mate Marmite'

Meanwhile, at BMP, there was plentiful evidence that the 'I Hate Marmite/My Mate Marmite' campaign was particularly successful. According to Research International, it was one of the most impactful campaigns they had ever tested. It achieved particularly high levels of awareness among adults (Figure 8 – 'pre' refers to opinions of the previous Marmite campaign). Tracking also showed that people were not merely aware of the campaign, but that most could also recall detail from the specific executions (Figure 9). In addition, the campaign was clearly a powerful and original piece of communication (Figure 10). As a result of this, claimed likelihood to eat Marmite increased (Figure 11).

Consumers' comments demonstrate how 'Hate/Mate' worked:

> 'It's going to make people sit up and talk about it.'
>
> 'It really did make me think, I don't hate it, I love it.'
>
> 'Puts you in mind to try it again.'
>
> 'It's the sort of humour people of our generation appreciate.'
>
> 'Original', 'Unique', 'It's true, isn't it?'

Sources: BMP Qualitative Research, RDS Open Mind

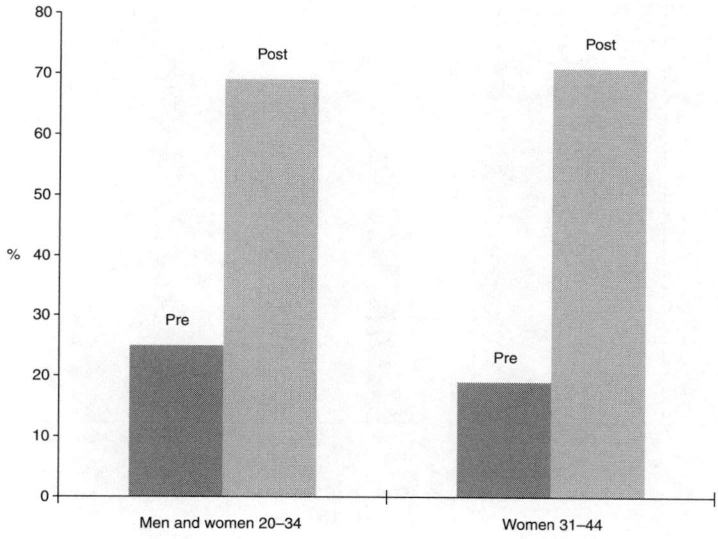

Figure 8: *Prompted TV ad awareness*
Source: Research International 1997

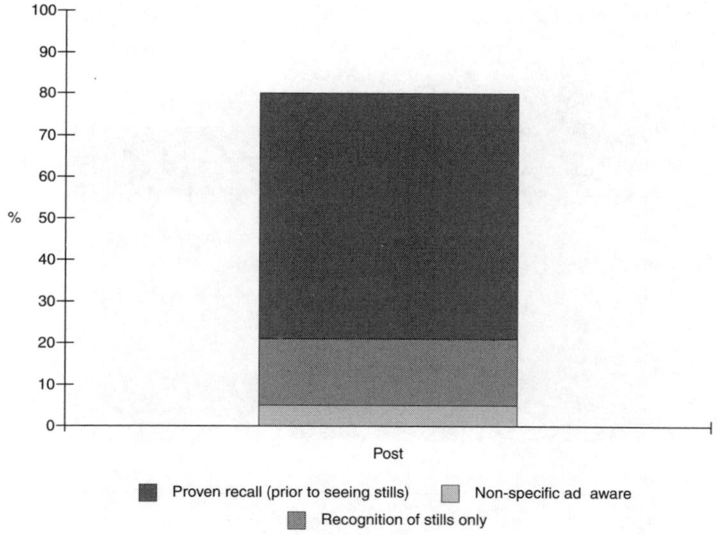

Figure 9: *Level/type of ad awareness*
Source: Research International 1997

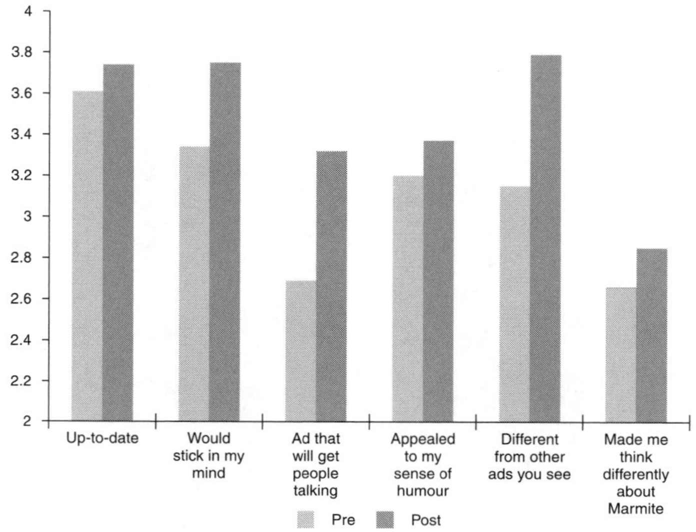

Figure 10: *Advertising descriptors*
Source: Research International 1997

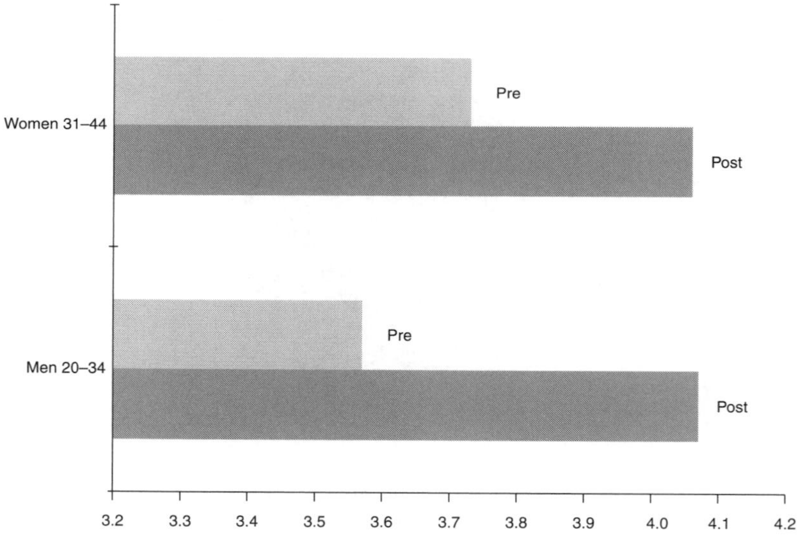

Figure 11: *Likelihood of eating Marmite*
Source: Research International 1997

THE CORRELATION BETWEEN ADS AND BEHAVIOURAL TRENDS

Consumption of Marmite

'Soldiers' and 'I Hate Marmite/My Mate Marmite' were intended to increase adult consumption of Marmite. There is strong evidence to show that both campaigns worked as expected. Consumption data from the 1980s confirmed that the 'Soldiers' campaign had coincided precisely with a significant increase in the proportion of Marmite which was consumed by adult households (Figure 12).[10]

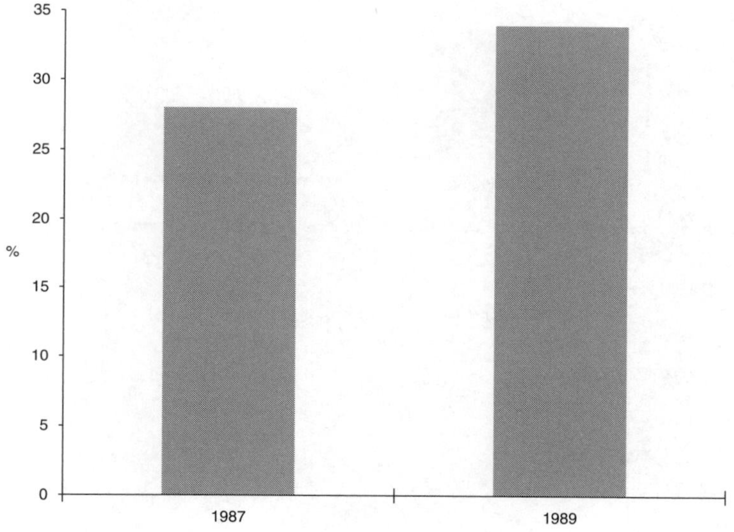

Figure 12: *The effect of 'Soldiers'*
Source: AGB

Meanwhile, consumption data from the time of the 'Hate/Mate' campaign also showed that adults, and men in particular (see Figure 13), consumed a higher proportion of the total Marmite eaten during the period of advertising than they did in the period prior to advertising.

Sales and Advertising

Furthermore, annual data also show that there is a long-term relationship between sales performance and levels of advertising support (Figure 14).

10. Two-person households are primarily two-adult households.

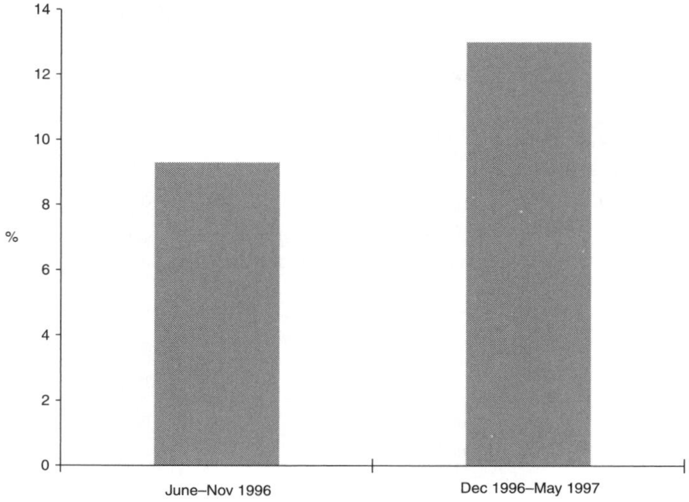

Figure 13: *The effect of 'I Hate Marmite/My Mate Marmite'; the increase of Marmite consumption by men aged 17–34*
Source: Family Food Panel

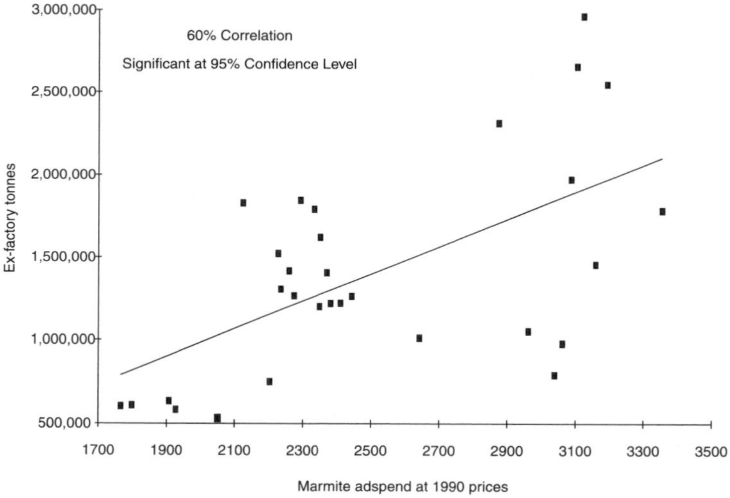

Figure 14: *The relationship between Marmite sales and advertising annual data, 1969–1998*
Source: CPC, Register-MEAL

REGIONAL EVIDENCE

Our search for evidence did not stop there however. More definitive proof that advertising was crucial to the Marmite life cycle and to Marmite's growth comes out of yet another peculiarity in Marmite's idiosyncratic history. Interestingly for us, an accident of history means that Marmite has been subjected to what must be one of the longest-lasting regional tests in marketing history.

Marmite's base of loyal users has historically been located in the southern areas.[11] Not surprisingly, advertising support was therefore concentrated in those areas. Hence, for over 25 years, they have been exposed to approximately three times as many TVRs as the northern regions.

Claimed Usage

Given the south's exposure to higher levels of advertising, one would expect the life cycle to have grown more in the south than in the north. Referring back to the 1982 U&A study, but this time dissecting the figures regionally, we can see that this was indeed the case.

Since 1982, the percentage of children eating Marmite has slightly increased in the south, whereas it has declined in the north. Meanwhile, the life cycle has also broadened out further to include more adults eating Marmite. Again, this trend is particularly marked in the south, but was also present in the north, which is not surprising given that most of the admittedly low-level advertising support which the north received focused on increasing adult usage.

	South		North	
	1982	1998	1982	1998
Children eating Marmite (1998 percentage indexed against 1982 percentage)	100	109	100	95
	1982	1997	1982	1997
Housewives eating Marmite (1997 percentage, indexed against 1982 percentage)	100	125	100	119

Source: U&A Study 1982, Audience Selection Omnibus 1997 and 1998

Meanwhile, heavier advertising support in the south has ensured that, today, a far higher percentage of southern 'Marmite babies' versus northern 'Marmite babies' feed their children Marmite and continue to eat Marmite themselves.

1. During Marmite's early history, its distribution through welfare clinics and associations was limited to the southern areas. Meanwhile, in Scotland, Marmite was only handled through an agent up until 1962. This therefore meant that most of Marmite's loyal users were primarily located in the southern areas. CPC and previous owners of Marmite have occasionally attempted to rectify this regional imbalance, but the relative sizes of the user bases in the different regions always meant that the largest short-term returns came from advertising in the south.

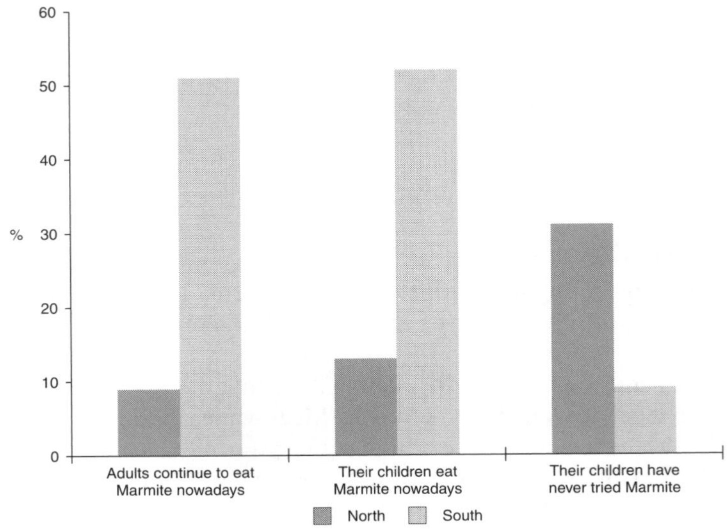

Figure 15: *Commitment to the Marmite lifecycle – adults who ate Marmite as children*
Source: Audience Selection Omnibus 1998

Penetration

Given the differences in advertising support, it was also unsurprising to see that household penetration had grown faster in the south than in the north.

Sales

If advertising has really driven growth, then one would expect the northern sales growth to have been poorer than that in the south, given that it has been exposed to far less advertising. This has indeed been the case, and the north's share of GB sales has steadily declined since 1979 (see Figure 16).[12]

Advertising Tests in the North

Moreover, we can also show that when the north has been supported by advertising, sales have responded to that support. In 1995 three regions (Scotland, the Midlands and the north west) received extra advertising support, and their performance immediately improved compared with that of the rest of the country. Figure 17 shows that there is a statistically significant relationship between the changes in advertising support and regional sales performance.

12. Unfortunately, 1979, rather than 1975, is the earliest year for which we have regional sales data.

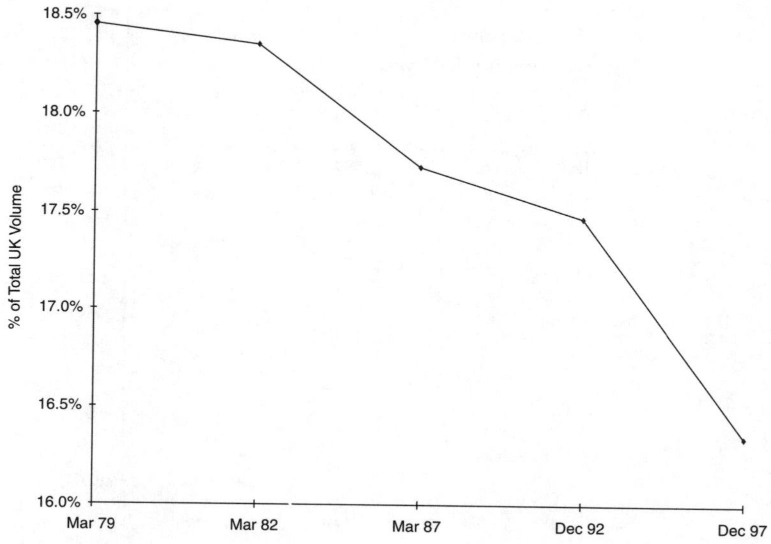

Figure 16: *The northern regions' share of Marmite sales*
Source: Nielsen, BARB, CPC

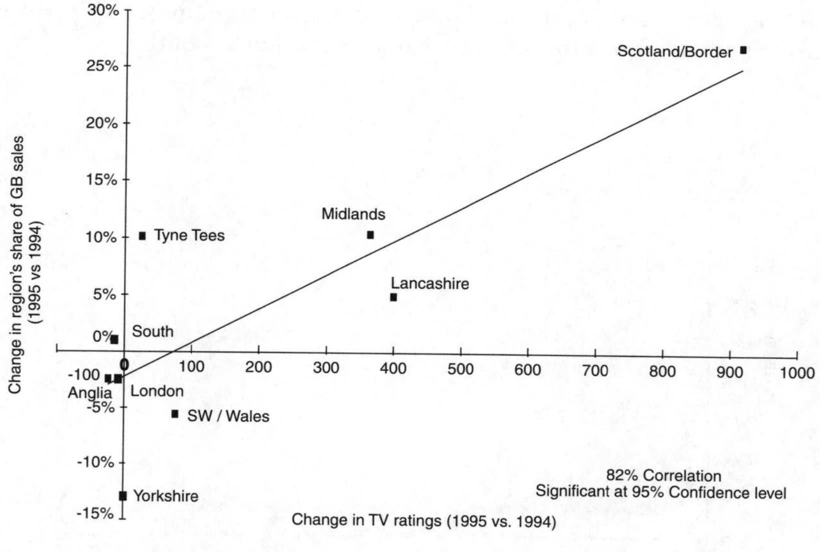

Figure 17: *The effect of the regional upweight test 1995*
Source: Nielsen, BARB

Furthermore, we can see from Figure 18 that when advertising support was withdrawn again, sales responded negatively. Advertising support was withdrawn from Scotland and the north west, while the Midlands only received a lower level of support. The sales performance slumped in the two non-advertised regions, while the Midlands saw a more moderate decline. Once again, the relationship is statistically significant.

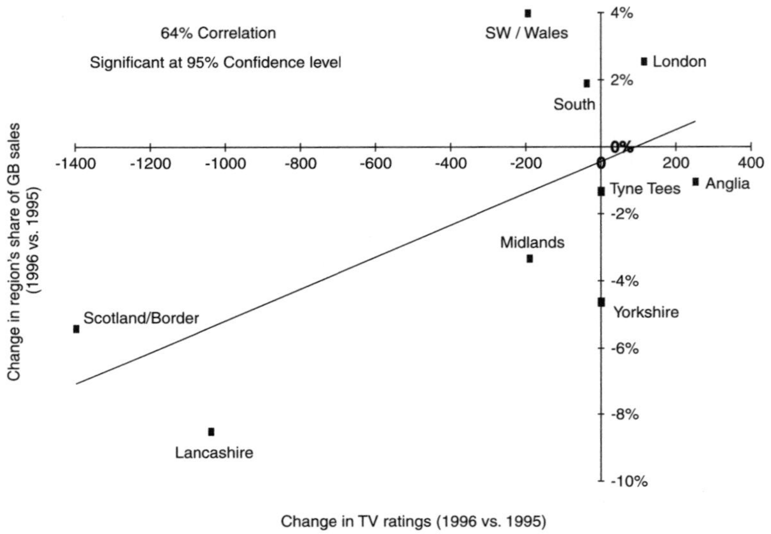

Figure 18: *The effect of withdrawing advertising from the northern test regions, 1996*
Sources: Nielsen, BARB

Figure 19 goes further, as it shows that the change in sales' performance matches the point at which the ads went off air to within a month.

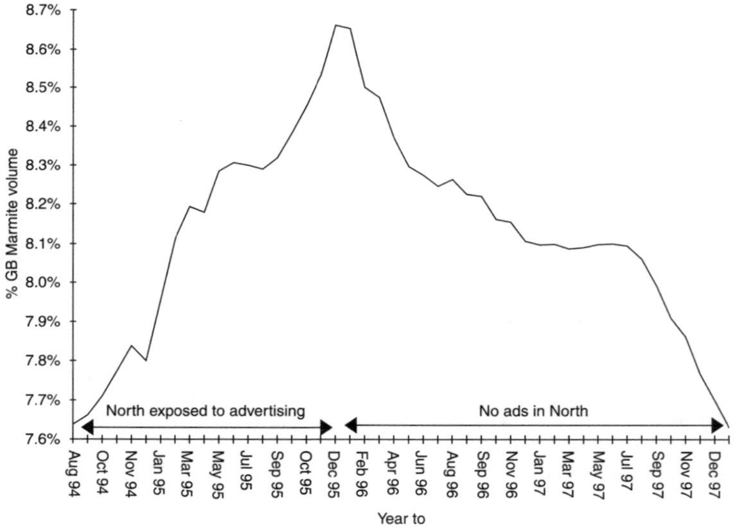

Figure 19: *The northern regions' share of Marmite sales during the test period*
Source: Nielsen

SUMMARY

We have shown that the life cycle is now functioning better in the advertised southern regions than in the north. We have also shown that sales have grown more in the southern regions, and that this is in direct response to advertising support.

We have also shown that bursts of advertising activity in the north do produce direct and positive results. The weight of this evidence clearly indicates that Marmite sales growth is intimately linked to advertising.

ELIMINATING OTHER FACTORS

Before we accept these compelling pieces of evidence, however, we should ask whether there are any other factors which could explain Marmite's growth as a whole and, in particular, the regional differences we have observed.

Product Changes

Overall, there have been no significant launches or new pack sizes which could have driven Marmite's growth. New introductions, such as Marmite cubes, are not the main drivers of growth and, in total, actually contribute less than 5% of the brand's volume sales.[13]

Meanwhile, there have been no significant changes to the product formulation or packaging.[14]

Promotions

Consumer promotions, meanwhile, have generally been on a relatively small scale. More importantly, however, these promotions have also been national, and therefore could not be responsible for Marmite's increased success in the southern regions.

13. Two pack sizes (8g and 600g) have been experimented with since 1975, but never contributed significantly to growth. Marmite cubes were launched in 1996, but again have not created any significant new growth. Meanwhile, at the time of metrication in 1987, the 113g jar was replaced by the 125g jar and the 227g jar was replaced by the 250g jar. Again there were no significant changes to growth.

14. The packaging was changed in 1984, when the original metal lids were exchanged for plastic lids. This change did not increase Marmite's growth, however, and was, in fact, initially met with an outcry of disapproval from Marmite loyalists.

PR

PR has perhaps played a more important role than promotions, as it has attempted to raise Marmite's profile and maintain its image as a healthy product. However, PR activities have again been national, and therefore can have had no role in generating the extra growth in the south.

Mother and Baby Distribution

When the original distribution of Marmite through health clinics and welfare associations stopped, Marmite tried to compensate with new distribution via bounty packs.[15]

While the introduction of bounty packs might have led to an initial step change in Marmite's growth rate, it could not have increased Marmite's growth rate continually from 1975, given that its distribution levels have not increased significantly since its introduction.

Finally, given that the bounty pack enjoys national distribution, if it is a powerful motivator to sales we would have expected it to even out the regional growth differences rather than exaggerating them.

Grocery Distribution

Distribution over the past ten years has been virtually static at 90%, and has been far eclipsed by growth in rate of sale (Figure 20). Any grocery distribution gains have also been almost entirely in the north, and so could have played no part in the growth of Marmite in the southern regions.

Price

Meanwhile, Marmite's real price did fall a little between 1987 and 1989, but since then the price has risen marginally faster than inflation. Yet, despite these price rises, the brand has managed to grow particularly fast.

We also know that price can have played no role in the regional divergence, as there have been no significant regional price differences.

---

15. Bounty packs are distributed nationally to mothers when they have children. Bounty packs contain samples of various products relevant to mothers, such as nappies and baby food. The packs also contain accompanying literature which gives guidance to new mothers. Tokens for Bounty packs are distributed to mothers, and can be redeemed for the actual packs at retail outlets, such as Boots.

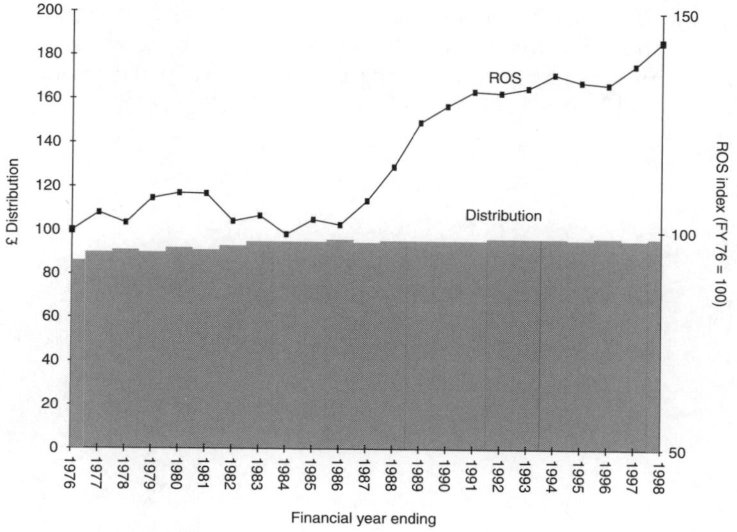

Figure 20: *Marmite distribution and ROS*
Source: Nielsen, CPC

Demographics

Overall, population trends have not been a significant factor in Marmite's growth, as sales of Marmite have risen much faster than the growth in population. In fact, as Figure 21 shows, sales of Marmite per head of the population have grown significantly, both nationally and also particularly in the south.

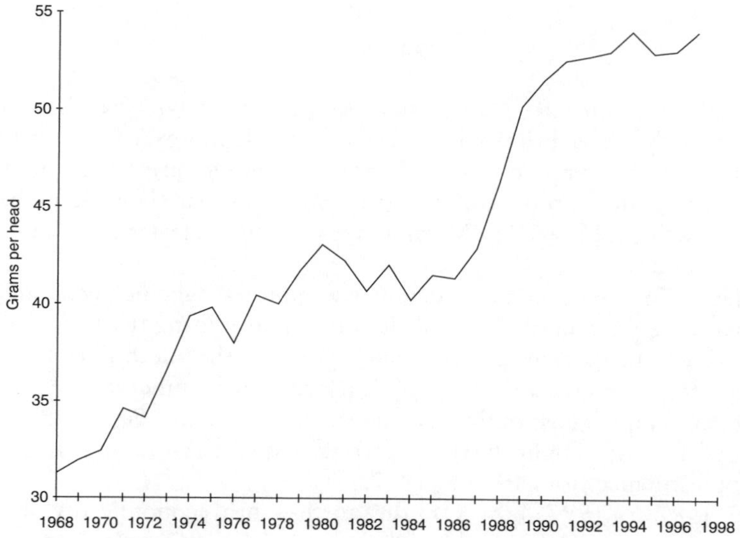

Figure 21: *Marmite sales per head of population*
Source: CPC Ex-factory, ONS

A more subtle criticism might be to suggest that the increase in the child population is responsible for Marmite's growth. As we have already pointed out, however, the birth rate has been declining through most of the period. Again, this decline has occurred in the south as well as nationally (Figure 22).

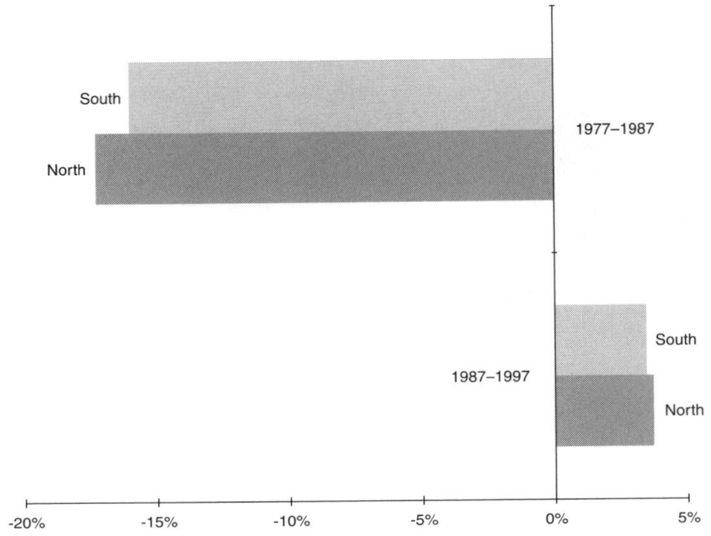

Figure 22: *Change in number of children per head of the population*
Source: ONS

We can therefore conclude that demographics cannot have been responsible for Marmite's growth, either nationally or in the south.

Economic Factors

It might seem plausible to suggest that Marmite's growth has been related to economic growth, since Britons have become much more affluent in the last 30 years. Intuitively, however, one would expect economic growth to benefit luxury items far more than a product like Marmite. It seems implausible to believe that economic growth could result in Marmite growing much faster than total consumer spending on foods.

Looking at this issue in more detail, we explored whether economic changes could explain the regional differential. It is true that, during the late 1970s and for much of the 1980s, incomes did rise much faster in the south than the north, but the actual effect on general consumption was more modest, perhaps because unemployment and the cost of living rose faster in the south (Figure 23).

Nevertheless, this might have helped to explain Marmite's relatively poor northern performance from 1979 to 1987.

During 1987 to 1997, however, the north–south economic divide narrowed, with the south hit harder by the last recession. Despite this, it is during this period that we see Marmite's southern growth surging ahead (Figure 24).

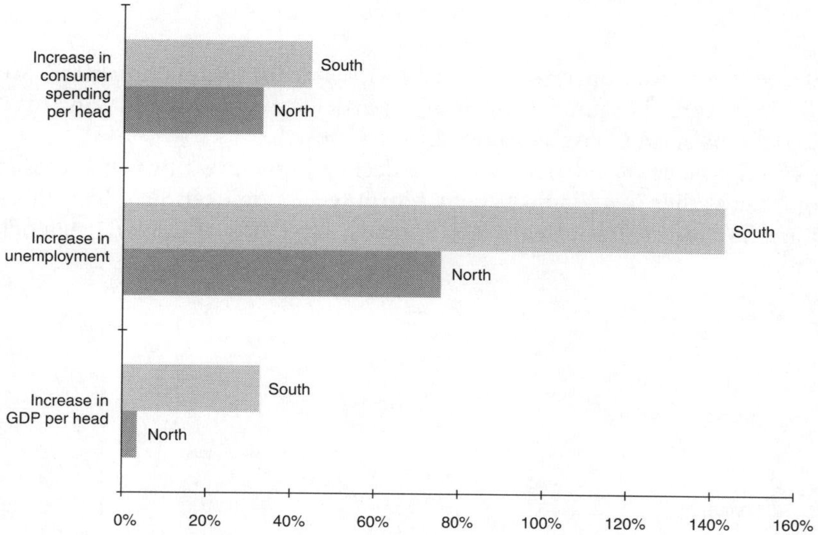

Figure 23: *The north–south divide 1977–1987*
Source: ONS

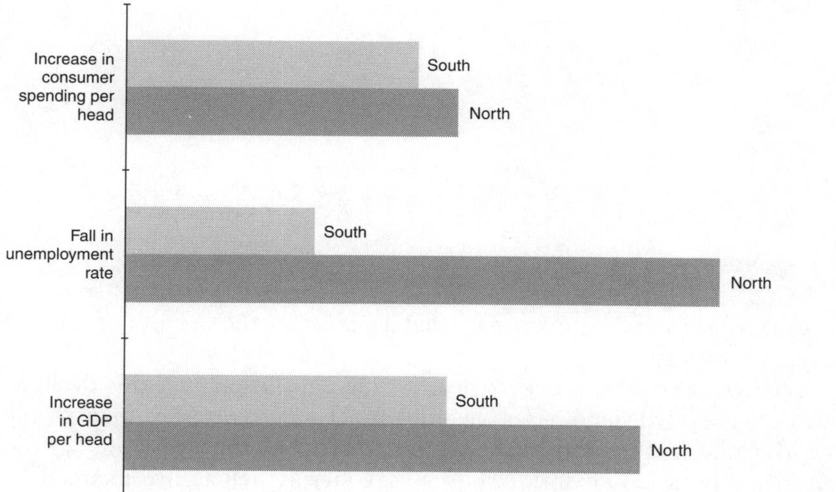

Figure 24: *The north–south divide narrows further, 1987–1996*
Source: ONS

We must therefore conclude that although increasing affluence is undoubtedly a factor in Marmite's success, it is only a minor one.

Food and Health Trends

Marmite, as we know, operates primarily as a spread, and at breakfast. So could changes in attitudes and behaviour, particularly a trend towards more health-conscious eating, have accounted for its growth?

It is certainly true that there has been a decline in the great British breakfast, and one might guess that this would benefit Marmite as a quicker, healthier alternative. Yet Figure 25 shows that cereals, not spreads, have been the main beneficiary of this trend.

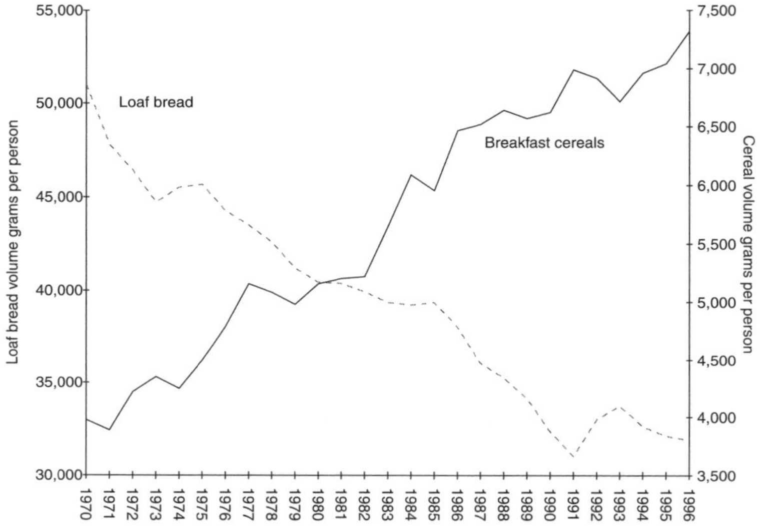

Figure 25: *Average consumption of loaf bread and breakfast cereals*
Source: National Food Survey

In fact, Marmite's growth has been achieved in the context of a massive decline in spreads overall.

The cynical might, however, leap to the conclusion that this decline in spreads was driven by a decline in less healthy sweet spreads, rather than savoury spreads like Marmite. Yet looking at the figures, we can see that Marmite's growth must be considered in the context of declines in savoury as well as sweet spreads.

The decline of spreads 1980–1996	
Sweet	-27%
Savoury	-9%

Source: National Food Survey

Dietary trends cannot therefore explain Marmite's growth.

Competition

Marmite has few significant competitors. While this might be used as a reason to explain why Marmite sales have not declined, it can by no means explain Marmite's growth, particularly as competitive presence has actually increased slightly over the period (Figure 26).

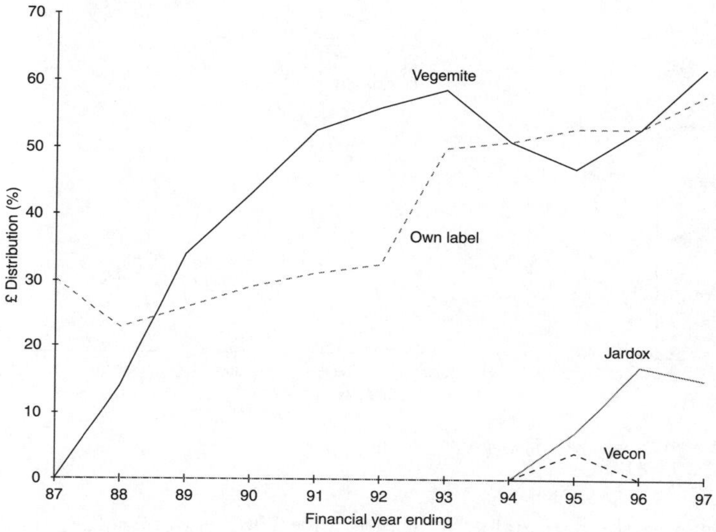

Figure 26: *Distribution of other yeast extracts*
Source: Nielsen

SUMMARY

The above analysis has clearly demonstrated that, although a number of factors such as income and price have undoubtedly contributed to Marmite's success over the last 25 years, they cannot explain the extent of the growth nor the regional sales patterns we have observed. In particular, we have shown that during the period of strongest growth (1987 to 1997) there were no factors, other than advertising, which could explain why sales grew so much faster in the south than in the north.

QUANTIFYING THE CONTRIBUTION OF ADVERTISING

The Contribution of Advertising to Revenue Since 1975

Since 1987, the south has been exposed to 6025 TVRs more than the north. As a result, the total growth rate (from 1987 to 1997) has been 38% in the south, compared to 25% in the north. This therefore suggests that 100 TVRs of advertising contributes around 0.2 percentage points to growth.[16]

Hence, if both north and south had had no TV advertising, then the national growth since 1987 would have been only about 17%.

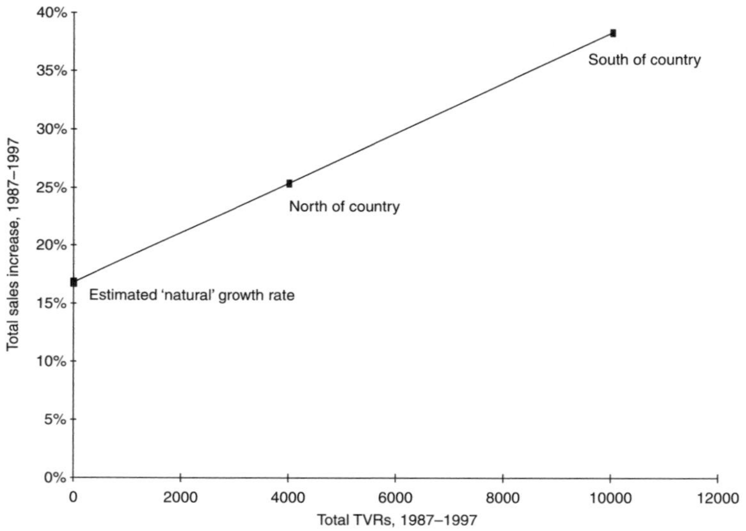

Figure 27: *Marmite sales growth versus advertising*
Source: CPC, BMP DDB

However, the national growth rate since 1987 is in fact 32%. Hence, advertising appears to account for around half of the sales growth seen since 1987.

Without disclosing sensitive information, we can confirm that the profit generated by this growth is greater than the advertising investment. Discounted cashflow analysis reveals that the average annual return on investing in advertising is, in fact, around 27%. This compares extremely favourably with the returns obtained on alternative investments (Table 1).

TABLE 1: AVERAGE ANNUAL RATES OF RETURN 1987–1998 (%)

Marmite advertising	27
Unit trusts	11–18
FTSE	14
Bonds	8
Bank/Building society deposits	5

Source: BMP Estimates

Furthermore, this figure is almost certainly an underestimate because:

1. It ignores the fact that there were several non-advertising factors that buoyed up the north in the period in question, and hence it underestimates the advertising's contribution to generating extra growth in the south versus the north.

16. (100 x (38 – 25)/6025) = 0.2.

2. It ignores the contribution of national non-TV advertising (yet we have included all non-TV advertising costs in our calculations).
3. It ignores the future consequences of the advertising on sales, particularly with regard to the mother-and-baby life cycle.
4. It does not attempt to quantify the effect of advertising creating a barrier to entry to the yeast extract market.

This last point is probably very significant, as the following section will show.

Advertising as a Barrier to Competition

Looking at Marmite since 1975, one is struck by how little competition Marmite faces, even though it is clearly profitable and the process of manufacturing yeast extract is by no means inimitable.[17] The presence of own labels seems particularly low when compared to the rest of the spreads market.

Perhaps more interestingly, though, levels of own label and Vegemite growth have been lower in the southern regions where Marmite advertising has been focused (Figure 28).

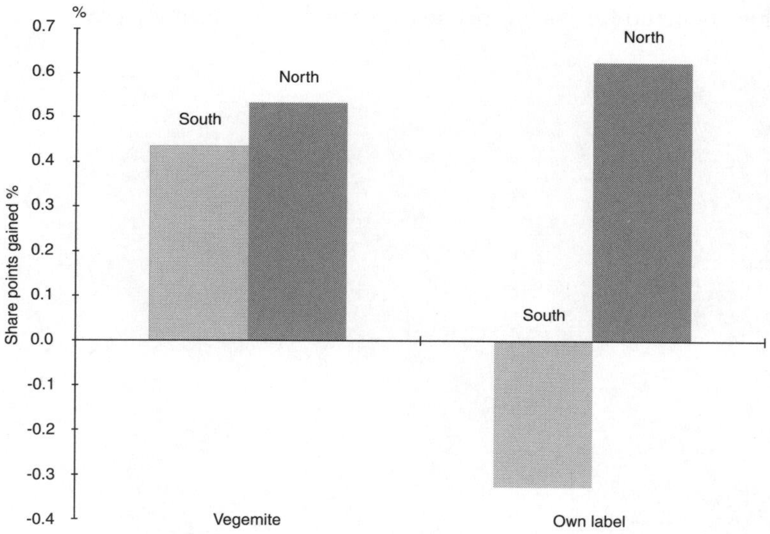

Figure 28: *Changes in competitors' shares of the yeast extract market 1995–1997*
Source: Nielsen

17. The process of regulating the texture of yeast extract is difficult, but by no means impossible to copy. Other competitors could also easily have secured yeast from other breweries to manufacture yeast extract, as Marmite by no means has a monopoly on purchasing the necessary yeast to make its yeast extract.

This indicates that Marmite advertising has indeed created barriers to entry to the yeast extract market, and this has in turn facilitated Marmite's past growth and its future growth potential.

CONCLUSION

Since Marmite's mid-life crisis in 1975, advertising has played a crucial role in preventing the collapse of the mother-and-baby life cycle and has also grown the brand among adults. Advertising has therefore clearly made a huge contribution to Marmite's growth and has also been extremely profitable.

Within the period, two campaigns have been particularly effective. These campaigns were Ogilvy & Mather's 'Soldiers' campaign and BMP's 'I Hate Marmite/My Mate Marmite'. Both campaigns were intended to increase adult usage and did so extremely successfully.

Furthermore, it is interesting to contemplate the potential effects of this Marmite advertising in the future. Given the Marmite life cycle, by which the Marmite 'habit' is passed on from generation to generation, the effect of current advertising may well have repercussions far into the twenty-first century, ensuring that Marmite's second century is as profitable as its first.

Overall, this paper demonstrates the importance of thinking long term in a world where demand for instant results is becoming increasingly prevalent.

7

National Dairy Council – the Milkman Relaunch

INTRODUCTION

Your client is the brand leader in a £3.2 billion food market. Because his competitors are far cheaper, he is losing more than a million customers a year. What could advertising do to help?

In this case the product was the milkman and the competitor the supermarkets.

The obvious answer was to target customers who were about to cancel their milkman. But we discovered that advertising could do little to dissuade them. It would be too little, too late.

Then we examined the move from milkman to supermarkets in more detail. We discovered that there was a *crucial first step* towards cancelling. This was when milkman customers started to buy some of their milk from the supermarkets on a regular basis. Here, it seemed, advertising could have an effect. By targeting these people advertising could not only return a very considerable short-term profit; it could also reduce the rate of cancelling in the future. In fact, we will show that advertising in this way actually halted the decline in the milkman's share during 1991.

What we learned was that you cannot assume the answer to a problem is always to confront that problem directly. In this case prevention proved far more effective than cure.

A HISTORY OF THE MILKMAN

- Door-to-door delivery of milk is a very old British tradition. It dates back to the last century, when handcarts were used to deliver the milk.
- After the Second World War the doorstep service was expanded to its current scale. War-time agriculture had created a huge milk surplus. The Milk Marketing Board (correctly) assumed that if milk was delivered daily, households would use more milk.
- As recently as 1980, almost 90% of households had a milkman.
- Since 1980 the milkman has been in steady decline, partly due to demographic and lifestyle trends but mostly due to competition from supermarkets, whose milk is cheaper.
- In the late 1980s the price gap between the milkman and the supermarkets became larger.
- As a result the milkman's decline accelerated (Figure 1).

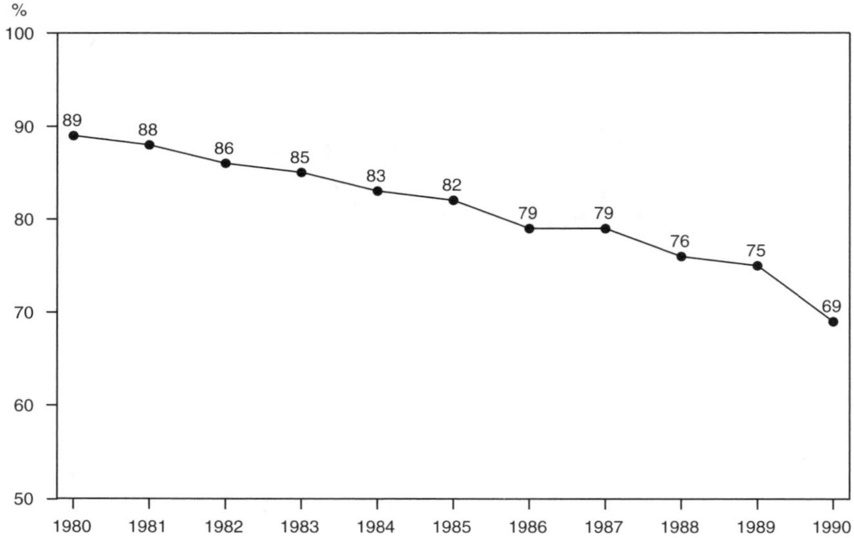

Figure 1. *Percentage of households who have a milkman nowadays*
Source: NOP

WHO CARES IF THE MILKMAN DECLINES?

The Milk Marketing Board (MMB)

— The MMB buys all the milk from the dairy farmers and sells it to dairies.

— The MMB operates, on behalf of farmers, to maximise consumption of milk products.

— Households which have a milkman use more milk. An econometric model in the late 1980s showed that, 'for every 1% fall in doorstep deliveries, milk sales will fall nearly 0.2%.' (MMD Ltd.)

— The reason for this is that daily milk delivery puts milk 'on tap'. Once bought it tends to get used up. Milkman customers are also less prone to running low and restricting consumption. (BMP Qualitative.)

The Dairies/Delivery Companies

— The dairies process, package and distribute milk. This is then sold through the dairies' own milkmen, or to independent delivery companies, or to retailers and wholesalers.

— The dairies and delivery companies make more profit if milk is sold through the milkman:

NDC estimates of dairy profits:

19.5p	Profit per pint sold through a milkman
7.5p	Profit per pint sold through shops
12.0p	Incremental profit per pint, if that pint is sold by the milkman rather than the shops

Source: NDC

— In addition the dairies have made a massive historical investment in doorstep delivery. Thousands of milkmen and dairy employees depend on it for a living.

In short, the whole milk industry (excluding the retailers) had a strong interest in stemming the decline of the milkman. All these groups contribute a levy for advertising to the National Dairy Council (NDC) which is our client. The NDC co-ordinates advertising, promotions, PR, sponsorship and education for the milk industry in England and Wales. (Separate Dairy Councils cover Scotland and Northern Ireland.)

WHY WERE MILKMAN SALES DECLINING?

It was clear that the milkman was losing both volume share and customers to its competitors; the supermarkets and small shops.

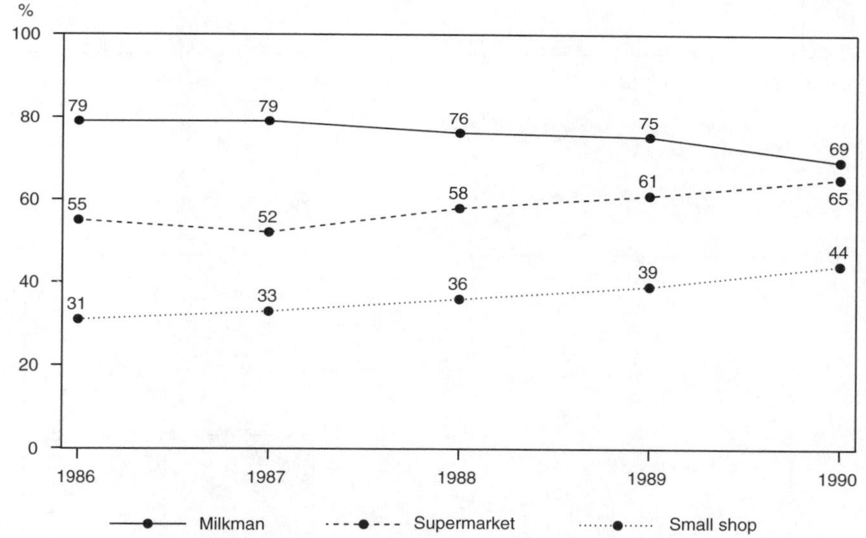

Figure 2. *Sources from which milk ever bought*
Source: NOP

The recent increase in small shop penetration is misleading – they only account for 10% of volume. The main problem was the supermarkets.

The question was, why was the milkman losing share to the supermarkets?

Price

Supermarket milk is much cheaper than milk from the milkman. Supermarkets sell milk at virtually cost price because they want to gain share of a £3.2 billion market. Milk is the biggest household staple and is bought frequently. Retailers could use milk to generate store traffic. Cheap milk could also add to their reputation for good value.

An econometric analysis (MMD Ltd) concluded that the price difference between doorstep and shop milk was responsible for two-thirds of the milkman's decline in 1989. Since then this price gap has widened further.

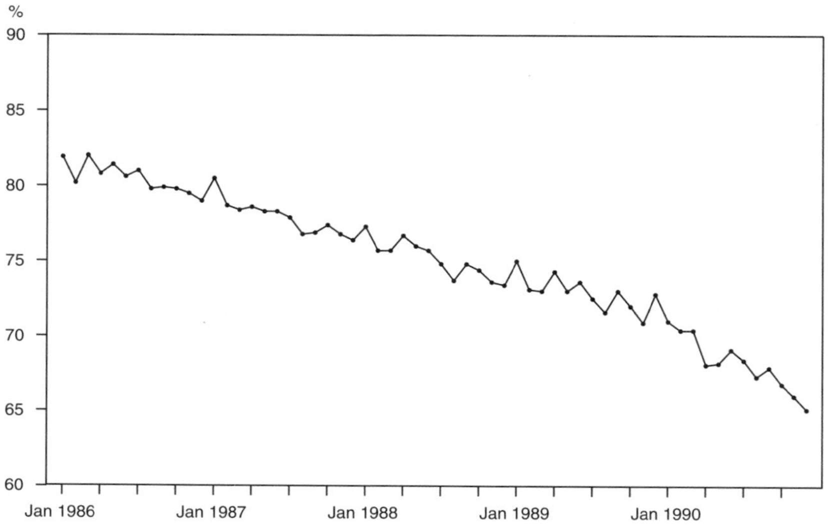

Figure 3. *Milkman volume share – doorstep proportion of household milk*
Source: MMB/Nielsen

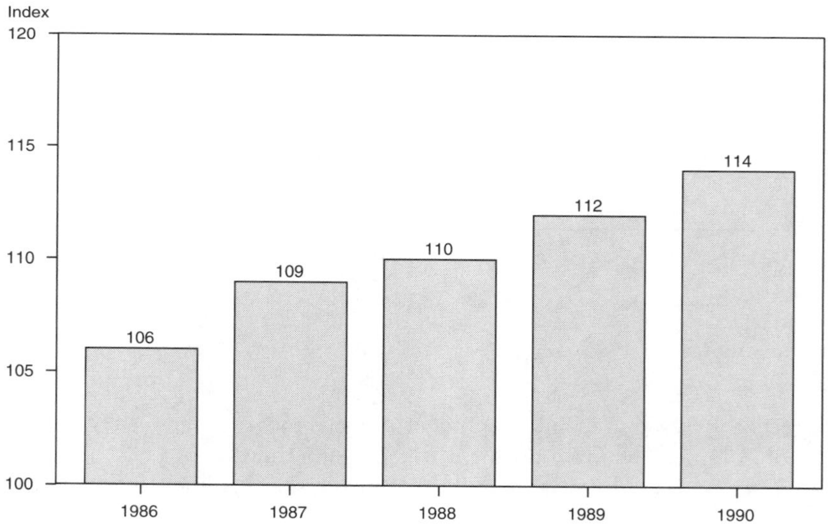

Figure 4. *Relative price of doorstep to supermarket milk*
Source: Nielsen/DTF

Supermarketing

As well as cut-throat pricing and promotions, the supermarkets have also invested in product quality (eg freshness); packaging (eg 4 pint containers); merchandising (eg prominent displays of low fat milks); advertising and leafleting to publicise their cheap prices. The growth of supermarkets, their improving image and the move to out of town shopping have also contributed to their increasing share.

Service

The quality of milkmen and service factors (eg frequency of delivery) affect the value of the milkman service and hence his share. For instance, with fewer customers, the milkman cannot afford to deliver as often. There is therefore a vicious spiral of falling share and reductions in quality of service.

WHAT DID WE THINK WAS GOING TO HAPPEN IN THE FUTURE?

Share had been steadily declining from 82% in 1986 to 65% by the end of 1990. The price gap between milkman and supermarkets was continuing to widen. The decline therefore was expected to continue and, probably, to get even steeper. It was reaching a level such that it became a priority issue for the NDC. Something had to be done to stem the decline.

WHAT COULD BE DONE?

Some of the factors affecting the milkman are out of the milk industry's control (eg supermarket price). There are only three important factors which the milk industry could control:

1. *Price*
   A substantial price reduction would be needed to influence people who were about to cancel their milkman. Unfortunately this reduction in price would obviously have to be offered to all customers, not just those about to cancel. Profitability would be decimated.

2. *Service*
   Improvements might increase loyalty. Various initiatives are now being tested (eg guaranteed early delivery). However, these changes take time (at least two years) to implement.

3. *Advertising*
   Given these stark choices, the milk industry agreed that if an advertising campaign could be developed which would help to stem the decline (at least until longer term solutions could be found) it would receive their full support.

DEVELOPING A MARKETING AND ADVERTISING STRATEGY

Marketing Objective

To slow down the decline in the milkman's share of total milk sales.

Interestingly, we found that with a sizeable advertising budget of £5 million we would only have to stem the decline by ½% share point for the advertising to pay back.

For advertising to repay a budget of £5 million:

½%	x	12p (incremental milkman profit – NDC estimate)
	x	8.9 billion pints (household milk volume – MMB)
	=	£5m extra profit

This equates to 45 million extra pints sold by the milkman.

Target Audience and Desired Change in Behaviour

The decline in the milkman's volume share was accompanied by a decline in the proportion of households having a milkman, from 82% in 1985 to 69% in 1990. Once these customers had been lost, the dairies knew (from experience of door-to-door canvassing) they would be very hard to get back. If the decline continued at its present rate then there would be no milkman customers left within 12 years. It seemed clear that there were two possible strategies:

1. Stop people from cancelling.
2. Recruit new milkman customers.

We were able to reject the second option because it was too small. The NDC estimated that at most only 2% of households are potential new milkman customers every year, whereas 6% of households had cancelled their milkman in the last year (Source: NOP). We decided that new customers were not a large enough audience to be the main focus of our advertising. (We have not completely dismissed this option. Later in 1992 advertising carrying a phoneline number was used to recruit new customers. This coincided with a major canvassing drive by the dairies.)

We were left with the first option, which was to stop customers cancelling. We needed to find out who they were and why they were cancelling. Equally we needed to find out why other customers weren't cancelling.

We therefore conducted some qualitative research among past and present milkman customers. What we found was that it was unrealistic to expect advertising to affect cancelling. But in the process we discovered another unexpected way to stem the decline.

What We Found

Research amongst those who had actually cancelled told us that:

— Consumers do not simply buy all their milk from the milkman, then suddenly decide to cancel.
— Those who cancelled had first gone through a phase when they had regularly bought extra milk from the supermarkets. Typically, they would 'stock up' with extra milk for the weekends – often buying 4 pint containers.
— Only when they had regularly bought from the supermarket for some time were they confident in this source of supply; its constant availability, its freshness, the convenience of picking it up 'when you're there anyway'.
— Because they bought regularly from both sources, these people became more aware of the price difference. Some then felt 'irresponsible' spending so much extra to have milk delivered.
— Even so, cancelling the milkman was a big decision. Many 'agonised' over it, weighing up their experience of each source. Some were also anxious about upsetting their milkman.
— They were often therefore prompted to cancel by an 'event'; eg a row with their milkman over the bill.

Source: BMP Qualitative

How could advertising influence people who had regular experience of both sources, who were fully aware of how much extra the milkman cost, who were virtually looking for an excuse to cancel anyway? Advertising had nothing new to tell these people. It was unrealistic to expect advertising to persuade them not to cancel. It would be too little, too late.

What Could We Do Then?

Past research had told us that most milkman customers buy from the shops occasionally, when they run out of milk. This latest research had told us that before cancelling, customers had first gone through a phase of buying quite a lot of milk from the supermarkets much more *regularly* (eg with their weekly shopping). In retrospect this was obvious. In fmcg purchasing people very rarely go from being 100% loyal to one brand to being 100% loyal to another brand. There is nearly always a period of trial and conversion.

This is the crucial finding that influenced our advertising strategy. It seemed that customers moving from the milkman to the shops followed a series of steps.

Milkman customers
(occasionally buy from the
shops as distress purchases)

↓ **'Drifting'**

Customers who still buy
most of their milk from the
milkman, but regularly stock up
from the shops

↓ **Cancelling**

Shop only customers

The key step we were interested in was when milkman customers moved from occasional distress purchasing to regular purchasing from the shops. We will call this step 'drifting' from now on, for the sake of brevity.

Before reaching the 'regular supermarket stage', milkman customers:

— were often unsure of the price difference (and often underestimated it);

— were not at all confident that the supermarkets could supply all their milk, (eg without shopping much more regularly).

Source: BMP Qualitative

Because they were 'drifting' into supermarket purchasing and were not yet strongly affected by price they seemed far more likely to respond to advertising.

The research told us that consumers tended to take their milkman for granted. They seldom saw their milkman apart from on pay day. They came to expect pints of milk just to 'turn up on the doorstep'. However, on probing they did recognise that there were strong rational and emotional benefits to having a milkman:

- The main benefit of the milkman service is the *considerable convenience* he provides; you don't have to carry all that heavy milk, you don't have to go out and get it, you don't have to worry about it, it's there in time for breakfast, etc.
- The milkman service also has warm *emotional values*; friendly, helpful, traditional, a family ritual, part of the local community ('like a village bobby').

Source: BMP Qualitative

If we could make these benefits more salient it could provide a strong counter argument against drifting into supermarket purchasing.

In addition, we had a number of new things to say in our advertising, which might lead to them buying more of their milk from the milkman instead of the shops.

- *Green*
  The green bandwagon was in full swing. Yet, because returnable glass milk bottles are so familiar, few had 'realised' they were better for the environment.
- *Low fat milks*
  Some weren't sure if the milkman sold these.
- *Weekend milk*
  They often didn't think about extra milk for the weekend until they reached the shops – but did find it heavy and bulky to get home. It would make more sense to leave a note for the milkman.

It seemed likely therefore that advertising *might work*, in deterring some of these consumers from 'drifting' into regular shop purchasing. We then needed to check if this was a worthwhile target.

Is This a Worthwhile Opportunity?

From an annual source of purchase data we were able to calculate that between June 1989 and June 1990:

- 9% of housewives 'drifted' into regular supermarket buying, while keeping their milkman.
- 6% of housewives cancelled their milkman.

(Source: NOP Annual Survey)

NOP also told us that on average the milkman customers who regularly purchased from the shops bought; eight pints a week from the milkman and four pints a week from the shops. We could therefore estimate how much volume per week was lost by the milkman, from the two migrations:

Drifting: 9% of 20 million households x 4 pints/week = 7.2 million pints/week
Cancelling: 6% of 20 million households x 8 pints/week = 9.6 million pints/week

Drifting was therefore responsible for nearly half the volume lost by the milkman.

Our research had told us that only those who had gone through a phase of regular shop purchasing tended to cancel their milkman. Our strategy aimed to reduce the number of milkman customers who entered this phase. It was therefore possible that any success would have an *additional long-term effect*, by reducing future cancelling.

In fact, there was evidence for just such a long-term process. MMD econometric modelling in the past had picked up a relationship between the amount of volume share lost in one year and further longer term losses. They call this the 'feedthrough effect'.

Summary of Creative Brief

Target audience	Housewives with a milkman who occasionally buy extra milk from the shops.
Who are they?	25–45 year old housewives, with children, heavier purchasers of milk.
Objective	Persuade them to continue buying from the milkman (or buy more from him) rather than drifting into the habit of regularly stocking up at the supermarket.
Proposition	Don't forget how helpful and convenient your milkman is.
Support	(i) The lovable, friendly, archetypal milkman – they've forgotten how wonderful he is. (ii) He delivers low fat milks. (iii) His returnable glass bottles are friendlier to the environment. (iv) He's more convenient for weekend extras than carrying heavy, bulky milk home.

Guidelines

A blockbusting relaunch was needed. One extra task, which was added to the brief at the suggestion of the client was targeting milkmen themselves (as a secondary audience) in order to improve morale.

Media Planning

TV was chosen as the only medium sufficiently impactful and involving to stage a major relaunch. The media target audience was housewives with children. The media plan is shown below.

Media timing/weights

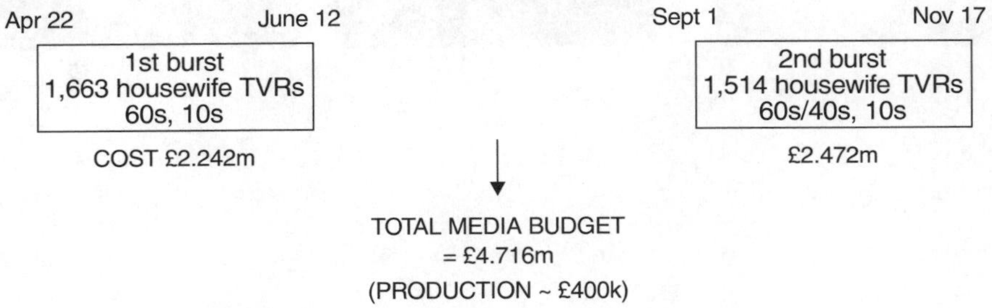

'DAYBREAK' ADVERTISING (60 SECONDS)

'DAYBREAK' ADVERTISING (10 SECONDS)

MVO: It's a lot easier to get all your weekend milk from your milkman.

VO: Whole milk, semi-skimmed, skimmed, your milkman can deliver them all.

VO: What's all this fuss about being green?

You've been returning our bottles for years.

Creative Development

The 'Daybreak' advertising was written to this brief. Most TV viewers now know this as 'the one with the dancing bottles'. The creative team had worked out roughly how many bottles of milk a milkman delivers a day (about 900). This impressive scale, plus the almost 'magical' way in which milk 'appears' on your doorstep inspired the main (60 second) commercial.

To keep the main ad as magical as possible, the rational support messages were relegated to 10 second ads. These were shown 'top and tail' with the 60 second (ie first and last ads in the commercial break).

This advertising became one of the most liked and noticed campaigns on TV. It also received recognition of the advertising industry, by winning Gold awards from the Creative Circle and British Television Awards. We believe that much of the credit for the advertising effectiveness must go to the creative team, for producing such a famous and distinctive, yet relevant campaign.

TABLE 1: THE TOP 10: SPONTANEOUS RECALL
Q: Thinking back over the past week, which commercials can you remember seeing or hearing?

	Account	Agency
1	Milk	BMP DDB Needham
2	Persil	JWT
3	Coke/Coca-Cola	McCanns
4	Radion	Ogilvy & Mather
5	Carling Black Label	WCRS
6	Fairy Liquid	Grey
7	Guinness	Ogilvy & Mather
8	British Telecom/BT	JWT
9	PG Tips	BMP DDB Needham
10	TV Quick	Lowe Howard-Spink

Source: *Marketing*, 27th June 1991

EVALUATION OF THE CAMPAIGN

Sales Results (MMB/Nielsen Data)

— Figure 3 showed that the milkman's share of household milk was in long-term decline. This decline continued up until April 1991.

— From January 1990–April 1991 the milkman's share declined at an average of 0.43% share points per month.

— However, from May–December 1991, when we advertised, this stabilised, resulting in a decline of only 0.01% share points per month, ie the decline had been almost completely halted in the advertising period.

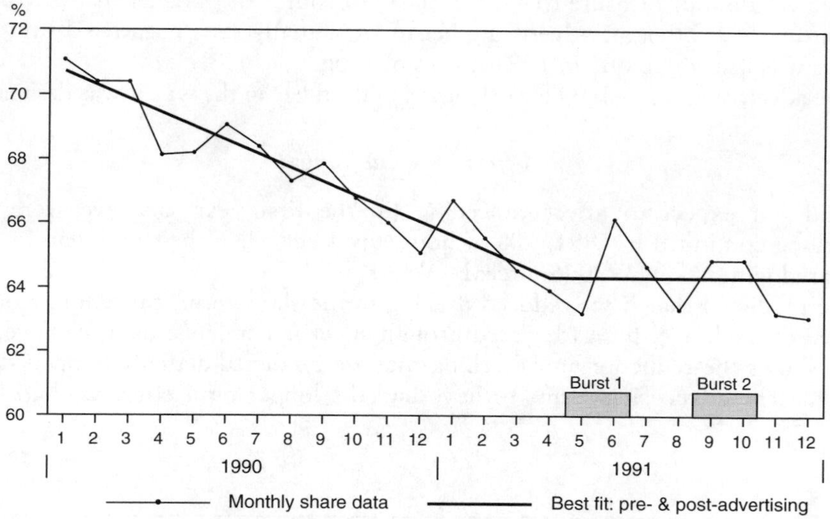

Figure 5. *Milkman volume share – doorstep proportion of household milk*

TABLE 2: AVERAGE MONTHLY RATES OF DECLINE
(Share points per month)

	Jan '90–Apr '91	May '91–Dec '91
Average monthly decline	–0.43 (Pre-advertising)	–0.01 (Advertising)

Source: MMB/Nielsen

— Not only did we see the milkman's decline nearly halted during the advertising period. We also saw two significant *increases* in milkman share, coinciding exactly with the advertising bursts.

Advertising burst	Milkman share
Apr–May	+ 2.9% pts
Aug–Sep/Oct	+ 1.5% pts

We do not have sales figures since December 1991, due to the time needed by the MMB to collect total milk market data. However, in only eight months, we have seen a very pronounced effect.

Effect on Drifting

TABLE 3: RATE OF DRIFTING

	June '89-June '90	Feb '91-Jan '92
% of households drifting	9%	–2%
(Sample)	(1,600)	(800)

Sources: NOP, Millward Brown

As we have seen from annual purchasing data, between June 1989 and June 1990, 9% of households (who had a milkman) drifted into regular shop purchasing. The advertising was designed specifically to combat this. We therefore set up a continuous measure (from February) of source of purchase using Millward Brown. In 1991, after the advertising began we actually saw 'negative drifting'. No volume was lost, therefore, in 1991 due to drifting.

The advertising seemed to be working very effectively in the way it was designed to.

Effect on Cancelling

We did not expect to affect cancelling (in the first year) and we were right. Cancelling continued in 1991; 7% of housewives cancelled their milkman in 1991, compared with 6% in 1990 (Source: NOP).

We predicted that if we reduced drifting in the short-term, cancelling would be reduced in the longer term (the 'feedthrough effect'). The latest data we have, from 1992, shows the reduction in cancelling that we predicted actually happened early in 1992. The advertising seems to have had the longer term effect we had hoped for.

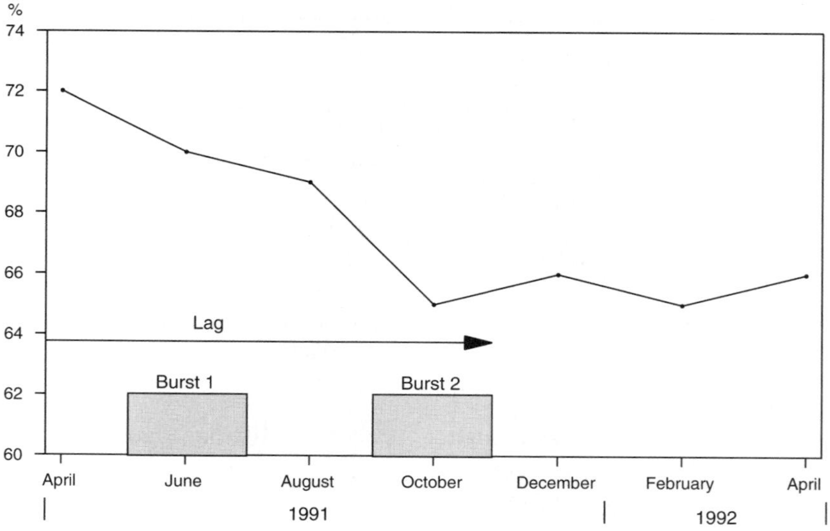

Figure 6. *Percentage of housewives who have a milkman*
Source: Millward Brown

The Unexpected Effect

— We assumed that, if we stopped drifting altogether, the best we could hope for would be to slow down share decline by nearly 50% (because in 1990 nearly half the volume lost by the milkman was through drifting). In fact it appears that we had underestimated the power of our advertising.
— Cancelling continued, yet share was flat rather than declining at half the previous rate.
— The only explanation is an effect we hadn't expected. We had thought of drifting in the absolute sense of changing source of purchase; rather than 'drifting' in the true sense of a continuum from occasional to regular shop purchasing.
— What appears to have happened is that those who still had a milkman but had not 'drifted' during 1991 (in the absolute sense) bought more milk from the milkman and less milk from the shops.
— This could explain why there were such immediate sales peaks during our

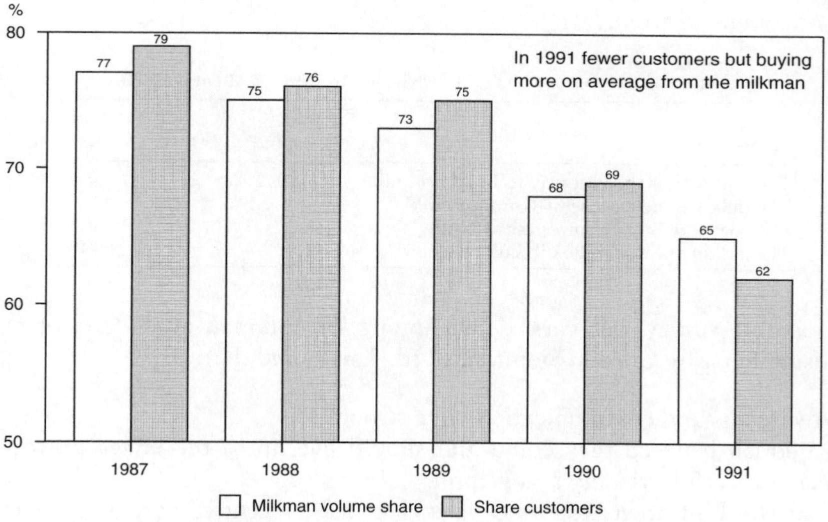

Figure 7. *Milkman volume share vs share of customers*
Sources: NOP, MMB/Nielsen

advertising bursts (eg milkman customers remembering to order extra from their milkman). In retrospect, this is how we should have expected the advertising to work – particularly the 10 second tactical ads.
— We can estimate the size of this effect from the fact that volume share only declined by 3% in 1991. From the rate of cancelling, we would have expected a decline of 7 or 8%:

Extra volume = 4% x 20 million households @ 8 pints
= remaining 62% x 20 million milkman customers @ ½ pint.

That is, every remaining milkman customer bought on average an extra pint every two weeks from the milkman instead of the shops.

Consumer Evidence of the Advertising Effect
Performance on the Advertising Tracking Study

The NDC has used Millward Brown for over ten years to monitor the performance of its advertising. In its first year, our milkman advertising achieved higher levels of spontaneous awareness and proven recall than any previous milk campaign.

TABLE 4: MILLWARD BROWN – AWARENESS LEVELS (end of 1st year)

(Housewives)	Spontaneous awareness	Proven recall
'Daybreak' campaign	60%	67%
Previous highest scores	48%	62%
Average (last 3 campaigns)	42%	48%

The communication objectives of the campaign were monitored by the following prompted statements. These showed an unprecedented strength and depth of communication.

TABLE 5: PROMPTED COMMUNICATION (MILLWARD BROWN)

(Housewives)	(Pre) Jan/Feb '91	(Post) Oct/Nov '91
'The milkman is the best way to buy fresh milk'	29%	56%
'The milkman delivers semi-skimmed milk'	9%	39%
'Milk delivery is environmentally friendly'	7%	40%
'The milkman can handle difficult orders'	4%	33%

A separate survey was carried out among 70 milkman at the end of the first advertising burst by Gordon Simmonds Ltd. This found that:

— Awareness and communication were strong.
— Milkmen believed they could and should live up to the image portrayed; in being cheerful, friendly and helpful.
— One-third of them reported sales increases recently, very few reported a decline.

Qualitative research was also conducted among housewives who had a milkman after the first burst, to check how the campaign was working;

— It was most repondents' favourite advertising on TV – 'straight away you have a smile on your face when it comes on, even if you're down.'
— The Disney-like imagery and music transported the viewer into childlike feelings of security and pleasure; these feelings were linked to having a milkman – a magical figure who has everything under control.
— Overall, the advertising made them feel good about having *their* milkman. It made them appreciate him and inclined to use him more. The 10 second ads (eg 'Green') provided extra (rational) reasons to do so.

Source: BMP Qualitative

ISOLATING THE ADVERTISING EFFECT

As we have seen in Figure 5 there were two significant increases in the milkman's share coinciding with our two advertising bursts. As a result the decline in milkman's share was halted.

We can eliminate all other factors which could possibly have caused this change in the rate of decline in the middle of 1991.

Price

The price difference between milkman and shops increased during the second half of 1991, when the ads were on air. If anything, therefore, the milkman share should have declined faster in the second half of the year.

TABLE 6: RELATIVE PRICE OF DOORSTEP TO SUPERMARKET MILK

	Jan/Apr '91	May/Dec '91
Index	112	115

Sources: DTF, Nielsen

Distribution

Nothing untoward happened (eg a strike at supermarkets or an increase in the number of milkmen) during 1991 to affect either source. If anything supermarkets should have gained share due to store openings and Sunday trading in the second half of the year.

Service

Presumably, those who thought their milkman service had improved might be responsible for a slowing down in the decline of milkman sales.

There has been a general drive within the milk industry to improve service, in response to falling sales. As a result there have been slight improvements in the perceptions of the service. However, there was no significant change in these improvements between the first and second half of 1991.

TABLE 7: BMRB TELEPHONE AD HOC 'SERVICE' SURVEY – SAMPLE 1000
('Over the past three months, would you say that the service your milkman has given you has:')

	Pre-advertising (Mar 91)	Post-advertising (Nov 91)
Improved	7%	8%
Stayed the same	91%	90%
Got worse	2%	2%

There is no evidence, therefore, that service changes had an increased effect on the milkman's share, after our advertising began.

Other Activity

There was no other national marketing activity supporting the milkman in 1991.

Any local activity which existing customers responded to favourably would have been seen by them as a service improvement.

But we know that service improvements did not have an increased effect after our advertising began.

Conclusion – Isolating the Advertising Effect

There were clear increases in the milkman's share of milk coinciding exactly with our two advertising bursts. As a result the decline in the milkman's share was halted in the advertising period.

No other factors which influence the milkman's share of milk changed in a way which could have caused this. In fact, the major factor which influences the milkman's share (ie price) changed in a way which should have increased the decline during the advertising period.

ESTIMATING THE OVERALL EFFECT OF ADVERTISING

Short-term Effect

— As we have seen the average monthly rate of decline in the milkman's share of volume from January 1990 to April 1991 was 0.43 share points.
— There is nothing to suggest that this rate of decline would not have continued through the rest of 1991. Indeed, the price increase suggests it might have got worse.
— In fact, share declined by 0.01 share points per month from May 1991 to December 1991.
— If we assume share would have continued to decline at 0.43 share points per month without the advertising then we can calculate the additional volume due to the advertising.

Average share May–December 1991

With advertising	Without advertising
64.2%	61.7%

Additional share points	=	2.5%
In 8 months, total household volume	=	5.95 billion pints
Additional milkman volume	=	2.5% x 5.95 billion
	=	150 million pints
Additional profit	=	150 million x 12p (NDC estimate of extra profit from milkman per pint)
	=	£18 million

As well as extra profit, we know that milkman sales bring extra volume because milkman customers use more milk; an extra 0.2% in milk volume for every 1% of extra milkman share (Source: MMD).

The milkman's share was on average 2.5% higher when we advertised, than expected from previous declines. We can therefore estimate the amount of extra milk consumption due to the advertising:

Additional volume	=	5.9 billion pints x 2.5 x 0.2%
	=	30 million pints
Extra profit	=	30 m x 15p (NDC estimate of average profit for milk)
	=	£4.5 million

The total extra profit was therefore £22.5 million. The total advertising spend was only £5.1 million. The advertising paid for itself more than four times over in 1991.

It had exceeded not only our objectives but our wildest dreams of what we could achieve.

Longer Term Effect

We had a theory that slowing 'drifting' in the short-term, would lead to a reduced rate of cancelling in the future ('feedthrough effect'). We have seen some earlier evidence that this was happening. This adds even more volume saved (and profit generated) by the advertising, in the longer term. And it contributes to the industry's longer term objective of turning around the decline.

SUMMARY

- The milkman was rapidly losing share to the supermarkets, which were cheaper. This had very big implications for the volume of milk used and the profit made by the dairy industry.
- We were briefed to develop advertising to stem this decline. Even ½% less share lost in 1991 would pay for our advertising.
- The obvious solution was to stop customers from cancelling. However, on further investigation it did not appear realistic that advertising could do this.
- We discovered that there was a crucial first step towards cancelling – when milkman customers started regularly purchasing extra milk from the supermarkets.
- This migration accounted for nearly half the volume lost in the short-term. It also gave us a way to nip future decline in the bud.
- This focused and innovative strategy was translated into advertising of the highest creative standards.
- The advertising slowed down the decline by 150 million pints. We can see this from the change in the rate of decline which occurred after the advertising started.
- Penetration data showed that the advertising worked as intended – in stopping consumers drifting more into regular shop purchasing. There also was an unexpected effect in increasing the amount of milk bought from the milkman by those customers who did not 'drift'.

— The advertising performed outstandingly on awareness and communication measures.
— We can demonstrate that the advertising was responsible for the sales effect, because nothing else changed in a way which could have caused it.
— The advertising paid for itself more than four times over, in extra profit saved by the milkman in 1991.
— There is some evidence that this effect led to reduced cancelling in the longer term which would mean further profit generated by the advertising.

CONCLUSIONS

We were given a very big task – to tackle what seemed a terminal decline within a £3.2 billion market. In only eight months we virtually halted this decline. Hopefully, with our advertising continuing, the milk industry may find a lasting solution to this problem.

There was no guarantee of success. A previous attempt to stem this decline (in 1984) targeted those who were about to cancel, with an exhortation not to 'let the milkman become a thing of the past'. There is no evidence that this had any effect. Only through the innovative strategy of targeting prevention rather than cure and through outstanding creative advertising, do we believe it was possible to achieve such remarkable results.

POSTSCRIPT

This case is based on 1991 data. In 1992 we continued to run the 'Daybreak' campaign. All the data so far indicate that the advertising has continued to be just as successful and profitable in its second year as it was in its first.

8

How the Chimps Kept PG Tips Brand Leader Through 35 Years of Intense Competition

INTRODUCTION

Our story begins in 1955, the year Brooke Bond relaunched PG Tips. Prior to 1955 it had been called 'Pre-Gestive' tea, a reference to the historical importance placed upon tea's dietary and medicinal properties.

The relaunch may have modernised PG Tips image but it didn't lead to a growth in its market share. Throughout 1955 and most of 1956, it remained number four brand.

Today, 35 years on, PG Tips is not just a player in this market, but also the dominant brand leader. How has this success been achieved and maintained?

Certainly, many things have changed over this period that might have affected the brand's performance. The nature of what the British eat and drink has changed substantially, as have fashions in the tea market and our social lives in general. Two things that haven't changed, however, are the campaign that first started in 1956 and the high level of media support given to the brand ever since.

In this paper we aim to prove that PG Tips *reached* this dominant position by 1958 because of the interest generated in the brand by the chimps advertising, then that PG Tips *maintained* its brand leadership by assimilating added value which enabled it to represent a more valued purchase to consumers, even though its absolute price has always been higher than its competitors.

After proving that added value has indeed been added, we then show that it is the chimps campaign that is primarily responsible for this addition of value.

Finally, we attempt to quantify the financial contribution of 34 years of the chimps campaign.

However, first we need to introduce them.

THE CHIMPS CAMPAIGN

A Unique Property

The original idea for the 'chimps' was chanced upon when a copy writer, charged with inventing the first PG Tips commercial, visited Regent's Park Zoo in 1956. The chimpanzees were enjoying a tea-party in front of a large crowd. A few months later, the first chimps commercial was shot in a stately home and featured a chimps tea-party accompanied by a voice-over by Peter Sellers.

This sixty-second commercial was designed to boost awareness of PG Tips and develop an original and inimitable property for the brand. At the time, it was believed that, on seeing the commercial, the obvious enjoyment of the crowd at the antics of the chimps in Regent's Park Zoo would be replicated in the homes of the viewers. Thus, it was hoped to establish a stronger relationship between brand, advertising and consumers.

'Stately home' first appeared on the nation's TV screens in the autumn of 1956.

Consistency

In all honesty, nobody at that time suspected that the chimps advertising would be so effective so quickly. Within two years, the brand had toppled Typhoo from the number one slot, on the way overtaking other erstwhile giants such as Brooke Bond Dividend and Lyons (Brooke Bond).

The agency and Brooke Bond soon realised that they had a hot property on their hands. As time passed with PG Tips still retaining brand leadership, faith in the long-term potential of the chimps campaign strengthened. They quickly became so popular that Brooke Bond conducted film shows in cinemas around the country.

Consistency has been maintained ever since with similar creative executions running over the whole 34 year period. By the time of the chimps' 30th anniversary in 1986, over 100 commercials had been made.

Consistency has been maintained not only in creative style but also in media presence. PG Tips has always retained the dominant share of voice in the tea market, only varying its advertising spend (in real terms) by a relatively small proportion from year to year whereas the competitors' spends have fluctuated much more dramatically.

Relevance

It would be tempting to believe that, having cracked a winning formula so early on, the agency's task would be solely to churn out more, very similar, chimps commercials. This of course is untrue for several reasons.

First, viewers need continually to be excited by new ideas.

Secondly, the chimps have lived through a period of exceptionally rapid social change. Making sure that they continue to reflect trends in society and do not become 'dated', has required constant change within the creative vehicle.

In the late 1960s, for example, the commercials reflected the self-expression of the times with two of them showing the chimps portraying a photographer and an artist.

'STATELY HOME'

Music: 'Greensleeves'
VO: The clock strikes four. In millions of English homes that means it's teatime

Teatime with its gleaming silver and tinkling teacups

What a happy time it is and how fortunate the hostess who knows that her favourite tea is also the favourite of her friends

For no matter how elegant the manners or charming the company

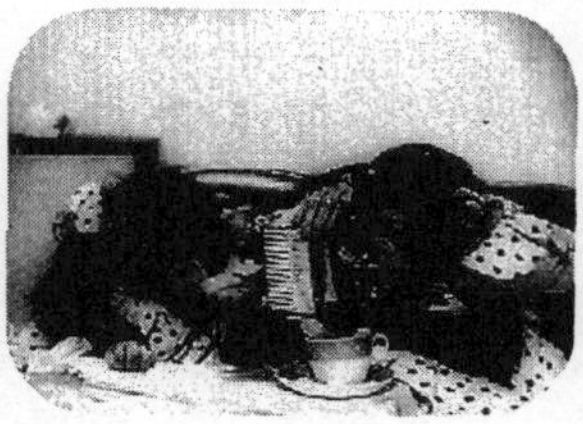

no guest is ever really happy without the right kind of tea

good tea, fresh tea, tea you can taste to

the last delicious drop

'He means Brooke Bond PG Tips. B-B-B-B-Brooke Bond'

Sound: Laughter from other chimps

In the 1970s, the chimps pastiched topical events such as the oil crisis and Ted Heath's preoccupation with his yacht, 'Morning Cloud'.

And of course, clearly observed sketches on the British character have always had the potential to attract enormous interest. 'Mr Shifter' who in 1972 coined the phrase 'You hum it son, I'll play it' and the 'Tour de France' cyclist with his 'Avez-vous un cuppa?' are two examples which have become part of the common vernacular.

The campaign has also adapted to take account of competitors' tactics. For example, in response to Tetley's greater emphasis on the advantages of their teabags' '2,000 perforations', the Bond series relaunched PG Tips with new 'Flavour Flow' teabags in 1981. 'Brooke Bond', a character based on James Bond, guarded the new teabags' secret.

'Ada and Dolly' formed the core campaign over the 1983 to 1985 period and were a deliberate move back to the chimps more traditional 'kitchen sink' territory, representing a retreat from the flash and spectacle of the Bond series. 'Ada' characterised the traditional packet tea user, 'Dolly' her more modern teabag-using counterpart. The appeal of old favourites still seemed to be strong however and therefore this series featured flashbacks to 'greatest hits' such as 'Mr Shifter' and 'Tour de France'. It was hoped that this would enhance the appeal of the campaign – reinforcing the campaign's and the brand's provenance.

Since then, development of the chimps has been driven by the desire to keep them in tune with ever more rapidly changing everyday life. Chimps are no longer shifting pianos but are flying on holiday to Spain, visiting health farms, doing their own DIY, making Board Room decisions and using computers.

This continual updating of the advertising has paid dividends throughout the 34 years of the campaign. As we shall show, the advertising's fame and appeal has remained consistently high.

THE TEA MARKET: 1956 – 1989

Like many British institutions during the 1960s, tea was challenged by the new liberalisation of the times. Sales gradually went into decline as coffee became more appealing to the younger generation and consistently, albeit very slowly, since then, its growth, and that of other substitutes has eroded tea consumption.

TABLE 1: DECLINE IN TEA

	1964	1974	1984	1989
Tea volume (million kg)	156	140	130	110

Source: Nielsen

Two major structural changes have occurred over the last 34 years – the introduction of the *teabag* and the introduction and steadily growing importance of *own label* teas.

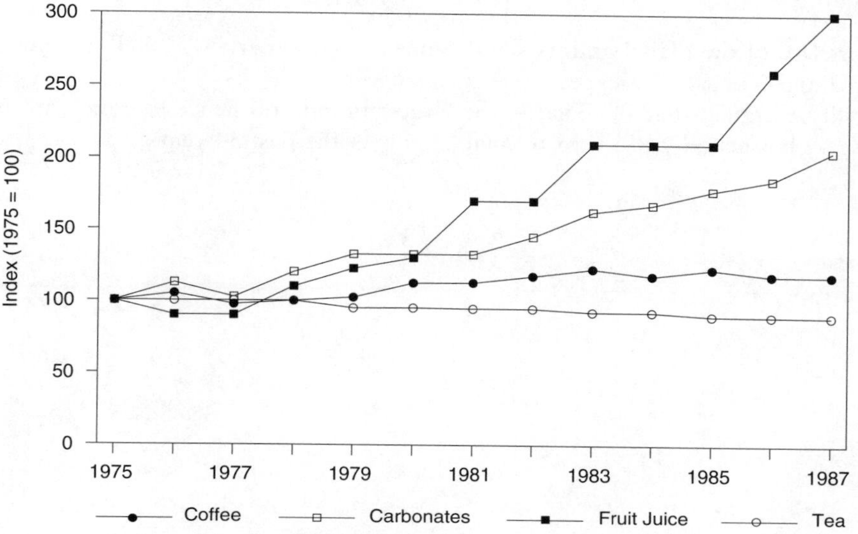

Figure 1. *Trends in drink consumption, average daily intake*
Source: NDS

The Teabag

Teabags, the single most important innovation in the market, were introduced in 1963. Their arrival heralded a format change which dominates today, accounting for 80% of the market.

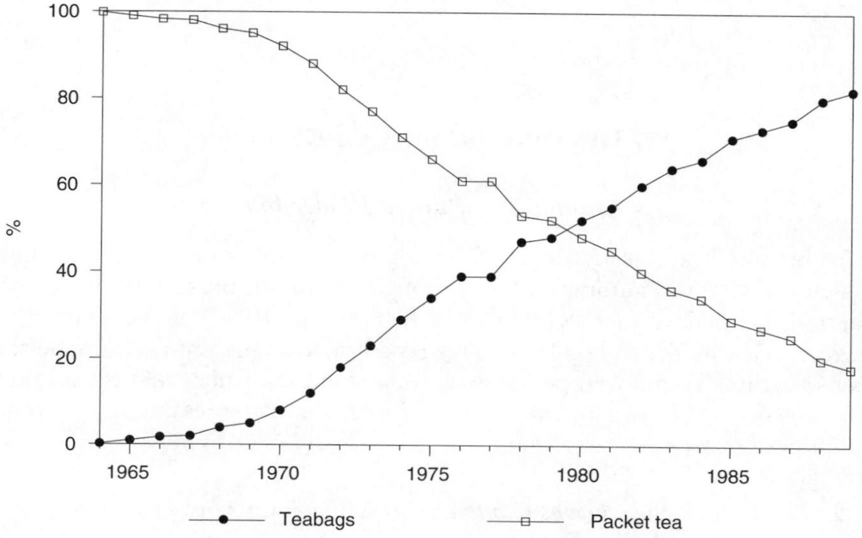

Figure 2. *The change in format, market shares of teabags and packet tea*
Source: Nielsen

The Rise of Own Label

The growth of own label and its significance in many markets is well documented. The tea market has not escaped.

It will be argued that PG Tips – the largest brand and hence the one with most to lose – has actually lost least to own label over the past 34 years.

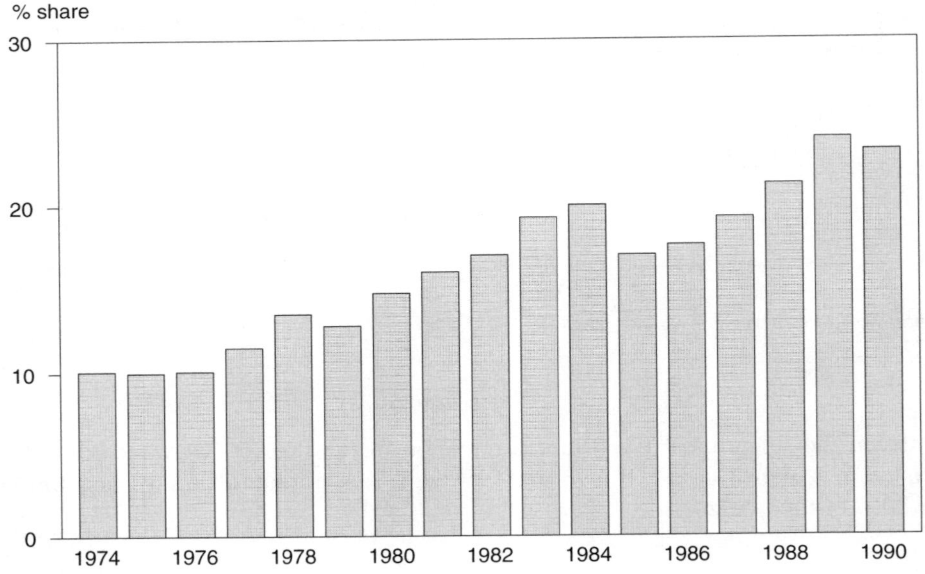

Figure 3. *Own label's advances, share of total tea volume*
Source: Nielsen

PG TIPS PERFORMANCE 1955 – 1958

Assumption of Brand Leadership

PG Tips became brand leader in 1958 having been number four before the chimps campaign rolled out in autumn 1956. Although we do not possess all the data from this period, we believe that PG Tips rose from about 10% volume share in early 1956, to c. 23% by the end of 1958. This represented at the time a dramatic shift in market structure. To put it in perspective, today (and remember that the market has shrunk since 1958) a gain of 13% volume share represents approximately £50 million of extra sales per annum.

The Role of the Chimps Campaign in Achieving Brand Leadership

It has proved impossible to trace accurate sales and other audit figures from the late 1950s. However, the following analysis eliminates other possible causes and suggests that the only causal variable for PG Tips' explosive growth in these two years was the advertising.

1. *Name Change* – Prior to 1955, Pre-Gestive was already colloquially shortened to PG by consumers, possibly because the P and the G were in bold type on the packet. Thus the name change is unlikely to have been such an important factor. Anyway, the change occurred a full year before the advertising started and share did not pick up as a result.
2. *Taste Change* – The blend was not changed at the time of the first chimps commercial.
3. *Distribution Change* – PG Tips was already in very strong distribution as the number four brand (aided by Brooke Bond Dividend's pre-eminence). As own label was not widespread at this time stocking four brands was perfectly normal.
4. *Price Change* – PG Tips was sold at the same price premium to the other brands before and after the advertising broke. So the growth was not caused by advantageous pricing.

What seems much more likely is that the advertising generated large increases in rate of sale.

Circumstantial evidence for the advertising being the root cause is also provided by the fact that this explosive volume share growth coincided with the most rapid increases in penetration of ITV and the chimps were the first TV tea advertising.

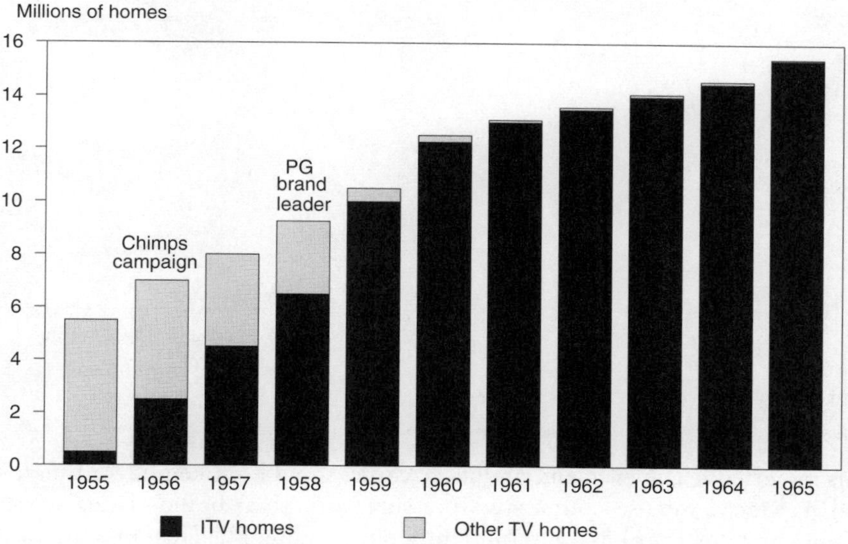

Figure 4. *The rapid growth in homes receiving ITV*
Source: ITV Association

Between 1956 and 1959, penetration of ITV grew fourfold, whereas between 1959 and 1962, it grew by only 35%.

Overall, although data inhibits our ability to 'prove' the claim conclusively, we believe that it is clear that it was the chimps TV advertising that thrust the brand from the number four slot to number one within the space of two years. Whilst the main theme of this paper is to demonstrate long-term advertising effects, we have also therefore shown that at one time the advertising had a very powerful and profitable short-term impact!

PG TIPS PERFORMANCE 1959 – 1989

Sustained Brand Leadership

Ever since PG Tips broke through into the number one position in 1958, it has maintained brand leadership with a consistently high and stable volume share. Unfortunately, we only have accurate share data available from 1968. However, this shows the robustness of the PG Tips performance from this date onwards.

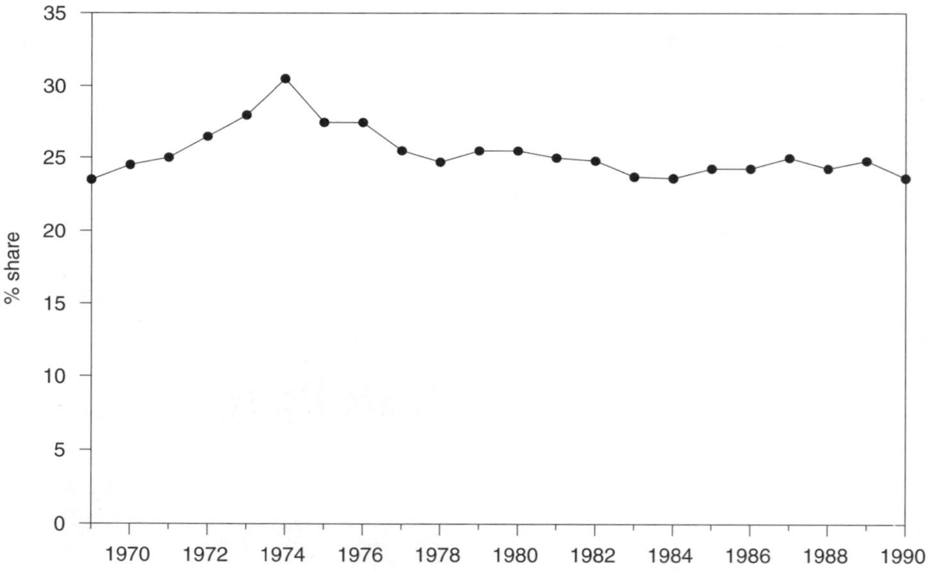

Figure 5. *PG Tips share of total tea market, year ending January*
Source: Nielsen, MEAL
Note: The unusual peak in 1974 coincided with one of the most popular ads, Mr Shifter, and with exceptional media weight

This remarkable achievement, and its rewards, should not be underestimated. The brand has faced intense competitive pressure with rival brands being relaunched (eg Quickbrew in 1986) and intermittently outspending PG Tips. In addition, every conceivable promotional weapon has been used by its rivals in an attempt to wrest away some of the PG Tips share.

The stability of the brand share over this period is evidence that these rival tactics have failed to dent PG Tips position over any significant length of time. Even when PG Tips share has dipped slightly, it has been able to bounce back shortly afterwards.

The Concept of Added Value

PG Tips has been able to maintain such consistent and dominant share leadership because it has assimilated, over the years, an increasing amount of perceived 'added value', which supplements the functional benefits of the product. We have already noted that the brand's functional benefits are essentially generic, we now intend to demonstrate that the brand possesses added non-functional values of sufficient worth to motivate consumers to buy PG Tips even when price and other factors may mitigate against such a decision.

Evidence of Added Value

The evidence that PG Tips has assimilated uniquely powerful added value over the past 34 years comes in many forms.

Branded Versus Blind Tests

Consumers find it very difficult to distinguish between the major brands in blind taste tests. For example, in 1983, when asked to rate tea tastes blind (on a scale of 1 to 7), the average consumer response for the top five brands was extremely similar – varying by only 1 or 2%.

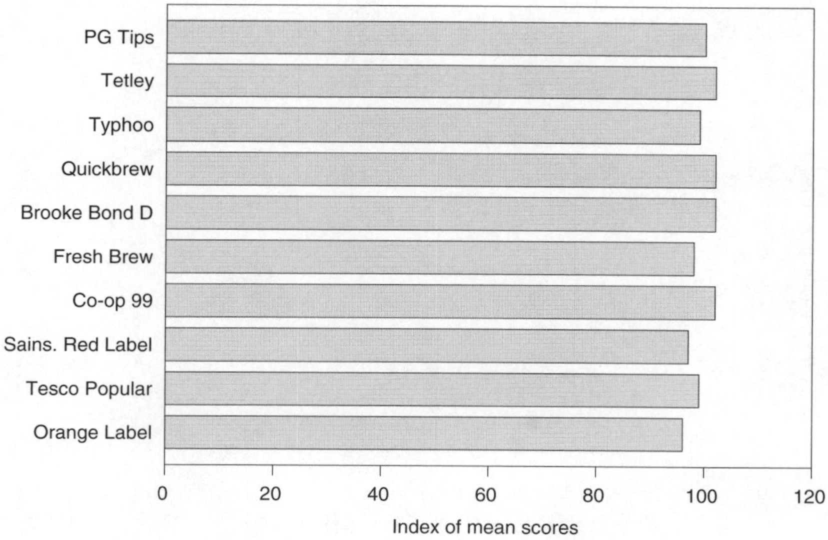

Figure 6. *Consumers find it difficult to identify teas in blind product tests*
Source: Millward Brown, May 1983

This has been the case throughout the brand's history.

However, in *branded* tests, throughout the latter part of the 34 year period, PG Tips has enjoyed the greatest preference.

Even after brand size factors have been eliminated, PG Tips is perceived to be the best tasting cup of tea.

TABLE 2: BRANDED TESTINGS

	PG Tips	Tetley	Typhoo
Best tasting cup of tea (indexed against PG)	100	85	40

Source: Millward Brown, March 1990

This indicates that the brand has indeed attained a perceived added quality which is not justified alone by functional characteristics.

Price Premium

Another significant measure of added value is whether the brand can justify a price premium and continue to sell in significant quantities while doing so – are consumers willing to pay more for a product that is functionally similar to its rivals? We have three pieces of evidence to suggest that PG Tips has succeeded in doing this.

First of all, a superficial glance at pricing data suggests that PG Tips does now command a price premium over the market average, and it does so whilst maintaining its share.

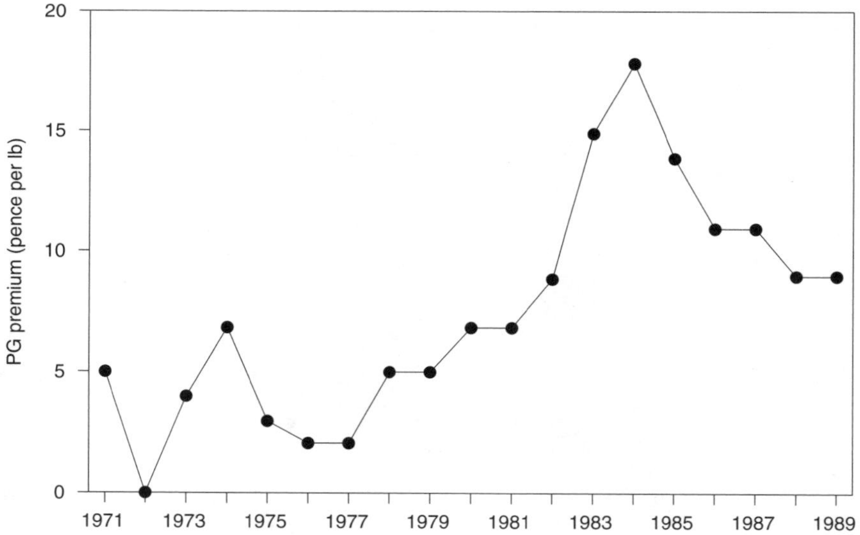

Figure 7. *PG Tips price premium vs market average at 1985 prices*
Source: Nielsen

Secondly, we have performed an econometric analysis using recent data from the teabag sector (now representing 80% of the market volume). This models PG Tips and Tetley's shares against relevant variables, details of which are given in the technical appendix.

The results show PG Tips to be much less sensitive than Tetley to price changes by both branded and own label competitors.

A 1% increase in the price of PG Tips relative to Tetley and Typhoo leads to a drop of 0.4 market share points. The effect of a similar increase in Tetley's price is much larger. A 1% increase in Tetley's price relative to PG Tips and Typhoo results in a downturn of 1.4 share points. We conclude that this is further evidence of the added value of the PG Tips brand compared with its major rivals since it implies that consumers are more likely to ignore price (in favour of other 'values') when it comes to purchasing PG Tips.

Finally, we have concrete evidence of the relative price insensitivity of the brand. In 1977, disaster struck both tea and coffee. Coffee bean and tea leaf prices rocketed. In the coffee market this provoked the introduction of cheaper, chicory based blends which grew to 30% of the market, hitting Nescafé, the brand leader, very hard.

Tea suffered too with market volume plunging by 10%. One might have expected the rapid rise in economy blends of coffee, at the expense of the brand leader, Nescafé, to be mirrored in the tea market with PG Tips. This did not happen. PG Tips retained its price premium and still held onto a 23% brand share – again demonstrating the added value justifying, even in times of crisis, a substantial price premium.

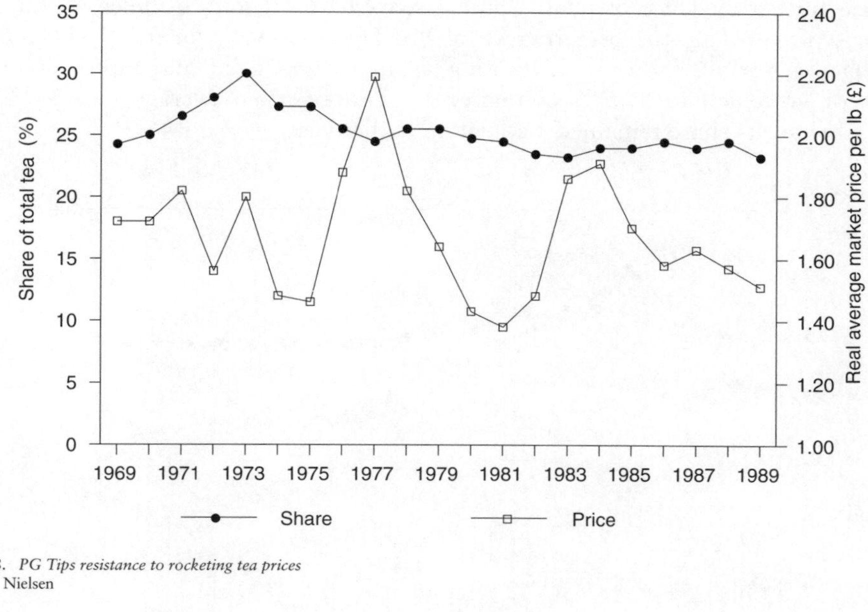

Figure 8. *PG Tips resistance to rocketing tea prices*
Source: Nielsen

Resilience in the Face of Short-term Reductions in Media Support

If indeed the brand has assimilated added values over the past 34 years, then this would suggest that it should be less sensitive to short-term declines in the level of its advertising support.

Our econometric modelling did indeed suggest that this is the case. When less is spent behind the chimps, there is only a very small decline in share in the short-term (0.07 of a share point per 100 TVRs). Similarly, when the Tetley Teafolk are on air there is only a small impact on PG Tips share (PG lose 0.3 share points per 100 TVRs of Tetley advertising), a small proportion of what Tetley gain from spending that amount.

Tetley is far more sensitive to short-term changes in advertising weight. An increase of 100 TVRs per month gives them an extra 1.7 share points. They forfeit similarly for a reduction (see appendix for technical details of how the model was constructed. The appendix also includes data from periods when PG Tips media was withdrawn for up to four months. This confirms that significant share is not lost as a result).

Given this, it is even more impressive that PG Tips can survive off air for a few months, without suffering any significant fallback in share when we know that Tetley's advertising is capable of stealing significant share (from others).

We suggest that this is a further strong indication of the existence and potency of PG Tips added value.

Having said this, there is some downside to having such strong long-term advertising effects. Gaining short-term share from increases in the chimps media weight is relatively expensive. Certainly share is also less sensitive *on the upside* to chimps advertising than Tetley share is to Tetley advertising.

Some further evidence of relative insensitivity to short-term declines in share of voice is provided by the performance of PG Tips following the 1979 ITV strike. During this period, the only advertising available was print and radio. PG Tips share of voice fell to 12.3% compared to a more usual average of 20 – 30%. Nevertheless, its share remained static at 25% that year.

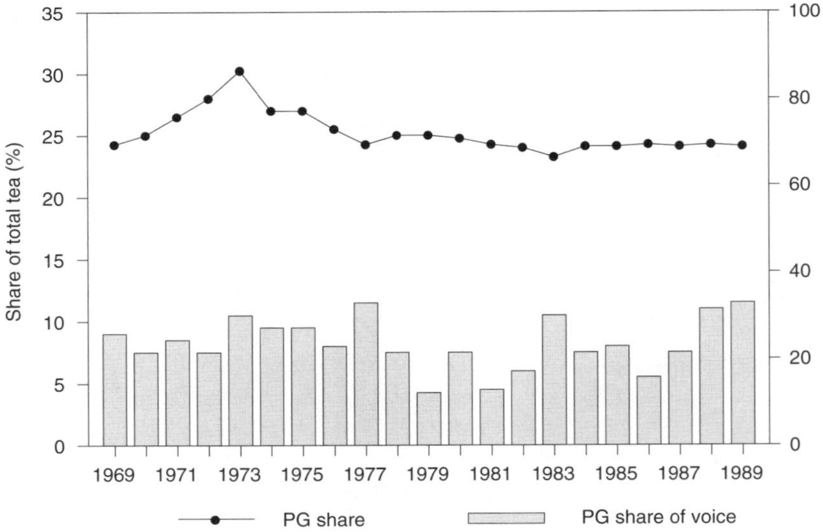

Figure 9. *PG Tips resistance to a low share of voice during the ITV strike in 1979*
Source: Nielsen

Saliency and Consumer Appeal of the Brand

PG Tips is a well known, well loved and well respected brand. All consumer audit data from the past 10 years suggests that it is consistently rated ahead of the competition on a whole raft of scores.

For example, during the whole of the 1980s, the brand has achieved higher spontaneous awareness than its nearest rivals.

TABLE 3: SPONTANEOUS BRAND AWARENESS 1981 – 1989

	PG Tips	Typhoo	Tetley
Average	100	91	58

Source: Millward Brown

In terms of perceived popularity, quality and taste, the brand continually outscores the competition.

TABLE 4: BRAND ATTRIBUTES, MARCH 1990

	Average percentage agreeing PG Tips	Tetley	Typhoo
Particularly popular	100	83	83
Particularly good quality	100	54	76
Best taste	100	85	40

Source: Millward Brown

Hijacking the Teabag Sector

The teabag arrived in 1963 as the product component of the new Tetley brand. Until then, Tetley had not existed as a tea brand at all and has never subsequently introduced 'packet-tea'.

At the time, Brooke Bond were cautious and delayed introducing a PG Tips competitive product. The reasons for this delay are now slightly obscure but three explanations seem plausible.

1. Initial growth of the teabag sector was small. This suggested at the time that Tetley's innovation may have elicited little genuine consumer demand.
2. The volume implications of teabags for the market were negative. When tea is brewed with loose tea, a pot is used which usually encourages waste, and of course, an extra teaspoon of tea is used 'for the pot'. When made with teabags, it is often done in a cup, with less likelihood of waste.
3. PG Tips was already brand leader so it was not in its immediate interest to promote another sector.

Whatever the reason, PG Tips didn't introduce teabags for four years. By then, even though teabags still accounted for a relatively small share of total tea (1.4%), they had been growing by 50% year on year and it was apparent that this share would continue to grow.

Tetley, the innovator in the market, had by then established a strong brand franchise and was brand leader in the teabag sector with a share of 71%.

However, despite the strength of Tetley's position, PG Tips grew steadily and when the proliferation of teabag brands accelerated, it was Tetley not PG that lost share.

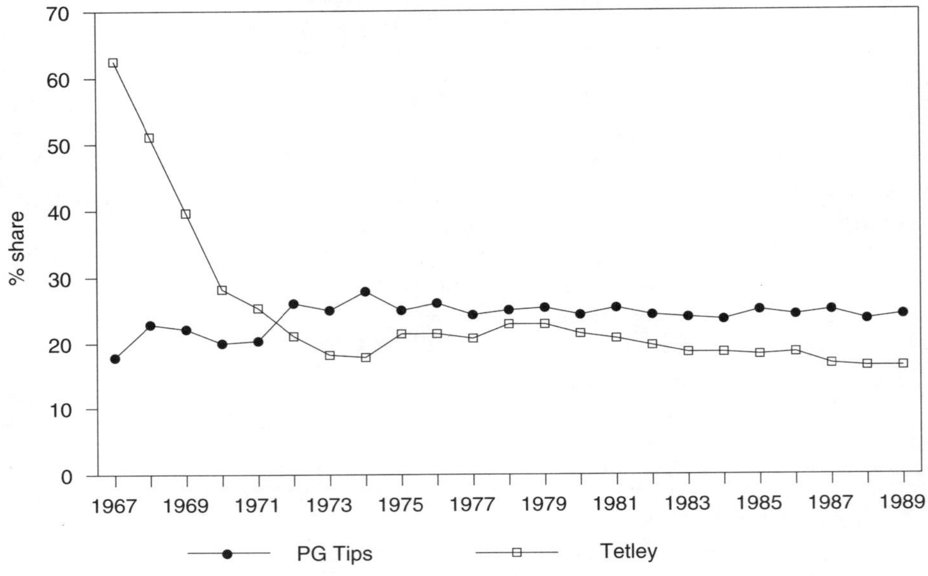

Figure 10. *Overtaking Tetley in the teabags market*
Source: Nielsen

We do not have media spend data for 1967 (the year of PG Tips bags launch) or 1968. However, during 1969, 1970 and 1971, Tetley bags *outspent* PG Tips bags on TV by 22%. Yet, by 1972, PG Tips had attained brand leadership.

The quality of Tetley and PG Tips teabags was equal. Distribution, if anything, favoured Tetley, as did price.

We conclude that this suggests that PG Tips already possessed significant added value compared with Tetley and that it was Tetley's lesser added values that made it the more susceptible of the two brands once competitive attack started in earnest.

Since we prove later that the brand's added value is largely due to the advertising, we can conclude that the advertising played a significant part in enabling PG Tips to hijack leadership in this sector.

The full significance of this is apparent when one considers that having grown from a meagre 1.4%, teabags now represent 80% of the market.

Resilience in the Face of Own Label

Own label's share of the market has grown considerably since the early 1970s as we saw earlier.

One might have expected PG Tips to have lost share to own label in proportion to the brand's size. Maybe, one would have expected it to lose even more since its price premium over own label is higher than for other brands.

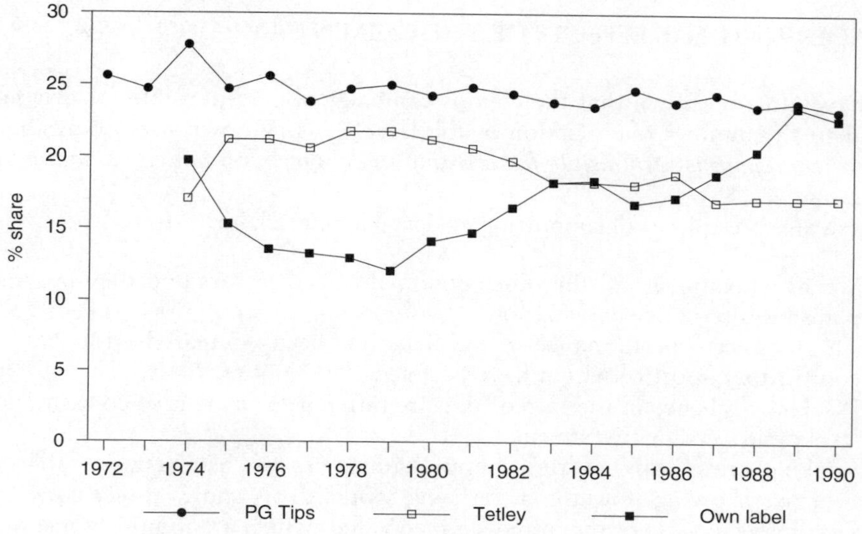

Figure 11. *The advance of own label teabags, PG Tips and Tetley vs Own label, year ending January*
Source: Nielsen

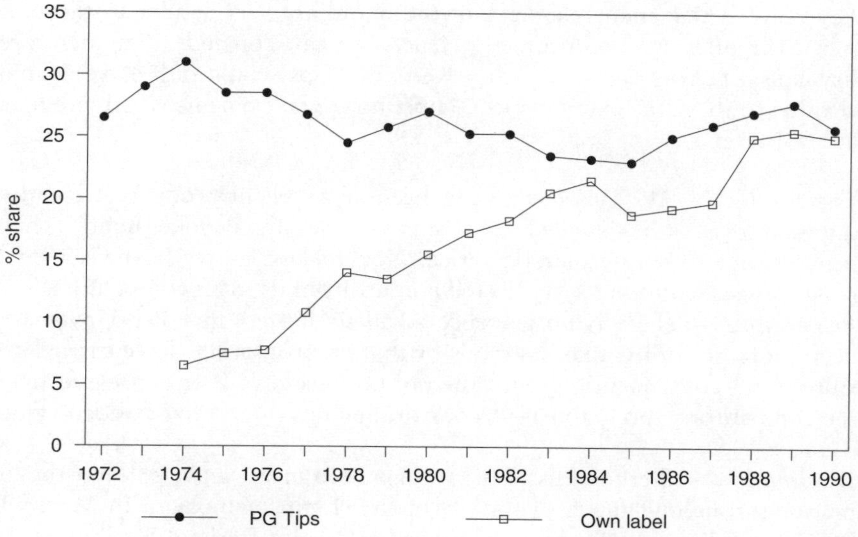

Figure 12. *The advance of own label packet tea, PG Tips vs Own label, year ending January*
Source: Nielsen

In fact, little of own label's growth has been at PG Tips expense. Instead, own label has eaten into the other brands in both packet and bags sectors.

Again, the clear conclusion is that PG Tips is more robust against price-led competition because it possesses added value compared with other branded teas. This enables the brand to offer a different, but very motivating, form of value for money to consumers.

ISOLATING THE EFFECTS OF THE CHIMPS CAMPAIGN: 1959 – 1989

We have already shown that the chimps campaign was responsible for driving the brand to the number one position in the late 1950s. We will now show that *the chimps campaign is responsible for creating the longer term added value the brand possesses.*

There are three pieces of supporting evidence for this claim.

1. We have examined all the other potential causal factors and they provide no plausible alternative explanation.
2. The long-term performance of PG Tips has been compared with that of its competitors, most of whom have declined. The only factors which can explain PG Tips resilience in the face of this are differences in creative content and the level of advertising investment.
3. Looking specifically at the chimps campaign, we have considerable 'soft' evidence showing how the advertising works. This shows direct correlations with many aspects of the brand's added values which are indirectly measurable via quantified consumer research.

Eliminating Other Factors

The key point is that many elements of the brand are very similar to those of our rivals in their offering to consumers. Hence, we can conclude that these are not primary causal factors because, if they were, PG Tips would only have assimilated added value to the same extent as its competitors. The elements which are matched by our rivals are:

1. *The Product* – PG Tips has always been an excellent product. A blend of 28 different teas, it is blended to a standard set by Brooke Bond's chief tea blender, not to a raw material price. Nonetheless, as we have seen, in blind product tests, consumers cannot tell it apart from its main competitors.
2. *Promotions* – There is no evidence at all to suggest that PG Tips has either been more promoted than its rivals or that its promotions have carried greater value. As a consequence, even if the promotions have been more effective than the competitors, surely this is a *result* of the brand's perceived added value, not a *cause*.
3. *Distribution* – Sterling distribution has been near universal for the major brands throughout much of the life of the chimps campaign. In March 1990, PG Tips, Tetley and Typhoo all enjoyed 90% plus sterling distribution. So we can exclude distribution gains.

4. *Price* – PG Tips has consistently maintained a 1% price premium over Tetley and Typhoo, its two closest rivals. Against own label, it has actually increased its premium over time – the brand was 57% more expensive than own label in September 1989 compared with 24% more in September 1971.
   Hence, price *cannot* have been a driving factor. Indeed the data suggests the opposite – that we have been able to enjoy a consistent price premium *as a result* of our added value.
5. *Packaging* – This is a more difficult variable to eliminate completely. The very nature of packaging means that the PG Tips pack is very different from its rivals – hence, it cannot easily be dismissed as a variable that is equivalent to that of other brands. Indeed, we feel that the PG Tips packaging – the tea-picker, red and green colour coding and 'PG Tips' block branding – and its consistency have played a part in building brand recognition for the brand, and its appearance must be an important factor.
   However, we also believe that the Tetley and Typhoo packaging elements are strong. It seems unlikely to us that PG Tips packaging alone could be so much more capable of adding so much value to the brand. This conclusion is circumstantially supported by the following chart which shows that claimed consumer appeal of these major brands' packs is roughly equal and certainly not significant in PG Tips favour.

TABLE 5: CONSUMER APPEAL OF PACKS 1981 – 1989

	Average percentage agreeing		
	PG Tips	Typhoo	Tetley
Has an attractive pack	100	94	114

Source: Millward Brown

6. *Repeat Purchase* – It is conceivable that consistent use of the brand will reinforce positive experience and build added value which will in turn prompt further purchase – almost a self-supporting system once it has started.
   This may be true. If it is, however, it is clear that advertising has played a role in this in two ways.
   First, the initial consumer franchise (in 1957/58) was largely attracted through the advertising.
   Secondly, we know that 'experience' of the brand in terms of all variables except advertising and packaging is matched by our rivals who have definitely not benefited in this way. Hence, if repeat purchase is a driving factor for added value then advertising is still largely responsible for this phenomenon.

Overall, this analysis leads us to believe that the only significant factors remaining which could have caused PG Tips assimilation of added value are the content of its advertising and the media weight behind it.

Comparison With Other Brands Performance

Many of PG Tips competitors have declined substantially over the last 20 or so years. The following table lists some of the losers.

TABLE 6: LONG-TERM SHARE TRENDS – STANDARD TEABAGS

	1975	1980	1985	1990
Tetley	21.2	21.1	18.1	17.2
Quickbrew	10.8	9.5	6.4	4.6
Typhoo/ Freshbrew	11.1	9.0	6.4	7.1

Source: Nielsen, year ending January
Note: We only have historical data for Typhoo and Freshbrew combined

What is interesting, however, is that before their major decline, all of these brands were approximately equal to PG Tips in terms of their product qualities, pricing and distribution. Packaging of course was different, but not significantly lower in 'quality' or appeal.

The declining fortunes of each of these brands correlates instead with a strategy of *chopping and changing the content* of the advertising and with *lower support* for the advertising.

Hence, this offers further proof that advertising can have a very significant effect in this market. We would suggest that this makes it even more likely that PG Tips has added value precisely because of the more consistent support of its highly impactful creative vehicle and heavier media weight.

How the Advertising Works

Further circumstantial evidence for the part advertising has played in growing the brand's added value can be seen in analysis of how consumers react specifically to this advertising.

Awareness and Appeal

The chimps campaign has the highest level of awareness of all tea campaigns.

TABLE 7: ADVERTISING RECALL INDICES 1981 – 1989

	PG Tips	Typhoo	Tetley
Prompted recall	100	51	77

Source: Millward Brown

It is also the most efficient campaign in terms of generating awareness. According to Millward Brown, PG Tips advertising index is the highest in the market. (This is defined as the percentage gain in advertising awareness that would be produced by

100 TVRs in a theoretical TV region where no advertising had previously been shown).

TABLE 8: ADVERTISING RECALL INDICES 1981 – 1989

PG Tips	Typhoo	Tetley
100	51	67

Source: Millward Brown

Combined with the heavy media weights of the past 34 years, it is hard to believe that such an impactful campaign as this had not had a significant impact on the consumer perception of the brand's value.

In addition, we know that the advertising is well loved.

TABLE 9: ATTITUDES TO THE ADVERTISING 1981 – 1989

	Market average	Chimps
Amusing	100	139
Better than other tea ads	100	146
Would enjoy seeing again	100	162

Source: Millward Brown

Given that consumers tend to talk about the chimps as part of the brand, it seems plausible that the above data suggests that the advertising is at least partly responsible for the brand's emotional appeal which in turn is surely what the added value of the brand is built on.

We also have further evidence of the advertising's inextricable role in building the brand's added value.

Communication of specific brand benefits

The chimps advertising has always claimed in one form or another that

'There is no other tea to beat PG .... It's the taste'.

We know from consumer response to the advertising in qualitative research that the chimps campaign is 'loved'. The frame of reference for describing the campaign is always one of affection and warmth. It seems clear that the entertaining and lovable nature of the advertising enables this message of extra quality to be accepted – surely this is one direct way in which the advertising can be seen to have added value to the brand.

Assumption of Tea Values

Finally, in qualitative research, many consumers describe the advertising almost as 'a pick-me-up'.

'It gives me a lift after a hard day'.

This is also in fact precisely how people talk about their preferred tea. It seems that the brand and the chimps have almost become one. It is easy then to see how the appeal of the advertising which we have shown can translate into appeal for the brand.

We suggest that 34 years of such a mechanic has indeed added value, beyond functional qualities, to PG Tips.

Summary

We have previously shown that the brand has assimilated added value over the past 34 years.

Later we demonstrated that this *added value was primarily built and sustained by the chimps advertising*. Therefore we can conclude that the advertising has played a fundamental part in producing and maintaining PG Tips dominance in this competitive market.

THE FINANCIAL CONTRIBUTION OF THE ADVERTISING

Since we have shown that the advertising was primarily responsible for investing the brand with the added value it now possesses, an analysis of the financial contribution should attempt to quantify financially this added value. The methodology to do this is not completely available to us. However, we can quantify three specific consequences of the power of the advertising and the added value it has generated. These instances alone suggest that the advertising has paid for itself many times over.

Financial Benefits of Long-term Brand Leadership

Without the short-term effectiveness of the chimps campaign from 1956 to 1958, it is unclear how PG Tips could have grown share substantially because the three brands above it at the time were all strong. Once it had achieved the number one position, we have already shown that the advertising played a primary role in maintaining that dominance.

Therefore, one way to evaluate advertising's contribution is to consider what revenue would have been lost if PG Tips had continued as the fourth brand.

From this it can be deduced that the chimps have helped the brand achieve an extra £2,000m sales over this 20 year period alone.

Brooke Bond are understandably unwilling to disclose margin data, but even on quite conservative estimates, the profit generated is much higher than the total of the amount spent on media and production over the whole 34 year period. The costs over the last 20 years at 1985 prices have been £86m (as measured by MEAL) on media and £6m on production.

Financial Benefits of Price Premium

It is possible that the above scenario shows the campaign's profit contribution in too positive a light. Maybe the brand would have grown without advertising or with a campaign run on a much lower media spend (although we doubt this). However, another way to evaluate the chimps' contribution is to look at the revenue generated over the 32 years since the brand reached number one, by the price premium that we believe that the advertising supported. If we assume that PG Tips could only have charged average branded prices to maintain its volume without the chimps, the extra revenue is still some £125m (at 1985 prices) over the last 20 years alone.

Financial Benefits of Hijacking the Teabag Market

Finally, we can look at the revenue generated by being able to assume brand leadership in the teabag market compared with what might have happened without the chimps.

If we assume that without the chimps, PG Tips teabags would have remained second brand to Tetley teabags with a share equivalent to the current number two brand, then PG Tips would lose £200m of revenue (at 1985 prices) which it gained because it assumed the number one position in 1972. This ignores the advertising costs of supporting the number two brand which would significantly increase this loss.

Summary

Whichever of these methods is used, the advertising's effect over the 34 year period more than justified its cost.

SUMMARY

Overall then there can be little doubt that PG Tips has been tremendously successful over the past 34 years. Brooke Bond has had the marketing foresight to continue to invest in rather than just milk, such a strong brand.

As a result, we have seen that PG Tips has remained brand leader over the whole of the period whilst fighting off fierce competitive challenges particularly in the form of Tetley's teabags and the growth of own label. Not only that, but it has remained price leader as well.

We have also seen that Brooke Bond have done this by investing the brand with added value that prompts consumers to continue buying even when more functional qualities of the brand suggest that other brand choices would be at least as satisfactory in purely functional terms.

This is perhaps the definition of what differentiates a true brand from a product.

And we have demonstrated that the chimps advertising has been the primary generator of this added brand value. Without it, or with advertising only as effective in the long-term as other tea brands it seems extremely unlikely that PG Tips would have been able to fight off such strong competitive activity.

Finally we have seen that quantifying the financial contribution of the advertising is difficult, but three methods have been used to show that it has generated a financial value for the brand well above its cost.

CONCLUSION

Brooke Bond have created in PG Tips a brand that has enormous value to consumers. As a consequence, more consumers choose it compared with its rivals even though it sells at a price premium.

In addition, the brand's perceived value is so strong that it can actually *exploit* a *rival's* innovation. In a market place where technical barriers to entry are very low, this ability is vital for the brand's long-term maintenance of leadership. After all, no brand, not even PG Tips, can have a monopoly on successful innovation over a long time period.

We believe that there are two key lessons to be learnt from all this, which are inter-related:

1. The importance of foresight. In maintaining brand leadership, a brand is going to encounter unexpected and unplanned for competitive activity. The only way to guarantee successful repulsion of these attacks is to have *already* built added values into the brand. Waiting until the threat is specifically known is costly and could be fatal.
2. The importance of consistent advertising support. If the paper has shown nothing else, it has shown that *consistency* in a very strong creative vehicle and in high levels of media weight can ensure the brand does indeed become invested with added value and can pay back dramatically over the long-term.

Taken together, these two points suggest the critical part treating advertising as a long-term investment can play in building and maintaining a brand's strength. PG Tips is and will continue to be a testament to that.

TECHNICAL APPENDIX

Ideally we would have wished to construct a very long run econometric model to try and test some of our hypotheses about whether, as PG Tips continued to advertise, its response to marketing variables was changing over time, eg whether it was becoming less price sensitive or less vulnerable to competitive activity. Our only available long-run of data however was annual and was not sufficient therefore in terms of the number of available data points to start constructing a complex model.

So, in order to investigate PG Tips responses, we tested our hypotheses 'cross-sectionally'. That is we constructed two models, one of PG Tips and one of

Tetley, and made comparisons of the market share responses of the two brands to the various pressures in the teabag market. From consumer data we knew that differences between the products were imperceptible and thus that any difference in terms of response to price etc was not a result of product difference.

The two models were estimated using 'ordinary least squares' on monthly Nielsen data from its start at the end of 1985 to December 1989.

For reasons of confidentiality, we do not wish to report the exact structures of the models. Both models, however, fitted the data well and performed very acceptably on a range of statistical tests. They included variables like branded competitive price, own label price, own label distribution, own and competitive advertising and the introduction of any line extensions/packaging changes.

In pricing terms, the models were similar in structure; the overall impact of price changes however differed markedly with PG Tips being much less sensitive to price than Tetley. Their response to advertising was quite different. Tetley was much more volatile, exhibiting marked short-term blips as a result of advertising but which died away quite quickly.

The following statistical tests and diagnostics for the fit and specification of both models were carried out and reported: R^2, standard error of the regression, sum of squared residuals, DW, Lagrange multiplier tests (portmanteau tests for higher order autocorrelation) with up to 1, 4 and 12 lags, ARCH tests for auto-regressive heteroscedasticity (1, 4 and 12 lags), the variance ratio test for homoscedasticity and the two Chow tests for post-sample predictive failure and for parameter stability and homoscedasticity respectively.

Both models have subsequently continued to predict the market well.

9

Anheuser-Busch

The launch of Bud Ice – how advertising helped strengthen rather than dilute the Budweiser brand

BACKGROUND

Introduction

When Anheuser-Busch launched Bud Ice in the summer of 1996, Budweiser, for the first time in the UK, became a 'stretched' brand.

It is sometimes feared that such a launch can dilute the main brand. This paper shows the opposite. It demonstrates that Bud Ice, when supported by appropriate advertising, not only was a major success in its own right, but also had a positive effect on its parent.

Market background

The Packaged Lager (PL) market is split into standard (SPL) and premium (PPL).[1]

In 1996, Budweiser was the number one PPL brand in the on-trade and number two in the off-trade.[2] However, compared with the four largest brewers, Anheuser-Busch was a relatively minor player, and hungry for further success.

Hence, the decision was made to grow Anheuser-Busch's share of the PL market, via a new PPL. Deciding which brand this should be was influenced by consumer motivations in this market.

1. PL is defined as all products which are lager, come in a can or bottle. SPL is defined as a PL comtaining less than 4.3% alcohol by volume (ABV). PPL is defined as a PL containing between 4.3% and 7.5%. Historically, there has been a gap of some 1+% ABV between the premium and standard brands. Recently the ABV's between the standard and premium lagers have narrowed, making an exact bifurication slightly more problematic. The PL market also contains the super-strengths (7.5%+ ABV).
2. The on-trade is where consumption is on premise (eg pubs), the off trade where it is off premise (eg supermarkets).

Attitudes to PPL brands

Put simply, our 18–24 year old male target audience (for it is they who drink by far the most PPLs) respect two different kinds of PPL brand: 'classic' and 'modern'. Being eclectic, most switch easily between the two. Hence, they are more correctly segmented by states of mind on particular occasions, rather than by actual groups of individuals.

Classic brands offer quality credentials. They have stood the test of time. They promise an authenticity and a provenance. Modern brands, conversely, gain their relevance directly from their modernity: manufactured for the now, directly for their target's needs – in a sense, deliberately artificial.

Classic brand	**Modern brand**
Consistent	Innovative
Heritage/authenticity	Now!
Provenance	Here!

By 1996, with its American heritage and provenance, Budweiser was the epitome of a 'classic' PPL brand. However, this meant it was not competing in the 'modern' sector.

Hence, a new 'modern' brand seemed sensible. Potentially, this would generate new sales while minimising cannibalisation.

The Ice market

Many of the successful 'modern' PPL brands until 1996 had been Ice brands.

Ice beers, pioneered by Labatt Ice at the end of 1993, are brewed using a new process in which ice particles are formed. This produces a refreshing, light and quaffable lager, which retains a strong alcohol content. Fosters Ice, the most successful by 1996, uses clear glass to display the light and refreshing looking liquid. The name, the taste and the packaging collectively suggest a particular type of occasion – perhaps on a hot dance floor or at a crowded party.

The Ice sector was growing and showed no signs of decline. Hence, in the summer of 1996, Anheuser-Busch launched its own version – Bud Ice.

TABLE 1: THE ICE SECTOR AT THE TIME OF BUD ICE'S LAUNCH

	Lanch dates	On-trade share[3]	Off-trade share
Fosters Ice	July 1994	3.8%	0.9%
Labatt Ice	December 1993	2.3%	0.4%
Carlserg Ice	September 1994	1.3%	0.2%

Source: Nielsen MAT vol. share[4]

3. All share figures in this paper show volume share of the total packaged lager market. Nielsen data is bi-monthly. The on- and off-trade are always a month out of synch with each other. So, while there is a off-trade data for the May/June bi-month, there is on-trade data for April/May.
4. MAT to May/June 1996 in off-trade, April/May 1996 is on-trade. Nielsen data is bi-monthly. The on- and off-trade are always a month out of synch with each other. So, while there is a off-trade data for the May/June bi-month, there is on-trade data for April/May.

Bud Ice was disadvantaged by being fourth into a market in which the incumbents had already had two years in which to establish themselves. Further, the other brands had already spent heavily on advertising to consolidate their positions: (Figure 1).

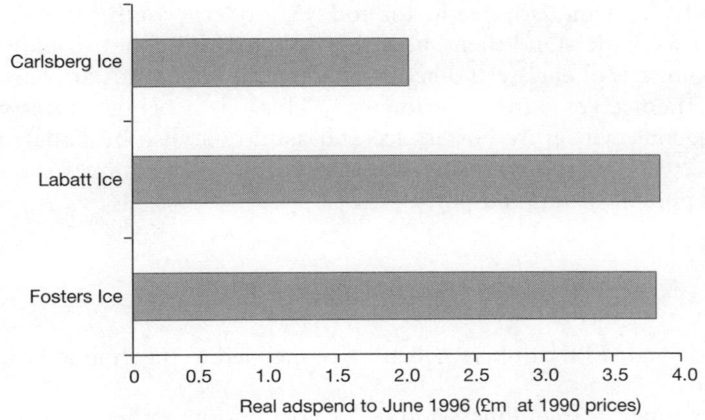

Figure 1: *Ice brands: total adspend since launch*
Sources: Register-MEAL, Advertising Association

Marketing objectives

In the on-trade, the tied system was likely to limit Bud Ice's distribution vis-à-vis the other Ice brands.[5] Hence, while in the off-trade share objectives were set, on-trade objectives were set in terms of rate of sale (ROS).

The marketing objective was to increase overall Anheuser-Busch share in the UK PL category, by:

1. Becoming number one Ice beer in the off-trade in volume share within two years.
2. Becoming number one Ice beer in the on-trade in ROS within two years.
3. Keeping the cannibalisation of Budweiser to a minimum in both on and off trades.

These were ambitious targets, given the disadvantages accruing from the late entry.

Given the level of competitive adspend, if Bud Ice was to meet these objectives, it seemed probable that its own advertising would have to play a major role. The brief was as follows.

5. The UK's four main breweries were vertically integrated businesses in a way Anheuser-Busch was not. Hence, a brewer such as ScotCo would stock its own Fosters Ice, and refuse to stock a competitor Ice. Even in the Independent outlets there were potential hurdles, with the larger brewers offering bulk deals on their portfolios (including draught and no-lager products, as well as PLs).

CREATIVE BRIEF

Opportunity

Because Bud Ice is a modern brand for today's modern youth, we need to show explicitly that we understand them, how they live, and how they drink.

The Ice promise is of energy and hedonism; and the Ice brands are ones which do not take themselves too seriously. This is being interpreted as laddish/outrageous/cynical by Fosters Ice and as ultra-stylish by Labatt Ice. While these have led to popular advertising, the richest vein for our target is quite simply the relentless pursuit of fun and party.

Target audience

18–24 year old male PPL drinkers, when more inclined to buy 'modern' rather than 'classic' brands.

They aspire towards friendliness and lack of pretension, rather than cynicism and laddishness – aspirations honed by the ethics of drugs culture, and the demise of the 1980s. Everyone's welcome – as long as they're not pretentious or a poser.

Proposition

Bud Ice is the party beer!

Support in image terms

1. It's a beer to have fun with, ideal for parties or nights out.
2. It's not a beer which takes itself too seriously.
3. It understands the happy-go-lucky culture of today's youth.

Support in product terms

It's perfect for parties and dance floors: refreshing, drinkable and cold.

Tone

Down-to-earth, fun, all-inclusive, optimistic.

Choice of media

Although the 18–24 male can be hard to reach by TV, it was decided that TV should be the primary medium. TV offered the opportunity to build coverage and frequency rapidly around the launch, and the best chance of producing 'talked about' creative.

With secondary media, we used selected press titles to ensure that we reached style leaders. Further, radio – a cost-effective method in reaching the 18–24 year old age group – was used to bolster total coverage.

ADVERTISING ACTIVITY

TV advertising

In the first execution, 'Ants', ants tip a Bud Ice bottle into their anthill in the middle of a hot desert before starting to party. 'Anteater' shows them getting one over on an anteater meddling in their fun. Both ads are set to popular 1970s disco tracks.

In the ants, we had a fun and instantly popular device to communicate the all-inclusive, hedonistic world of our consumers.

Consumer response

> The ants are us!
>
> They work hard and play hard – and that's what we do too.

Source: BMP Qual

Radio advertising

Radio used a translation of the TV work – with the retention of the 'Get Down Tonight!' track, and skits on partying ants.

Press advertising

An insert was included in listings magazines and style press, in the form of a Bud Ice branded luggage tag. It invited readers to fill in their name and address, and attach it to themselves.

Media schedule

From launch in June 1996 until the end of 1997, the majority of spend was on TV.

TABLE 2: MEDIA SPEND

	Spend (£000s)	Share of Bud Ice spend
TV	1,840	88%
Press	122	5%
Radio	80	3%

Source: Register-MEAL

The schedule was as follows:

	6 96	7 96	8 96	9 96	10 96	11 96	12 96	1 97	2 97	3 97	4 97	5 97	6 97	7 97	8 97	9 97	10 97	11 97	12 97
TV			XXX	XXX	XXX								XXX	XXX	XXX	XXX	XXX	XXX	
Press					XXX		XXX	XXX											
Radio												XXX	XXX	XXX	XXX	XXX	XXX	XXX	XXX

There were two bursts of TV activity. A limited budget meant we had to spend wisely. As 20% of PL volume went through London, and London was a strong Fosters Ice region, only London received advertising support in the first TV burst.

In the larger, second burst, there were resources for light, national advertising with strong regional upweights. Scotland as well as London was upweighted. This was because Scotland was a relatively strong Anheuser-Busch area in which Bud Ice had been growing slower than anticipated.

The other regions received no support at all in the first TV burst, and less support than London and Scotland in the second. We will term these other regions, collectively, as the 'control'. Bud Ice TVRs are shown in Figure 2.

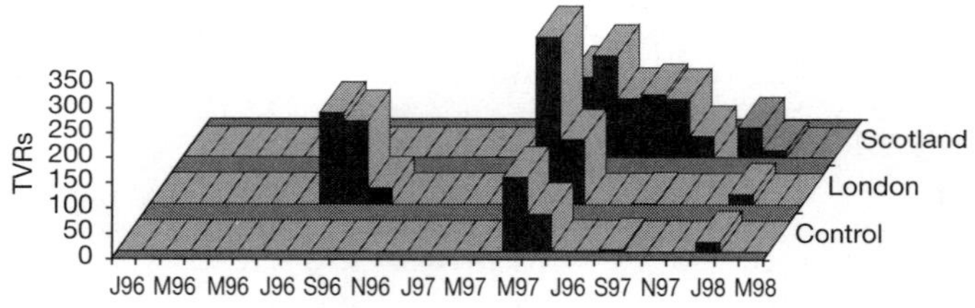

Figure 2: *Bud Ice TVRs by region*
Sources: BARB

PERFORMANCE AGAINST OBJECTIVES

Overall objective

To increase overall Anheuser-Busch share in the Packaged Lager market.
Anheuser-Busch did achieve a step change in share after the Bud Ice launch (Table 3).

TABLE 3: STEP CHANGE IN SHARE AFTER BUD ICE LAUNCH

	On trade A–B share	Off trade A–B share
August 1995–July 1996 (pre)	21.7%	2.4%
August 1996–July 1997 (post)	25.7%	3.3%

Source: Nielsen

Although share was also growing before the launch due to Budweiser's success, the *rate* of share increase also increased dramatically as can be seen in Table 4, Figure 3, Table 5 and Figure 4.

TABLE 4: ANHEUSER-BUSCH SHARE OF PL MARKET OFF-TRADE

Off-trade	A–B market share	Share change
August 1994–July 1995	2.2%	Pre: +0.2pp[6]
August 1995–July 1996	2.4%	
August 1996–July 1997	3.3%	Post: 0.9pp

Source: Nielsen MATs

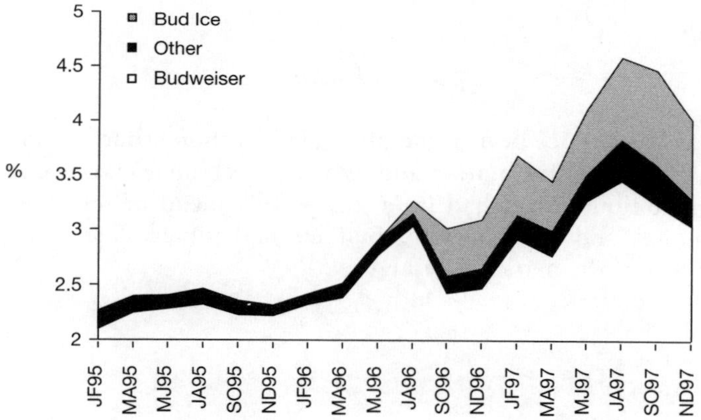

Figure 3: *Anheuser-Busch share of PL market off trade*
Sources: Nielsen

TABLE 5: ANHEUSER-BUSCH SHARE OF PL MARKET ON-TRADE

On-trade	A–B market share	Share change
August 1994–July 1995	19.1%	Pre: +2.6pp[6]
August 1995–July 1996	21.7%	
August 1996–July 1997	25.7%	Post: 4.0pp

Source: Nielsen MATs

6. pp = percentage points.

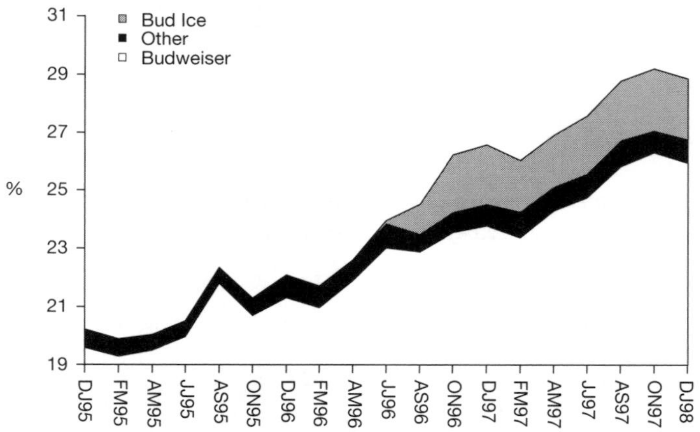

Figure 4: *Anheuser-Busch share of PL market on trade*
Sources: Nielsen MATs

Specific objective 1

To become number one Ice beer in the off-trade in volume share within two years. Despite being fourth into the market and two years behind everyone else, by the end of 1997 this ambitious target had been met – well ahead of schedule. Fuelled by strong distribution and ROS growth, Bud Ice had joined Fosters Ice as market leader, with 0.8% of the market (see Figure 5).

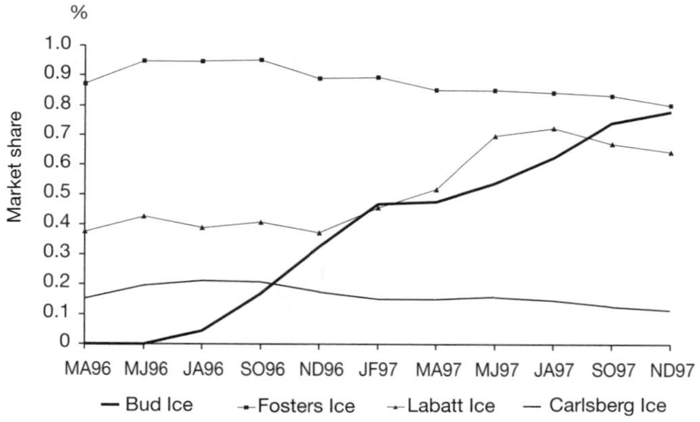

Figure 5: *Ice brands: market share off-trade*
Sources: Nielsen – rolling six monthly data

Specific objective 2

To become number one Ice beer in the on-trade in ROS within two years.

Due to the tied brewery system, distribution was indeed very hard to come by here (Table 6).

TABLE 6: DISTRIBUTION OF ICE BEERS

On-trade	Distribution[7]
Fosters Ice	16%
Bud Ice	8%
Labatt Ice	8%
Carlsberg Ice	6%

Source: Nielsen latest six months data[8]

However, the second market objective was met. By the end of 1997, earlier than planned, Bud Ice had succeeded in becoming the Ice beer with the highest ROS as can be seen in Figure 6.

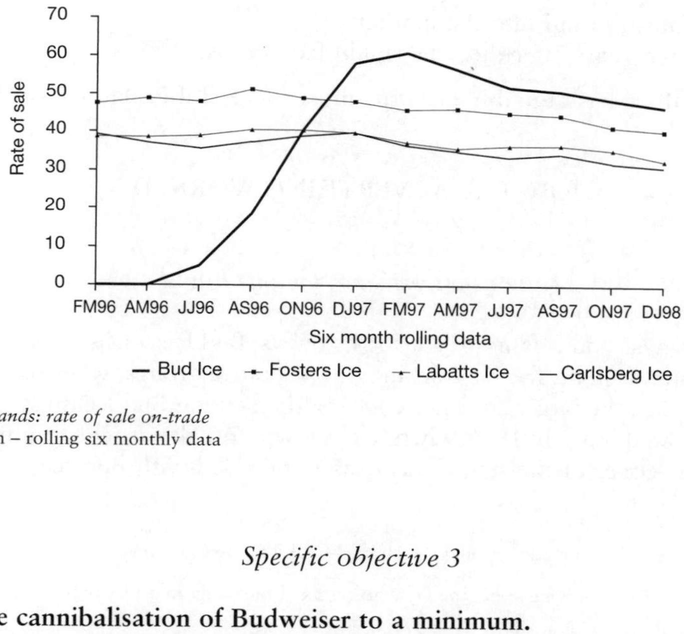

Figure 6: *Ice brands: rate of sale on-trade*
Sources: Nielsen – rolling six monthly data

Specific objective 3

To keep the cannibalisation of Budweiser to a minimum.
Budweiser kept growing just as strongly after Ice was launched, and in the off-trade the rate of growth actually accelerated (Table 7 and Table 8). Hence we would suggest that cannibalisation was minimal.

TABLE 7: ON-TRADE RATE OF GROWTH

On-trade	Budweiser market share	Rate of share change
August 1994–July 1995	18.5%	+2.6pp
August 1995–July 1996	21.1%	
August 1996–July 1997	23.6%	+2.6pp

Source: Nielsen MATs

7. Numeric distribution.
8. Up until the latest available bi-monthly data point – Nov/Dec 1997 in the off-trade and Dec 1997/Jan 1998 in the on-trade.

TABLE 8: OFF-TRADE RATE OF GROWTH

Off-trade	Budweiser market share	Rate of share change
August 1994–July 1995	2.2%	+0.2pp
August 1995–July 1996	2.4%	
August 1996–July 1997	2.8%	+0.4pp

Source: Nielsen MATs

Summary of performance

Within a year and a half of launch, Bud Ice had equalled or bettered the market leader in terms of share in the off-trade and ROS in the on-trade. Furthermore, this was achieved in just a year and a half – well ahead of the (ambitious) two year schedule. And this was despite:

1. being the fourth brand into the market;
2. launching two years after the other main Ice brands.

Given this, Bud Ice has arguably been the most successful PL launch of the 1990s.

HOW THE ADVERTISING WORKED

Famous advertising, famous brand

The advertising was and is famous. During its bursts, Bud Ice consistently outperforms the other Ice brands in awareness tracking. In qualitative groups, when asked to recall their favourite ads, the target audience consistently mention Bud Ice most frequently.

This culminated in early 1998 when 'Get Down Tonight' reached number two in the charts. The cover of the single was heavily branded with Bud Ice, the ants and the anteater.

> We've heard of music from ads topping the charts – well this owes its very being to the telly ad
>
> Livingstone, the DJ who remixed the song, in a recent BBC1 radio interview

This has had repercussions for the brand, where a quick build in awareness was a key element to the success of the launch. Despite the length of time they have existed, Bud Ice is more highly recalled than Labatt Ice or Carlsberg Ice – and is now just a little behind Fosters Ice in awareness measures:[9] Table 9.

TABLE 9: BRAND AWARENESS

	Bud Ice	Fosters Ice	Labatt Ice	Carlsberg Ice
Prompted awareness	93	96	93	n/a
Spontaneous awareness	7	10	5	2

Source: Millward Brown

9. If measures such as spontaneous awareness are to an extent a function of the brand being seen around, this is particularly impressive given Bud Ice's inevitable distribution disadvantage in the on-trade.

There are two pieces of evidence demonstrating advertising's role in this.

1. Timing of bursts

Nationally, there is a very clear correlation between the advertising bursts and uplifts in Bud Ice awareness.

When the first burst began, spontaneous awareness built immediately. When the burst finished, it settled. It began to rise again the very week the second burst began. Once again, as the advertising declined, so did the awareness (Figure 7).

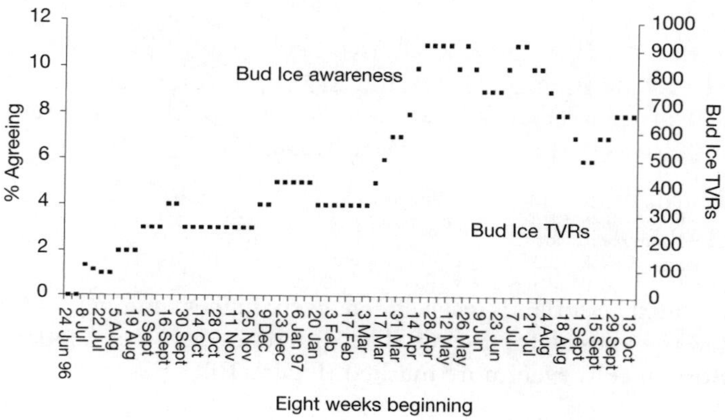

Figure 7: *Bud Ice spontaneous awareness vs advertising*
Sources: Millward Brown, BARB

2. Regional analysis

In burst one, London was the only region supported with TV. There, the increase in spontaneous awareness outstripped the control many times over (Figure 8).

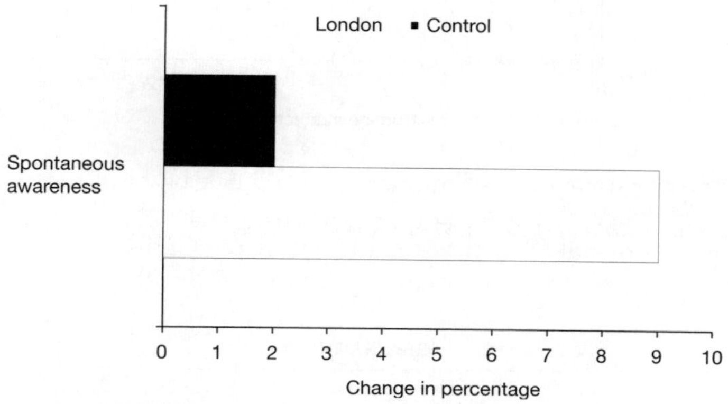

Figure 8: *Changes in Bud Ice awareness*
Burst 1: London vs control area
Sources: Millward Brown – 8 weeks to 19 August 1996 vs 8 weeks to 4 November 1996

During the second burst, all regions were supported with TV, but London received a higher number of ratings than the Control regions. Once again, London outperformed the Control (Figure 9).

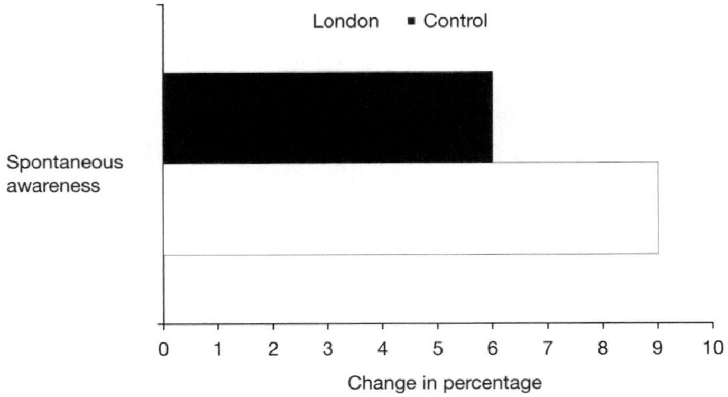

Figure 9: *Changes in Bud Ice awareness*
Burst 2: London vs control area
Sources: Millward Brown – 8 weeks to 28 April 1997 vs 8 weeks to 23 June 1997

In the second burst, Scotland received an even higher number of ratings than London, and was exposed for longer. The difference between Scotland's and the Control's performance is even more marked (Figure 10):

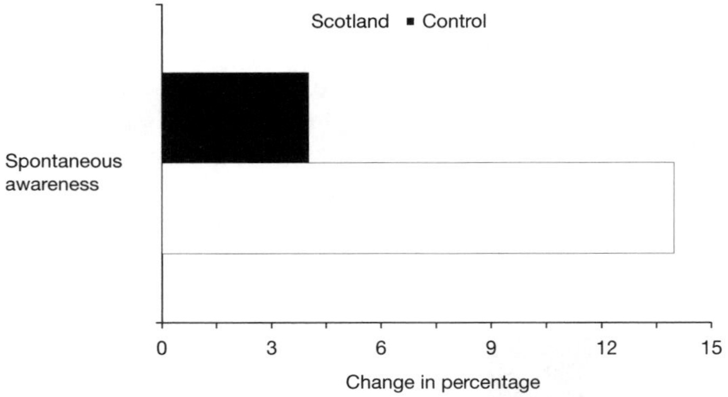

Figure 10: *Changes in Bud Ice awareness*
Burst 2: Scotland vs control area
Sources: Millward Brown – 8 weeks to 28 April 1997 vs 8 weeks to 11 August 1997[10]

Popularity

Qualitatively, the identification of the target with the ants, the cartoon humour, and the fashionably retro disco tracks made the ads extremely popular.

10. Burst two lasted longer in Scotland than it did in London, hence slightly different dates have been used for the two regions.

Quotes from 2CV's qualitative research

It's brilliant. I saw it once on satellite and I'm waiting for it to come on again so I can tell my mates. They think I'm making it up.

The anteater is the establishment, and the ants are going sod you, we're going to party.

The ants are getting pissed on Bud Ice and having a party. It's simple. That's what it's all about.

Quantitatively, while 'Ants' was not Millward Brown LINKTM tested, 'Anteater' received an enjoyment rating of 4.32 out of 5 – compared with a Millward Brown average against lager ads of 3.24. This put Anteater in the top 2% of ads Millward Brown had ever tested.

Creating relevant attitudes towards the Bud Ice brand

Returning to the brief, the advertising was intended to show how Bud Ice:

—Understood the attitudes and lifestyle of late 1990s youth.

—Was the epitome of an Ice product.

The tracking measures which were designed to measure our success in these areas were: 'is fashionable', 'is for style conscious people', and 'is refreshing'.

In both 'fashionable' and 'is for style conscious people' Bud Ice is now the lead brand. While it has been harder for Bud Ice to own the more Ice-generic refreshment measure, it has still overtaken Labatt Ice on this.[11] (See Table 10.)

TABLE 10

	Bud Ice	Fosters Ice	Labatt Ice	Carlsberg Ice
Fashionable	35	32	33	n/a
For style conscious people	28	27	19	n/a
Particularly refreshing	17	19	11	n/a

Source: Millward Brown

Again there are two pieces of evidence demonstrating advertising's role:

1. Timing of bursts

There is a similar correlation between these measures and advertising as the one seen for awareness.

Table 11 shows the percentage point *change* in these measures.

11. All tracking figures are from Millward Brown. This is 16 week rolling as of beginning of January.

TABLE 11

	Burst 1	Off air	Burst 2
Refreshing	3	–1	6
Fashionable	3	–1	18
Style conscious	1	–6	14

Source: Millward Brown[12]

2. Regional analysis

As with awareness, the uplifts in the supported regions increase far more than in the control regions (see Figure 11, Figure 12 and Figure 13).

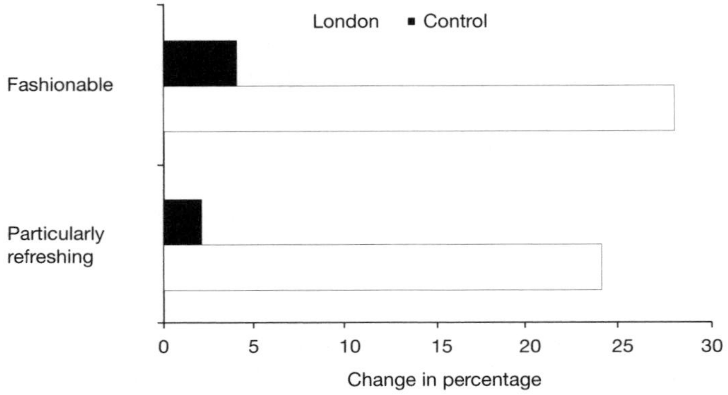

Figure 11: *Changes in Bud Ice image*
Burst 1: London vs control area
Sources: Millward Brown – 8 weeks to 19 August 1996 vs 8 weeks to 4 November 1996

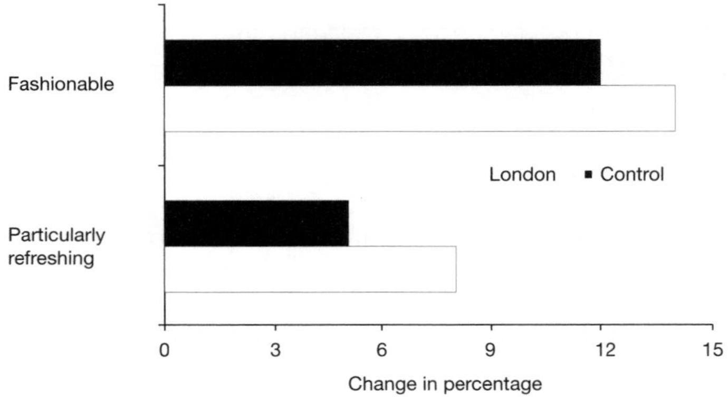

Figure 12: *Changes in Bud Ice image*
Burst 2: London vs control area
Sources: Millward Brown – 8 weeks to 28 April 1997 vs 8 weeks to 23 June 1997

12. The burst one figure is the change from 19/08/96 to 04/11/97. The off air figure is the change from 11/11/96 to 21/4/97. The burst two figure is the change from 28/04/97 to 21/07/97.

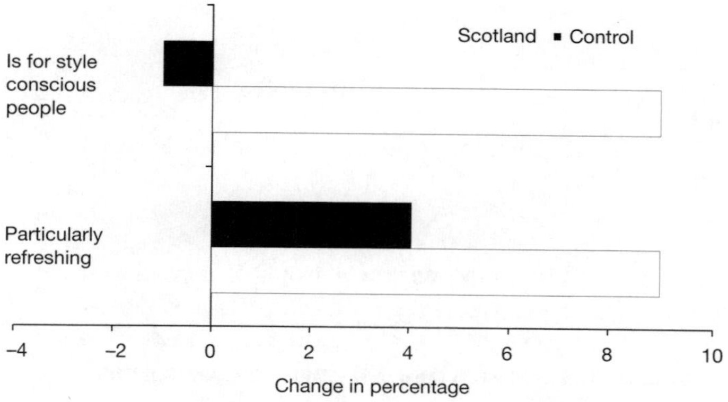

Figure 13: *Changes in Bud Ice awareness*
Burst 2: Scotland vs control area
Sources: Millward Brown – 8 weeks to 28 April 1997 vs 8 weeks to 11 August 1997[13]

Conclusion

The advertising was famous, loved, and communicated the correct things about brand and product. It will now be shown how this contributed to the outstanding *business* performance.

ISOLATING THE ADVERTISING CONTRIBUTION IN THE ACHIEVEMENT OF THE MARKETING OBJECTIVES

The advertising was a major factor in enabling Bud Ice to meet its marketing objectives. The advertising directly influenced both ROS (consumer demand) and distribution (trade response). This resulted in significant share growth.

Rate of sale

There is a strong correlation between advertising activity and ROS increases.

Both trade sectors tell the same story – although the trend is more pronounced in the off-trade.[14] There ROS built quickly after launch, supported by the advertising. When the advertising stopped, ROS began to decline.

When the larger second burst began there was an immediate response, and ROS *doubled* in four months. When the advertising support was decreased, ROS began to fall away once again (see Figure 14 and Figure 15).

13. Burst two lasted longer in Scotland than it did in London, hence slightly different dates have been used for the two regions.
14. This is not surprising, as on-trade data is based on sales in to the trade, rather than sales out to consumers. Throughout our investigations, we found that sales movements matched the pattern of advertising support less closely in the on-trade than they did on the off-trade.

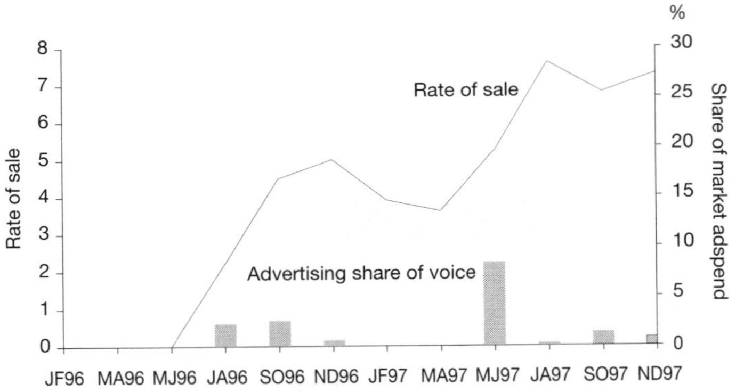

Figure 14: *Bud Ice rate of sale vs share of voice off-trade*
Source: Nielsen, Register – MEAL

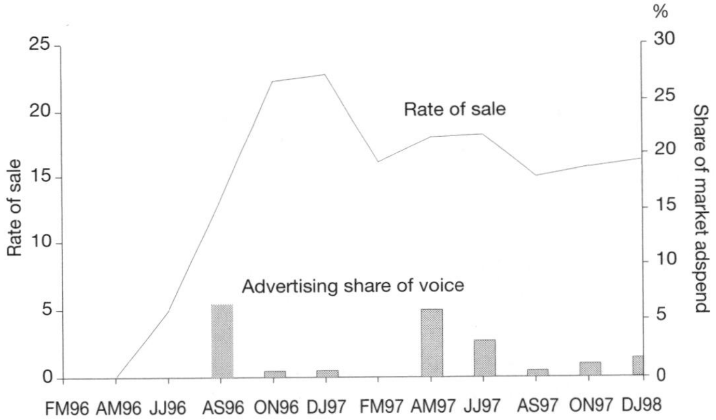

Figure 15: *Bud Ice rate of sale vs share of voice on-trade*
Source: Nielsen, Register – MEAL

It is likely that the high ROS of sale immediately after the first burst can be attributed in part to some kind of 'launch effect' independent of advertising – especially in the on-trade.[15] However, while this is true, the increase in ROS after the second burst strongly suggests an advertising effect. Moreover, there are clear regional variations in ROS, which can only be explained by advertising.

ROS in London vs Control in the first and second bursts

London was the only region to be supported in the first burst, and was upweighted in the second. In all, London received nearly four times as much as the Control

15. There is more likely to be a significant 'launch' effect in the on rather than off-trade because of how the data is collected. Hence there is the possibility of an initial ROS spike at launch as the trade buys in stock from nothing.

regions (Table 12).

TABLE 12

	Cumulative TVRs in both bursts
London	849
Control Regions	229

Source: BARB

As a consequence, ROS is now much higher in London than in the Control (see Figure 16 and Figure 17).

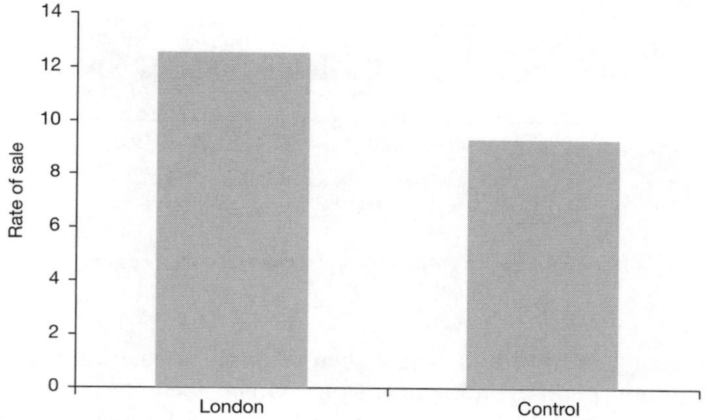

Figure 16: *Bud Ice rate of sale post second burst off-trade*
Source: Nielsen September/October 1997

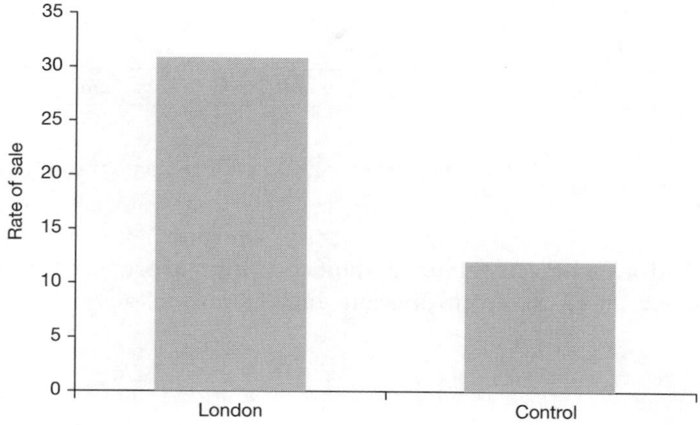

Figure 17: *Bud Ice rate of sale post second burst on-trade*
Source: Nielsen September/October 1997

ROS in Scotland compared with Control regions in the second burst

During the first advertising burst neither Scotland nor the Control regions were supported. During this time, the Scottish off-trade performed admirably. However, by 1997, it became clear that Bud Ice was under-performing in the Scottish on-trade vis-à-vis the Control (see Figure 18).

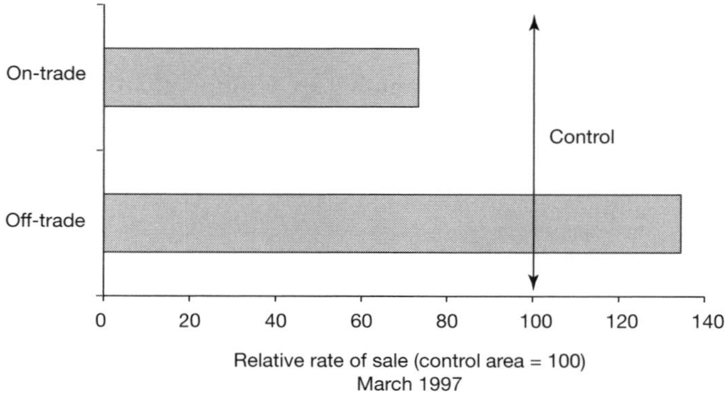

Figure 18: *Bud Ice rate of sale in Scotland indexed against control area prior to second burst*
Source: Nielsen[16]

With Scotland an historically strong Anheuser-Busch area, this was a worrying development - but perhaps not surprising. Miller Genuine Draft's success in Scotland vis-à-vis the rest of the Britain, and in the Scottish on-trade compared with the off trade, was probably instrumental in producing these disappointing on-trade results.[17] Hence, it was decided that in the second (national) burst of advertising Scotland was to be upweighted alongside London (Table 13).

TABLE 13

	Cumulative TVRs in 2nd burst
Scotland	776
Control regions	229

Source: BARB

The activity had a favourable effect in the Scottish off-trade, stretching Bud Ice's advantage there vis-à-vis the Control (see Figure 19).

16. The latest data points before second burst are Feb/Mar is off-trade March/April in on-trade.
17. Miller Genuine Draft had already been successful in establishing itself as the number one on-trade PPL in Northern Ireland. In Scotland, a combination of good word of mouth, a sweet taste well suited to the Scottish palette, popular advertising and very aggressive pricing into the on-trade ('buying distribution') combined to make it second only to Budweiser in the on-trade PPL. In contrast, to date. Miller has only targeted the English market to a minimal degree.

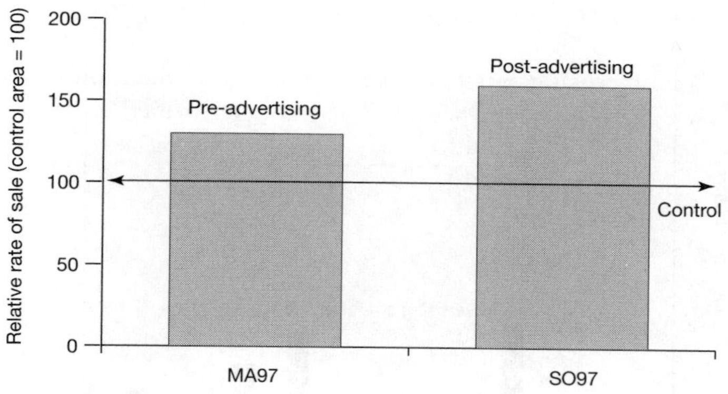

Figure 19: *Bud Ice rate of sale in Scottish off-trade indexed against control area*
Source: Nielsen[18]

Obviously, the task for advertising in the Scottish on-trade was the more difficult one where it needed to raise ROS from a very low level. This it succeeded in doing (see Figure 20).

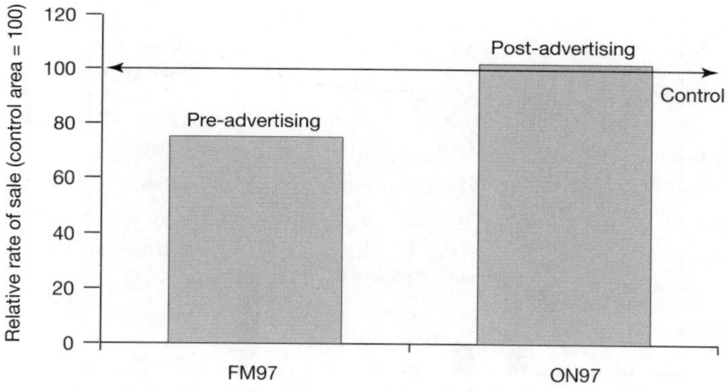

Figure 20: *Bud Ice rate of sale in Scottish on-trade indexed against control area*
Source: Nielsen

Distribution

There is a correlation between advertising bursts and distribution gains, similar to that seen with ROS. In both on and off trade, distribution builds strongly after launch, supported by the advertising. It then levels off, and begins to build again after the second burst begins (see Figure 21 and Figure 22).

18. Sep/Oct in the off-trade and Oct/Nov in the on-trade is just before the end of the Scottish advertising burst.

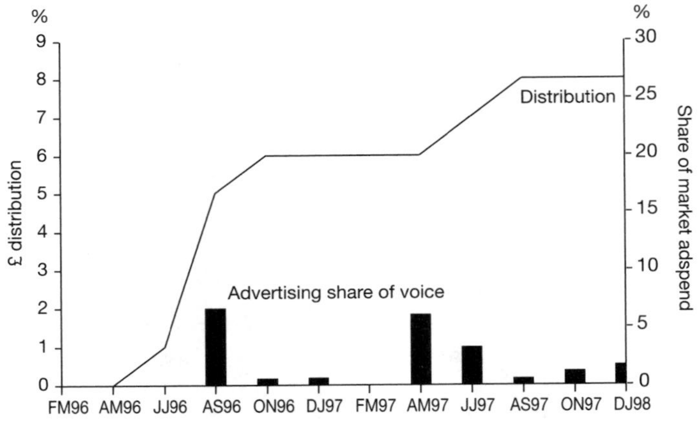

Figure 21: *Bud Ice distribution vs share of voice on-trade*
Source: Nielsen, Register – MEAL

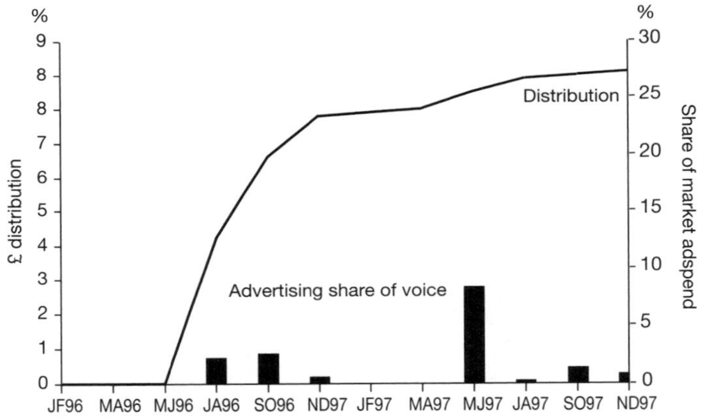

Figure 22: *Bud Ice distribution vs share of voice off-trade*
Source: Nielsen, Register – MEAL

Distribution in London vs Control in the first and second bursts

There are distinct regional differences here as well. In the year and a half since launch, Bud Ice has built greater distribution in London than in the Control regions (see Figure 23 and Figure 24).

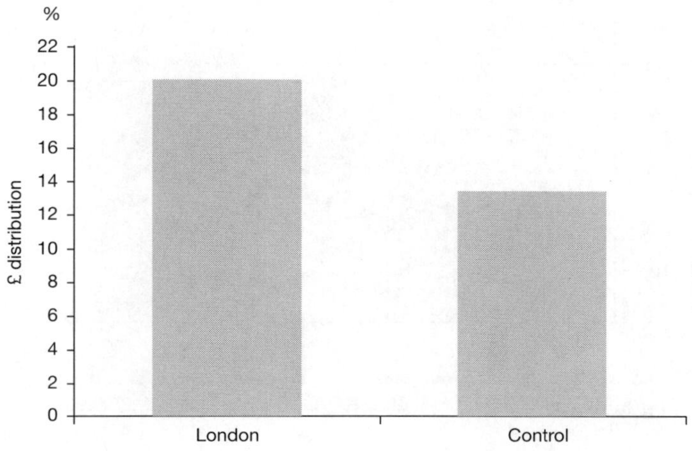

Figure 23: *Bud Ice distribution post second burst on-trade*
Source: Nielsen, October/November 1997

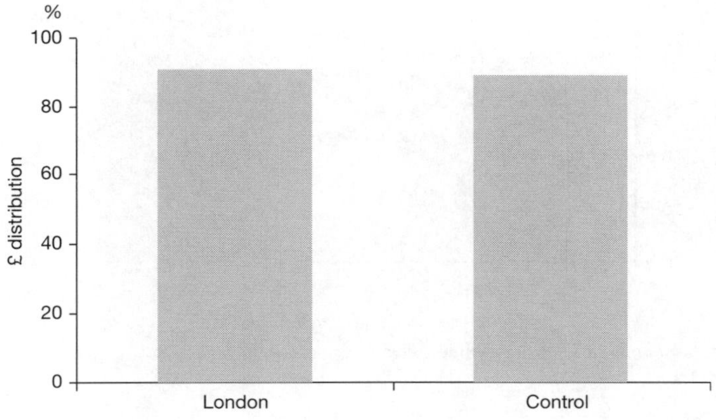

Figure 24: *Bud Ice distribution post second burst off-trade*
Source: Nielsen, September/October 1997

Distribution in Scotland vs Control in the second burst

Before Scotland received advertising support, on-trade distribution (mirroring ROS) was lower than in the Control regions. Unlike ROS, off-trade distribution was also lower. The more competitive environment created by Miller Genuine Draft was also having a detrimental effect on distribution.

However, post the advertising burst, Scotland had not only caught up the distribution levels in the control, but had actually surpassed them (Figure 25 and Figure 26).

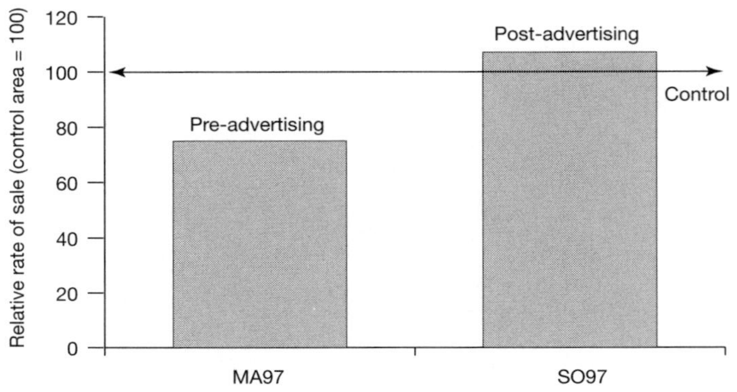

Figure 25: *Bud Ice distribution in Scottish off-trade indexed against control area*
Source: Nielsen

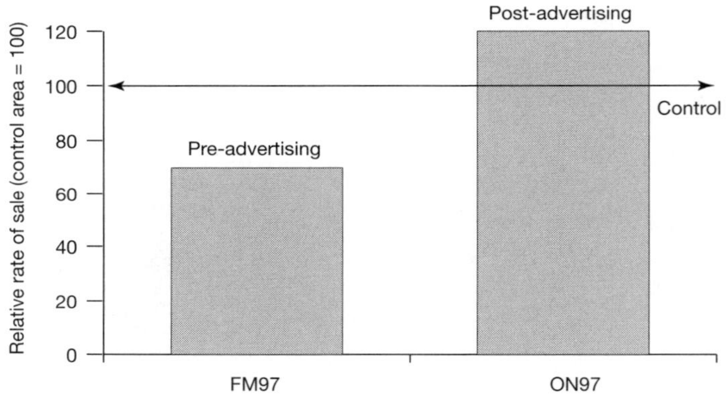

Figure 26: *Bud Ice distribution in Scottish on-trade indexed against control area*
Source: Nielsen

How the advertising worked in influencing distribution

1. *Directly through the trade* – The trade both see the advertising directly and is informed of it via trade press and salesforce. They suspect that, all else being equal, advertised brands sell better than non-advertised brands. Hence, advertising could increase their propensity to stock.
2. *Via the consumer* – We have shown how advertising affected consumer demand for Bud Ice. The trade, keeping abreast of their customer's desires and actions, can discover the best brands to stock – through conversations with their customers, visits to more popular venues, and knowledge of what's selling in other outlets.

See Figure 27.

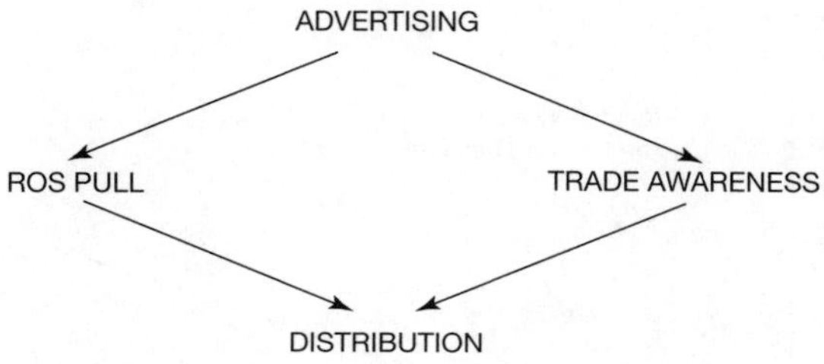

Figure 27

Summary – the net effect on share

Given that the advertising affected both ROS and distribution, one would expect a marked effect on share. This has indeed been the case. We can demonstrate this simply and briefly through regional analysis.

There were marginal differences *within* the regions making up the control. Hence, we can model advertising weight against share growth using nine data points.

For both trade sectors, there is a statistically significant correlation between the share Bud Ice captured in each region and the level of advertising used to support the launch there (see Figure 28 and Figure 29).

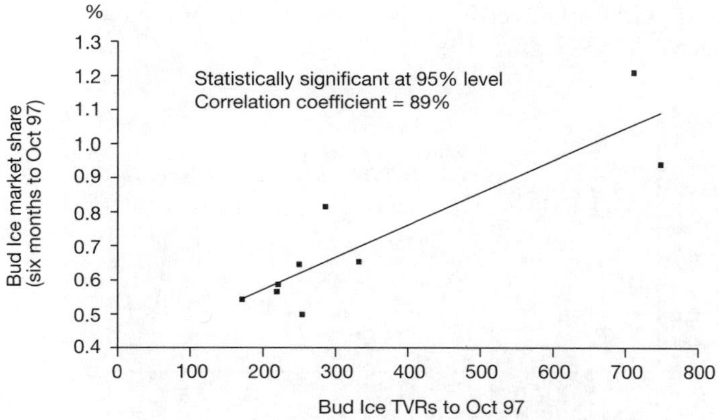

Figure 28: *Change in Bud Ice share vs TVRs off-trade*
Source: Nielsen, BARB

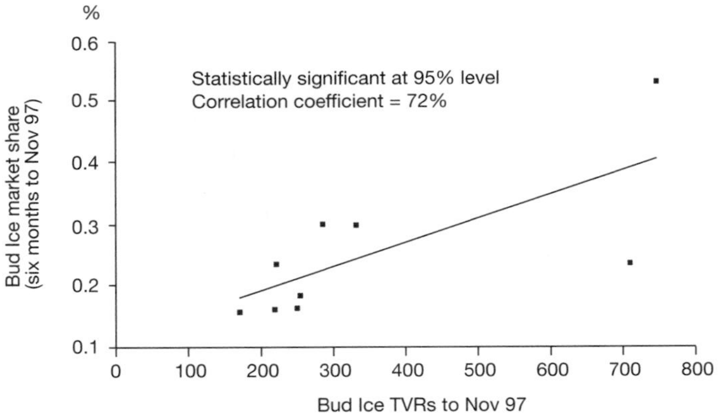

Figure 29: *Change in Bud Ice share vs TVRs on-trade*
Source: Nielsen, BARB

Econometrics

The final proof that the advertising boosted sales comes from econometrics. In the off-trade[19] we have weekly sales data covering most of the period since launch.[20] An econometric model of Bud Ice's market share clearly shows that the advertising had a significant effect on sales. At its peak, the advertising caused a 40% uplift in share. This means that without advertising Bud Ice would not have met its off-trade marketing objective[21] (see Figure 30).

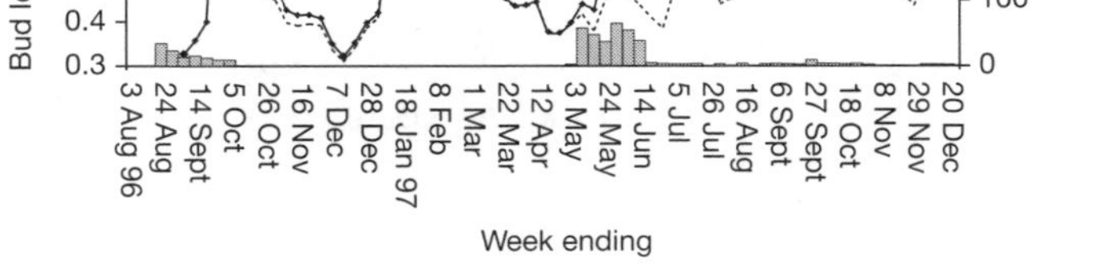

Figure 30: *The effect of advertising on Bud Ice market share off-trade*
Source: Nielsen, BARB, Econometric Model

19. On-trade data was unsuitable for modelling.
20. This enables us to look at the relationship between sales and advertising in detail.
21. And almost certainly not its on-trade marketing objective either (although this has not been proved econometrically).

ADVERTISING EFFICIENCY

It has now been shown that the advertising was instrumental in achieving the marketing objectives. However, this was a launch, and so (it could be cynically argued) *any* advertising would have resulted in these uplifts. However, the soft measure above would strongly suggest this was not the case. Moreover, the information below gives further evidence that this advertising was *abnormally* successful.

Awareness

The Bud Ice TV advertising was exceptionally efficient at generating awareness compared with other lager advertising.

Quote from Millward Brown

The executions are extremely efficient at generating branded advertising associations. The Awareness Index of 12 is amongst the highest ever recorded in the category.

Sales

The most obvious comparison here is with the efficiency of other advertising in generating sales for other Ice brands at *their* launches.

The end of 1997 marked 18 months since the launch of Bud Ice. The charts below compare Bud Ice with the other Ice brands 18 months after *their* launches. For the reasons outlined earlier, whilst we can look at share in the off-trade, the fairest measure in the on-trade is ROS.[22]

TABLE 14

	Spend after 18 months (£)	Market share in off trade[23]	Advertising efficiency[24]
Bud Ice	**£2.0 million**	**0.6%**	**7.1**
Fosters Ice	£3.9 million	0.6%	3.7
Labatt Ice	£1.8 million	0.2%	2.6
Carlsberg Ice	£2.4 million	0.1%	1.0

Source: Nielsen, Register MEAL

TABLE 15

	Spend after 18 months (£)	ROS in on-trade[25]	Advertising efficiency[26]
Bud Ice	**£2.0 million**	**1.4**	**1.7**
Fosters Ice	£3.9 million	1.4	1.1
Labatt Ice	£1.8 million	1.2	1.6
Carlsberg Ice	£2.4 million	1.0	1.0

Source: Nielsen, Register – MEAL

22. The respective periods being compared are: July 1996–December 1997 for Bud Ice; July 1994–December 1995 for Fosters Ice; December 1993–May 1995 for Labatt Ice; September 1994–February 1995 for Carlsberg Ice.
23. Over respective first 18 months.
24. Cumulative market share over cumulative advertising spend, indexed to Carlsberg Ice (= 1.0).
25. ROS over respective first 18 months, indexed to Carlsberg Ice (= 1.0).
26. ROS over advertising spend, indexed to Carlsberg Ice (= 1.0).

In the off-trade, Bud Ice spent less per share point gained than any other Ice beer. And in the on-trade it spent less in achieving its ROS.[27] All else being equal, Bud Ice advertising has worked harder.

ELIMINATION OF OTHER FACTORS FROM THIS SUCCESS

Nothing else could have caused these results. We will show that other potentially influential factors:

— were constant or negligible over time (hence not responsible for uplifts around advertising bursts);

— were constant or only negligibly different across regions (hence not responsible for regional disparity);

— would not have given Bud Ice an advantage relative to competitors at their launches (hence not responsible for differences in advertising efficiency).

1. *Products* – Blind taste testing suggests consumers can tell little difference between the different Ice beers.
2. *Price* – Due to corporate policy of keeping premium price, Bud Ice operated at a price disadvantage to the other Ices (Table 16).

TABLE 16

	Average price per bottle Off-trade	Average price per bottle On-trade
Bud Ice	**98p**	**£1.85**
Carlsberg Ice	98p	£1.85
Fosters Ice	97p	£1.78
Labatt Ice	87p	£1.81

Source: Nielsen latest six months data

3. *Bud Ice packaging* – This did not change over time or region. However, it *is* popular – at least as popular and impactful as Fosters, and preferred to Carlsberg and Labatt.[28] However, Bud Ice's packaging probably lacks *some* of the novelty value which surrounded the packaging of other Ice beers at *their* launches – particularly Fosters Ice.
4. *Competitive advertising spend since Bud Ice's launch* – With the exception of Carlsberg Ice, Bud Ice has actually had the lowest advertising spend since its launch:

27. The comparison is particularly telling against Fosters Ice, which had the same share in the off-trade and same ROS in the on-trade.
28. Bud Ice's packing consists of a bright multi-coloured label and clear 'ice chunk' bottle. The ice chunk bottle was an innovation in the category.

TABLE 17

	Spend in £000s
Fosters Ice	4,419
Labatt Ice	2,758
Bud Ice	**2,638**
Carsberg Ice	7

Source: Register – MEAL

5. *PR and below-the-Line* – The small amount of non-advertising PR was even over time and appeared nationally. There was below-the-line material, but again, its availability was constant, and would not have advantaged Bud Ice unduly over the competition who also used below-the-line.
6. *Sponsorship* – Bud Ice sponsored two festivals in May and August 1997. While 70,000 attended, this probably included only some 25,000 of our core 18–24 males. This only represents some 1% of total 18–24 males – and hence can be regarded as an extremely minor effect compared with the advertising. Also, it could well be argued that any minor effect was in part an advertising one, as much of the branding was based on the ants – for example, a giant ant as a meeting point and the 'Ant-arctic' chill out room.
7. *Possibility of London and Scotland being naturally stronger regions for packaged lager* – While London *does* have the highest PL ROS in the on-trade, it does not in the off-trade (all regions are quite similar), where there was a similar uplift. Scotland is not as strong as London. Further, inherent regional strength could only influence ROS, not share – but we saw clear advertising effects for share too.
8. *The salesforce* – There is no evidence that the competence or performance of the salesforce has varied over region or time.
9. *Seasonality* – There are PL ROS uplifts around the summer and Christmas periods. However, these uplifts are less than the uplifts of Bud Ice around its advertising. Also, seasonality would not have an effect on share, distribution, or the regional analysis.
10. *The novelty of the category* – It could be argued that Bud Ice had the advantage of entering an established category, which the others did not. But, this argument would make more sense in a category where the consumers needed an initial *education*. The fear was actually the opposite: that, by entering late, Bud Ice might have missed out on the novelty value which surrounded the initial launches.
11. *The number of brands in the category* – There were more brands fighting for share at the time of Bud Ice's launches than at other launches. This would have worked *against* rather than for Bud Ice.

EVIDENCE OF ADVERTISING EFFECT BEYOND THE STATED OBJECTIVES

So, the marketing objectives were met, and advertising played a large part in making this possible. However, additionally, the advertising had an effect on Budweiser itself. Given that the worry was about *cannibalisation*, this was hardly an effect we had been expecting.

Awareness

The first clue was the awareness data. There was a correlation between Budweiser's spontaneous awareness and its own advertising – but there were also peaks which could not be explained by this. In particular:

1. *Between* the Budweiser bursts of May/June 1996 and October/November 1996, Budweiser's spontaneous awareness rises sharply.
2. Budweiser awareness grows on the back of Budweiser's March/April burst. However, it *continues* to grow after this burst has subsided, but before Budweiser's June/July burst.

See Figure 31.

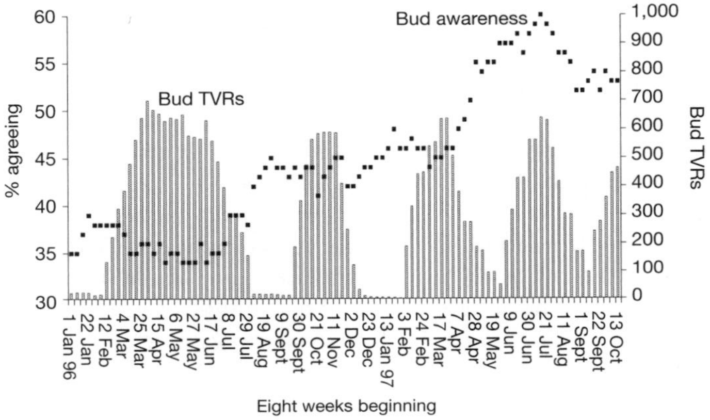

Figure 31: *Budweiser spontaneous awareness vs Bud advertising*
Source: Millward Brown, BARB

Only when the two Bud Ice TV bursts are considered, do these trends make sense. They coincide with both of the unexplained uplifts outlined above (see Figure 32).

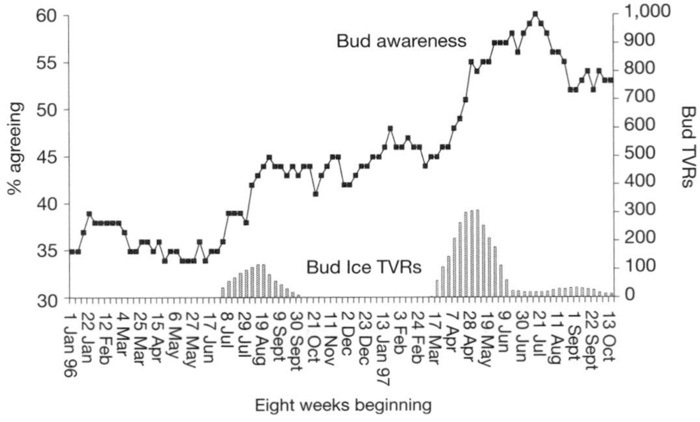

Figure 32: *Budweiser spontaneous awareness vs Bud Ice advertising*
Source: Millward Brown, BARB

We examined other Budweiser tracking measures, but there were no similar trends. The Bud Ice advertising, then, did not made people think differently about Budweiser (indeed, it could be worrying if Bud Ice *had* influenced Budweiser's brand identity) but it *had* brought Budweiser top of mind.[29]

Budweiser share

Given that the Bud Ice advertising affected Budweiser's salience, it seemed possible there was a sales effect too.

Investigation revealed a correlation between Budweiser share and Bud Ice advertising in both trade sectors – although the effect on the off-trade is more marked.[30] There are two points of correlation here:

— In both bursts of Bud Ice advertising, there is a corresponding increase in Budweiser share.

— In the much larger second burst, the increase in Budweiser share was greater than during the smaller first burst.

See Figure 33 and Figure 34.

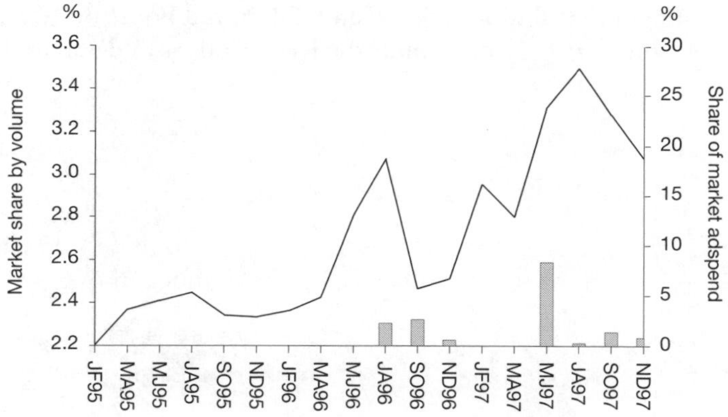

Figure 33: *Budweiser market share vs Bud Ice share of voice off-trade*
Source: Nielsen, Register – MEAL

29. The link between spontaneous awareness of an established brand and it sales performance is not necessarily an obvious one. However, there are often few brand cues when the choice between PL brand is made. First, the numerous PLs are not always easy to differentiate between. Second, buying in rounds means the choice is often made away from the bar. This makes the link between salience and sales a more intuitive one.
30. See footnote 13 above.

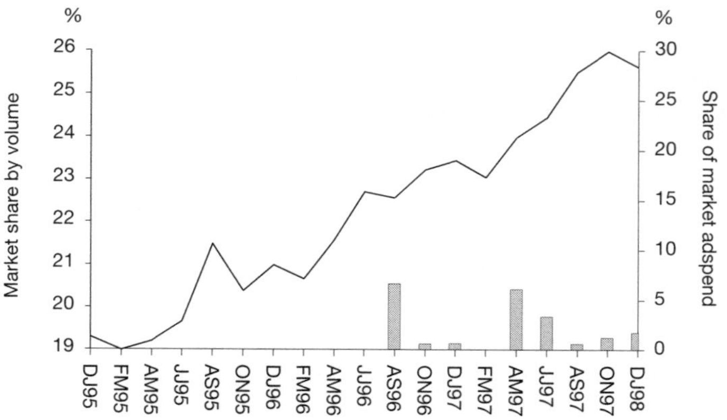

Figure 34: *Budweiser market share vs Bud Ice share of voice on-trade*
Source: Nielsen, Register – MEAL

Econometrics

In order to decide whether the apparent sales effects were genuine, econometrics was used. By constructing a model of Budweiser's market share over the last five years, we have shown that Bud Ice advertising did indeed boost Budweiser share. In fact, the effect is quite large. At one point, the Ice ads boost Bud's share by 14% (see Figure 35).

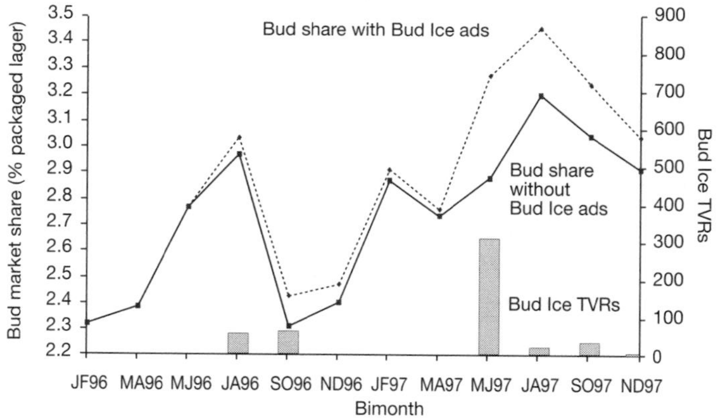

Figure 35: *The effect of Bud Ice advertising on Bud market share off-trade*
Source: Nielsen, BARB, Econometric Model

Further, the model shows that as Bud Ice gains distribution, sales of Budweiser are slightly depressed. This is important. If the advertising had been absent from the Bud Ice launch, sales of Budweiser would have decreased. In other words, cannibalisation does occur after all, but the advertising effect on Budweiser offsets this.

Elimination of other factors

1. *Timing of Budweiser advertising* – Budweiser advertising also correlates with uplifts in Budweiser share. However, this cannot explain the *disparity* between the share uplifts. Budweiser advertising was actually heavier during the smaller of the two uplifts which correlated with Bud Ice advertising. Also, Budweiser advertising is fully accounted for in the econometric model.
2. *Variations in effectiveness of Budweiser advertising* – Budweiser did not change campaign over this period. Further, there is no evidence suggesting that executions varied significantly in terms of appeal or awareness.
3. *Price* – There were no significant variations in Budweiser's price relative to the PL market over this period.
4. *Sponsorship* – Budweiser's only major sponsorship over this period was that of the Olympics. However, this was in 1996 where the *smaller* of the two uplifts occurred.
5. *Change in format* – Budweiser introduced a new larger 440ml format. However, this has been available since May 1996 – ie, throughout the period we are studying. Moreover, this would not effect the on-trade.
6. *Budweiser Packaging and Product* – These stayed the same in all important aspects over this period.

OVERALL EFFECT OF THE ADVERTISING

Econometrics allows us to quantify the combined effect of advertising on Bud Ice and Budweiser. Figure 36 shows the extra sales generated by the advertising.

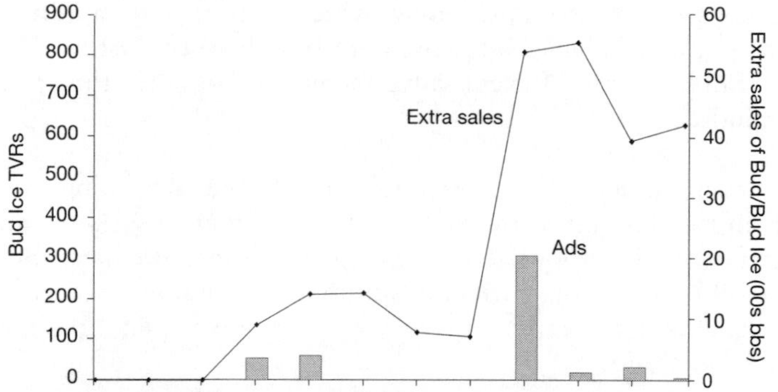

Figure 36: *Total extra sales generated by Bud Ice advertising off-trade*
Source: Nielsen, BARB, Econometric Model

According to the model, by December 1997, Bud Ice advertising was responsible for selling an extra 17 million PPLs for Anheuser-Busch in the off trade, at a retail value of £15.5 million. Furthermore, the model predicts that, even if advertising support had been withdrawn at the end of 1997, the ads would have continued generating extra sales worth £7.9 million during 1998 to 2000. Thus the advertising would have contributed £23.5 million worth of extra off-trade business in its first four and a half years. On-trade effects, although not formally quantified, are likely to be more than 1.5 times as much again, given that the on-trade accounts for 60% of Bud Ice value (and even more for Budweiser).

We cannot disclose the margin of any Anheuser-Busch products. However, as Anheuser-Busch only spent £3.2 million on advertising during 1996/97,[31] we can deduce from the model that the advertising would have paid for itself if the gross margin were 5.5% or more. The average margins in the industry as a whole are around 10% (Sources: CAMRA, Mintel). Hence, if Anheuser-Busch margins are in line with industry margins, the advertising has paid for itself very comfortably indeed.

CONCLUSION

This paper has demonstrated the considerable role advertising has played in making Bud Ice arguably the most successful PL launch of the 1990s. Without the advertising, or with more averagely effective advertising, Bud Ice would have not have met its ambitious marketing objectives.

As important, we have shown that Bud Ice advertising has increased sales of the parent brand. If advertising had been absent, the smaller gains would have been outweighed by cannibalisation.

Moreover, if we use industry profit margin averages as an indication,[32] the advertising comfortably paid for itself.

In summary, two factors contributed to this success:

1. A strong consumer-based positioning which appealed to a different market segment to Budweiser, hence allowing both brands to flourish.
2. Excellent, famous and efficient advertising to establish this positioning in people's minds.

In a world where much of the literature on brand stretching pessimistically concentrates on the dilution of the parent brand – either in sales or image terms – there are significant conclusions to be drawn here. In fact, we have shown that the opposite is possible. When the correct positioning is communicated via outstanding advertising, benefits can accrue not just for the advertised brand but for the business' wider portfolio.

31. Production and media spend (source: BMP).
32. Anheuser-Busch's profit margins are confidential.

10

Felix Advertising 1989–95

How the cat that crept got the cream

INTRODUCTION

Can you think of a grocery brand in a mature and established market that, after spending years as a relatively insignificant minor player, suddenly started to grow rapidly, overtaking the market leader in less than five years? More specifically, can you think of a brand that has achieved all this without significantly revamping the product, with parity pricing and with, at best, parity levels of distribution to its rivals?

If you can't, here's one: Felix. This paper will show how advertising featuring a mischievous black and white cat was the catalyst to this remarkable success story.

THE WET CATFOOD MARKET

In 1989, when our story begins, the UK wet catfood[1] market was worth over £400 million a year. Although a mature market with almost 100% penetration among cat owners, it had grown steadily through the 1980s, driven by an increase in the cat population. This growth plateaued towards the end of the decade and during the period covered by this paper (up to August 1995[2]) the market was static.

The market was segmented as follows:

— Expensive super-premium brands, usually served as treats.

— Premium brands served daily.

— Sub-premium brands, which were less palatable[3] and cost significantly less than the premiums.

---

1. In volume terms, wet catfood accounts for roughly 88% of the catfood market, the remaining 12% coming in either dry biscuit or 'semi-moist' formats.
2. This cut-off point was chosen due to alterations in our principal data sources.
3. 'Palatability' is a reasonably objective index of product quality in the catfood market. Manufacturers tend to measure it in two ways: (i) using cat owners to assess in-home how much their cats appear to like unbranded samples, and (ii) in the laboratory (or 'cattery') by recording the speed and manner with which cats eat samples of products – known in the trade as 'cat attack'.

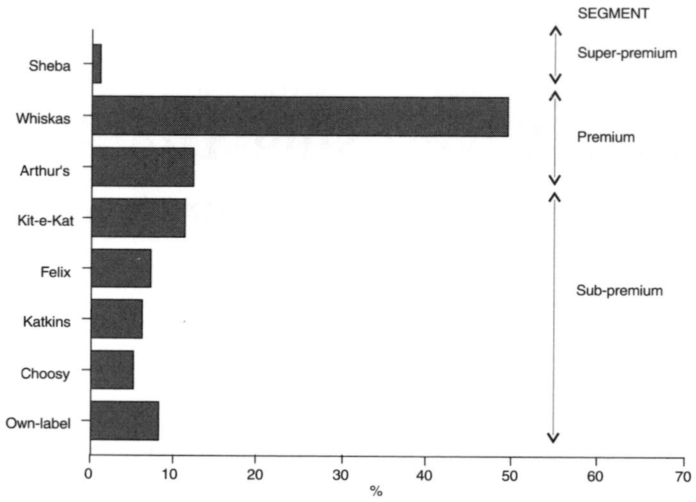

Figure 1: *Catfood brands volume share and market segment, year to January 1989*
Source: Nielsen

Whiskas Supermeat was the market leader with a share of nearly 50%. This premium brand had dominated the market since the 1970s and its position seemed as secure as Kellogg's Corn Flakes or Coca-Cola in their respective markets.

FELIX UNDER PRESSURE

Felix was bought by Quaker[4] in 1970 and positioned in the sub-premium market sector. The brand grew steadily through the early 1980s, helped by distribution gains but, by 1989, its share had levelled out at around 6.5%.

Although its share was steady, two trade developments raised the worrying possibility that Felix might start to lose listings:

— The major multiple retailers wanted to allocate more shelf space to the highly profitable super-premium sector (launched in the mid 1980s).

— They were also keen to sell more own-label catfoods.[5]

Felix was in a particularly weak position to face such a threat.

4. Quaker Petfoods was bought by Spillers in February 1995.
5. In 1989, the own-label catfood sector was relatively underdeveloped in comparison with other fmcg sectors.

— It came in only six flavours, making it a relatively uncompetitive range to stock.[6]

— Unlike all the other major brands, it had never received advertising support.

— From a consumer perspective, it lacked a distinctive identity.

Action had to be taken. As Quaker Petfoods' commercial director put it: 'The alternative of doing nothing would have meant we wouldn't have had a brand within two years.'[7]

THE FELIX RELAUNCH

Hence, the decision was taken to relaunch Felix in May 1989.

— The product was reformulated.

— Three new flavours were introduced.[8]

— The packaging was redesigned.

— For the first time in the brand's history, it received a £250,000 budget for advertising.

The relaunch marketing objective was to increase volume share to 10% over two years by getting non-users to try Felix and by building purchase levels among existing users. In reaching such a position the hope was that Felix would challenge Kit-e-Kat's placing as the third-largest brand in the market, thereby securing its listings and, ultimately, its long-term future.

DEVELOPING THE ADVERTISING

In January 1989, BMP was asked to develop the advertising for the relaunch. The primary advertising objective was to make Felix a credible brand, to endow it with an identity that would give non-users a reason to try it and users a reason to use it more regularly. This was a challenging brief!

All the major brands in the sector advertised heavily so there was no question that our combined media and creative solution had to be highly distinctive. If it was

---

6. By contrast, Kit-e-Kat came in nine flavours, Arthur's in ten and Whiskas Supermeat in twelve. (Source: *The Grocer Price List*, 1 April 1989).
7. *Marketing*, 3 December 1992.
8. Trout & Shrimp, Duck & Heart and Beef & Liver (replacing Liver). This took the number of flavours in the range up to eight.

not, our plaintive meowing risked being drowned out by the roar of our competitors, especially Whiskas which spent the equivalent of our entire budget every eight days.[9]

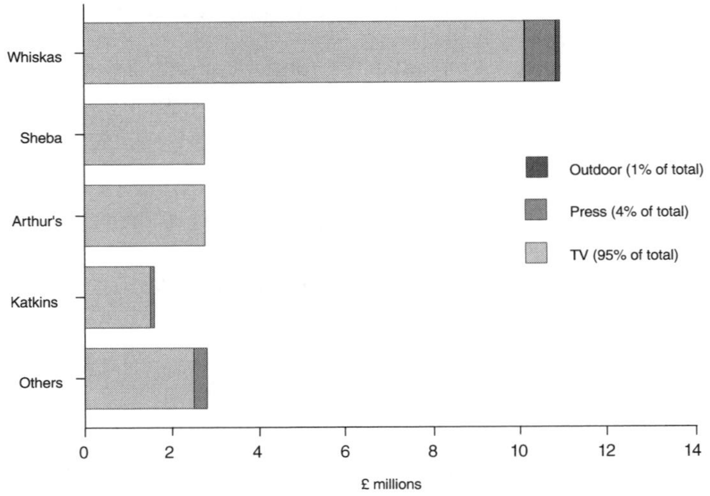

Figure 2: *Catfood brands adspend 1988*
Source: MEAL

To answer the trickier question of exactly what form this distinctiveness should take, we scrutinised our competitors' habits and got under the skin of cat owners.

The Creative Strategy

We found that most catfood advertising at the time sought to reassure owners that their cat would be eager to eat the brand being advertised.[10] It attempted to do this in a very rational manner using owner endorsements, lingering shots of catfood being forked from tin to bowl, and voice-over information about vitamins and minerals. These product stories were accompanied by idealised images of immaculately groomed cats and owners.

However, as soon as we started talking to owners, we realised that there was a gap between how these ads portrayed cats and how a great many owners actually felt about them.

9. Even Katkins, the smallest spender among our main competitors, spent around four times our budget annually.
10. This need to reassure was understandable; unlike dogs, who will eat almost anything, cats frequently turn up their noses at something that they were happy to eat the day before. However, owners are (excusably) reluctant to sample brands and flavours on behalf of their unpredictable pets.

At the warm-up stage of our first group discussion, we naïvely invited respondents to tell us what it was like having a cat – little knowing the difficulty we would have in getting them to stop! They reeled off dozens of amusing cat anecdotes.[11] This enthusiasm was shown by almost everyone we spoke to: they liked their cats *not* because they were affectionate bundles of pretty fluff (as represented in the competitive advertising), but because of their mischievous characters and frequently exasperating exploits.

Quotes from Cat Owners

'He's an absolute nutter, he terrorises the other cats.'

'My cat is a real cow first thing in the morning and it's bedlam.'

'They're mischievous, aren't they? Whatever you're doing they'll come and mither at you.'

'When they've done something wrong they give you a look that says "What are you going to do about it?" '

'They do what they want, when they want, and the odd thing is you forgive them for it. No idea why!'

Source: BMP Qualitative Research

We felt we had spotted a gap in the market: the most effective way to give the Felix brand a distinctive and motivating identity was to target these people and talk their language. We did not need to talk about vitamins, minerals and flavours to persuade them their cats would like to eat Felix, we could persuade them by showing we understood what cats were *really* like.

The Media Strategy

Before incorporating this learning into a creative brief we needed to have a clear idea about where the advertising ought to appear. Indeed, to maximise our limited budget, it was critical that our creative and media strategies reinforced each other as much as possible.

Initially, we could not afford to advertise on television – nor did we want to since that was where our competitors spent most of their money. Instead, we chose to start the campaign in national newspapers. No other catfood brands advertised in this medium so we would be able to dominate it as our own. Furthermore, by choosing to advertise in only a small number of titles, we could afford to maintain a continuous weekly presence all through the year. This allowed us to:

11. For example, about how little Rambo had swiped the Sunday roast off the sideboard, about Smudge's weakness for squirrels, or about Tibbles and her disastrous attempt to scale the Christmas tree.

— Echo the regular weekly timing of the catfood purchase cycle.

— Maximise the chances that advertising would catch owners when they were most vulnerable to brand switching.[12]

— Produce many *different* executions, to help flesh out the personality that lay at the heart of our creative strategy.

— Expose our target to a regular succession of executions, helping to boost Felix's brand stature in their eyes.

Despite these benefits, this 'targeted drip' approach was quite risky; the only way we could afford such a prolonged presence was to sacrifice coverage and appear in a limited number of newspaper titles. However, we believed the benefits of the strategy far outweighed any potential disadvantages: if 'Eight out of ten cat owners (who expressed a preference)' preferred Whiskas, we were happy just to talk to the two out of ten who did not.

We were now able to write the creative brief.

Creative Brief

Requirement
Black & white national press campaign.

Target
Cat owners, mainly women, who appreciate their cats for who they are.

Proposition
If your cat is like the Felix cat then he or she will like Felix catfood.

Support
Show the sorts of things mischievous everyday moggies get up to.
Show that those sorts of cats like to eat Felix.

Tone
Cheeky and down to earth.

12. Namely whenever their unpredictable cat started refusing to eat a brand it had previously liked.

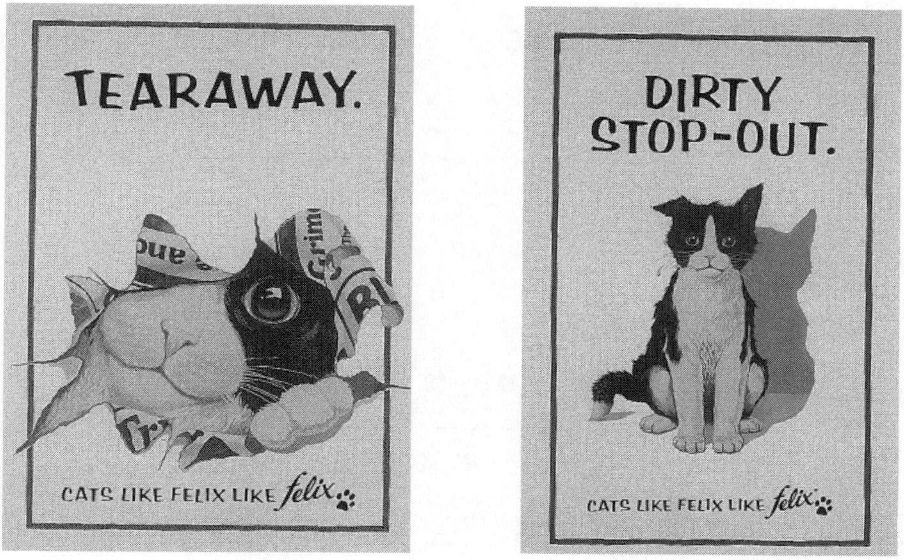

FELIX 'PERSONALITY' NEWSPAPER ADS

FELIX 'TOPICAL' NEWSPAPER ADS

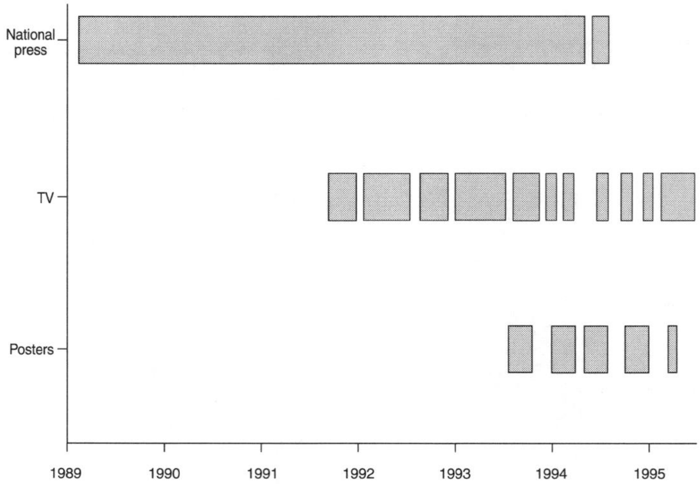

Figure 3: *Felix media plan: September 1989 to August 1995*
Source: MEAL

The Creative Work

We had found in research that many cat owners liked the black and white cat on the new Felix packaging. The creative team christened him Felix and decided to bring him to life.[13] The ads they came up with showed Felix either engaged in, or coming home from, various roguish tricks and, now, wanting to be fed. These featured the end-line *'Cats Like Felix Like Felix'*.

The team also created a series of cheekily topical ads, to be used on particular days during the course of the year.

CAMPAIGN DEVELOPMENT

Felix in the Newspapers

From mid-September 1989, Felix appeared in two daily titles.[14] As the brand grew, increased budgets allowed us to broaden our coverage, while maintaining frequency, by moving into additional titles.[15] The press buying brief was *be cheeky*: like hungry cats around meal times, the press ads popped up everywhere.[16]

13. After experimenting with photographs of black and white cats they decided an illustrated cat would – paradoxically – be more characterful. Certainly, it was much easier to 'direct' than a real cat.
14. The *Daily Express* and the *Daily Star*.
15. The *Daily Mirror*, the *Sun* and the *Daily Telegraph*.
16. In November 1992, we even bought every space in a single title, the *Daily Mirror*, a tactic subsequently adopted by Microsoft for the launch of Windows 95, Mercury for the launch of the Oliver and Claire campaign, and Pepsi for the launch of its blue can. We were, we believe, the first brand to do this.

Felix Goes On Telly

In October 1991, the budget became large enough for us to increase our coverage further by moving onto television. We still wanted to avoid the competition, create the impression among a discrete set of cat owners that Felix was a bigger brand than it actually was, and echo the catfood purchase cycle. So, instead of adopting a more conventional burst strategy, we continued with our tightly targeted drip approach.[17] Again, as budgets increased, we broadened our coverage by moving into additional programmes and dayparts.

Felix Goes Outside

From March 1993 the television and press work was supplemented by regional poster activity designed to boost brand awareness and further build Felix's brand stature.[18]

Spillers deserves praise for its audacity. It did not choose the obvious advertising solution. Instead, it consistently invested in work that broke many catfood advertising precedents:

— It did not show the product or talk about its contents.

— It focused on real rather than idealised cat behaviour.

— It illustrated these (ironically) with an 'unreal' cat.

— It appeared initially in a medium where catfood had never previously been advertised.

— It was bought in a manner where frequency and consistency of presence took priority over coverage.

RESULTS

Spillers' audacity has been extremely well rewarded.

17. Translated into the new medium, this initially involved buying one spot every week in *The Bill*, supplemented by further spots in the Breakfast TV daypart.
18. Again, as far as is possible with posters, we tried to use them in a suitably mischievous manner. For example, when one of our competitors sponsored the 1993 Cat Show at Olympia, the first thing spectators saw as they arrived and departed were two Felix ad vans parked outside the front entrance. This feat was topped at the same event two years later by our projecting Felix onto the exhibition hall itself.

'SMOOTH OPERATOR'

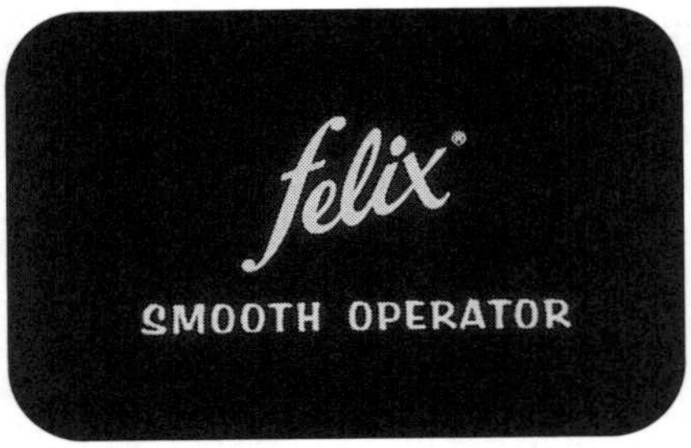

SOUND: Telephone rings

Hello...oh hi...yes...

Oh, I see...did you...?
SOUND: Dial tone.

Come on...

FVO: Cats like Felix like Felix.

Sales

There was an immediate uplift in Felix's sales after the advertising began in September 1989. Within only 16 months, eight months earlier than planned, the relaunch objective of achieving 10% share was met.

This growth continued: by August 1995, volume and value share had increased by a further 145% and 158% respectively (Figure 4).

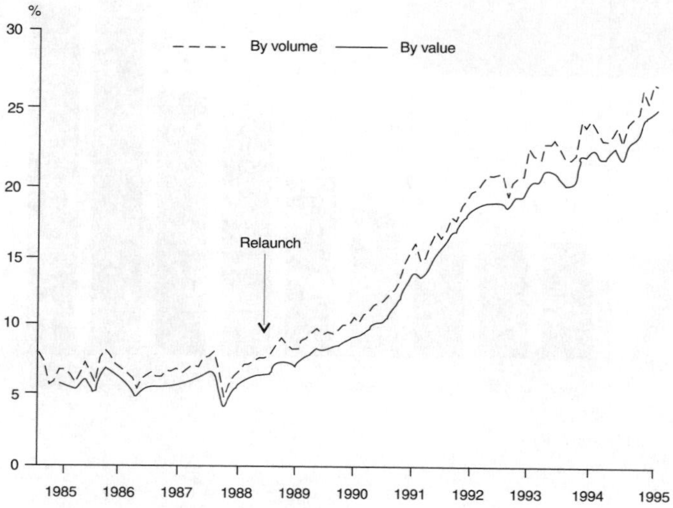

Figure 4: *Felix market share 1985–95*
Source: Nielsen

Felix did not simply catch up with the number-three brand, Kit-e-Kat, in December 1990 it overtook it. Then, 14 months later, it overtook the number two brand, Arthur's. And, in January 1994, it overtook the previously dominant market leader, Whiskas Supermeat.

It was not only by the standards of the catfood market that Felix's rate of growth was impressive: in 1991, Felix was the fourth fastest-growing brand in *any* grocery category; in 1992, the second fastest-growing brand; and, in 1993, the third fastest. This moved it from being the 80th biggest brand in the country before the relaunch to being the 27th biggest by 1995.[19]

19. This put Felix ahead of Gold Blend, Weetabix, Fairy Liquid, and Mars Bar. Source: *Checkout* magazine/Nielsen Biggest Brand Survey.

Consumer Behaviour

As planned, Felix's growth was driven both by large increases in penetration and loyalty levels. The brand's user base tripled in size (see Figure 5).[20]

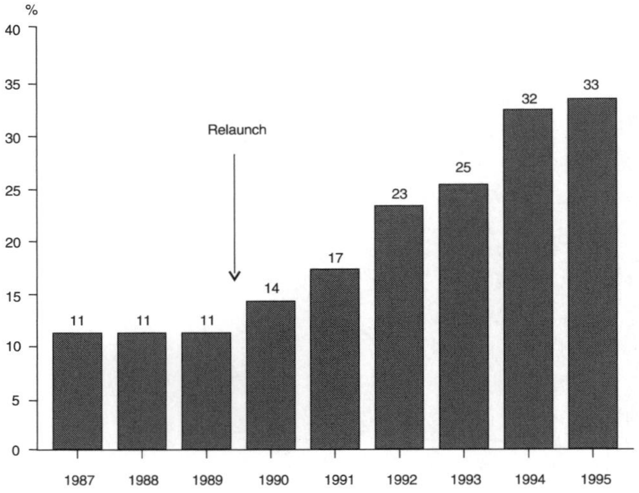

Figure 5: *Felix penetration 1985–95*
Base: Catfood buyers

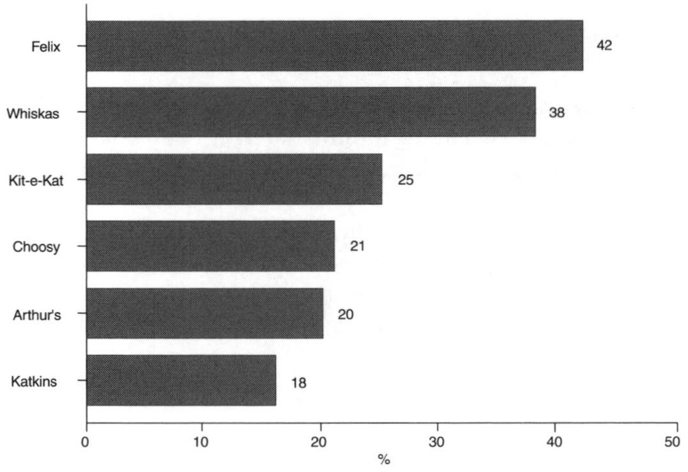

Figure 6: *Share of repertoire occupied by brand*
Base: All buyers of brand during survey period
Source: AGB Superpanel 20 w/e 27 August 1995

20. Since the TGI measuring year runs from April through to the following March, the 1989 figure can be regarded as a clean pre-relaunch measure.

And Felix's share of repertoire among catfood buyers doubled from 21% in 1988 to 42% in 1995, putting it ahead of all of its competitors (see Figure 6).[21]

Consumer Perceptions

In terms of how consumers view the Felix brand, spontaneous and prompted awareness increased significantly.

TABLE 1: FELIX BRAND AWARENESS

	November 1989 %	August 1995 %
Spontaneous	29	49
Prompted	87	94

Base: Housewives with cats
Source: Millward Brown

Perceptions of Felix's quality and stature, likewise, increased:

TABLE 2: THOSE AGREEING WITH FELIX BRAND IMAGE STATEMENTS

	November 1989 %	August 1995 %
'It is particularly good quality'	17	35
'It is becoming more popular nowadays'	9	18

Base: Housewives with cats
Source: Millward Brown

Furthermore, Felix was given a distinctive and highly characterful identity within the catfood market (see Figure 7).[22]

Overall, then, the marketing objectives following Felix's relaunch were not simply met, they were dramatically exceeded.

21. Source: AGB Superpanel, 28 w/e April 1988 versus 20 w/e August 1995.
22. We didn't have enough money to conduct awareness and image research before the relaunch and the advertising. The earliest measure we have comes from early November 1989, roughly six weeks after the advertising started. Accordingly, the baseline against which we are judging Felix's performance is likely to be higher than an absolutely clean pre-relaunch measure. This suggests that these figures underestimate the extent to which Felix's awareness and image measures have grown.

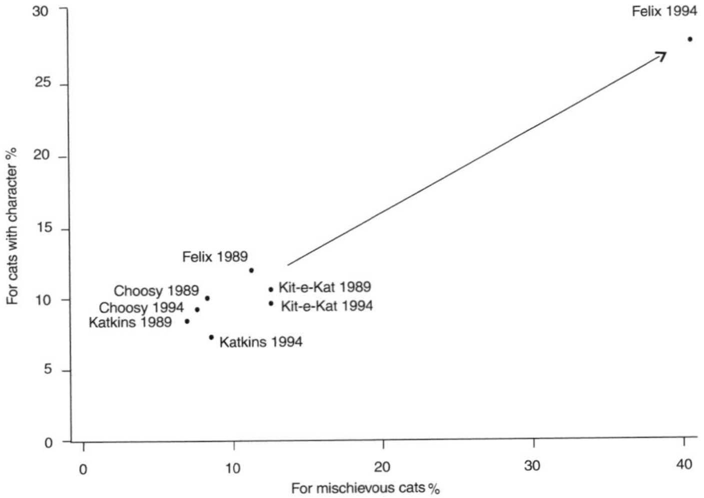

Figure 7: *Catfood brand identity Nov 1989 versus Nov 1994*
Base: % Housewives with cats who agree with image statement
Source: Millward Brown

THE CONTRIBUTION OF ADVERTISING

Felix's fortunes may have been transformed but what evidence is there to link this transformation of the brand to its advertising? We have four reasons to believe such a link exists.

— Consumers responded to the advertising exactly as we had planned.

— Cross-media and cross-regional analyses show correlations between the advertising and Felix's sales and penetration growth.

— We can rule out the contribution of non-advertising factors.

— Econometric modelling.

CONSUMER RESPONSE TO THE ADVERTISING

The newspaper and TV advertising was impactful, enjoyable, empathetic, and communicated clearly.

Within just two years of the start of the campaign, and only a month after it had first moved onto television, it had become the second most-noticeable catfood campaign (see Table 3).[23]

TABLE 3: ADVERTISING AWARENESS (IN ANY MEDIUM)

Whiskas	67%
Felix	30%
Kit-e-Kat	25%
Arthur's	21%

Base: Housewives with cats
Source: Millward Brown, November 1991

Crucially, for a campaign which was meant to tap into owners' positive feelings towards their cats, the advertising was enjoyed by cat owners (see Table 4). More specifically, over 50% of them spontaneously commented that they liked the Felix cat, and 30% said it reminded them of exactly how their cat behaves.[24]

TABLE 4: ENJOYMENT OF FELIX TV ADVERTISING

Enjoyed a lot	28%
Quite enjoyed	42%
Total	70%

Base: Housewives with cats who have seen Felix TV advertising recently[25]
Source: Millward Brown (campaign norm up to 7 May 1995)

In terms of communication, the Felix newspaper and TV ads established the type of cat which was most likely to want to eat Felix, as well as more 'generic' quality credentials (see Figures 8 and 9 overleaf).

Further evidence for the campaign's impact, enjoyability and clarity of message comes from qualitative research.

Consumer Comments on Felix Newspaper and TV Advertising

'The other adverts all look the same. I haven't seen a style like this before, it's quite a revolution.'

'You can relate to having a cat like that. I can see my cat in there, the way he jumps up.'

'It's part of the charm of the ad, he's got a character like a cheeky little child.'

'He's not one of those posh cats that lie around on the sofa. He's mischievous William Brown – I can see the catapult in his back pocket.'

'He's got that look on his face as if to say "Well, I've been out all night and now I want feeding!" '

23. Although, strictly speaking, this is more an indication of efficiency rather than effectiveness, it is worth noting that the Felix campaign has been a remarkably cost-effective generator of advertising awareness. For example, in May 1995 it was scoring 12 on Millward Brown's Awareness Index compared with Kit-e-Kat's 4 and Whiskas' 1.
24. Source: Millward Brown, May 1995. Base: Housewives with cats who have seen Felix advertising recently.
25. We do not have comparable quantitative data for the Felix press advertising.

'He always wants feeding and he always manages, whatever the situation, to be fed.'

'The food's so good he can't wait to get stuck into it.'

Source: BMP Qualitative Research 1990–95

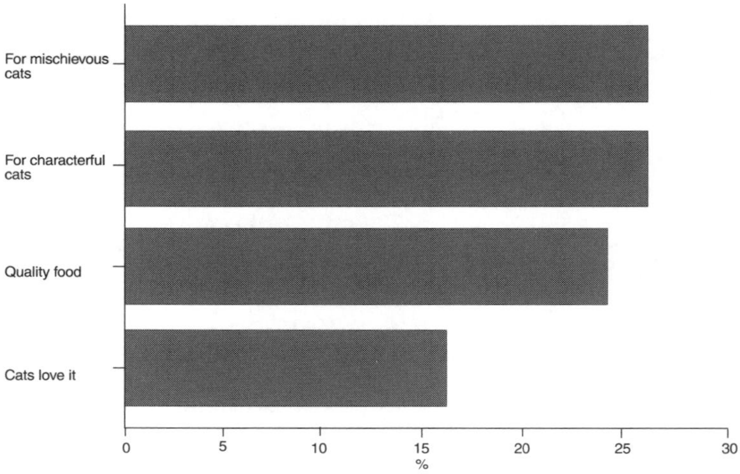

Figure 8: *Prompted impression: newspaper ads*
Base: Housewives with cats who have seen Felix advertising recently
Source: Millward Brown, June 1991

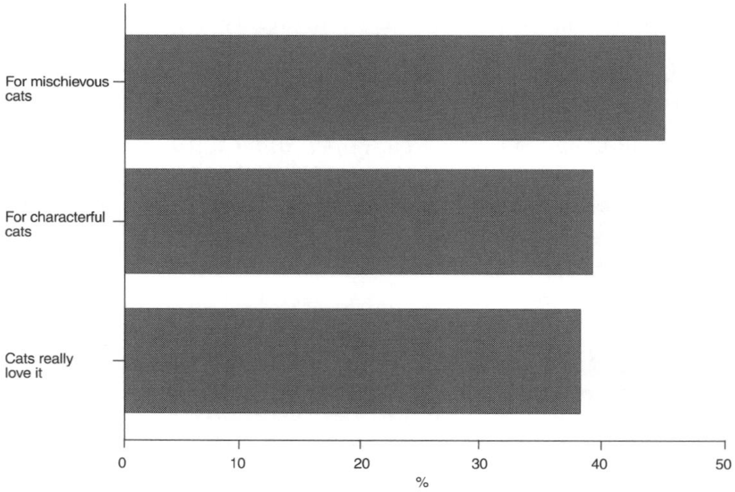

Figure 9: *Impressions from Felix TV ad*
Base: Housewives with cats who have seen Felix TV advertising recently
Source: Millward Brown, 13 March–7 May 1995

TABLE 5: FELIX BRAND IMAGE: ADVERTISING AWARE VERSUS UNAWARE

Those who agree	Aware %	Unaware %
'It is for mischievous cats'	42	22
'It is for cats with character'	32	18

Base: Housewives with cats who do/do not recall having seen Felix TV advertising recently, mean score September 91–July 95
Source: Millward Brown

Comparing perceptions of Felix's brand image among advertisement-aware versus unaware cat owners suggests strongly it was the advertising that built and reinforced the brand's distinct identity (Table 5).[26]

Taking all this information together, it is clear that the changes in consumer perceptions towards Felix are largely due to the advertising, which worked exactly as we had hoped.

CROSS-REGIONAL AND CROSS-MEDIA ANALYSES

During the period of our press advertising, before we began to advertise on television, the regional differences in Felix's share growth correlated with the regional differences in its newspaper advertising weights (Figure 10).

Again, prior to the move onto TV, Felix's penetration levels among readers of titles where we advertised grew faster than among readers of non-advertised titles (Table 6).

TABLE 6: FELIX PENETRATION AMONG READERS OF NEWSPAPERS WHERE THE BRAND ADVERTISED

	Ever read %	Never read %
1989	11.6	11.2
1990	16.8	13.3
1991	21.4	15.6

Base: Housewives with cats who ever/never read the *Daily Mirror*, *Daily Express*, *Daily Star*.
Source: TGI

Following the brand's move onto TV, regional differences in the cost of airtime resulted in regional differences in Felix's share of voice. These correlate with regional differences in the brand's penetration growth (Figure 11).

26. The IPA's *Guide To Authors* stresses that 'differences in behaviour or attitudes between those who claim recall of advertising and those who do not will not be regarded as proof of advertising effectiveness, largely because of the contaminating influence of intervening variables like product usage and selective perception. Thus, while it is true that usage and perceptions of Felix's quality are higher among cat owners who are aware of its advertising, we *won't* cite this as evidence that the advertising was responsible. However, perceptions of *Felix's character* are highly unlikely to have been influenced by product usage, so we can legitimately claim that advertising is the only thing that can have driven these particular brand image dimensions.

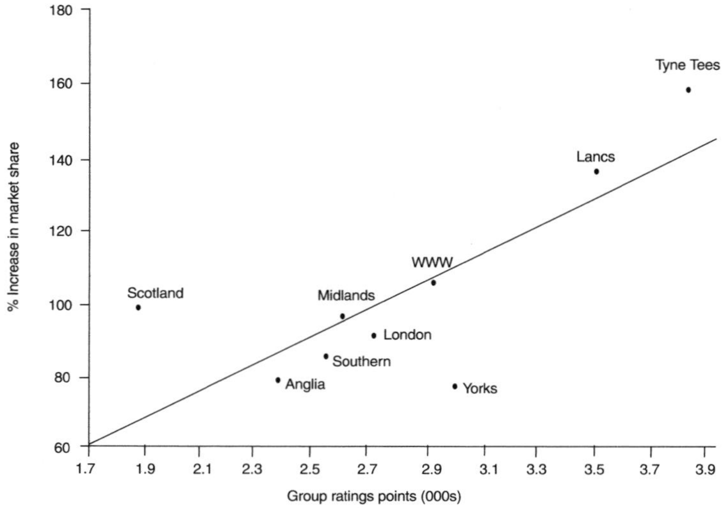

Figure 10: *Felix share gains versus press ratings by region, 1989–91*
Sources: Nielsen, BMP

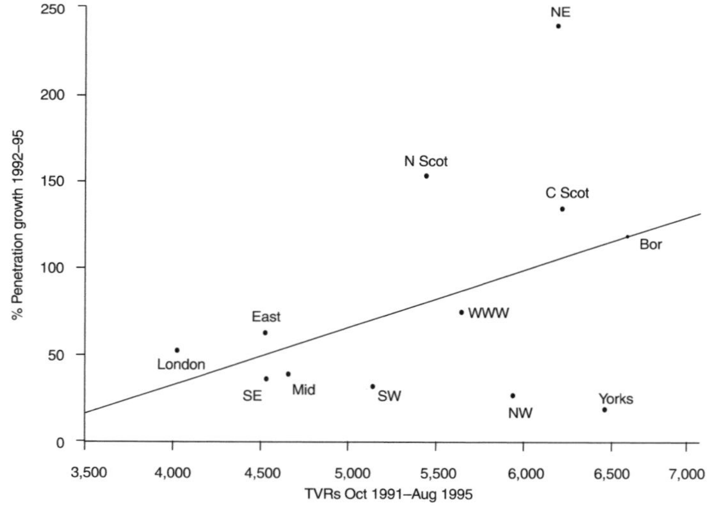

Figure 11: *Felix penetration growth versus TVRs by region*
Sources: MEAL, TGI

Overall, looking at the entire campaign period (up to August 1995), there was a 95% correlation between Felix's monthly share and the amount spent on advertising during the *previous* year (Figure 12).

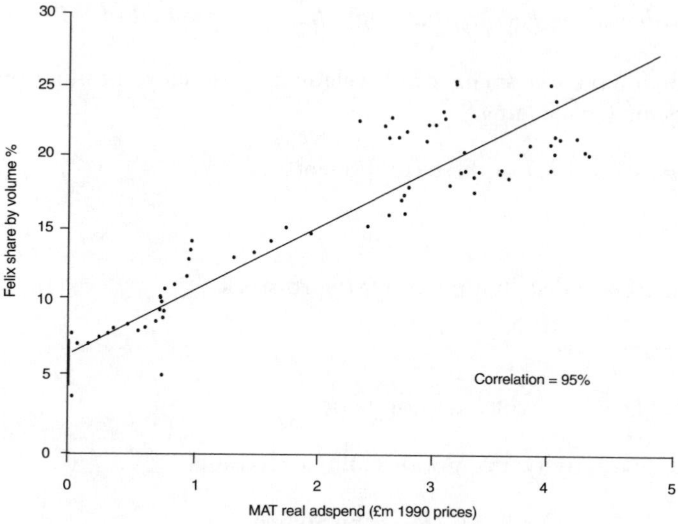

Figure 12: *Felix share versus adspend*
Sources: Nielsen, Register/MEAL

It appears, then, that there is very strong correlational evidence to link advertising to Felix's sales and penetration growth[27]. Can we make this evidence more compelling by ruling out other factors which might also have influenced that growth?

THE CONTRIBUTION OF NON-ADVERTISING FACTORS

Looking at all the non-advertising factors that might have exerted an influence, we found that, although some elements in the marketing mix could have contributed to brand performance, either individually or in combination, advertising is by far the strongest candidate when it comes to isolating the key driving factor behind Felix's success.

---

27. Further evidence – albeit inferential – for the effectiveness of Felix's advertising comes from the 1989 Choosy relaunch. A strong case has been made that the advertising accompanying that relaunch was effective (see 'The relaunch of Choosy catfood', *Advertising Works 6*, pp 302–322). Since Felix's growth considerably outstripped Choosy's in the 12 months post relaunch, when the brands are most comparable, it seems fair to infer that Felix's advertising was even *more* effective.

Non-advertising Factors that might have contributed to Felix's Growth

a) The individual components of the relaunch: product reformulation, new flavours, new packaging.

b) The *combined* effect of these components.

c) Pricing.

d) Trade presence: distribution and forward stocks.

e) Range extensions.

f) The UK black and white cat population.

g) Competitive activity: promotions and advertising.

h) The purchase of Quaker Petfoods by Spillers.

The Individual Components of the Relaunch

Product Reformulation

Perhaps Felix's success was due to straightforward product superiority, either in terms of cat palatability or human appeal.

Although we do not have relative palatability data for all the major brands covering the entire 1989–1995 period, we do have enough to draw some conclusions. Felix's reformulation at relaunch improved its palatability, putting it ahead of Kit-e-Kat. However, this advantage was only temporary. Within 11 months of the relaunch (and seven months after Felix began to advertise), Kit-e-Kat too reformulated and caught up again. More importantly – contrary to some reports – until summer 1992, Felix was consistently *less* palatable than Whiskas Supermeat, the brand from which it appears to have taken most share up to that date (see Figure 13).[28] So, this rules out product superiority as a factor.

As for human appeal, at the time of its relaunch, Felix's chunks-in-jelly format was noticeably different from the meaty-loaf products of Kit-e-Kat, Whiskas Supermeat and Arthur's. However, there are three reasons to believe that Felix's cosmetic appeal was not the key driver of the brand's growth.

28. Source: Quaker/Spillers cattery tests, March 1989, April 1990, February 1992, May 1992, June 1992, August 1992. Interestingly, in August 1992, Whiskas launched a new chunks variant, Select Cuts. This new product outperformed Felix cosmetically and in palatability terms, but its arrival on the market did not reduce Felix's rate of growth.

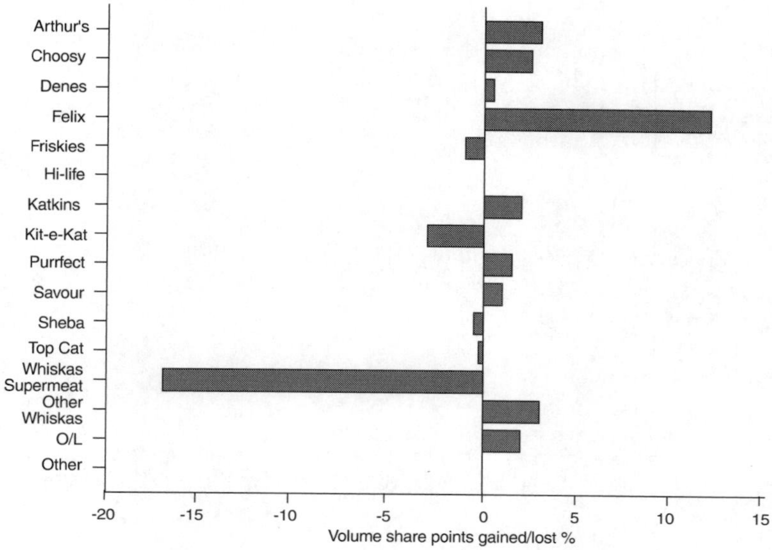

Figure 13: *Share gains April 1989–August 1992*
Source: Nielsen

— Felix had been in this format *unchanged* since September 1982.

— Katkins was also available in the chunks format, yet it did not enjoy similar growth.

— Whiskas, Kit-e-Kat, and Arthur's have all launched chunks-format brand variants since Felix's relaunch, yet none of these has grown to the same extent as Felix.

New Flavours

Cat owners want to give their cats a varied diet so it is possible that some of Felix's growth was driven by its availability in new flavours (Figure 14).[29] However, there are three reasons to believe that this was not a significant factor behind the brand's success. First, the sales for the flavours which had been available *before* the relaunch continued to grow after it.

Second, the *rate of sale* of Felix's original flavours also grew after the relaunch – indeed, by 1992, two of them had become the country's fastest sellers (see Table 7).

29. As well as the three flavours introduced at the relaunch, three more were launched in September 1991, and a further three in March 1993.

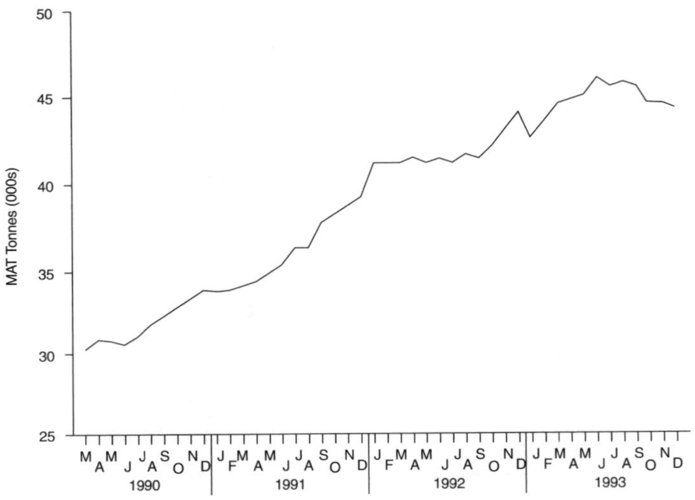

Figure 14: *Felix ex-factory sales, original flavours*
Source: Spillers

TABLE 7: ORIGINAL FELIX FLAVOUR'S RATE OF SALE RANKED VERSUS OTHER CATFOOD BRANDS' FLAVOURS

	Pre-relaunch (Year to 6/88)	Post-relaunch 1 (Year to 6/91)	Post-relaunch 2 (Year to 6/92)
Chicken	33	15	1
Beef	28	16	2
Tuna	39	18	9
Rabbit	36	17	12

(ie in 1988 Felix Chicken was the 33rd fastest-selling flavour in the country, in 1992 it was the fastest seller).
Source: Nielsen
Base: 1988 and 1991 TOPS, 1992 Key Accounts

At no point between 1989 and 1995 did Felix have more flavours in its range than any of its main competitors.

As for *type* of flavour, there is no reason to believe that Felix's flavours were significantly more alluring to cat owners than those of its competitors.

Packaging

There is little evidence to suggest that Felix's packaging was a key driver of brand growth:

— For much of the 1989–95 period, many of Felix's competitors enjoyed the practical advantage of having easy-to-open ring-pull tops.

— According to a quantitative study conducted by Quaker in spring 1989, the revised label did *not* increase owner's 'propensity to purchase' Felix.

— The post-relaunch label, while obviously different from the pre-relaunch design, still followed the conventions of the market.

Figure 15: *Felix pack design, pre-relaunch versus post-relaunch*

That said, Felix's packaging did differ from its competitors in one respect after the relaunch: a paw-print and the phrase 'Tasted and Approved' were printed on the can lid. It is possible that the introduction of this paw-print and phrase could have led to a one-off step change in Felix's performance. However, it is highly unlikely that such a minor difference could have driven Felix's growth for a full *six years*.

The Combined Effect of the Relaunch Components

It may be possible to discount the non-advertising relaunch components individually, but perhaps they worked together *synergistically*. Fortunately, there was a four-month gap between the relaunch and the start of the advertising which allows us to examine the relaunch effect in isolation.

The relaunched product had entirely replaced the pre-relaunch version on shelf by the end of May 1989. Figure 16 shows that, although Felix's share grew in June and July, it fell back in August and September, and did not start to rise again until the advertising began.

This suggests that there *was* a non-advertising relaunch effect but that it was relatively short-lived. Like the paw-print on the can lid, Felix's relaunch might explain a one-off step change in the brand's performance but not six years of sustained brand growth.

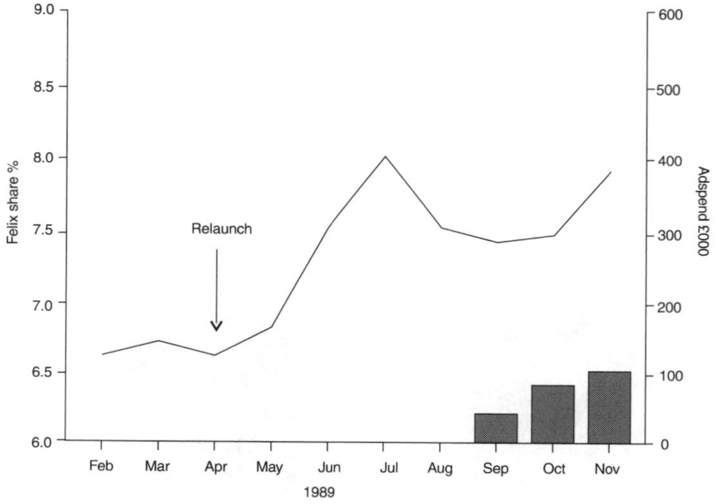

Figure 16: *Felix relaunch 1989*
Sources: Nielsen, Register/MEAL

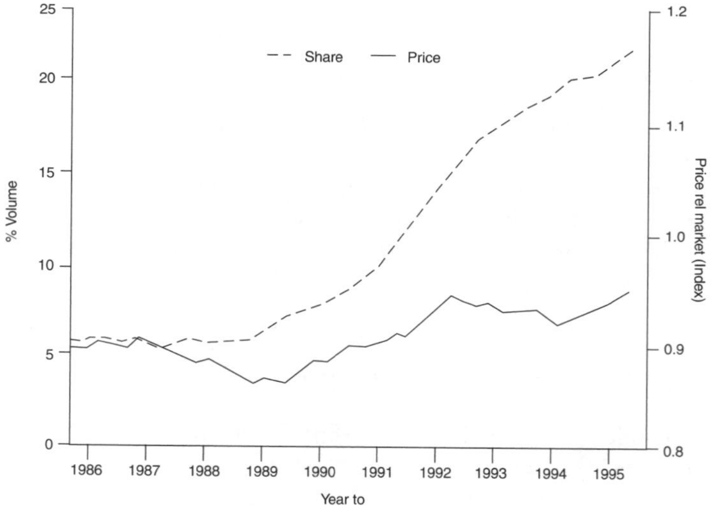

Figure 17: *Felix share versus relative price MATs*
Source: Nielsen

Pricing

Although the catfood market is highly price sensitive, price cutting did not drive Felix's growth: its price *increased* relative to its key competitors (Figure 17).[30]

Trade Presence

Distribution

Felix increased its sterling distribution between 1989 and 1995, but this increase does not appear to have driven the brand's growth. Indeed (as Figure 18 shows), distribution growth lagged *behind* share growth.[31]

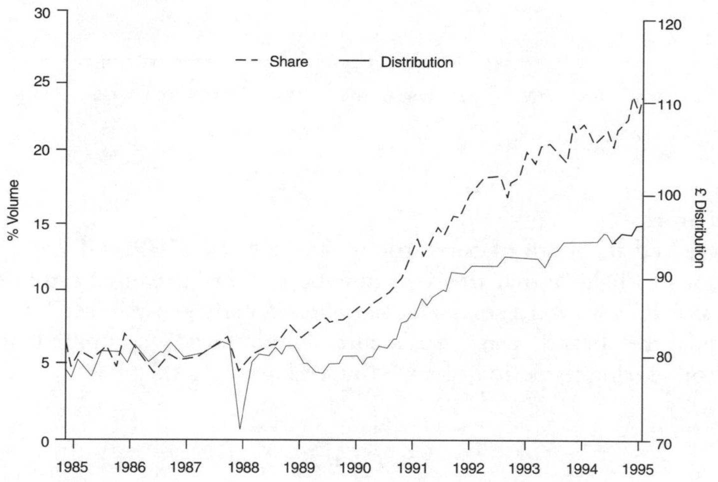

Figure 18: *Felix share versus distribution*
Source: Nielsen

Further evidence showing that distribution was not a factor comes from Felix's rate of sale, which has risen consistently since the advertising began (Figure 19).

30. This pattern of growth could be interpreted in another way: it might be argued that increasing the price improved consumers' perceptions of Felix's quality. This may or may not be true at a perceptual level, but econometrics shows that, all other things being equal, increasing price actually depresses sales. This is true of all catfood brands (and, indeed, nearly all goods and services). However, even if Felix was one of those rare products with a 'positive price elasticity', the price increase could still not explain its sales growth: prices started to rise about a year after the brand started growing.
31. This lag suggests that increases in Felix's sales may have driven the distribution gains.

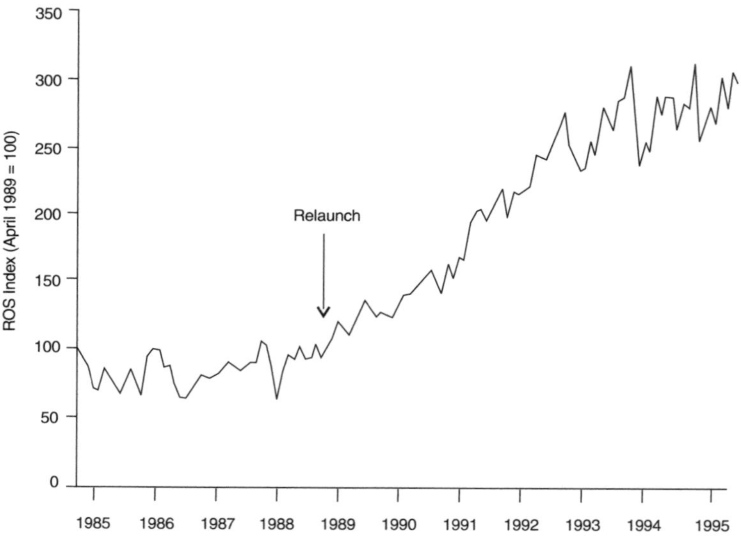

Figure 19: *Felix rate of sale*
Source: Nielsen

Forward Stocks[32]

Felix increased its share of forward stocks between 1989 and 1995 but there are two reasons to believe that this was not the primary driver of brand growth. First, growth of Felix's forward stocks *lagged behind* share growth (see Figure 20).[33]

Second, the brand was consistently 'underfaced' compared with its main competitors during its period of growth (see Figure 21).[34]

Range Extension

There have been two Felix range extensions since the 1989 relaunch:

— From May 1994, the brand was available in a chunks in *gravy* format in addition to its original chunks in *jelly* format.[35]

— From July 1995, the brand was available as a kittenfood variant.

These extensions may have contributed to some of Felix's growth between May 1994 and August 1995. However, since they only accounted for 14% of the

32. A brand's 'forward stocks' can be defined as the total number of cans on display in Britain's shops at any given time. 'Share of forward stocks' expresses that as a percentage of all the catfood brands on display.
33. Suggesting, as with distribution, that the brand's gains in shelf space have been driven by its growing rate of sale.
34. That is, it didn't receive shelf-space allocation commensurate with its volume share.
35. It was the fourth brand to enter this sub-sector of the wet catfood market after Whiskas, Kit-e-Kat and Arthur's.

brand's overall volume by this time, this contribution is unlikely to have been significant.

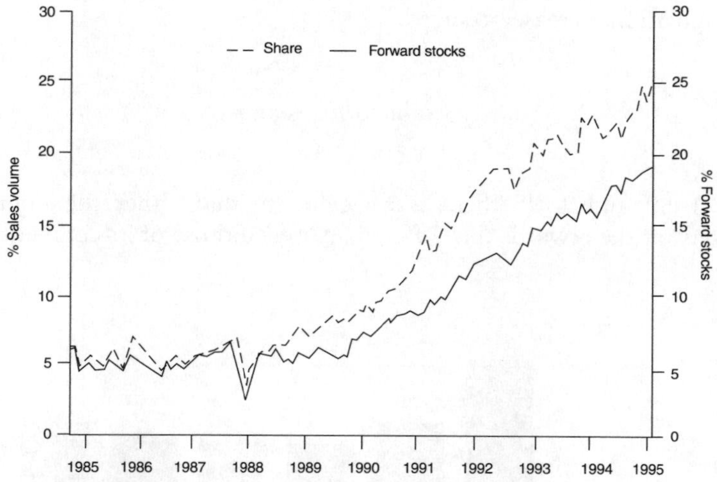

Figure 20: *Felix share versus forward stocks*
Source: Nielsen

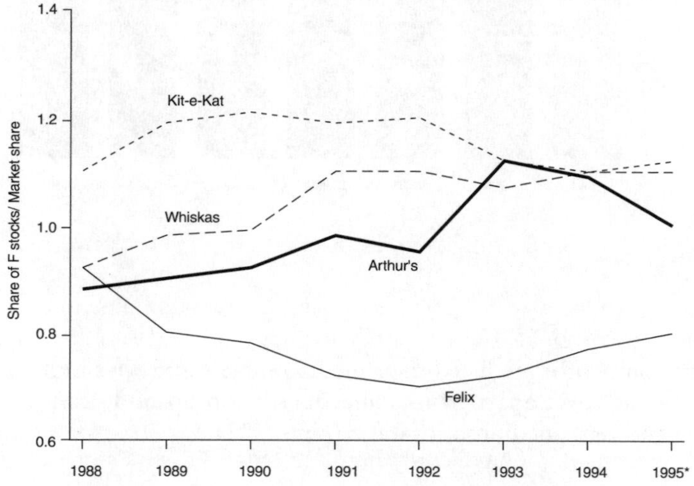

Figure 21: *Forward stocks to share ratio*
Source: Nielsen
* Year to August

The UK Black and White Cat Population

Felix's growth could have been driven by an increase in the proportion of black and white cats within the UK cat population. However, there is no reason to believe such a population increase occurred.[36]

Competitive Activity

Promotions
Between 1989 and 1995 there is no evidence that either the number of Felix promotions, or the rewards they offered, exceeded those of its competitors.

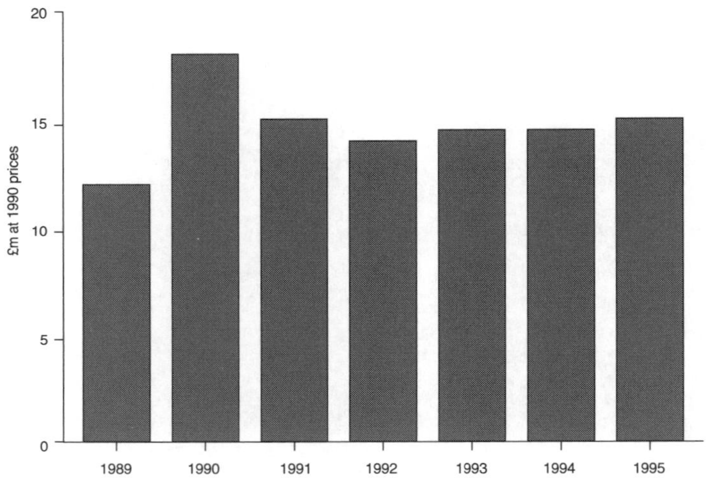

Figure 22: *Competitive adspend*
Source: Register/MEAL, AA

Advertising
Perhaps our competitors reduced their media budgets and we simply outspent them. This was not the case, apart from some fluctuation around 1989 and 1990, their combined spend remained broadly static (Figure 22).

The Purchase of Quaker Petfoods by Spillers

Following Felix's acquisition by Spillers in February 1995, it became part of the same catfood brand portfolio as Arthur's and Choosy, suggesting that some of its

36. Sources: the Cats Protection League, the General Council Of Cat Fancy, the Black and White Cat Club.

growth might have been due to the 'managed decline' of these brands. However, we can state that deliberate portfolio management was not a factor.[37]

Overall, then, we can discount all the factors which might have contributed to Felix's growth.

ECONOMETRICS

The direct and inferential evidence presented so far suggests strongly that advertising has played a key role in Felix's remarkable success. However, to dispel any remaining doubts, we constructed an econometric model of Felix's market share, taking account of all the factors which might have influenced sales over the last ten years. This model provides the final confirmation of advertising effectiveness, demonstrating that Felix's advertising did indeed have a strong and direct effect on the brand's sales.

RETURN ON INVESTMENT

Overall, the model estimates that the £17 million[38] spent on Felix's advertising between 1989 and 1995 increased sales by *£108 million*. Although we cannot reveal profitability figures, margins in the catfood market are sufficiently high for us to say that Felix's advertising more than paid for itself. Indeed, in investment terms, the return from advertising 1989–95 was almost *four times* greater than investing in the FT ordinary share index over the same period.

TABLE 8: COMPARATIVE RETURN ON INVESTMENT PER ANNUM 1989–95

Felix advertising	49.6%
Shares	13.0%
Bonds	9.1%
Bank deposits	9.3%

Source: BMP Estimates

Furthermore, there are good reasons to believe that the true payback is even greater:

— The model shows that the advertising effect is quite long-lasting; even if the ads had stopped in 1995, they would still be generating extra sales for several years to come. Using a reasonable set of assumptions, modelling estimates that the

37. Given that we have already ruled out product quality, trade presence, advertising weight, and pricing as drivers of Felix's growth, it is hard to conceive what form such 'portfolio management' could have taken.
38. Source: MEAL/Media Register. This figure doesn't include production costs. However, these are more than counterbalanced by substantial discounts achieved in buying the Felix press advertising.

extra sales generated between 1995 and the year 2000 by previous advertising would probably be worth a further £90 million.[39]

— As well as direct advertising effects, the ads may have had an *indirect* effect on brand growth by helping to persuade retailers to stock more Felix.[40]

— Econometrics suggests that Felix's price elasticity has fallen since 1989, reducing the impact of price increases that have taken place since. Although we cannot quantify its contribution, it seems likely that advertising was partly responsible for this.

— All of the above calculations assume that, without advertising, Felix's sales would have been roughly static. However, there is good reason to believe that, had we not taken action in 1989, Felix might have eventually been delisted. In that case, advertising may have made the difference between having sales of £111 million a year and having no sales at all.[41]

CONCLUSION

IPA effectiveness papers often end with a pertinent marketing moral. In the case of Felix, it is hard to know which one to choose. We could stress the David and Goliath side of the story: that advertising can be an extremely powerful business tool in markets which appear to be 'sewn up', even when the budget is tiny in comparison with the competition. We could talk about the benefits of 'joined-up thinking', emphasising the integration of creative and media planning, where the latter is used as a tool to reinforce the content of the advertising rather than simply as a way of delivering it efficiently to the target audience. Or we could point out the virtues of a continuous but tightly targeted media presence, even when this means coverage figures end up looking a little thin.

However, if forced to highlight just one lesson from the Felix story, it would be that the advertiser who dares wins: breaking the advertising conventions of a market can be highly effective in business terms, provided your rule-breaking is based on rock-solid consumer insight.

---

39. 1990 prices.
40. The model shows that some of Felix's extra sales were due to increases in forward stocks. However, forward stocks in this market are principally determined by historic sales levels, suggesting that Felix's stock gains were largely a knock-on effect of the brand's early share gains. We know from the modelling that many of these share gains were, in turn, due to advertising, so some of the extra sales attributed by the model to stock gains were almost certainly due to advertising. Without modelling forward stocks, it is impossible to quantify this indirect effect, but it may well be as big as the direct effect.
41. Although the value of Felix's equity has not been formally audited it is also worth noting that in February 1995 Spillers paid £442 million for the Quaker Petfood business and its two principal brands, Felix catfood and Chunky dogfood.

11

The Volkswagen Golf 1984–1990

INTRODUCTION

In the IPA booklet 'How to Win – A Guide to Authors' it is stated that, 'Allowance is made for how difficult it is in each case to isolate advertising effect. In some cases eg car campaigns, it is fiendishly difficult.'

In the introduction to a number of recent 'Advertising Works' volumes, comment is made about the need for new ways of looking at how advertising works and how to *prove* advertising works: 'Over time we must expect to see a development and a broadening of what is submitted and what is rewarded and published in these Awards, otherwise the advertising business will fall into the trap of believing that it has already solved all the intractable problems of measuring effectiveness.'

In this paper, we aim to address both of these points. We hope to demonstrate that:

1. Using conventional means to isolate the advertising effect of a car campaign in any long-term sense (ie not a '0% Finance' offer), is even more than 'fiendishly difficult' – it may well be impossible.
2. That a car campaign can convincingly be shown to have been effective if a new approach is taken to proving its effectiveness.

WHY IS PROVING ADVERTISING EFFECTIVENESS IN THE CAR MARKET SO DIFFICULT?

Before demonstrating how we believe a car campaign can convincingly be shown to have been effective we must explain why, in our view, isolating advertising effect in the car market is so difficult.

Our explanation concentrates on two areas:

1. The nature of the purchase process.
2. Attitudes to a marque.

The Purchase Process

The key point here is that:

1. It is a long and complex process with many stages coming between advertising and a sale.

Because

2. A car is an infrequent high risk, expensive purchase, akin to choosing a new house. If you get it wrong, you have to live with your mistake for a long time.

The implication is that trial purchasing, in the sense used in fmcg markets, does not really exist in the car market. People won't buy a car just to give it 'a go' as they might with a newly advertised lager or toilet cleaner. Hence, the usual method of showing a clear link between a particular piece of advertising causing an immediate uplift in sales followed by repeat purchase and loyalty measures, will not work in the car market.

Attitudes to a Marque

The point we want to make here is that even if we had a complete set of data covering the so called 'soft' measures of effectiveness (which we do not), it would not be particularly helpful in demonstrating the effect of advertising.

It is our contention that there is one factor of overwhelming importance that dictates imagery and attitudes to a marque or model and that is the reality of the product itself. Our analogy involving house purchase may help to explain this view. Choosing a particular model of car – say a VW Golf – is analogous to choosing to live in a particular area – say Hampstead. (The particular variant, colour and extras you choose would then be analogous to the particular house or flat you choose.) To keep the analogy fair, let us assume we have an audience of people who are already aware of Hampstead*. Now, we would suggest that it would be entirely unreasonable to expect an advertising campaign to significantly alter the image of Hampstead and people's attitudes to it.

The reality of the architecture, the local amenities, the heritage of the area and the prices of the housing will not have changed and will be too powerful to be overshadowed by paid for communication from an interested party.

On the other hand, to make the point from the opposite direction, an example would be Docklands in the mid 1980s. In Docklands, the 'product' *was* significantly altered. Redevelopment, refurbishment, new local shopping and transport facilities were all introduced and, consequently, the imagery of Docklands and people's attitudes to it changed enormously.

Together, we hope these two analogous examples show that image and attitudinal measures are of little value in proving advertising effectiveness in the car market because they don't change unless the product changes (see later). In fact, large changes in these measures would be a much better argument for the existence of improved product 'effectiveness' ie the effect of introducing better product.

* Awareness of Golf is close to 100%

We can demonstrate quite clearly this point that it is *the standard of the product* that determines attitudes to a marque by using one of the few measures we have (since 1982) for most marques. Fortunately, it is an important measure being, in our view, the summation of all attitudes to any marque*. The measure is that of propensity to consider. The question asked of 1,200 nationally representative car owners who bought new in the last five years is: 'Suppose you were going to buy a new car tomorrow. Which makes would you seriously consider?'

For virtually all manufacturers (we shall come onto the one exception later), this measure does not change to any significant degree. Figure 1 shows the sort of variation that is typical. This relative stasis (which corresponds to very slowly changing market share for a marque) raises a large question that relates back to our analogous examples of Hampstead and Docklands.

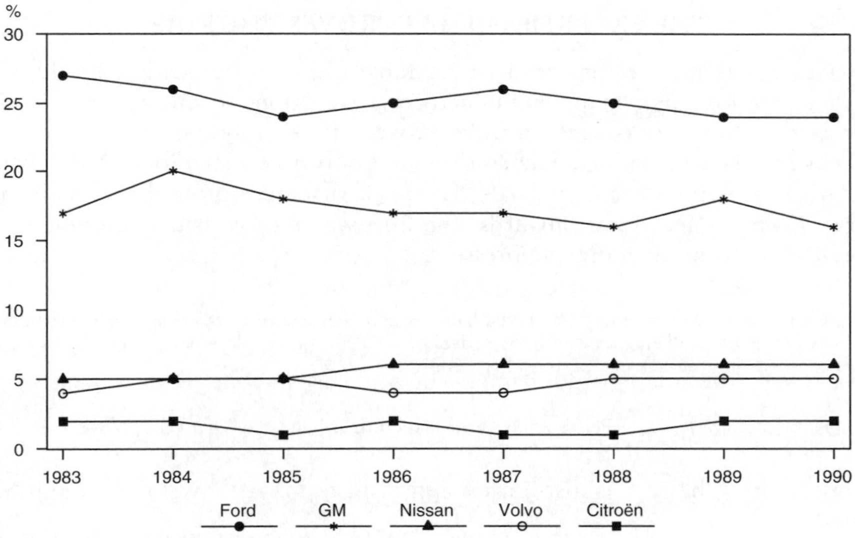

Figure 1. *Propensity to consider (Percentage share 1983–1990)*
Source: VW

After all, 'redevelopment' is a feature common to all car marques. New models costing billions of pounds in development costs are launched every year. Hundreds of millions of pounds are spent on advertising and promotions every year singing the praises of these new cars. And yet the propensity to consider or 'desirability' of a marque seems to move slowly if at all. Why should this be? The answer lies in the fact that *all* car manufacturers are continually 'redeveloping', not just the odd one or two.

Consequently, what the propensity to consider question is measuring is *relative* desirability at any given time. And, it is a fact of the marketplace that *relative* desirability doesn't change much because the *relative* strengths of different cars don't change much. It is exorbitantly expensive to design an entirely new car, and manufacturers are rightly wary of alienating the customers they already have.

* All our 'soft' data are for marques rather than models. But since Golf accounts for over half of all Volkswagens sold and is by far the best known model VW make, 'VW' is a good proxy for 'Golf'.

Hence, most new cars are simply subtle evolutions or updates of what has come before – slightly different curves reflecting changing fashion or developments in aerodynamic theory; incorporation of peripheral new technology such as ABS or lean burn engines; an improved interior. In most cases, the name is not even changed (eg Escort, Golf, Granada, Astra etc). In addition to their natural wariness, another factor is at work. All major manufacturers are working on new products using the same computers, complying with the same legislation, targeting the same audience and jealous of their competitors' previous technical advances.

The only time a given car has an advantage over its competitors is when it is new and its competitors aren't. However, this is only sustainable up to the point at which the new competitor is launched and at that point the advantage shifts to the competitor. And so it repeats itself.

THE EXCEPTION THAT PROVES THE RULE

We have said that new cars tend to resemble old cars but with the addition of today's technology. For major manufacturers, exceptions to this rule are rare and, as far as the 1980s are concerned there is, we believe, only one. The manufacturer was Peugeot, the car the 205. The 205 was not only a vast step forward for Peugeot (ie relative to its predecessor the 104), it was a vast step forward for small cars in general. From its inception onwards, the 205 was met with unconditional praise and adulation from the motoring press:

> 'In years to come 1983 may well be looked back on as something of a watershed time in the design and marketing of small cars. For with the arrival of the Peugeot 205 the small car can be seen to have come of age.' What Car?, November 1983

> 'It must be the surest winner Peugeot have ever had on their hands.' *What Car?*, November 1983

Importantly, the 205 is also an exception in terms of how long its appeal has endured:

> 'Eleven (sic) years old and the Peugeot 205 still drives rings round the opposition. Can anything beat this car?' Performance Car, June 1992

> 'The best car of the '80s and still going strong. Not many family hatches have this sort of staying power: a testimony to the design's original quality of "rightness".' Autocar and Motor, May 1992

Remembering that the propensity to consider question measures a marque's desirability *relative* to its competitors it seems clear that with the 205 we would expect Peugeot's desirability to leap up after 1983 and to continue rising as more and more people become aware of the change that had occurred. This is precisely what we do in fact see (Figure 2). The proportion of new car buyers that would consider a Peugeot increases from 3% in 1983 to 14% in 1990. Quite clearly (Figure 3), this increase in the number of people who would consider a Peugeot translates into remarkable growth through the 1980s for Peugeot.

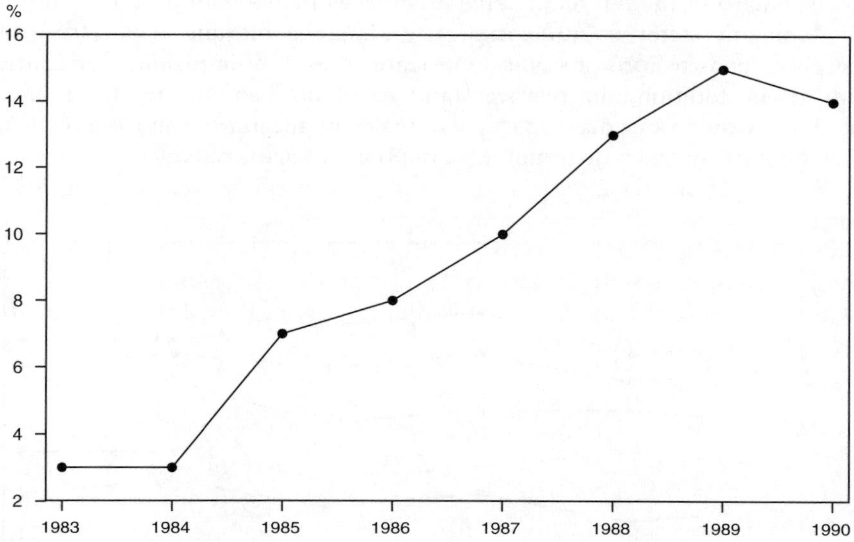

Figure 2. *Propensity to consider Peugeot*
Source: VW

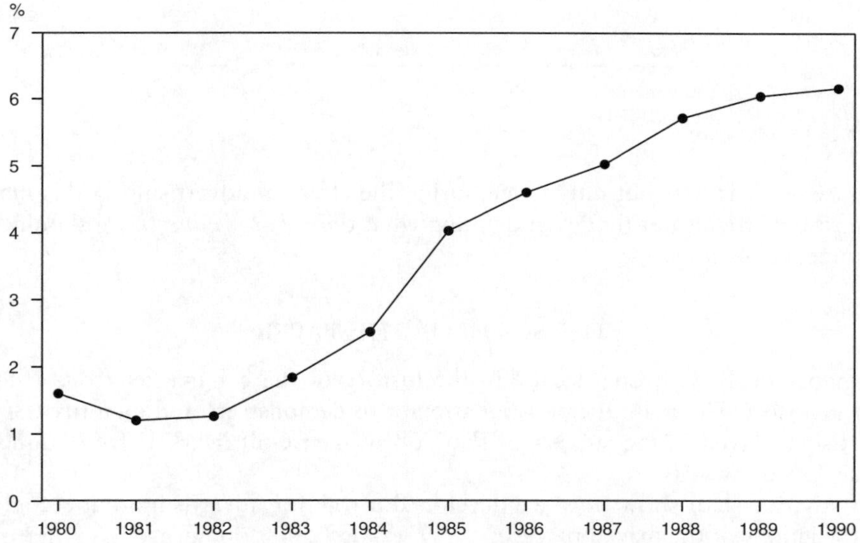

Figure 3. *Peugeot market share (1980–1990)*
Source: SMMT

SUMMARY

Measuring advertising effectiveness in the car market is very difficult.

There is no such thing as 'trial' and hence changes in sales, repeat purchasing and loyalty are difficult to attribute to particular pieces of advertising.

The standard of the product relative both to its predecessor and the competition is the dominant factor in influencing attitudes to a marque. The nature of the marketplace tends to force a situation of status quo in both products and attitudes (Figure 4). In addition, the relative standard of product dictates the number of people who would consider a particular make in the future and hence this also tends to be static unless a quantum leap, in product terms, is made.

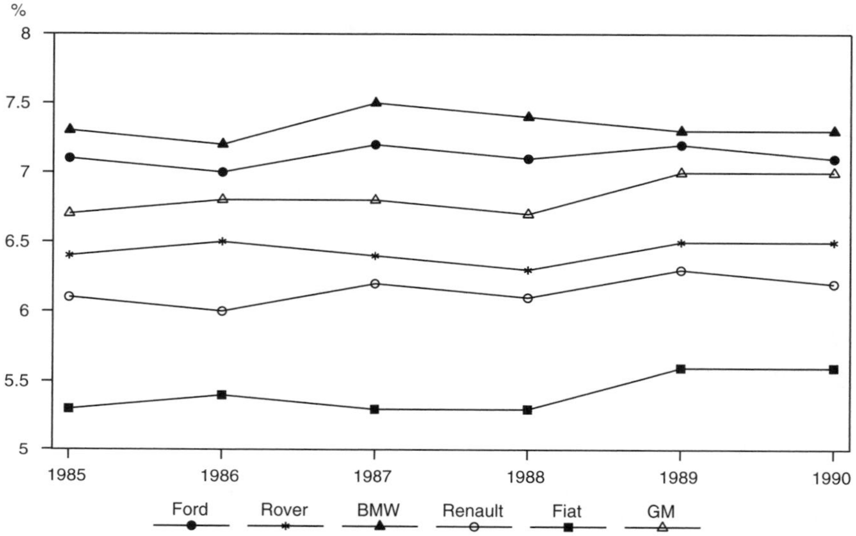

Figure 4. *Overall attitude to marque (1985–1990)*
Source: VW (average of all scores)

It seems clear that not only is measuring the effect of advertising in this market going to be difficult but that even defining what the *role for advertising* should be is by no means obvious.

THE SCOPE OF THIS PAPER

This paper deals with one decade in the history of the car market from 1980 to 1990 inclusive. The main theme is an attempt to demonstrate and quantify the part advertising played in the success of the Volkswagen Golf Mark II from launch in March 1984 onwards.

Firstly, we shall show how we developed a role for advertising that recognised the restrictions of the marketplace.

We shall go on to demonstrate the effectiveness of this advertising by developing a simple model that predicts *any* new car's behaviour in share terms. We shall show that any new car behaves (in share terms) in a well-defined way and that this behaviour is easily understood. Finally, we shall show that the Golf is the *only* car that breaks the 'laws' of the car market and that the only credible explanation for its anomalous performance is its advertising.

DEVELOPING A ROLE FOR ADVERTISING

We have written a lot about what advertising can't do or can't be seen to do. Specifically, we have shown how advertising can't overpower the reality of the product and hence significantly alter attitudes to it. We have also shown how advertising can't be seen to directly influence or cause a particular sale (because of the peculiarities of the purchase process). So what can advertising do? What could be the role for advertising?

At the time of the launch, the role for advertising is clear and simple. Namely, to build rapid awareness of the existence of the *new* car. However, assuming this role has been fulfilled, the future role for advertising is less obvious.

The answer, for VW, lies in us returning to our house buying analogy. Whilst our potential Hampstead resident may be fully *au fait* with the rational attributes of the area – the analogues to 'good performance', 'technically advanced cars', 'reliable' and 'safe' – what he or she can't know is what it *feels* like to actually live there. In other words, what does moving to Hampstead imply about him or her as a person? This is clearly a much more subjective and emotional dimension than the realities of house prices, local amenities and architecture. It was from these ideas that the advertising strategy for Golf was developed. The strategy was linked to Volkswagen's 'reliability' positioning through the idea, 'You (the driver) can rely on it (the car)'.

Role for Advertising

The role for advertising was to make our audience *like the idea* of owning a Golf more than would be expected from the reality of the car.

Target Audience

People who would consider a Golf for their next car.

Advertising Objective

To make people who would consider a Golf more likely to actually buy one, ie to provide a marginal reason for choice of a Golf rather than an Escort or Astra.

Advertising Strategy

By making the idea of being the sort of person who owns a Golf more appealing.

THE ADVERTISING

The brief for 'Casino' (see storyboard) was a copy of Rudyard Kipling's poem *If*. The task was to present the hero of the poem as the sort of person who would choose to drive a Golf. The creative team elaborated on one particular part of the poem and it was this that generated the ad:

> 'If you can risk all your winnings on one turn of pitch and toss. And lose and start again at your beginning and not breathe a word about your loss.'

'CASINO'

This is a man who put a million on black

and it came up red

This is the man

who married a sex kitten just as she turned into a cat

This is the man who moved into gold just as the clever money moved out

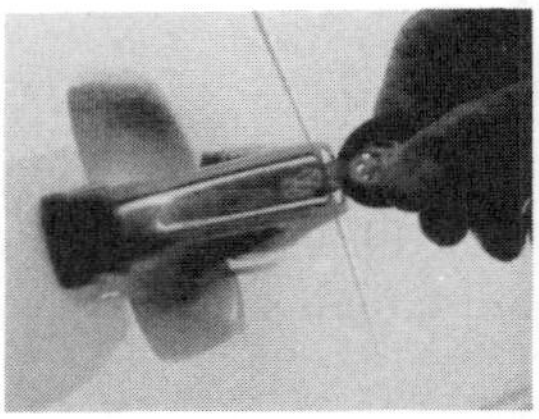

This is the man

who drives...

...a Volkswagen

Everyone must have something in life he can rely on.

'CHANGES'

Everyone is going through changes

and no one knows what's going on

and everybody changes places

but the world still carries on

Love must always change to sorrow

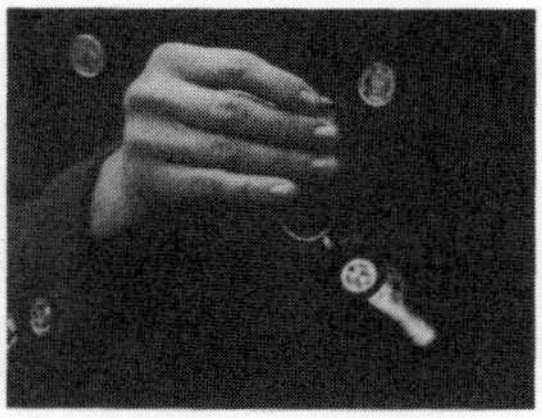

and everyone must play the game

it's here today and gone tomorrow

But the world goes on the same

Music fades

For 'Changes' (see storyboard), the brief was simply to do another 'Casino' but with a woman in it!

Both ads were solely about the drivers of the car. In the context of the product focused ads produced by competitors, they were revolutionary.

How We Thought the Advertising Would Work

Impulse purchase is not a feature of the car market. People usually end up with two or three cars that they find acceptable, each of which will have, in their minds, particular strengths and weaknesses. Anything that can add to the marginal appeal of one of their potential choices may well be enough to solve their dilemma and tip the balance in favour of that car. It seems reasonable to suppose that if someone is happy, on functional grounds, with either a Golf or an Escort, then their final decision may well rest on whether the *idea of being a Golf owner* is more or less appealing than being an Escort owner. It was this marginal factor that we hoped to influence.

THE MEDIA

The nature of the media strategy was dictated by three factors:

1. We wanted to reach the biggest, broadest possible audience, most of whom would not be replacing their car for some time.
2. We wanted to be as intrusive as possible.
3. We wanted to make our audience *feel* what it was like to be a Golf owner.

For these reasons, TV was felt to be the most appropriate medium. Golf is a mass market car, hence we went for a mass market car buying audience of ABC1 adults.

Between 1985 and 1989, 'Casino' and 'Changes' were given eight bursts of national TV airtime.

Total media spend as follows:

'Casino'	£5.2m
'Changes'	£5.7m
Total	**£10.9m**

Source: MEAL

DEMONSTRATING ADVERTISING EFFECT

Developing a Lifecycle Model

In order to demonstrate the effect of the Golf's advertising we must first develop a predictive model of the 'shape' of a new car's share performance following launch. The reason we need this model will become clear as we develop our case.

— *The General Case*

From our understanding of the market, we can state a few key facts:

(i) A new car's main competitive advantage is, simply, that it is new.

(ii) The cyclical nature of new car launches means that this advantage will only be held for at most two or three years and will then be lost to some other manufacturer's new car.

(iii) In general, new cars are subtle evolutions of what came before and do not fundamentally upset the status quo.

(iv) Consequently, the total number of people who would consider buying one does not increase significantly, ie total potential demand is flat.

Taking these four facts it seems clear that, following launch, one would predict a couple of years of increasing share followed by gradual share decline up to the point of launch of the new car's replacement (Figure 5).

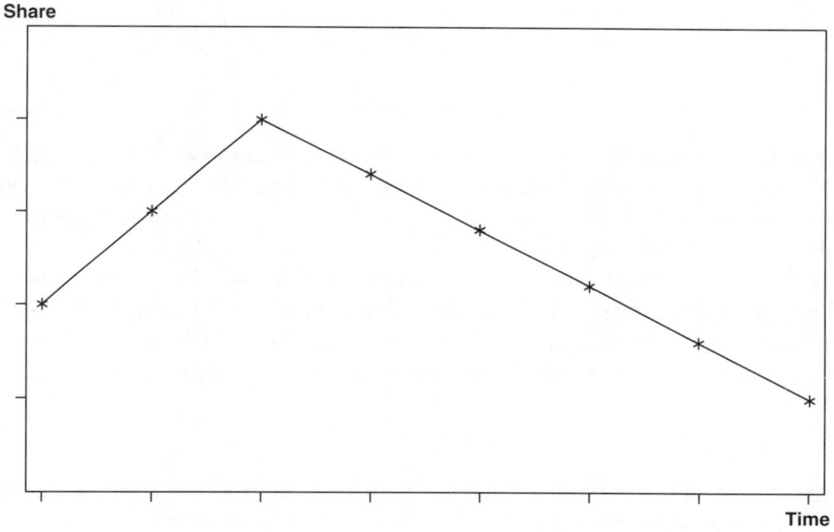

Figure 5. *The general case – predicted share pattern*

— *The Exceptional Case*

Very occasionally, facts (iii) and (iv) must be substituted for as follows:

(iii) The new car *is* a quantum leap forward relative both to what the manufacturer had produced before and to the competition. The new car fundamentally upsets the status quo.

(iv) Consequently, as awareness of this unexpected upset to the status quo grows, the number of people who would consider buying one also grows, ie total potential demand grows.

Taking these facts into consideration, it seems clear that, following launch, one would predict steadily increasing market share, perhaps beginning to tail off as the effect of the age of the car increasingly counters the effect of increasing potential demand (Figure 6).

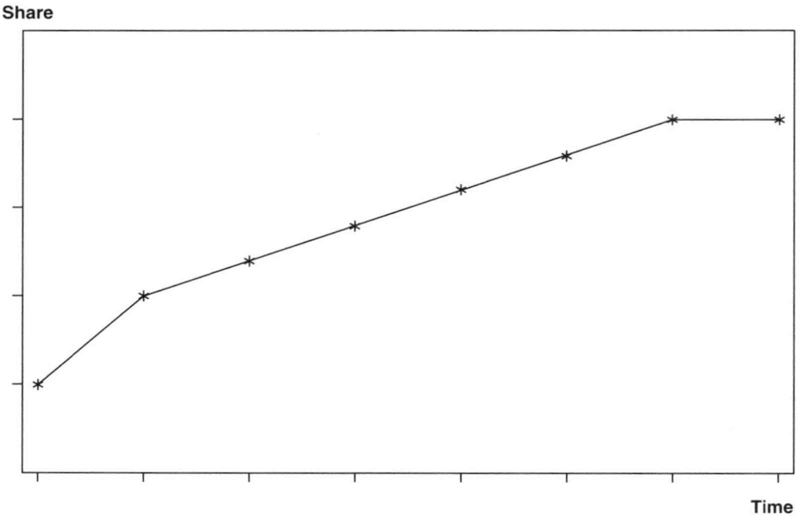

Figure 6. *Exceptional cases – predicted share pattern*

The Model

We now have a simple predictive model for the 'shape' of *any* new car's share performance from launch onwards. The model depends on only one variable, namely whether or not the new car is a dramatic leap forward both for its manufacturer and for the market.

If it is not a dramatic leap forward, as is almost always the case, then we would predict two or three years of share growth followed by gradual decline. If it is a dramatic leap forward then share should continue rising for longer with the rate of growth slowing (and maybe finally reversing) as the car's age catches up with it.

Testing the Model

To test our model, we have looked at a large sample of new car lifecycles. We confined ourselves largely to the first half of the decade for three reasons:

1. To keep the task manageable.
2. To look at the Golf's nearest contempories.
3. To provide enough time for a fully-developed lifecycle to emerge.

We tried to ensure our sample was as representative as possible by looking at:

— Both British and imported marques.
— Models launched under new names (eg Citroën Visa, Ford Sierra etc) as well as familiar ones (eg Escort, Renault 5 etc).
— Cars from every major sector of the market.

(The one major area we will ignore is Japanese manufacturers since the quota agreements mean that UK sales of Japanese cars are almost entirely supply, rather than demand, driven.)

We already know, both from our general market knowledge as well as more crucially from the potential demand data (ie propensity to consider) that only the Peugeot 205 fits into our 'exception' category. For all other cars, therefore, we would expect to see a quick rise followed by gradual decline. As can be seen (Figures 7-13) this is exactly what we find (bar the odd fluctuation probably caused by a facelift, a special edition model, or a price promotion).

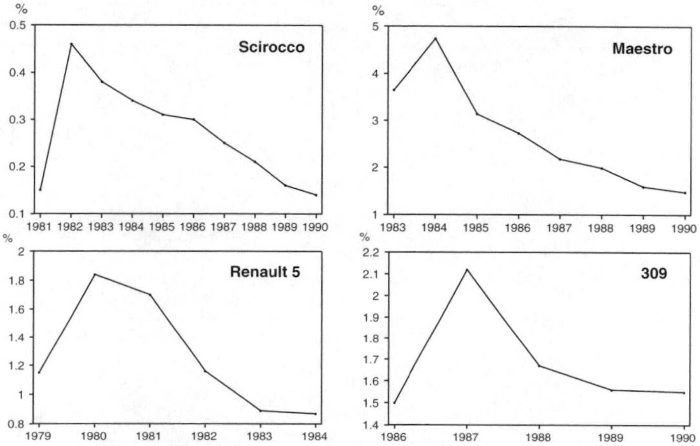

Figure 7. *Market share – Scirocco, Maestro, Renault 5, 309*
Source: SMMT

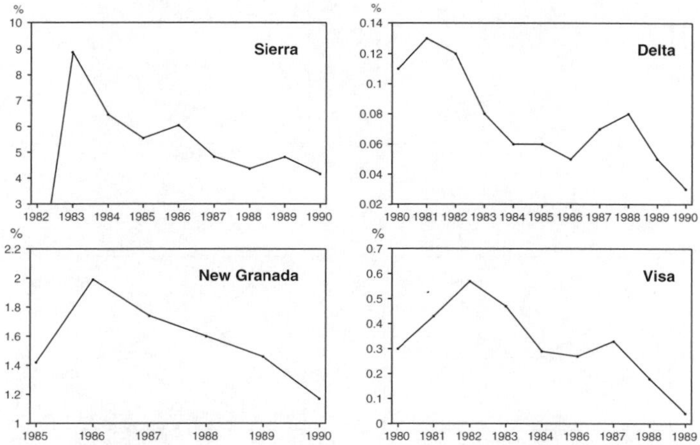

Figure 8. *Market share – Sierra, Delta, New Granada, Visa*
Source: SMMT

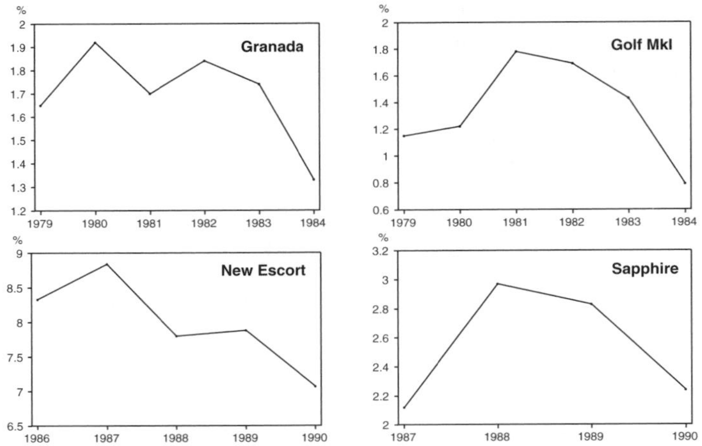

Figure 9. *Market share – Granada, Golf Mk I, New Escort, Sapphire*
Source: SMMT

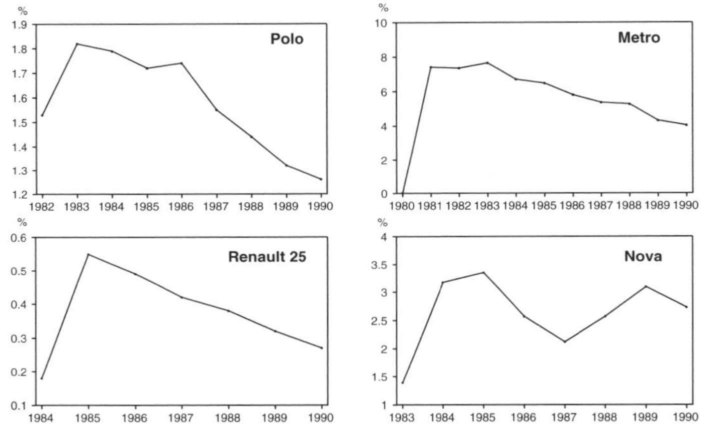

Figure 10. *Market share – Polo, Metro, Renault 25, Nova*
Source: SMMT

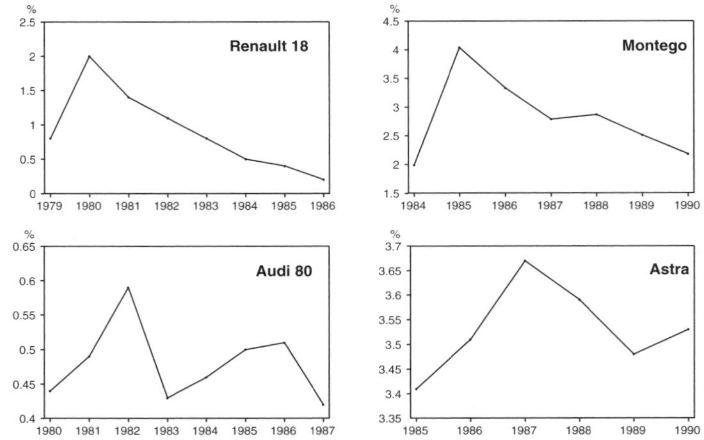

Figure 11. *Market share – Renault 18, Montego, Audi 80, Astra*
Source: SMMT

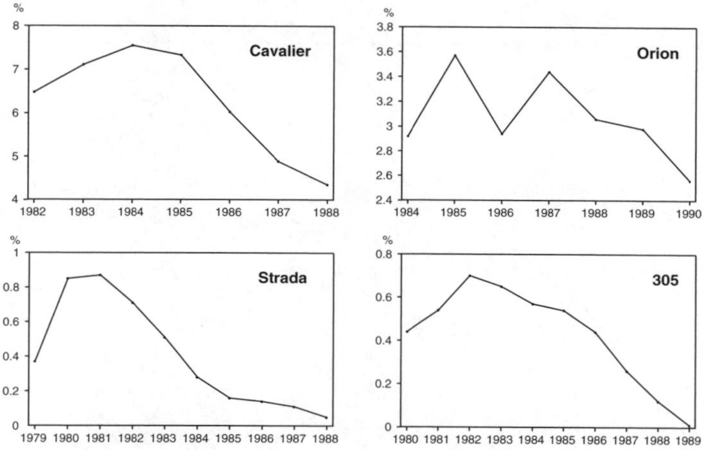

Figure 12. *Market share – Cavalier, Orion, Strada, 305*
Source: SMMT

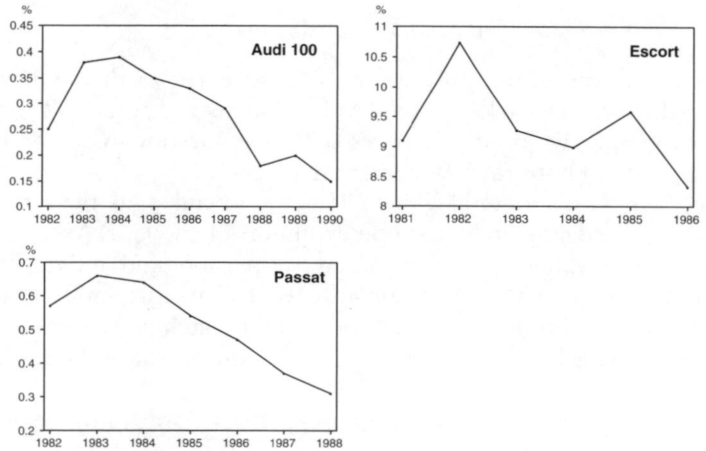

Figure 13. *Market share – Audi 100, Escort, Passat*
Source: SMMT

What is remarkable is that the model works on only one variable. The new cars that we looked at display the same basic share performance shape:

- Regardless of manufacturer.
- Regardless of British or import origins.
- Regardless of market sector.
- Regardless of whether the new model retains the name of its predecessor (Escort) or breaks all links with the past (Metro).

Our exception, the 205, also performs as we would expect given the nature of the product and the consequent increase in potential demand (Figure 14). In fact, the 205 almost singlehandedly accounts for Peugeot's spectacular share growth as a marque.

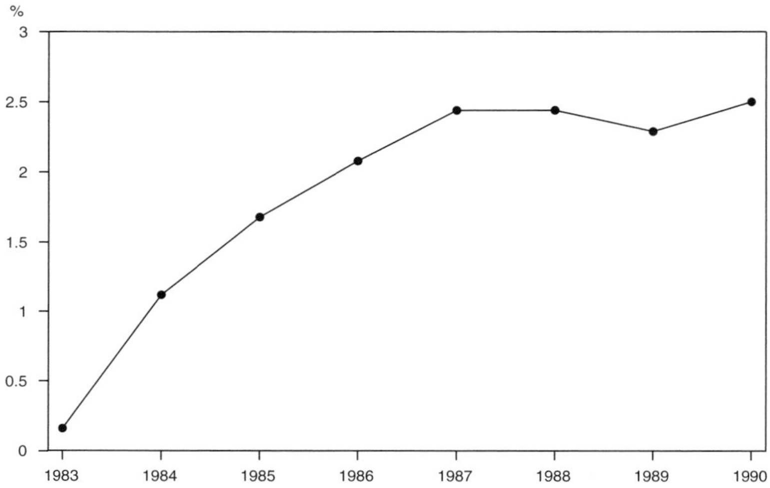

Figure 14. *Market share – Peugeot 205 1983–1990*
Source: SMMT

The Model Applied to Golf

We are now in a position to apply what we have learnt to the Volkswagen Golf Mark II, launched in March 1984. To decide what sort of future VW should have predicted for their car we need to answer only one question 'Was the new Golf a dramatic leap forward both for VW and for the market?'

The new Golf was not, unlike the 205, ever intended to be a revolutionary vehicle. It was quite deliberately a subtle evolution of the Golf Mark I. The main changes were more cabin space, reworked suspension and a larger fuel tank. Cosmetically, the lines of the car were softened for a more modern appearance. Crucially though, the car was still a 3 or 5 door hatchback, came in the same variants from the base level CL, through the GL and up to the GTi, and was still called Golf.

Contemporary reviews in the motoring press reflect how cautious VW had been:

> 'Then came the new Golf. The shock was the extent to which it deliberately looked like the previous model. In essence, the new Golf is little more than the old one, stretched in the wheelbase, its screen more steeply raked and its nose smoothed over for the sake of lower drag.' *Car*, March 1984

> 'A feeling of disappointment almost clouds our judgement on the new Golf; disappointment that the new model breaks little new ground, simply reinforcing existing strengths.' *What Car?*, April 1984

> 'There is no breathtaking thrill of innovative styling, no obvious new techniques of engineering, and little sign of any special new cult appeal which might develop.' *What Car?*, April 1984

In product terms, then, the Golf Mark II was no 205; like its competitors the new Escort and Astra, it fitted squarely into the 'maintaining the status quo' bracket.

From this, we would predict two things. The first is that the new Golf would have little or no effect on propensity to consider a Volkswagen. This proves to be the case (Figure 15). The second is that, in share terms, we would expect Golf to follow the common pattern of rapid growth followed by gradual decline. What actually happens (Figure 16) is completely unexpected. Share climbs steadily during the six years following launch and only dips slightly in the seventh. (As we shall see later, the drop in the seventh year was caused not by a tailing off of demand but by an extraordinary and unplanned for supply problem.)

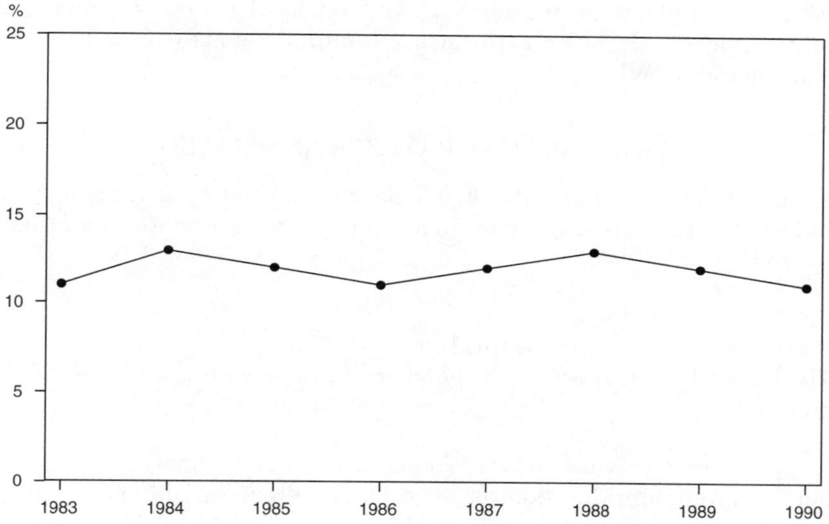

Figure 15. *Propensity to consider VW*
Source: VW

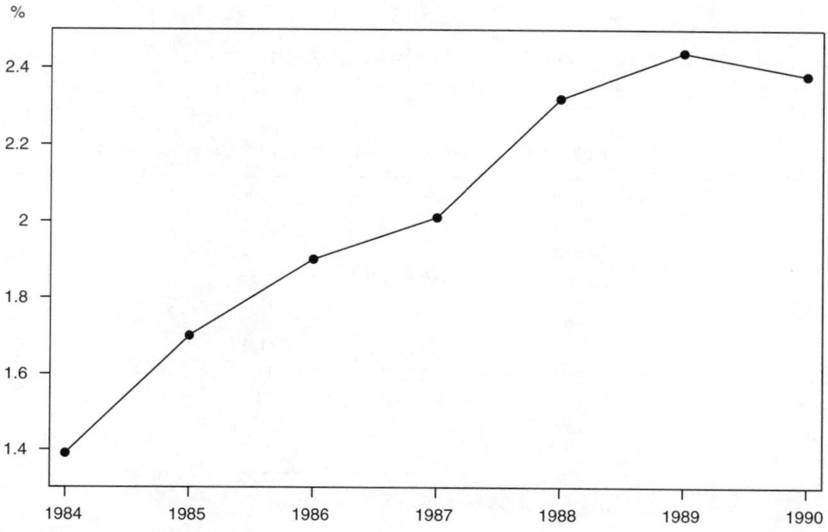

Figure 16. *Golf Mark II market share 1984–1990*
Source: SMMT

The difference between what we would expect to see and what we actually see cannot be overstated. We are not looking at a difference of degree but a fundamental change of structure. It demands an explanation. After all, in every respect Golf fits perfectly the pattern of the vast bulk of new cars:

— It is an evolutionary model.
— It has little/no effect on propensity to consider.

In fact, judging by the press comment, Golf fits in with the potentially less successful new products on the market. And yet its share performance seems to deny all the evidence. Its share performance is a total anomaly. Clearly we need to answer the question 'Why?'.

THE SEARCH FOR OTHER ANOMALIES

In fact, the search is not that difficult. We have already eliminated the main area – the product. We have seen, through three sources, that the cause cannot lie in the product itself:

— The Golf is evolutionary.
— The press response supports this fact.
— The launch has no effect on the number of people who would consider buying one.

What we are left with are the other areas of the marketing mix: price, distribution, promotion. In addition, there is one other variable pertinent to cars (especially from foreign manufacturers) which is supply (ie availability). Finally, we need to also look at competitive activity in terms of new car launches.

Price

Perhaps Golf grew share through massive price reductions as the car grew older. As is clear from Table 1, this is not the case.

TABLE 1: GOLF PRICE INDEXED ON AVERAGE OF KEY COMPETITORS*

1981	103
1982	102
1983	100
New Golf	
1984	106
1985	107
1986	109
1987	112
1988	111
1989	108
1990	104

Note: * (Escort, Astra, Maestro etc)

Distribution

Volkswagen share of distribution has remained more or less constant throughout the decade. In absolute terms, the number of VW dealerships has fallen from 354 in 1984 to 343 in 1990.

TABLE 2: VOLKSWAGEN DEALERS AS PERCENTAGE OF ALL CAR DEALERS

	%
1981	4.1
1982	4.3
1983	4.1
New Golf	
1984	4.0
1985	4.1
1986	4.2
1987	4.3
1988	4.3
1989	4.2
1990	4.3

Supply

In the first two or three months of its life, as with any new car, production problems with the new Golf had to be ironed out and supply was affected. This is expected when any new model is introduced.

Beyond this, there were no problems with supply to the UK until, ironically, towards the end of its lifecycle. When the Berlin Wall came down in November 1989, Volkswagen in Germany saw a massive new market open up. Their urgent desire to supply this new market resulted in an increase in factory time devoted to left hand drive production. Supply of (right hand drive) Golfs to the UK was significantly reduced.

Competitive Launches

As we have shown, the effect of new car launches tends to be counterbalanced by the fact that all manufacturers are continually developing new products. The period following the launch of the Golf was as rich in new car introductions as any other. Clearly, the anomaly we are searching for is not a lack of competitive product.

SOME MAJOR MODEL LAUNCHES PRE AND POST GOLF

1979
Fiat Strada
Ford Granada
Renault 5
Renault 18

1980
Peugeot 305
Audi 80
Austin Metro
Lancia Delta
Citroën Visa

1981
Scirocco
Ford Escort

1982
GM Cavalier
Audi 100
Passat
Ford Sierra

1983
Peugeot 205
GM Nova
Austin Maestro

1984
Austin Montego
Renault 25

1985
GM Astra
Renault 5
Ford Granada
Mazda 323

1986
Ford Escort
Ford Orion
Fiat Croma
Nissan Sunny

1987
Citroën AX
Toyota Corolla
Ford Sapphire

1988
Fiat Tipo
Colt
Peugeot 405
Seat Marbella

1989
Ford Fiesta
Renault 19
GM Cavalier
Proton

We now know at least what does *not* account for Golf's extraordinary performance:

— It was NOT the product itself.
— It was NOT its price.
— It was NOT distribution.
— It was NOT supply.
— It was NOT a lack of competitive products.

We are left with a completely anomalous share performance for which we cannot find a corresponding anomaly in any of the areas we have looked at so far.

However, there remains one final area in which to search.

THE ADVERTISING

Following some fairly undistinguished launch advertising in early 1984, the Golf was supported from 1985 to 1989 with two of the most popular and unprecedented pieces of TV advertising ever made for a car. As we shall show, this is not only our view but the view of the people who saw the ads.

It is unfortunate that VW have no tracking data prior to 1990 nor any qualitative research reports from the time.

However, what we do have is the results of groups conducted amongst mixed new car buyers in early 1992. The two ads were shown once and respondents were simply asked to comment on them. The first surprise was the extent to which the advertising was universally recognised and acclaimed:

> 'I remember it, I think it's wonderful.'
> 'You could run that ad now and it would still be brilliant.'
> 'Was it that long ago, 1985, I can't believe it.'
> 'I'd describe it as timeless.'
>
> (Casino)

> 'It's difficult to be objective now because it gets played on every review of great ads you ever see on TV.'
> 'That's one of my favourite ads ever.'
>
> (Changes)

> 'I can't remember any other car ads.'
> 'They definitely stand out in my mind.'
> 'They're brilliant, fantastic.'
> 'They're streets ahead of other car advertising.'
>
> (Both)

Both ads were felt to stand radically apart not only from other car advertising but from other advertising in general.

What was striking about the ads was the way in which they talked about the car indirectly, through the person who would drive it:

'I very strongly identify with it because I'd like to make lots of money and be very successful but I probably won't be but one of the few things that is within my control is the kind of car I buy. That says a lot about the sort of car I'd buy.'
'It's about his way of life, his style.'
'It's chin up, carry on. If at first you don't succeed and all that. It's inspiring.'
'It makes you believe the car is good. They don't even need to talk about it.'

(Casino)

'It concentrates on the buyer rather than the car. It identifies a set of values that you would identify with when you bought the car, do you see what I mean, instead of talking about 0-60 or anything like that.'
'It makes the car the woman's friend. That's very appealing.'
'It tells me everything I want to know about the car without telling me anything!'

(Changes)

'I love both of those. Especially at that time when everyone was going in the opposite direction.'
'It's streets ahead. Every other make does driving on the continent through twisty lanes. It's just on a completely different plane.'

(Both)

In addition, the ads seemed to make people emotionally closer to VW as a manufacturer. This is probably the key source of their enduring strength:

'It makes you like VW for its understanding of you.'

(Casino)

'It makes you feel really good.'

(Changes)

'They tap a real emotional vein.'
'You feel good when you watch them. A hell of a lot better than you would watching a car driving up a mountain.'

(Both)

It seems clear that the new Golf had not one, but two anomalous aspects to it:

— An extraordinary share performance.
— Extraordinary advertising.

WHAT EVIDENCE IS THERE OF DIRECT ADVERTISING EFFECT?

Despite the problems that exist in trying to directly show advertising effect, we believe there are a few clues that suggest the advertising worked in the way we had hoped.

As already stated, in general, attitudes to VW did not change and should not be expected to change. The bulk of the measures covered areas such as:

'Is very safety minded.'
'Makes mechanically reliable cars.'
'Makes cars which are reasonably priced.'
'Makes technically advanced cars.'
'Offers cars with good workmanship' etc.

These were measures of people's perception of reality and hence were most strongly influenced by reality. Taken as a whole, this battery of measures varied across the 1980s by an amount statistically equivalent to zero. Given what we know about the marketplace and the fact that respondents were inevitably scoring VW *relative* to the competition, this result is not surprising.

Fortunately, we have three measures available for VW since 1982 that are a little less rational in nature and hence may provide evidence of a change in the way people *felt* about VW.

The first two of them are included in the attitudes battery and ask respondents to mark VW out of 10 for: 'Makes cars that have personality and character' and 'Is a prestige make'.

Whilst the changes in score against these measures are undramatic, in the context of the stability of all other measures, they are significant. (Figures 17-19).

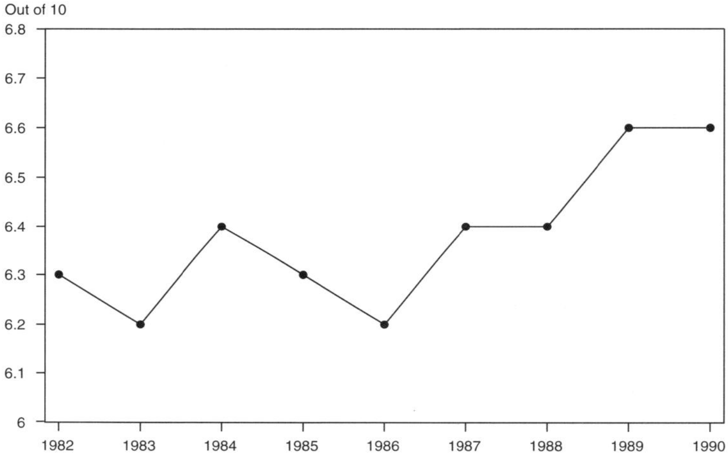

Figure 17. *Attitudes to VW – 'Cars with personality and character'*
Source: VW

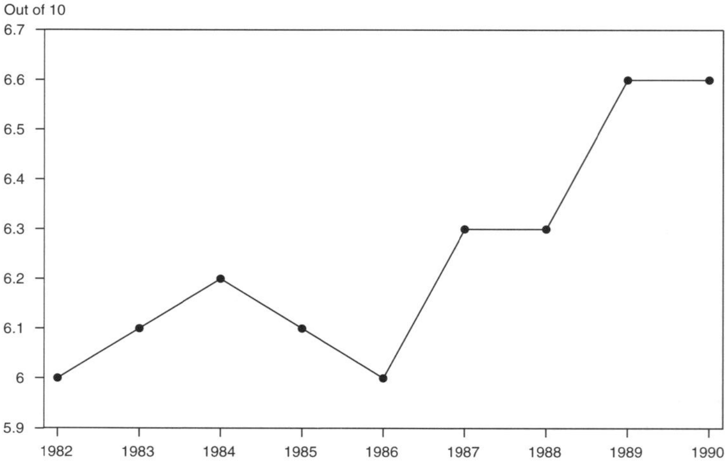

Figure 18. *Attitudes to VW – 'Is a prestige make'*
Source: VW

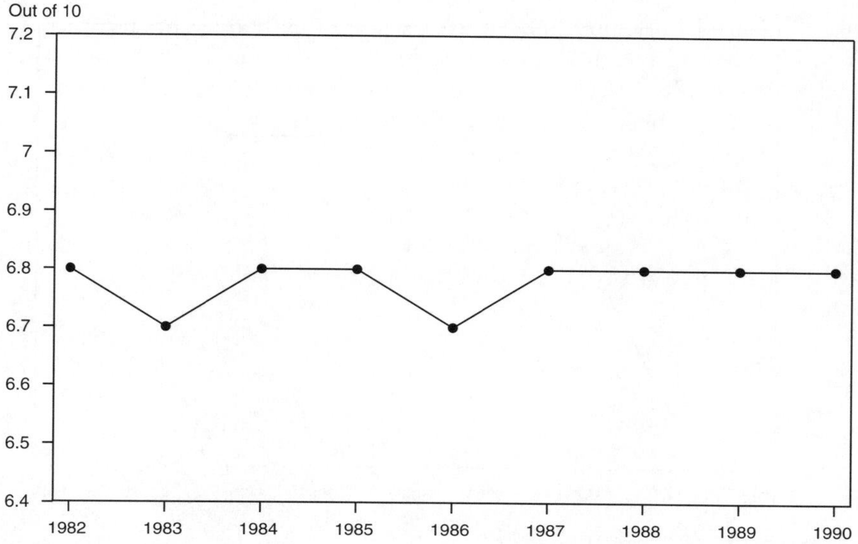

Figure 19. *Average of attitudes to VW (excl 'prestige' and 'personality')*
Source: VW

The third measure we have is also probably the closest we have to measuring the effect we wanted. This measure is 'overall liking for VW', again scored out of 10. Once again, the movements aren't spectacular but are significant (Figure 20). The increase of 'liking' for VW relative to other marques also increased (Figure 21) so this was not a market-wide effect.

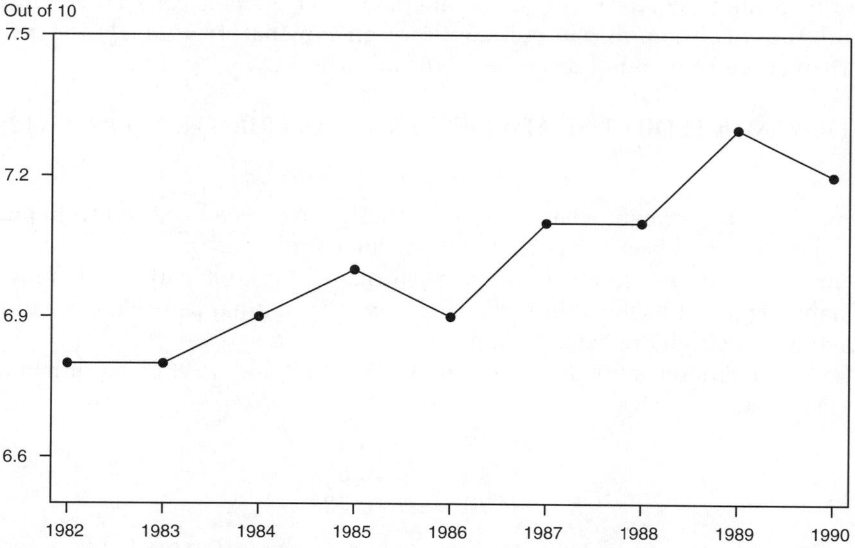

Figure 20. *VW marque 'liking' (1982–1990)*
Source: VW

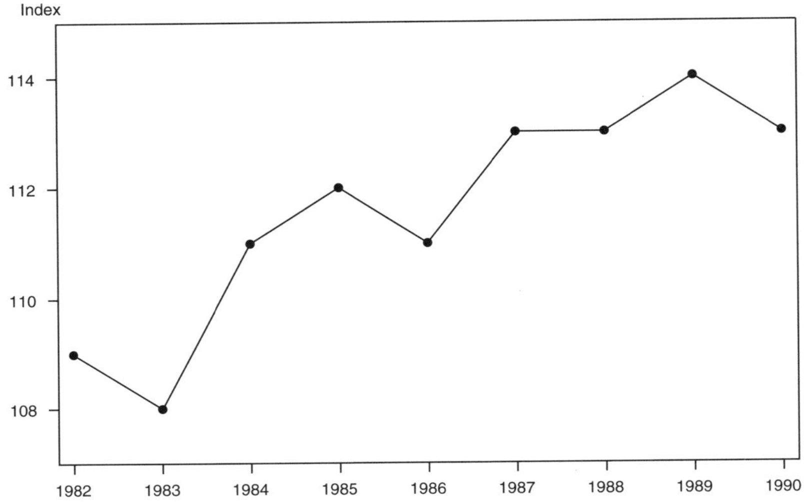

Figure 21. *VW 'liking' relative to all marques (1982–1990)*
Source: VW

We believe these three measures, together with the qualitative results, provide all the evidence we are ever likely to find that the advertising worked in the way we had hoped. We were never going to make someone who wouldn't consider buying a Golf suddenly consider it. But we could make someone who would consider a Golf more likely to ultimately choose one.

We are left with two choices. We can ignore the compelling evidence of the 'laws' of the car market and dismiss the Golf's share performance as just 'one of those things' and the advertising as an unrelated coincidence. Alternatively, we are left with the conclusion that in our search for an explanatory anomaly for the car's performance we have found only one – the advertising.

HOW MUCH DID THE ADVERTISING CONTRIBUTE TO PROFIT?

How Big was the Effect?

It is very hard to estimate what could reasonably have been expected to happen to Golf's share if it had been supported with 'ordinary' advertising.

Being as optimistic about the share performance of Golf without the ads as is reasonable, Figure 22 shows the difference between what happened and what might reasonably have been predicted to happen.

There is a difference in share only in 1988, 1989 and 1990. The difference in each case comes to:

1988	:	+0.4%
1989	:	+0.6%
1990	:	+0.7%

In terms of number of vehicles, this equates to 36,720 extra Golfs across the period 1988–1990 or around £30m additional gross profit. With an advertising spend against Golf of only £10.9m from 1985 to 1989 this is clearly a good

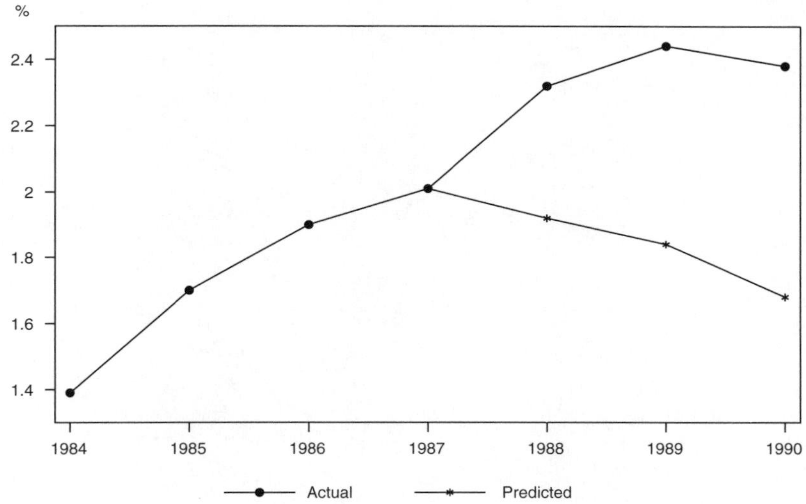

Figure 22. *Golf Mark II market share (predicted vs actual)*

investment. In addition, with loyalty averaging around 50% in the car market, any additional sale today generates at least half an extra sale in the future. This would increase the financial value of the advertising still further.

Where Did the Extra Sales Come From?

We know that the Golf's main competitors are Escort and Astra so most of the Golf's extra sales will have almost certainly come from them. Across the three years 1988–1990, a total of 821,550 Escorts and Astras were sold. The Golf's extra 36,720 sales are therefore equivalent to less than 5% of people who 'ought' to have bought an Escort or Astra buying a Golf instead. We suggested we were looking for a marginal effect and that seems to be exactly what we have got.

SUMMARY

We have shown that new cars in the car market behave in a well defined and predictable way. All the cars we looked at fit the pattern of behaviour that we described except two – the 205 because of a remarkable product and the Volkswagen Golf because of remarkable advertising. In addition, we have shown how this advertising worked by breaking the product-focused 'rules' of the market and concentrating instead on the owner of the car. Finally we have demonstrated that, even by the most conservative estimate, the advertising was a commercially successful investment.

CONCLUSION

We hope we have shown conclusively that a car campaign has been effective. However, we were lucky in that we were dealing with extraordinary advertising. Advertising that caused a change in the 'structure' of Golf sales through its lifecycle.

Proving the long-term effectiveness of more 'run of the mill' car advertising is a challenge that has yet to be answered.

12

HEA AIDS Advertising

The effective use of mass media advertising to meet the challenge of AIDS

INTRODUCTION

In the UK there is a new generation with different sexual behaviour because of the threat of HIV and AIDS.[1]

Partly as a result of this, the UK is now "a low prevalence country in a high prevalence world", its AIDS prevalence dropping from 93% of the twelve EC countries average rate in 1984, to 54% in 1993.[2]

This case will argue that this is at least partly a result of the government's mass media advertising through the Health Education Authority (HEA) around AIDS which achieved its two primary objectives:

i) preventing HIV/AIDS slipping off the public agenda; and
ii) encouraging condom use among young heterosexuals.

We will evaluate the HIV/AIDS advertising developed by BMP DDB Needham on behalf of the HEA from December 1988 to December 1993.

The focus will be on the campaigns run in general public media. It excludes advertising targeted specifically at gay men which ran in gay clubs and press.[3]

---

1. Source: National Survey of Sexual Attitudes and Lifestyles ('National Survey') as published in: Johnson A, Wadsworth J, Wellings K, and Field J (1994) *Sexual Attitudes and Lifestyles* Blackwell Scientific Publications. (All subsequent references to the National Survey are from this publication.) The National Survey represents the first comprehensive survey of UKs sexual behaviour and attitudes. It interviewed a representive sample of 18,876 men and women aged 16-59. Interviewing took place from May 1990 to November 1991 (and hence overlapped with the largest period of HEA advertising activity).
2. Source: WHO European Centre for the Epidemiological Monitoring of AIDS. Quarterly report no.40 (31.12.93). Analysis: HEA. Behaviour change among gay men and the success of needle exchange schemes have also kept AIDS prevalence in the UK low.
3. The advertising to gay men was designed for an audience at a very different stage of awareness and understanding about the risks of HIV. Moreover, promoting 'safer sex' to this audience primarily involved promoting non-penetrative sex. Only latterly (1992 onwards) has HEA advertising focussed on advice on condom use for gay men.

THE EARLY DAYS: 1986–1988

By the mid 1980s AIDS was seen by the government as one of the greatest threats to the UK's public health this century, and significant public education campaigns preceeded the work developed by BMP and the HEA.

In 1986 and 1987 the Department of Health (DOH) through TBWA dramatically announced the arrival of AIDS in the UK. The campaign, featuring apocalyptic images of tombstones and icebergs, stressed the seriousness of AIDS, and that everyone was at risk. The multi media advertising was supported by a leaflet distributed to all 23 million households in Britain.

The high level of awareness and anxiety generated by this campaign proved a double-edged sword. It was impossible for the government to continue publicity at this level. In fact there was a twelve month gap before further advertising appeared. But because publicity stopped, people believed the threat of AIDS had lessened.

The HEA was created in 1987, and took over responsibility for all aspects of AIDS public education[4].

Its first work (through TBWA) attempted to address some of the problems it had inherited. Swings in public concern from alarm to complacency needed replacing by more reasonable levels of concern amongst the relevant group, ie sexually active young heterosexuals. Two commercials ran in Spring 1988, 'Flat' and 'Disco'.

Tonally, however, the advertising remained sombre and threatening, echoing TBWA's earlier work.

By mid 1988 the HEA was seeking a more balanced and factual advertising approach. BMP were appointed in the autumn of 1988.

THE NEW APPROACH TO HIV/AIDS ADVERTISING

Autumn 1988 to December 1993

To prevent the transmission of HIV, the HEA wanted to encourage young sexually active heterosexuals (demographically 16-34 year olds with two or more sexual partners in the last 12 months) to use condoms.

The development of advertising strategies to achieve this was guided by behavioural models, notably the 'Health Belief Model'[5]. This states that to change their behaviour:

> "individuals must have sufficient concern about health issues and believe that:
> — they are susceptible to the illness and hence perceive a threat;
> — illness would be avoided with appropriate behaviour change;
> — behaviour can be changed at an acceptable cost."

---

4. With the exception of drugs, the responsibility for which remained with the DOH.
5. "Health Belief Model" (Rosenstock, Strecher and Becker) as quoted by McEwan R and Bhopal R (1991) *HIV/AIDS health promotion for young people: a review of theory, principles and practice* HEA AIDS Programme Paper No.12. See also Wellings K (1992)
Assessing AIDS Prevention in the General Population. Report for the EC Concerted Action (I UMSP, Lausanne)
It should be noted there are criticisms of this model, not least that it oversimplifies the social and psychological complexities around behaviour change (in much the same way as models of consumer purchasing behaviour in FMCG markets do).

Advertising therefore had to work on two levels.

a) To maintain 'sufficient concern' around HIV/AIDS, advertising needed *to prevent HIV/AIDS slipping off the public agenda*. The nature of HIV (its long incubation period and the inability to tell by sight if someone is infected) meant:
— many were likely to be positive without knowing it;
— thousands who had been diagnosed often chose not to disclose their HIV status for fear of being marginalised.
These factors resulted in
— no 'visible' evidence of AIDS for most of the general population;
— generally 'low' official statistics exposed by the press.
Advertising had to impress upon the general public:
  i) AIDS was a serious ongoing threat;
  ii) it was an increasing problem relevant to heterosexuals;
  iii) the link between HIV and AIDS (to explain the apparent 'invisibility' of AIDS).

b) For 16-34 year olds with 2+ partners we needed to *encourage them to use condoms* by creating the conditions for behaviour change suggested by the Model. Thus advertising was used to:
  i) encourage them to believe they personally could be at risk from HIV;
  ii) promote condoms as the primary means of prevention; and
  iii) reduce some of the 'barriers' around condom use, as a means of removing their emotional 'cost'.

Achieving both sets of objectives, particularly from 1989 to 1992, also involved targeting those with an influence upon the sexually active young. High profile, mass market media such as TV and national press were used for large parts of the campaign to reach beyond young heterosexuals to the broader public. (See Figure 1.)

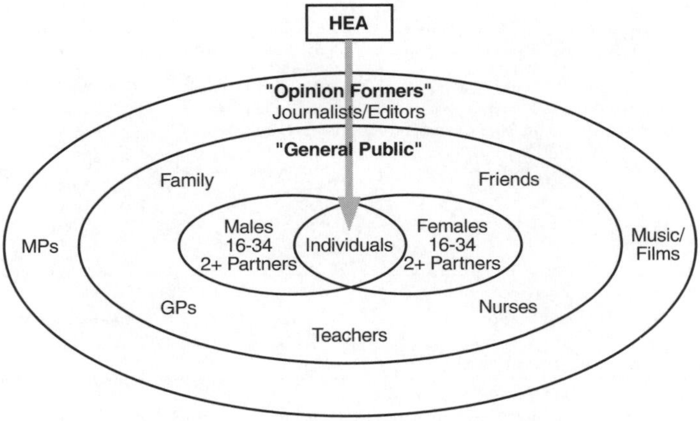

Figure 1.

CHRONOLOGY OF THE CAMPAIGN

Tables 1 & 2 provide a summary of the HEA's HIV/AIDS advertising in wider media from December 1988 to December 1993[6]. Broadly the advertising since 1988 can be grouped under three headings:

— keeping HIV/AIDS on public agenda and encouraging perceptions of risk among heterosexuals;
— reducing the barriers to condoms;
— safer sex on holiday.

TABLE 1: HIV/AIDS CAMPAIGN CHRONOLOGY: DECEMBER 1988 – DECEMBER 1993

Timing	Campaign Title	Target	Specific Objectives	Media	Spend
December 1988-March 1989	HIV Facts	General public 16-34s, 2+ partners	Keep HIV/AIDS on public agenda. Link HIV to AIDS.	National Press	£1.8m
Spring/Summer 1989	Empowerment	Young women	Help breakdown barriers to condom use	Women's Press	£179k
Summer 1989	Travel	Young holidaymakers	Reminder to use condoms on holiday	Poster/Tubecards	£171k
World AIDS Day 1 December 1989	WAD	General public 16-34s, 2+ partners	Keep HIV/AIDS on public agenda. Link HIV to AIDS.	National Press	£179k
February-March 1990	Experts	General public 16-34s, 2+ partners	Re-establish importance of AIDS. Reassert heterosexual risk.	TV National Press	£2.9m
Summer 1990	Travel	Young holidaymakers	Take condoms on holiday	Posters near airports Tubecards/Radio	£313k
Autumn 1990	'Hands'	Behaviourally bisexual men	Identify with HIV risk	Special interest male press	£47k
December 1990-March 1991	'Testimonies I'	General public 16-34s, 2+ partners	Keep HIV/AIDS on public agenda. Personalise risk for young heterosexuals and promote condoms	TV	£2.3m
December 1990-February 1991	Mrs Dawson	16-34s, 2+ partners	Normalise condoms	Cinema	£431k
July-August 1991	'Testimonies II'	General public 16-34s, 2+ partners	Keep HIV/AIDS on public agenda. Personalise risk for young heterosexuals and promote condoms	TV Radio	£1.58m
July-August 1991	Mrs Dawson	16-34s, 2+ partners	Normalise condoms	Cinema	£120k
Summer/Autumn 1991	'Hands'	Behaviourally bisexual men	Identify with HIV risk	Male Press/ Supplements	£95k
December 1991-February 1992	'Testimonies III'	General public 16-34s, 2+ partners	Keep HIV/AIDS on public agenda. Personalise risk for young heterosexuals and promote condoms		
	PLUS				
	Mrs Dawson	16-34s, 2+ partners	Normalise condoms	TV	£1.24m
December 1991-February 1992	Mr Brewster	16-34s, 2+ partners	Normalise condoms	Cinema	£167k
June-August 1992	Mr Brewster	16-34s, 2+ partners	Normalise condoms	Cinema	200k
August-October 1992	AIDS Can Affect Anyone	Black and minority ethnic groups	Raise profile of AIDS as issue for this target	Posters	£215k
July-December 1992	How Far	Young women	Help negotiate condom use	Womens Press	£110k
July-December 1992	Immortal	Pre-scene young gay men	Safer sex information	Youth Press	£131k
December 1992-March 1993	Mrs Dawson and Mr Brewster	16-34s, 2+ partners	Normalise condoms	TV	£2.6m
Summer 1993	Travel	Young holidaymakers	Take condoms on holiday	Posters near airports Airport washrooms Tubecards/Radio	£338k
Autumn 1993	How Far	Young women	Help negotiate condom use	Women's Press	£300k
				Total Gross Spend (incl VAT)	£15.4m

6. Targeting specific messages in wider media.
At certain points in time advertisements have appeared which contained specific messages (usually different to the heterosexual/general public message) for specific target audiences, but which had to be placed in wider media in order to reach those audiences, and therefore will have been seen by the 'general public' and considered part of the overall campaign.

TABLE 2: HEA HIV/AIDS ADVERTISING APPEARING IN WIDER MEDIA
December 1988 – December 1994

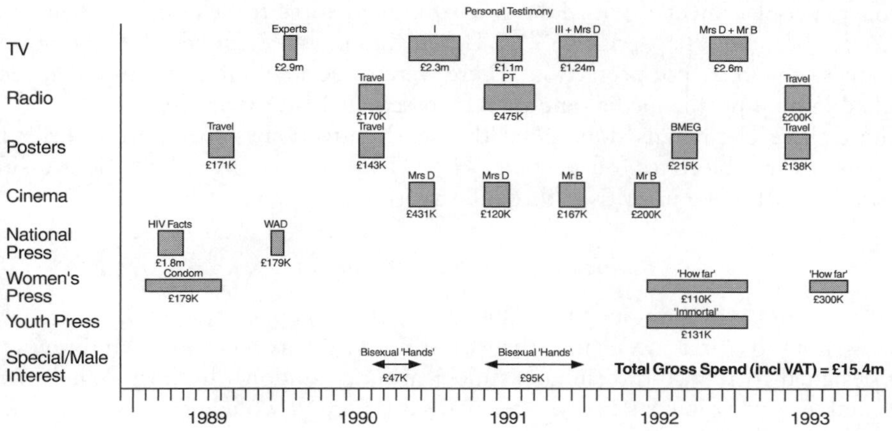

Keeping HIV/AIDS on public agenda and encouraging perceptions of risk among heterosexuals

'HIV Facts', 'Experts' and the 'Testimonies' advertising all used high profile mass media and were expected to reach each of the 'rings' described in figure 1.

'HIV Facts' was a national press campaign communicating the link between HIV and AIDS. It ran from December 1988 to March 1989.

Through 1989 and into 1990, however, public concern about HIV/AIDS waned, fuelled by press coverage of three issues which appeared to suggest there was no HIV risk for heterosexuals:

— a parliamentary question from Lord Kilbracken which highlighted the very low number of people known to have been infected via vaginal sex with partners with no other 'risk factor'[7]:
— The Sunday Times serialisation of Fumento's 'The Myth of Heterosexual AIDS'[8]:
— a government report revising downwards estimates and predictions of levels of HIV infection[9].

National press advertising ran in support of World AIDS Day in 1989 as a counter balance to the negative press coverage, and in February and March 1990 the 'Experts' campaign set the record straight. Leading experts reiterated the known

7. This received a great deal of news coverage – for example, the front page of the Daily Mail. The advertising always had to bridge the gap between current levels of infection and future potential of the epidemic.

8. Michael Fumento's book was originally published in the US in the autumn of 1989, and controversially rejected by UK publishers.

9. *Acquired Immune Deficiency Syndrome in England and Wales: Projections using data to end September 1989 (PHLS)* – also known as the 'Day Report'. Stood as the successor to a previous report, *Short Term Prediction of HIV Infection and AIDS in England and Wales 1988* ('Cox Report') which had predicted the number of people in Britain with HIV to be between 20,000 and 50,000.

facts around HIV and AIDS, emphasising the risks to heterosexuals. This advertising ran at peak times and high weights.

Having re-established on a factual level that HIV posed a risk to heterosexuals, the advertising from December 1990 to February 1992 used the testimonies of 'ordinary' people, infected with HIV to encourage people to believe "someone like me could become HIV positive"[10]. The testimonies concluded by promoting condoms as the means of protection. There were three stages to the campaign, each launched in high profile media, and then focussed on 16-34 year olds.

These three campaigns dominated the yearly advertising spend from 1989 to 1991, as their objectives of keeping HIV/AIDS on the agenda and stressing heterosexual risk were prioritised through that time.

Reducing the barriers to condoms

A range of work was developed to tackle the barriers to condom use.

Most notably, first in cinema, then on TV, 'Mrs Dawson' and 'Mr Brewster' were designed to reduce the embarrassment around condoms by positioning them as normal, everyday items ('condom normalisation'), and women's press advertising was used to help young women use condoms.

Through 1992 and 1993, once perceptions of risk had been considered to have been pushed as far as credible, these condom campaigns formed the bulk of the advertising.

Safer Sex on Holiday

Each year, advertising has run urging young holidaymakers to take and use condoms on holiday.

Since Winter 1992/1993 there has been no large, high profile advertising campaign for HIV/AIDS. The successes of the UK's preventive efforts have been such that UK prevalence of AIDS is low, and levels of HIV infection are estimated at lower levels than those previously predicted.

Attention is now turning to other aspects of sexual health, with the structure of the HEA altering accordingly. The expectation is that mass media will continue to be used as a key sexual health education tool in the UK.

10. The advertising featured a range of testimonies and included gay men infected with HIV. This campaign provided the first opportunity to talk to gay men without risking the marginalisation of AIDS as a gay-men only problem.

'SASKIA'

Consecutive right hand pages

'HOW FAR'

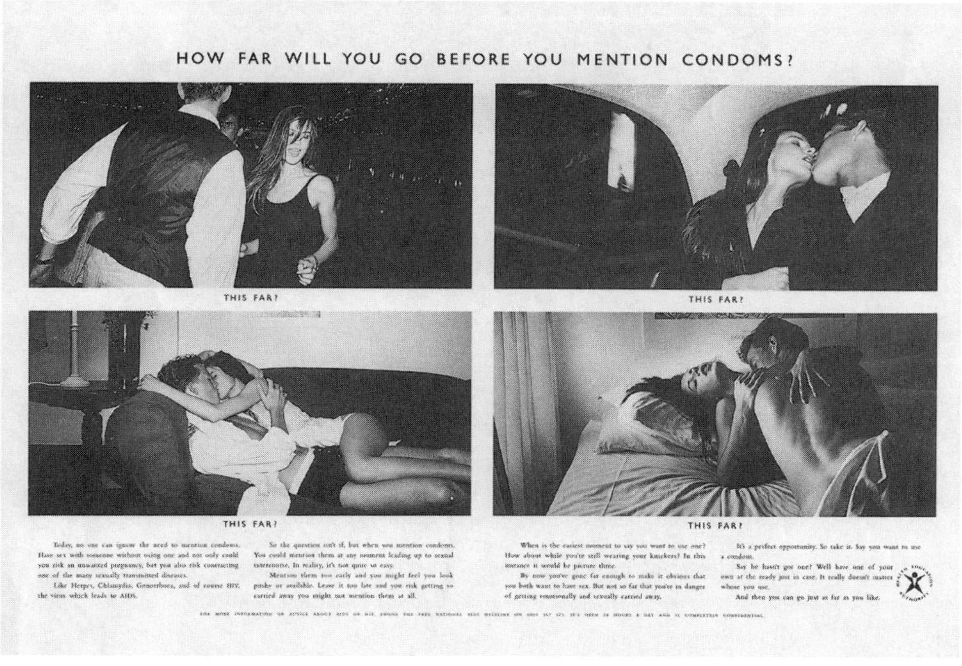

'STEVE'

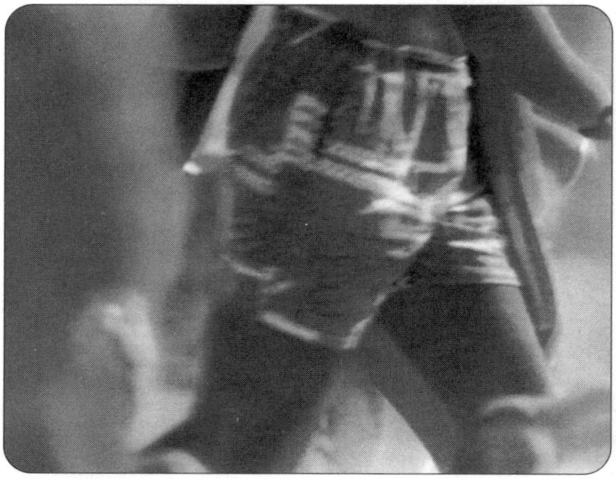

"Had a drink in the hotel and I met this girl at the bar and we got on really well. She was the picture of health, very pretty. I suppose the little devil inside my head would have been saying "go on, son". So I suggested we went upstairs. We had a drink and Bob's your uncle. That's what it's like on holiday. I mean, I really wish that I'd taken some condoms with me but, it's easy to say that now."

MVO: Steve is 28, heterosexual and HIV positive.

'PAUL'

"We'd lived together for a little while and it didn't work out … and I didn't expect to meet up with him you know. But we went for a few beers … then one thing led to another … and I'd known him, you see … and it were the last thing that entered my head that he's positive. But I just didn't think it could happen to me. But it happened, you know."

MVO: Paul is 22, gay and HIV positive.

'EXPERTS I'

"We know for certain that HIV, the virus that causes AIDS, is spread by sexual intercourse from man to man, from woman …

… to woman and from woman to man. It is also spread by sharing syringes and needles during drug abuse."

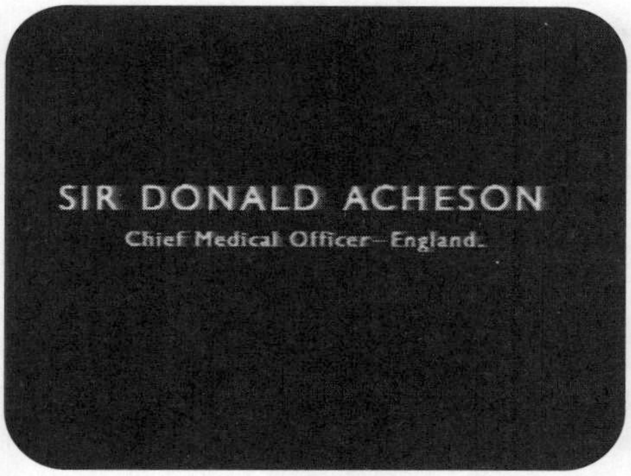

"It's possible for someone to have the virus for up to ten years without knowing it and during that time they can pass it on to others through sexual intercourse."

"It may not seem very serious now, like the greenhouse effect, but if we do not act, it could have a disastrous effect on the future of our children and grandchildren."

'MRS DAWSON'

"Of course, working here we're the first to notice the change in people's behaviour.

We're making more of these things than ever before.

Obviously it's down to AIDS and HIV.

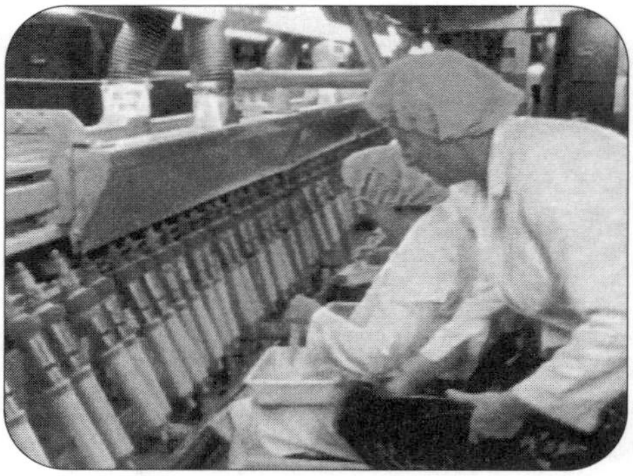

Young people can't afford to take chances these days.

Seems they've got their heads screwed on though. I've never been so busy."

EVALUATING THE EFFECTS OF THE HEA'S ADVERTISING

It is difficult to isolate the advertising's contribution.

i) Advertising about HIV/AIDS has never taken place in a vacuum. Media coverage, school lessons, even what Madonna writes on the inside cover of 'Like A Prayer' has had its part to play. Indeed, as has been explained, part of the advertising's objectives has been to affect and stimulate these other influences.[11]

ii) The HEA's press office continually supported advertising's messages, talking to journalists, editors, programme makers and parliamentarians. As a result the HEA has been able to benefit from 'unpaid for' media.

iii) The HEA has been scrupulous in fulfilling its remit on a national basis. No region has been omitted or upweighted: the imposition of tests and controls in health education is difficult to justify on ethical grounds.

iv) There are issues around key data sources[12]. There have been three major quantitative studies commissioned by the HEA over the period in question with differing samples and questionnaires, making long term analysis problematic.

However, we will argue that advertising achieved the objectives set and so represented the catalyst for behaviour change. Without this advertising it is likely that AIDS in the UK public's perception would have 'gone away' and any appropriate attitude changes unsustained, resulting in significantly less condom usage among young, sexually active heterosexuals.

WHAT HAS BEEN ACHIEVED?

There is evidence of achievements against both sets of objectives: the maintaining of HIV/AIDS on the public agenda, and behaviour change involving condom use among the sexually active young.

Preventing HIV/AIDS Slipping Off The Public Agenda

This has represented a constant challenge for the HEA in the face of a public and press eager to believe that AIDS isn't the problem originally suggested.

---

1. Hence, for example, the launch of major campaigns around World AIDS Day (1st December), to benefit from and contribute to a yearly crescendo of 'noise' around AIDS. This makes it difficult to separate out the effect of the advertising from the 'seasonal' effect of World AIDS Day.

2. The HEA has monitored public awareness and understanding of AIDS and the response to the advertising via three commissioned quantitative studies.
i) BMRB AIDS Strategic Monitor (December 1987 - February 1991)
ii) ICM Waves (December 1989 - September 1991)
iii) BMRB Communications Monitor (October 1991 onwards)

AIDS as a serious ongoing threat

The 1986/1987 DOH campaign had over-emphasised the seriousness of AIDS. It dominated public concern in November 1986.

TABLE 3: PUBLIC HEALTH CONCERNS
Diseases or infections that might seriously affect the health of people in the UK
Base: All respondents

	Feb 1986 %	Nov 1986 %	Dec 1987 %
AIDS	34	83	53
Cancer	73	65	54

Source: BMRB for COI

However, as concern began to fall away in 1987, the objective was prevent it slipping to previous lows. Since the HEA/BMP campaigns began the proportions of people rating AIDS as a "disease or infection that might seriously affect the health of people in the UK" never fell below 41%, and was consistently rated second only to Cancer.

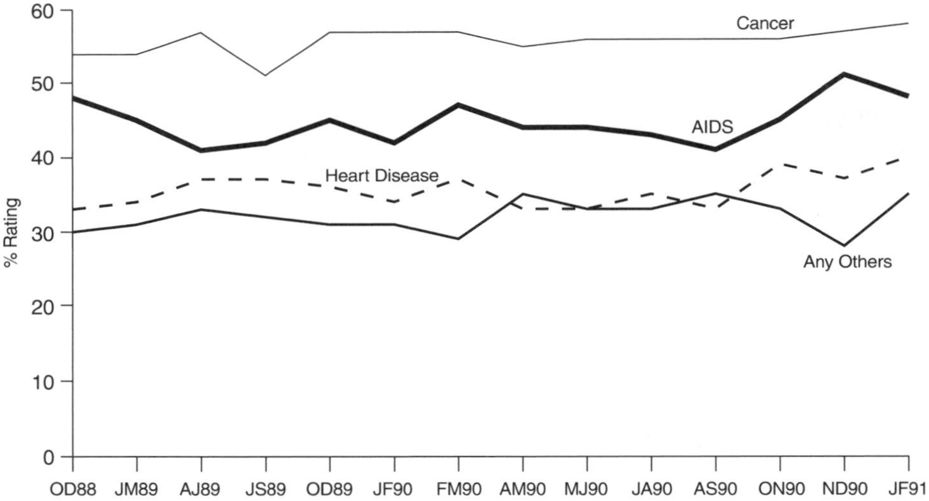

Figure 2. *Diseases or infections that might seriously damage health of people in UK*
Source: BMRB Strategic Monitor, all adults aged 13+

With the change in research methodologies at the end of 1991, the question was re-framed as "factors having a great deal of influence on long term health". Throughout 1992 and 1993 "whether people practise safer sex or not", (the AIDS-linked statement) has remained second only to "whether people smoke or not", (the Cancer-linked statement).

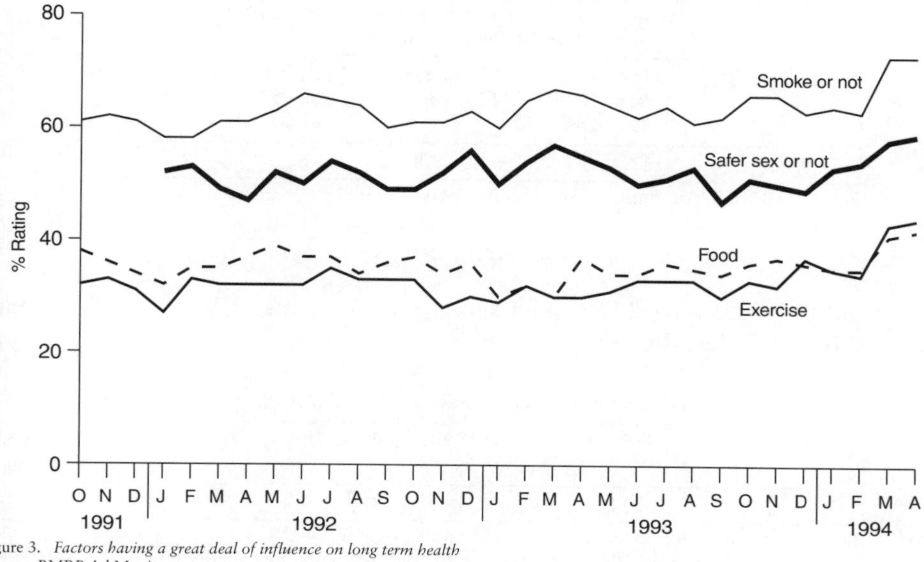

Figure 3. *Factors having a great deal of influence on long term health*
Source: BMRB Ad Monitor

AIDS had been retained as a key health concern in the public mind.

Understanding AIDS as an increasing problem relevant to heterosexuals

Keeping HIV/AIDS on the public's health agenda has involved sustaining the perception that AIDS is a growing problem among heterosexuals.

Throughout the period tracked by the Strategic Monitor, the majority of the public believed it would be "much more common" over the next few years (albeit with a dip in 1989, a reflection of the public scepticism generated in that year described earlier).

TABLE 4: 'AIDS MUCH MORE COMMON OVER NEXT FEW YEARS'
Base: All adults aged 13+ who have heard of AIDS

	1988 %	1989 %	1990 %
Agreeing	64	59	61

Source: BMRB Stragetic Monitor

The Communications Monitor, introduced in November 1991, asked people's agreement with the statement "more and more people in this country are getting HIV from sexual intercourse between men and women". From November 1991 to February 1993 (the last major burst of TV advertising) between 85% to 87% of all adults (16-54) agreed.

TABLE 5: "MORE AND MORE PEOPLE IN THIS COUNTRY ARE GETTING HIV FROM SEXUAL INTERCOURSE BETWEEN MEN AND WOMEN"
Base: All adults aged 16-54

	Nov '91 %	Nov '91-Feb '92 %	Feb '92-May '92 %	July '92-Aug '92 %	Dec '92-Feb '93 %
% Agreeing	87	86	85	85	86

Source: BMRB Communications Monitor, AIDS Module

Linking HIV with AIDS

By the end of 1988, only 24% could spontaneously name HIV as the virus that leads to AIDS. This has risen dramatically.[13]

TABLE 6: SPONTANEOUS NAMING HIV AS AIDS VIRUS

O/D'88 %	O/D'89 %	O/D'90 %	N/F'92 %	D/F'93 %	D/J'94 %
24	38	51	87	87	90

Source: 1988-1990: BMRB Strategic Monitor, all adults aged 13+
1992-1994: BMRB Communications Monitor, all adults aged 16-54

This is a considerable achievement. Understanding HIV is an important starting point for understanding the risks posed by AIDS.

We have demonstrated that the first set of the HEA's objectives have been met. AIDS has been prevented from slipping off the public agenda. The backdrop of 'sufficient concern' around AIDS had been set as a context for appropriate behaviour change.

Condom Use Among Sexually Active Young

Recent evidence from the 'National Survey' confirms that today's 16-34 year olds use condoms to an extent their predecessors didn't.

The proportion of people using a condom the first time they have sex has risen noticeably each year amongst those first having intercourse from 1985 onwards. (See Figure 4.)

Commenting on the increase, the National Survey concludes: "This supports the view that the revival of the method in the 1980s was largely attributable to AIDS public education, suggesting considerable success in motivating public response"[14].

This survey also provides the link with behaviour change because of AIDS.

When asked "Have you changed your own sexual lifestyle in any way or made any decisions about sex because of concern about catching AIDS or HIV virus?" 19.5% of men and 14.2% of all women said 'Yes'. (See Table 7.) This rises among younger respondents[15] and among men and women with two or more heterosexual

13. NB: The changes of sample from all adults aged 13+ to 16-34 year olds will have exaggerated the changes: the inclusion of older respondents (55+) in earlier monitoring reducing overall levels of awareness. Direct comparison of 16-34 year olds is not possible. Nevertheless, 16-34 year olds across both samples still reveals a doubling of the percentage able to name HIV as the virus leading to AIDS.

14. National Survey, Chapter 4, p88.

15. Some allowance must be made for the 1% of the male sample (n = 118) reporting behaviour change who have had a homosexual partner, 65% of whom have changed lifestyle, 68% of which named condom use.

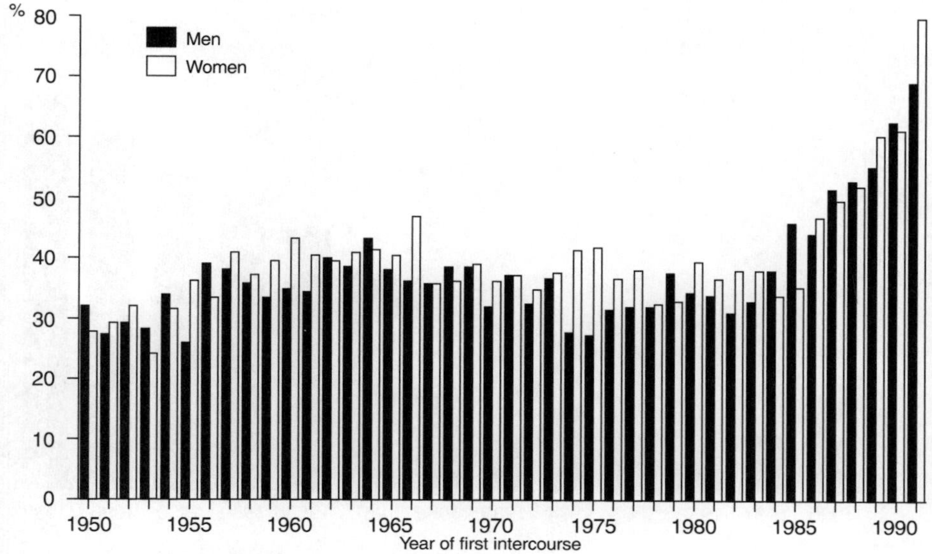

Figure 4. *How many poeple used a condom when they first had sex?*
Source: National Survey of Sexual Attitudes and Lifestyles

partners in the last five years. The majority of that change is represented by condom use.

TABLE 7: PROPORTION WHO REPORT SEXUAL LIFESTYLE CHANGE BECAUSE OF AIDS BY AGE GROUP

	Men			Women		
	16-24 %	25-34 %	All %	16-24 %	25-34 %	All %
Any change	**36.2**	22.9	**19.5**	**29.7**	15.7	**14.2**
Using condoms	26.4	13.7	12.1	16.8	7.5	7.1
% change accounted for by condom use	75%	60%	62%	57%	48%	50%

	Men 2+ heterosexual partners (all ages) %	Women 2+ heterosexual partners (all ages) %
Any change	**38.3**	**36.8**
Using condoms	26.2	20.5
% change accounted for by condom use	68%	56%

Source: National Survey of Sexual Attitudes and Lifestyles

A tangible indicator of increased condom use is the remarkable and continued growth in the sales of condoms. Approximately 40 million more condoms were sold in 1992 than in 1986.

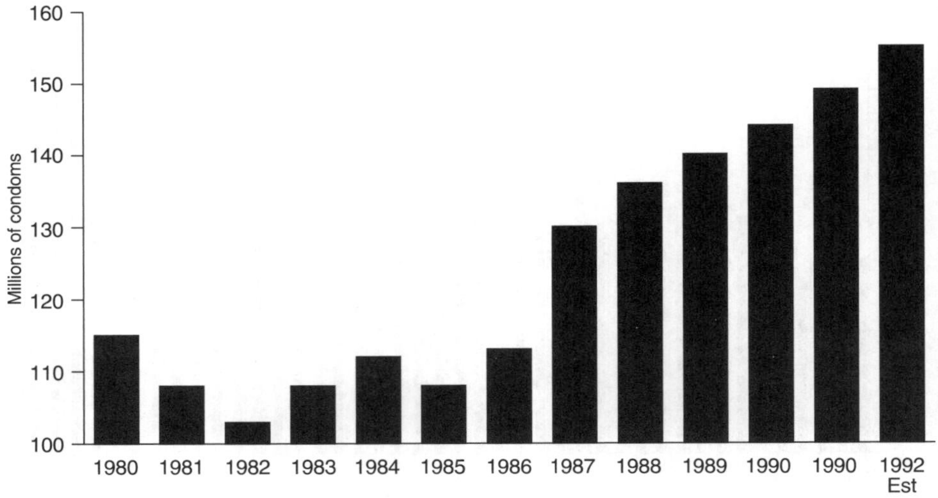

Figure 5. *Condom sales*
Source: Pre-'87: LRC
'87 Onwards: Mintel

EVIDENCE OF ADVERTISING'S ROLE

As has been said, it is difficult to isolate the contribution of advertising to these considerable achievements. Nevertheless the campaigns can be demonstrated to have had a role in the successes against both sets of objectives.

Advertising and the Public Agenda

Seeing AIDS as a serious threat

Whilst AIDS concern has never slipped down to February 1986 lows (Table 3 and Figure 2), it has nevertheless fluctuated, primarily in response to advertising or the lack of it.

The upward movements, representing a re-establishment of the importance of AIDS, coincide with periods of TV advertising and higher levels of the public's advertising awareness.[16]

The relationship exists (albeit to a lesser degree) with the reframing of the question to "Factors having a great deal of influence on long term health". (Figure 3). Noticeably "whether people practise safer sex" was in the public's view becoming less important through 1993, following lower weights of advertising and hence less advertising awareness.

16. An important learning made early on in BMP's work for the HEA was that even heavy weight national press did not appear to sustain AIDS on the public agenda; it had to be TV.
The peak around Oct-Dec '89 can therefore only be attributed in part to the running of advertising on World AIDS Day. It is also likely to reflect the noise and debate created around the Kilbracken affair.
The fall back to 48% following the 'Testimonies' launch can be explained by the way in which the media for the campaign was bought. The launch of the campaign was geared around re-raising the profile of AIDS. As the campaign progressed towards the Spring of '91, the media schedule focussed on 16-34 year old programming.

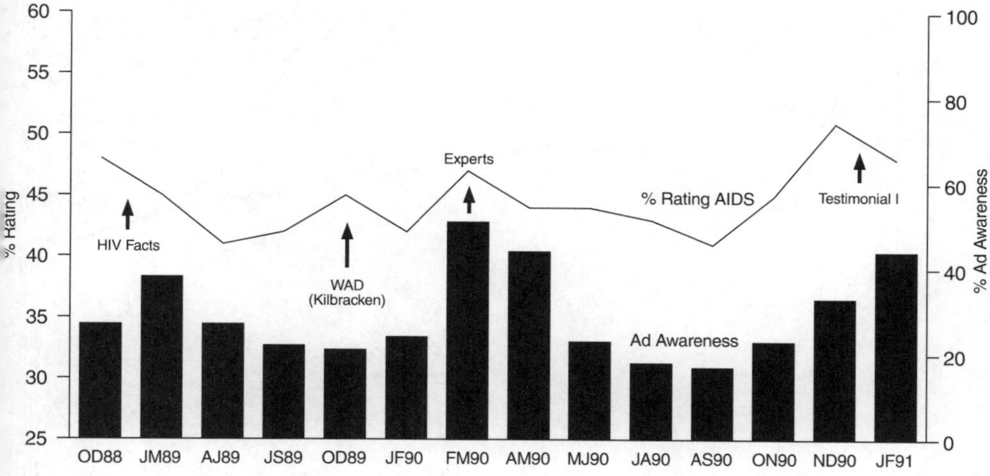

Figure 6. *Relationship between advertising and perceptions of seriousness of AIDS*
Source: BMRB Strategic Monitor, all adults aged 13+

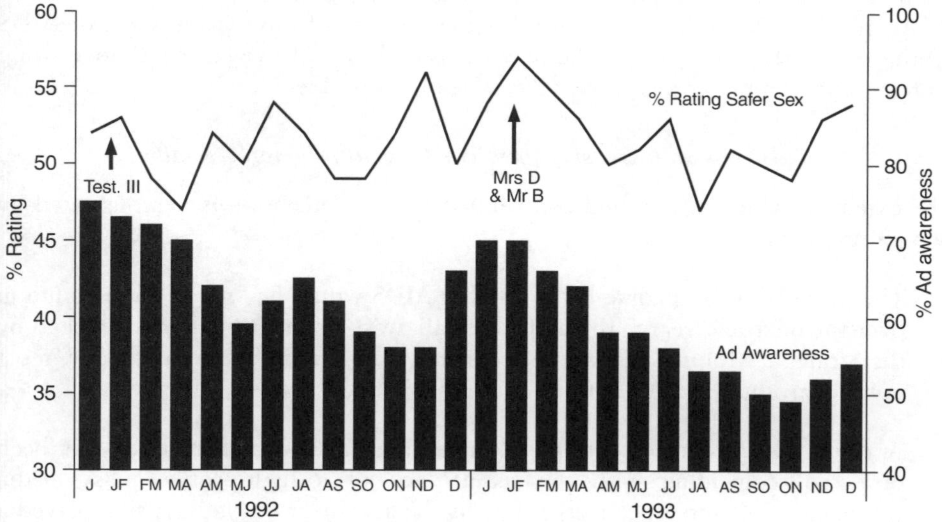

Figure 7. *Advertising and perception of safer sex as important to long term health*
Source: BMRB Advertising Monitor, 16-54 year olds

The topicality of AIDS as an issue (newly tracked by the Communications Monitor) also appears to respond to advertising and the lack of it. (See Figure 8.)

An increase is shown alongside the final 'Testimonies'. Media scheduling from then on became focussed on 16-34 year olds, and the topicality of AIDS among the general public begins to decline. Then, with no TV advertising for AIDS, the decline accelerates.

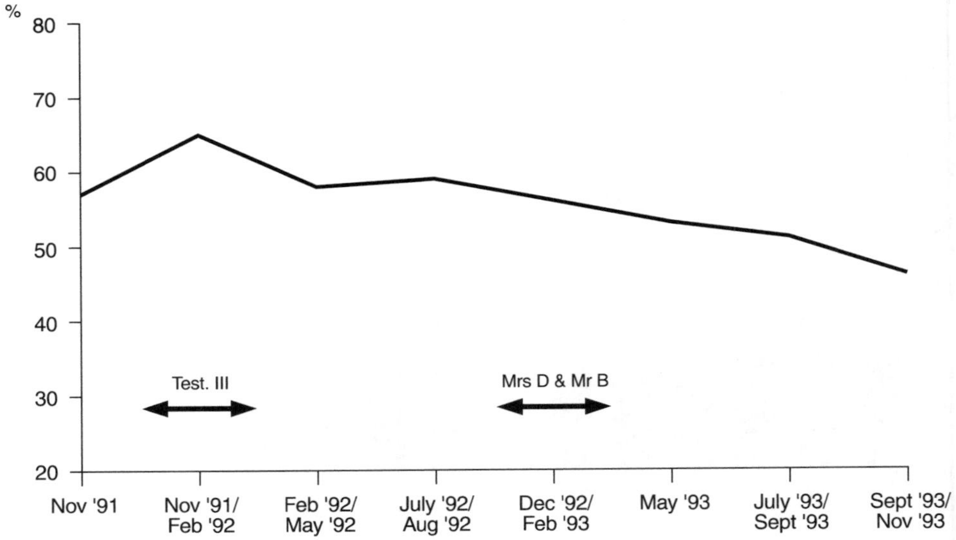

Figure 8. *"I can remember talking about AIDS recently with friends or family or people at work"*
Source: BMRB Communications Monitor, 16-54 year olds

These relationships all suggest advertising is the key (if not solus) driver of the public's perception of the importance of the disease.

As an HEA Paper has observed: "In the absence of any visible signs of AIDS around them, the press and public may be using levels of 'government' advertising on television as a proxy measure of the scale of the problem".[17]

AIDS as an increasing problem relevant to heterosexuals

The extent to which advertising contributed to this perception is demonstrated by two pieces of evidence.

a) The proportions of people believing that AIDS would be "much more common over the next few years" threatened to fall away through the period tracked by the Strategic Monitor but were successfully reasserted by key campaigns, most notably around the 'Testimonies' campaign launch.[18] (See Figure 9.)

b) A recent *decline* in perceptions of increasing heterosexual infection has been observed, coinciding with the recent lack of a high-profile, mass media campaign. This retrospectively supports the argument that advertising played a key role in achieving this objective. (See Figure 10.)

In summary, there are relationships in the data which suggest key campaigns were responsible for either reasserting or enhancing the desired attitudes around AIDS among the general public, preventing AIDS from slipping off the public agenda.

17. Perl S, *Reflections on using mass media for AIDS public education.* HEA AIDS programme Paper No. 13.

18. As 16, the media strategy explains the slight fall back on this dimension for the *general* public.

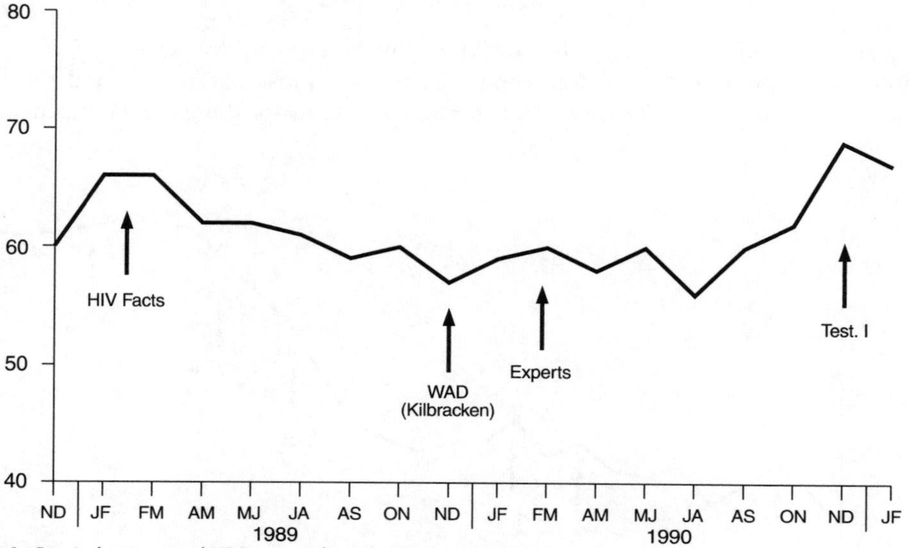

Figure 9. *Perceived commoness of AIDS over next few years: "Much more common"*
Source: BMRB Strategic Monitor

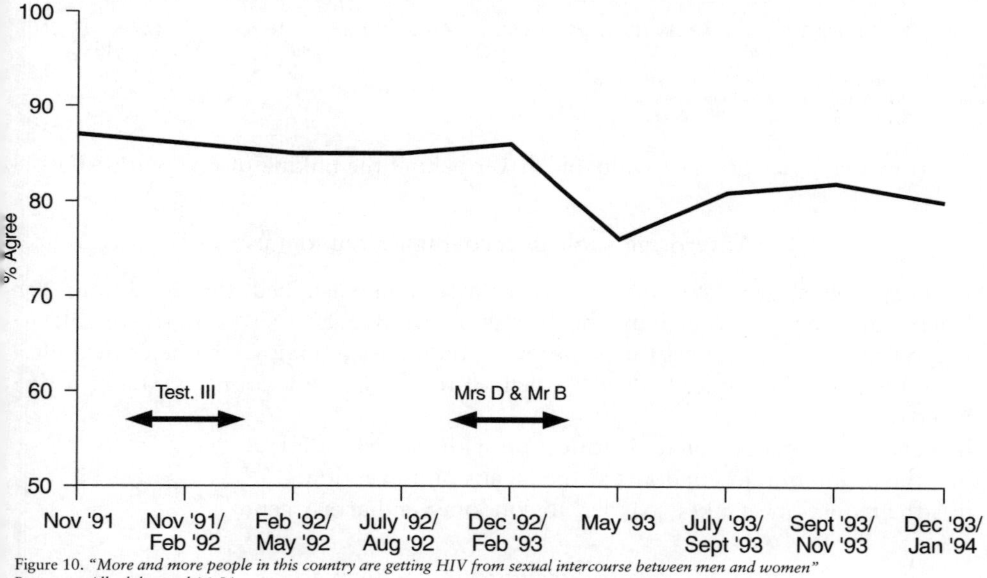

Figure 10. *"More and more people in this country are getting HIV from sexual intercourse between men and women"*
Base: *All adults aged 16-54*
Source: BMRB Communications Monitor

Linking HIV to AIDS

Advertising's role in linking HIV to AIDS can be seen by the *acceleration* of the ability to name the virus at key campaign times – most notably around the first wave of 'Testimonies'. (These all end stating the person speaking is HIV positive.)

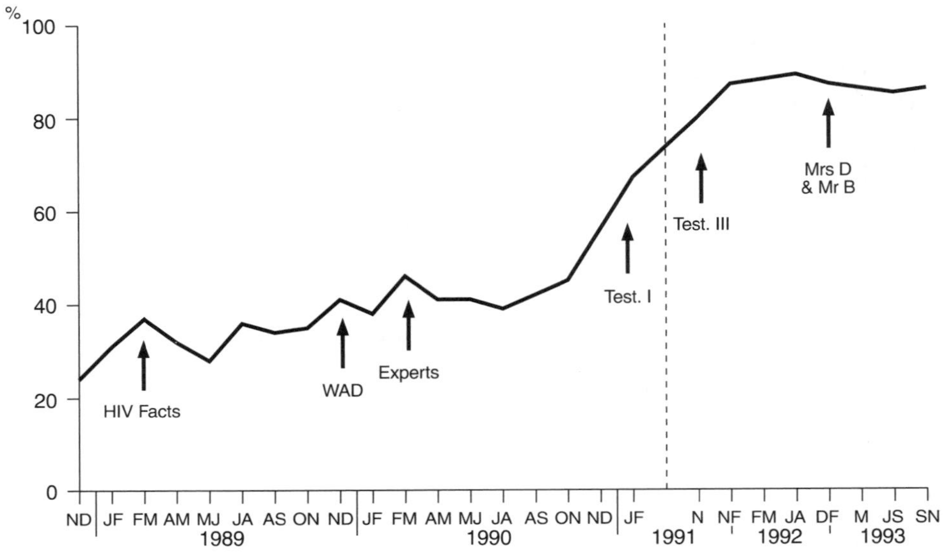

Figure 11. *Spontaneous naming of HIV as virsus that leads to AIDS*
Source: BMRB Strategic Monitor, all adults aged 13+
BMRB Communications Monitor, all adults aged 16-54

Advertising has proven a valuable driver behind the linking of HIV with AIDS.

Advertising's role in encouraging condom use

If it can be shown that advertising created and sustained the conditions for behaviour change outlined by the Health Belief Model, then it is reasonable to suggest that advertising helped encourage condom use among young heterosexuals.

Advertising has indeed played a demonstrable part for young, sexually active heterosexuals in

i) encouraging a personal identification with the risk of HIV;
ii) the promotion of condoms as the means of prevention;
iii) the reduction of a key 'barrier' to condoms: embarrassment.

Personal identification with risk

The proportion of 16-34s denying the risk (ie agreeing "I don't believe I'll ever get HIV" – Figure 12) declined from 77% in 1989 to around 56% by Nov-Dec 1991, the final round of TV advertising specifically designed to encourage a personal identification with risk.

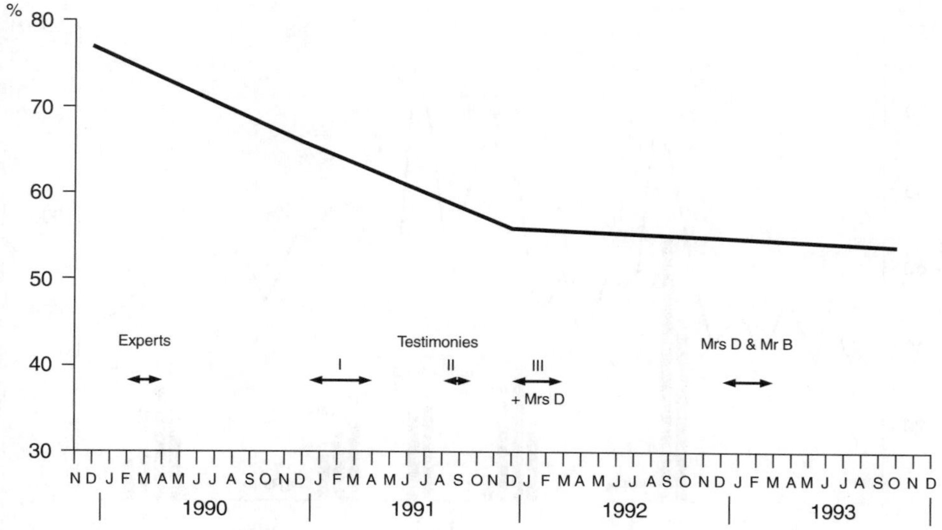

Figure 12. *"I don't believe I'll ever get HIV": Percentage of 16-34 year olds agreeing*
Source: BMRB Strategic Monitor
BMRB Communications Monitor

The latest point at which the question was asked shows that this level has been broadly maintained. Unsurprisingly, campaigns focussing on reducing the 'barriers' (eg 'Mrs Dawson') have not increased peoples perceptions of risk in the way in which the 'risk' campaigns did (eg 'Testimonies').

Another measure of personal risk taken during the ICM Waves (pre 'Experts' to post 'Testimonies II') indicates an increasing perception of risk over the time of campaigns focussing on this objective.

TABLE 8: PERCEPTION OF RISK
"With your present lifestyle, how much risk are you at personally of catching HIV (the AIDS virus) in the future?"
Base: 16-34 year olds, 2+ partners

% agreement	W1 Dec '89 %	W2 Apr '90 %	W3 Dec '90 %	W4 Mar '91 %	W5 Sept '91 %
Greatly at risk	3	3	4	3	4
Quite a lot at risk	**9**	**12**	**14**	**17**	**17**
Not very much at risk	50	50	50	50	49
Not at risk at all	**33**	**30**	**25**	**24**	**23**

Proof of a *direct* link between the advertising and the increase in peoples sense of personal risk is the large increases in calls to the National AIDS Helpline (NAH)[19] around these 'risk' oriented campaigns.

Figure 13 demonstrates the increase in number of calls prompted by 'Experts' and the 'Testimonies' campaigns.

The first four weeks of the 'Experts' campaign averaged 20,895 calls per week, nearly doubling the 1989 weekly average of 11,839 calls, and surpassing even the

19. The National AIDS Helpline is a free 24 hour telephone advice service, supported by the HEA and promoted as a referral point in all TV advertising for AIDS.

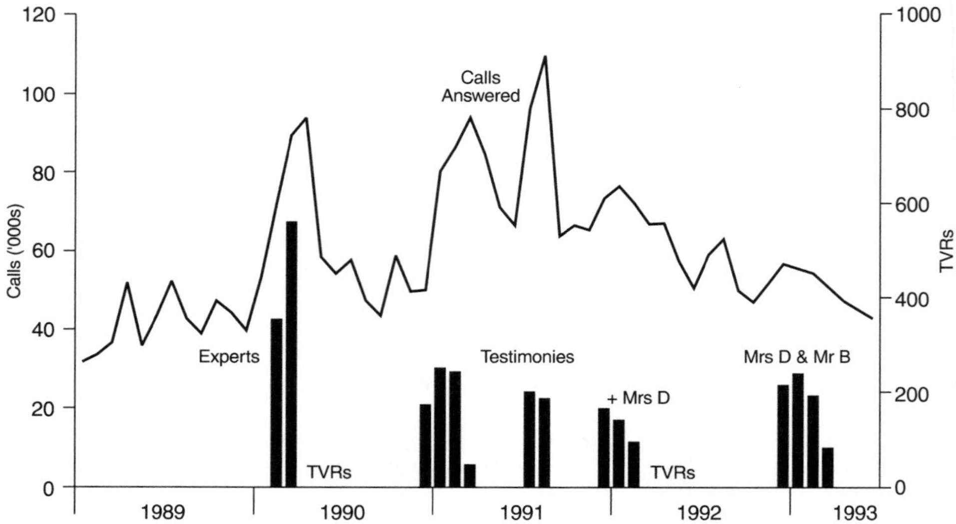

Figure 13. *Calls to national AIDS Helpline*
Source: NAHUK

busiest week of 1989 (16,455 calls). Callers were asked where they'd got the number: 60% cited advertising. 86% of callers in this period were heterosexual. The NAH observed an effect of the campaign:

> "During the course of the HEA campaign in Spring 1990 a subtle change in attitude become apparent. Many callers decided that they had been, or probably had been, at some risk. There was a high incidence of callers who had already decided to take an HIV test. The question itself has changed from 'Should I take a test?' to 'Where can I have a test?'"
>
> NAH 1990 Report

In 1991 the weekly average rose to 18,542 (vs 14,057 in 1990 and 11,839 in 1989). A similar proportion of callers were heterosexual. (Source: NAH[20].)

Condoms as solution

Nowadays there is an almost exclusive association of safer sex with condoms.

However, early in the epidemic's history a range of other risk reduction strategies were also talked about in press and advertising, including a reduction in the number of partners and "being careful who you slept with".

20. *National AIDS Helpline 1992 Report*
1992 and the first 6 months of 1993 saw a tailing off of the calls to the Helpline. The lesser effect of the final burst of testimonies supported the view that 'risk' had been pushed as far as it could go. It is unsurprising that there is less prompting of calls from condom normalisation advertising (which 'Mrs Dawson' and 'Mr Brewster' represent). In itself this lesser reaction is confirmation of the success of 'Personal Testimonies' and 'Experts' in encouraging heterosexual audiences to identify with the risk of HIV infection.

Condoms as the primary means of protection from HIV was increasingly singlemindedly promoted by the HEA in its advertising[21], and this is recognised by the consumer, as a recent piece of qualitative research points out:

> "The condom message has now become a familiar part of the campaign in its own right. It was in fact this message that identified the ads as being from the HEA rather than the use of the HEA logo itself"
>
> Strategic Research Group
> *Condom Climate Part III*, January 1994

The National Survey proves the link between safer sex and condoms is very strong. (Table 9) Over 75% of men and 80% of women say "use a condom" when asked "From what you have heard or read, what does the phrase 'safer sex' mean to you?" (This was the only open-ended question asked in the survey.)

TABLE 9: MEANING OF PHRASE 'SAFER SEX' BY AGE GROUP

	16-24 %	25-34 %	All Ages %
Men			
Use a condom	75.6	79.0	75.3
Restrict no. partners	31.8	28.6	27.1
Know partner	21.5	22.8	20.4
Women			
Use a condom	80.5	84.8	81.0
Restrict no. partners	44.5	37.3	35.6
Know partner	28.4	26.1	23.2

Source: National Survey of Sexual Attitudes and Lifestyles

The HEA's ICM surveys show a similar if less pronounced picture. Importantly, "don't sleep around/have fewer partners" declined in importance from 32% to about 24%.

TABLE 10: "YOU MAY HAVE HEARD OF THE TERM 'SAFER SEX'. WHAT DO YOU UNDERSTAND THIS TO MEAN?"

	W1 Jan/Feb '90 %	W2 Apr '90 %	W3 Nov/Dec '90 %	W4 Mar '91 %	W5 Sept '91 %
Use condoms	62	60	62	61	66
Don't sleep around/have fewer partners	32	28	23	23	25
Take precautions/Use contraception	16	11	21	21	15

Source: ICM: 16-34 year olds, 2+ partners. Self-completion survey

21. It must be noted that this single-minded promotion of condoms is in itself the subject of debate and criticism. There are concerns that it could be seen as an encouragement to 'promiscuity' (ie it doesn't matter who or how many, as long as you use a condom). However the HEA firmly believed condom use was the form of prevention that would be both safer and acceptable to the target ("being careful who you sleep with" is unsatisfactory from a safer sex point of view as there is no way of telling by sight who is infected, and the HEA recognised that abstinence was unlikely to be accepted by a target already sexually active). The HEA was careful to ensure its advertising did not appear to condone or encourage promiscuity.

Table 10 suggests a relationship between 'condom use' being increasingly the take-out of the advertising, and understanding of condoms as safer sex.

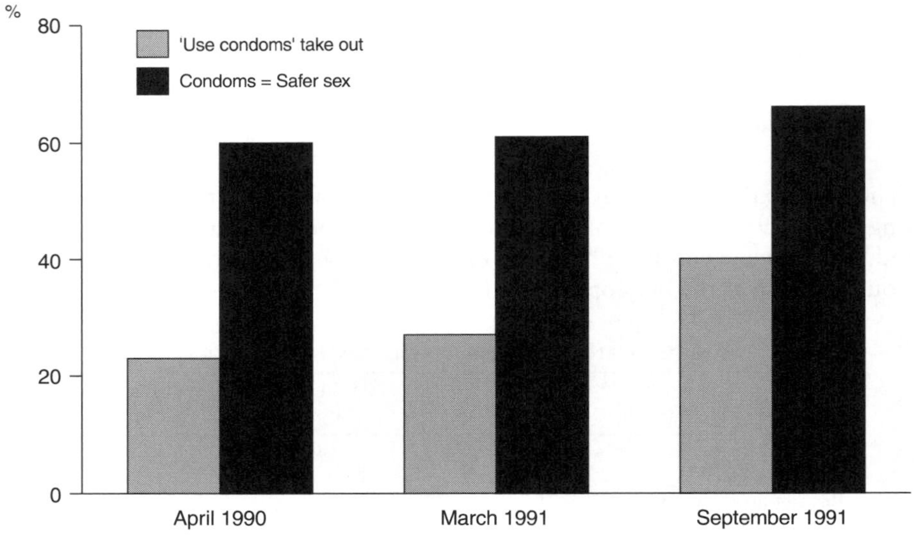

Figure 14. *"Use condoms" – Relationship between key take-out from ads* and understanding of safer sex*
Note: ** All claiming to have seen ads*
Source: ICM: 16-34 years olds, 2+ partners

A further indicator of the success of 'Testimonies' in suggesting condoms as the solution is the way in which they not only maintained but strengthened the target's intentions to use condoms with a new partner.

As can be seen in Table 11, at Wave 3, the pre-stage of the ICM's monitoring of the campaign, 67% agreed: "If I had a new partner I would definitely use a condom". This significantly increased to 72% at the post stage and was maintained at Wave 5 – confirming the role the advertising had in promoting condoms as the primary means of prevention.

TABLE 11: "If I had a new partner I would definitely use a condom"

	W1 Dec '89 %	W2 Apr '90 %	W3 Dec '90 %	W4 Mar '91 %	W5 Sept '91 %
Agreeing	68	67	67	72*	71

Note: * Statistically significant change at 95% confidence level

Source: ICM: 16-34 year olds, 2+ partners

If it is, as we believe, a result of the HEA advertising's singleminded promotion of condoms that condoms are seen as the primary means of prevention, then the advertising must have contributed to the increased use of condoms nowadays.

Reducing the 'cost' of the solution: Normalising condoms

It is not enough for people to understand that condoms are the solution. As the Health Belief Model suggests, the 'cost' of the solution needs to be acceptable. For condoms, the 'costs' are primarily social and emotional.

It was through qualitative work that these costs were usefully understood and monitored.

Evidence of the successful removal of embarrassment around condoms comes from a debrief of a large piece of qualitative research[22]:

> "Attitudes evidenced in this sample demonstrated that condoms have become 'normal' both in the realm of conversation and the realm of understanding. The only evidence of unease was in communication between parents and children, and teachers and students.
>
> At this juncture it could be said that the establishment of knowledge and awareness proved to be a more or less completed task"

Strategic Research Group, March 1993

This report makes explicit reference to the advertising's role:

> "Recall of current advertising ('Mrs Dawson' and 'Mr Brewster') was strong across all groups in the sample. Opinion was that these have succeeded in going some way towards establishing condoms as normal, everyday items in that condoms have entered everyday vocabulary and do not, in themselves, constitute embarrassment".

Strategic Research Group, March 1993

Mintel's 1992 Contraceptives report offers further evidence of successful 'condom normalisation'. They point to the changing share of condom sales by the various outlets (Table 10) as indicators that condoms are a less embarrassing and more everyday purchase, notably the large increases in the share of grocery stores.

TABLE 12: SALES OF CONDOMS, BY TYPE OF OUTLET, BY VOLUME, 1989 AND 1991

	1989 %	1991 %	% point change
Chemists & drugstores	55	49	–6
Vending machines	14	16	+2
Grocery stores	10	15	+5
NHS	11	9	–2
Service stations	3	3	–
Mail order	3	2	–1
Others	4	6	+2
	100	100	

Source: Mintel, 1992

Condoms are now a 'normal' part of everyday life – and we believe advertising has had a key part to play in making them so.

We have shown how advertising has played a vital role in the prevention of HIV transmission – by preventing AIDS from slipping of the public agenda and encouraging condom use among young heterosexuals.

However, before concluding, we will first eliminate the possibility of other factors playing this key role.

22. Strategic Research Group *Condom Climate Advertising Research* March 1993. An extensive sample comprising: 7 peer group discussion, 17-34 year olds; 2 Family group interviews; 2 'couples' depth discussions; 1 male friendship depth discussion; 3 minority ethnic group discussions; 1 'health professional' extended group and 1 'opinion formers' extended group.

WHAT ELSE MIGHT HAVE ACHIEVED THESE RESULTS?

Preventing AIDS slipping off the public agenda

One could contend that it was press coverage of AIDS, not the advertising which has kept AIDS 'top of mind'.

Press coverage of AIDS has increased over the years[23]. However, whilst advertising awareness appears to correspond with people's perceptions of the seriousness of AIDS (Figures 8 and 9), the peaks and troughs in press coverage do *not*. (See Figures 15 and 16.)

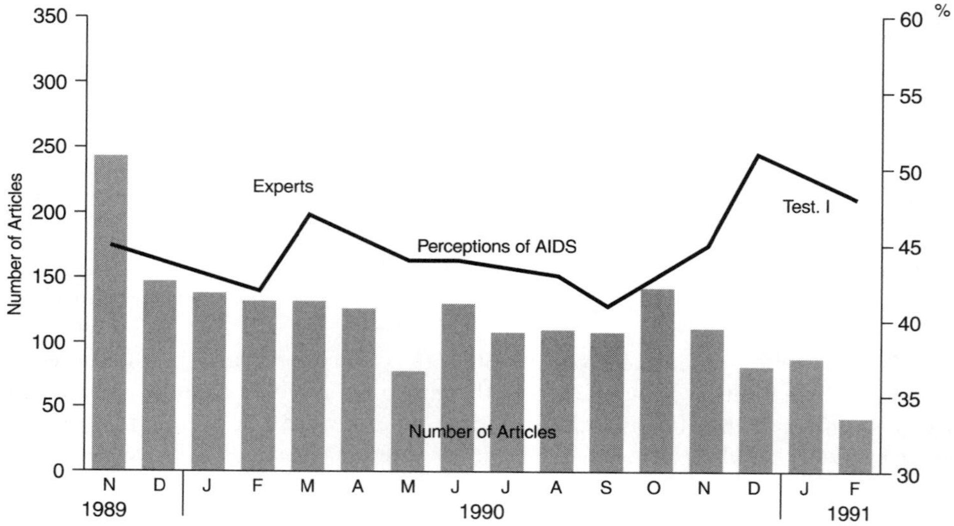

Figure 15. *Perceptions of seriousness of AIDS* vs amount of press coverage*
Note: ** As "disease/infection that might seriously damage health of people in UK".*
Source: BMP Press Audit/BMRB Strategic Monitor, all adults aged 13+

It would therefore seem reasonable to conclude that press coverage is a support rather than a driver of the public's awareness of AIDS.

23. BMP Press Audit monitored number of articles about HIV/AIDS from November 1989 to July 1993, on behalf of HEA. The Audit only tracked National Press coverage (dailies and Sundays), and doesn't comprise magazine articles and local press.

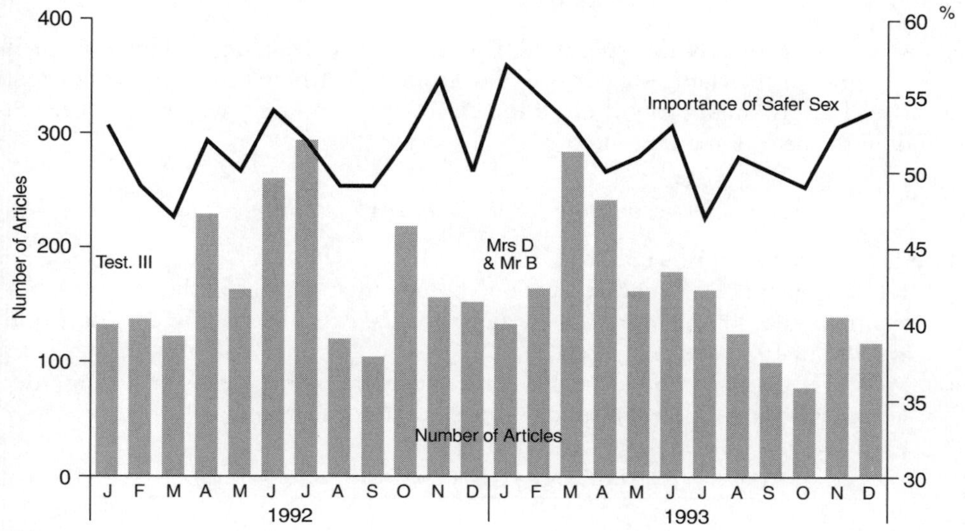

Figure 16. *Importance of safer sex* vs amount of press coverage*
Note: ** As "factor having great deal of influence on long term health of UK"*
Source: BMP Press Audit/BMRB Communications Monitor, all adults aged 16-54

Encouraging condom use

Advertising from condom manufacturers

Durex, Mates and Jiffi have advertised over the last five years. (Table 13), and two new condom launches received advertising support.

TABLE 13: CONDOM MANUFACTURER ADVERTISING SPEND

	1989 £m	1990 £m	1991 £m	1992 £m	1993 £m
Durex	0.4	0.2	0.4	*	*
Mates	0.6	0.4	0.2	*	*
Jiffi	–	–	*	*	0.2
LeCondom	–	–	0.1	–	–
Femidom	–	–	–	0.8	0.9
HEA[24]	3.6	3.7	3.8	2.1	1.7

Note: * = < £100K

Source: Register-MEAL

However, condom manufacturer spends, even in total, were small in absolute terms and minimal relative to the HEA's levels of spend. It is therefore unlikely this activity can take the credit for increased condom sales.

24. Register/MEAL spend differs from actual spends previously quoted:
– likely to be about 30% under-reported because of premiums paid due to programming constraint;
– actual spend is gross, and includes VAT and COI commission.

Education in schools

Many schools probably incorporate AIDS into their curriculum[25]. However, it is unlikely that all the changes described above can be attributed to school education, given a relatively small proportion of the 16-34 year old target would have been at school in the period in question.

Gay men accounting for the majority of condom sales

Two factors suggest this is unlikely:

i) 1.1% of men (16-59) had at least one homosexual partner in the last year. For less than 200,000 men to account alone for the extra 40 million condoms sold in 1992 vs 1986 seems unlikely[26];

ii) Moreover non-penetrative sex has increasingly become a means of having safer sex for gay men (Table 14) much more so than for heterosexuals.

TABLE 14: REPORTED BEHAVIOUR CHANGE BECAUSE OF AIDS

	Men Homosexual Partners %	Men 2+ Heterosexual Partners %
Using a condom	44.2	26.2
Avoiding some sexual practices	40.2	5.5

Source: National Survey of Sexual Attitudes and Lifestyles

Condom sales would have continued to grow without subsequent advertising

A sizeable increase in condom sales occurred in 1987 in response to the advertised 'advent' of AIDS.

We believe that this increase would not have continued without our advertising, as demonstrated, sustained perceptions of risk of HIV/AIDS despite negative press coverage and no 'signs' of AIDS in daily life.

This suggests 'natural' condom sales trends would have been downward or static after 1987 in the absence of continued advertising.

25. Sex education in schools during the period covered by the paper was discretionary with no fixed curriculum. Qualitative evidence suggests many schools did not choose to cover issues relating to safer sex and condom use.

26. The National Survey found 1.1% of men aged 16-59 had a homosexual partner in the last year. Number of men in UK in 1991 aged 15-59 = 16.8m (OPCS Census figures).

COST EFFECTIVENESS

We have shown that the advertising achieved its objectives. But was it money well spent?

A strong case for the advertising spend representing a sound investment can be made wholly on the basis of the primary reason for the spend alone: AIDS prevention.

The estimated cost of supporting an individual with AIDS is about £30,000 per annum[27]. (This is a very conservative estimate of the cost, as it does not include HIV related illnesses.)

Prognosis for people with AIDS varies, but we have assumed for the purposes of this calculation, that the average is 2 years from diagnosis.

Based on this assumption, the total spent on advertising (about £15.4m) can be considered to have 'paid back' if it has contributed to the prevention of, on average, 51 cases of HIV infection a year[28].

Without a national HIV testing programme we do not know how many people are HIV positive, or the likelihood of a heterosexual encounter involving someone who is infected. Nevertheless, the National Survey suggested 26% of men and 21% of women with two or more heterosexual partners in the last five years use condoms because of AIDS. This amounts to 2.3 million people[29], (and considerably greater number of sexual occasions during which HIV could otherwise have been transmitted). Given this degree of behaviour change it is likely that the commitment to prevention programmes have been more than justified in terms of monetary cost effectiveness.

SUMMARY

The concept of financial 'pay-back' for an investment in any public health concern seems brutal. The real cost savings from investing in AIDS prevention are of course human.

We will never know what would have happened if we hadn't used advertising as the primary 'driver' of the AIDS prevention programme.

We hope to have demonstrated convincingly, however, our belief that advertising *was* a key driver, maintaining an appropriate level of public concern regarding AIDS and against this backdrop encouraging condom usage amongst young people at risk.

If this advertising had not achieved these aims, the situation we face today in the UK as a 'low AIDS prevalence' country, might have been very different.

27. Source: House of Commons, Committee of Public Accounts, *HIV and AIDS related health services*. London HMSO, 1992.

28. Based on the current assumption that HIV invariably leads to AIDS.

29. Calculation based on:
OPCS: men, 15-59 in UK in 1991 = 16.8m; women, 15-59 in UK in 1991 = 17.0m
National Survey: 34.7% men had 2+ partners in last 5 years, of which 26.4% claimed to have condoms because of AIDS; 23.5% of women had 2+ partners in last 5 years, of which 20.5% claimed to have used condoms because of AIDS.

13

Meat & Livestock Commission

Pulling round the red meat market

ABOUT THE PAPER

This paper is different and we believe unique. There are no brands. Instead we show how advertising supported a market from enormously powerful competition – not in the form of other brands – but from a barrage of negative forces.

The Competition to Meat

Red meat has faced two main problems. First, long-term, 'chronic' forces; social, demographic, ethical, economic, and health related. Second, a shorter-term, 'acute' event; perhaps the biggest health scare to hit any food market – BSE.

We show how a change of advertising succeeded in reducing the impact of these forces and restored the market to year-on-year growth.

Results and Payback

A model shows that the total media spend of £36.2 million spent on red meat advertising between 1994 and 1997 resulted in additional red meat sales of £739 million at retail value – a return of nearly 18:1.

The extra £621 million retail value of GB-produced red meat due to advertising resulted in an additional revenue to farmers of £155 million. Using the average gross margin of 59%, this resulted in an additional £91 million gross margin to farmers (£51 million after subtracting advertising media and production expenditure).

The red meat industry in total is a huge one. Apart from the farmers, there are large numbers of other stakeholders in the carcass red meat market – a chain from auction markets to abattoirs to meat processors to butchers and multiple retailers. All of these businesses' fortunes are harnessed to the fortunes or otherwise of red meat retail sales. Thus, beyond the retail sales benefits, there are huge knock-on effects for retail markets (ready meals, burgers and so on) as well as many other sectors such as catering and fast food, brought on from the advertising effects shown.

INTRODUCTION

We are all familiar with the way advertising can support or grow brands at the expense of competitor brands. Or even how it can help a brand grow a market.[1]

This paper is different and, we believe, unique. There are no brands. Instead we show how advertising from 1994 to 1997 supported a *market* (the red meat market) against enormously powerful competition – not in the form of other brands – but from a barrage of negative forces:

1. Long-term 'chronic' forces – social, demographic, ethical, economic, and health-related.
2. A shorter-term 'acute' event – perhaps the biggest health scare to hit any food market: BSE.

We show how a change of advertising, against all the odds, succeeded in reducing the impact of these forces – slowing the rate of decline in red meat eating and in 1997, restoring the market to year-on-year growth. This, in such a huge market (£2.1 billion in 1997[2]), resulted in significant additional profit to the whole beleaguered farming industry dependent on these sales – not only to the farmers who directly funded the advertising but also to the many other stakeholders (a chain from auction markets to abattoirs to meat processors to meat retailers).

The evaluation task is difficult:

— The market is mature.

— Sales trend lines do not conveniently uplift with advertising bursts.

— Advertising runs virtually year round – ie, no bursts.

— Promotions run simultaneously with advertising.

— Unforeseen 'events' have thrown plans off course.

This paper sets out to show how, despite these challenges, evaluation of the advertising contribution has been achieved.

The Meat & Livestock Commission (MLC)

The MLC is a body set up by the Government in 1967. It is funded by a statutory levy paid by farmers and abattoir owners for each animal slaughtered.

This levy funds all the MLC's activities (covering veterinary research, NPD activities, economic analysis, advertising and promotion and so on). The advertising described in this paper is however funded by the levy paid by farmers.[3]

---

1. BT Grand Prix Paper in 1996 Advertising Effectiveness Awards.
2. Retail red meat carcass sales 1997 (AGB).
3. Abattoirs' levy payments do contribute to the advertising budget, but their proportion of this relative to the farmers' payments is minimal. So for the purposes of this paper, we assume that the advertising is funded solely by the farmers' levy payments.

This paper presents an unusually pure example of advertising effect because the MLC has no direct control over the supply side of the product in question.[4] All it can attempt to influence is the demand.

Focus of the Paper

The primary focus of the MLC's promotional activities (and hence this paper) is in-home consumption of carcass red meat – pork, beef and lamb[5] (which we will call the 'red meat market').

This focus is because:

— This 'market' accounts for the greatest volume of red meat.

— It is where the volume decline has been focused.

— Any uplifts in demand in this area generate greater increases in red meat volume than in other areas such as ready meals.[6]

— Any imagery improvements in this area tend to ripple out into processed meat (but not vice versa) because it is the heart of the 'brand'.

LONG-TERM NEGATIVE PRESSURES

The MLC has a tough job. Red meat suffers from a debilitating range of long-term negative pressures.

Price of Red Meat versus Poultry

Since 1970, red meat prices have steadily increased relative to poultry (Figure 1).

New Poultry Products

Helped by the low cost of raw material, poultry producers have launched an extensive range of value-added convenience food products.[7]

4. The Common Agricultural Policy (CAP) and other intervention mechanisms put supply and price outside the MLC's control, and likewise product quality, presentation and distribution are beyond the MLC's direct control.
5. Not game or poultry, and not processed meat – like ready meals.
6. There is more red meat in a portion of roast meat than in a portion of a lasagne ready meal.
7. Child-oriented products like chicken nuggets have been particularly successful.

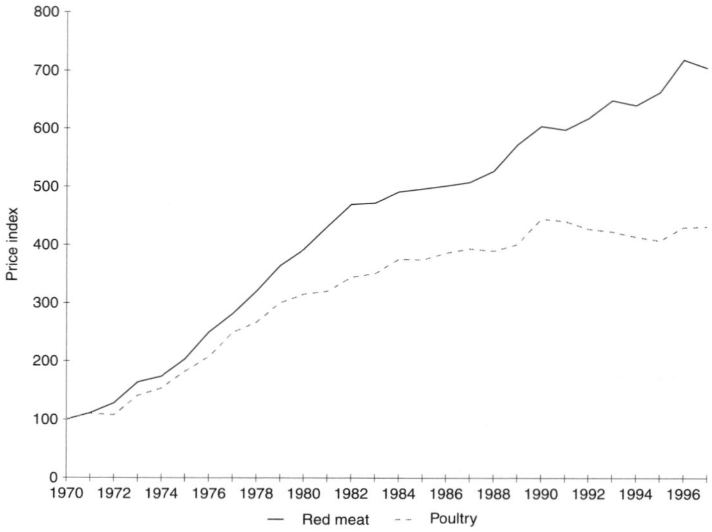

Figure 1: *Prices – red meat versus poultry*
Source: ONS, MLC

Growth in Ready Prepared Food

We are all familiar with the reasons for this.

— More money and less time have fuelled the *demand* for these products, facilitated by the growth of freezers and microwaves.

— Food technology improvements (like chilled processing) and the growth in availability through supermarkets have fuelled the *supply*.

Growth of Supermarkets

The switch to supermarket buying directly depresses red meat sales – due to the juxtaposition of red meat with a vast array of convenient alternatives as well as the loss of the advisory role of the local butcher.[8]

Growth in 'International' Food

Our tastes are broadening. Increasingly we are cooking more 'international' meals.[9] These are more likely to contain little or no red meat compared with 'British' meals.

8. BMP econometric modelling shows that a 1% increase in grocery shopping purchases through supermarkets results in a 1.3% decrease in red meat volume. Sales of red meat through butchers are in decline – having fallen to around 16% of all red meat sales by 1998.
9. Italian, Indian, Chinese, and so on.

Ethical/Health Concerns

Other reasons have encouraged some people to consciously cut down or cut out red meat or even all meat.

— Ethical
Although it is difficult to quantify genuine 'vegetarianism' precisely, *claimed* vegetarianism is increasing, and the rate of growth is also increasing (Figure 2).

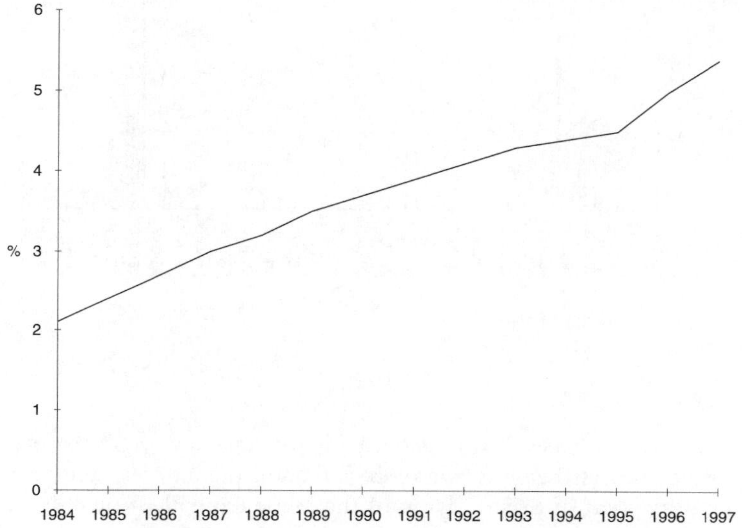

Figure 2: *Claimed vegetarians as a % of population*
Source: Mintel

— Health
Over the past 20 years, a succession of health scares have been associated with red meat: cholesterol levels, animal growth hormones, E Coli, cancer, abattoir procedures, Chernobyl affected sheep, and so on.

BSE

On top of these long-term structural factors affecting all red meat have been the shorter-term problems caused by BSE – affecting beef.

There have been two key phases of media-led BSE consumer concern: the first in 1990 the second in 1996 (Figure 3).

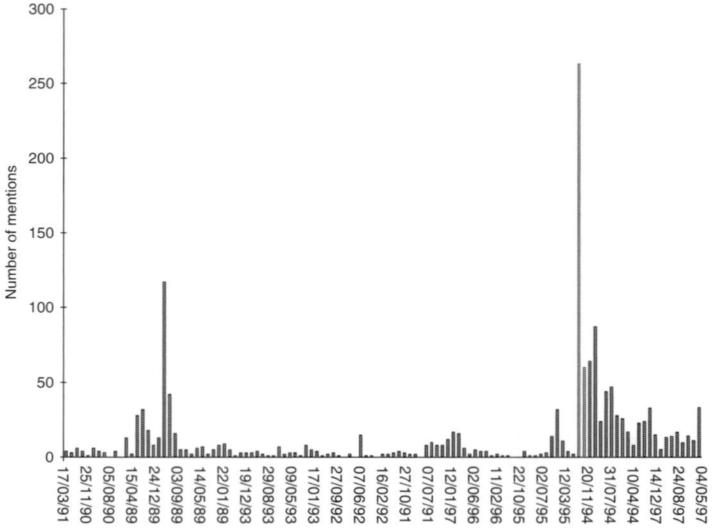

Figure 3: *National press mentions of BSE*
Source: MMD, MLC

1990

Although the cattle disease BSE had been identified a few years before, it was in June 1990 that the first heavy wave of BSE related media coverage occurred. This was prompted by a cat in Bristol dying of the feline equivalent of BSE – raising, for the first time, the terrifying possibility that this type of disease could cross species barriers (and by extension could affect humans).

However, the outbreak of the Gulf War at the end of 1990 wiped BSE off the front pages, although coverage continued at low levels over the next five years.[10]

1996 – The Major BSE Crisis

Catastrophic shock waves were felt after the announcement by Stephen Dorrell in March 1996 that there may after all be a link between BSE and the human equivalent disease, CJD.[11]

10. Largely featuring the ongoing debate and conflicting views about the cause and human implications of BSE.
11. This, in fact, only confirmed what the public had suspected all along but had always been denied by politicians/health officials prior to this announcement.

BACKGROUND TO THE NEW CAMPAIGN 1993

Hence, back in 1993 (even before the major 1996 BSE crisis), things looked fairly bleak from the MLC's point of view.

The long-term trends outlined above had resulted in household consumption of red meat declining since the 1960s. In addition, the rate of decline in red meat sales seemed to be accelerating (Table 1).

TABLE 1: HOUSEHOLD CONSUMPTION OF RED MEAT

	Red meat volume (million tonnes)	% change
5 years to 1988	4.3	-11
5 years to 1993	3.3	-22

Source: AGB

In 1993, the MLC appointed BMP to help undertake a major review of strategy. BMP research revealed that behind the accelerating sales decline were worrying attitudinal problems too.

Product Issues

In addition to the discrete health scares mentioned (like E Coli) over the 1980s, red meat had come to acquire an image as more unhealthy (particularly, higher in fat and cholesterol) than chicken, fish or non-meat meals. We often found that there was no real factual basis for these beliefs – just half-remembered scare stories, confusion over types of fat and, most importantly, a lack of effective counter messages from red meat.

User Image Issues

Red meat eaters were consistently portrayed by consumers in research as overweight, old-fashioned and unsophisticated (Les Dawson), while chicken or fish eaters were seen as controlled, virtuous and contemporary (Selina Scott). As a result, people were embarrassed to admit to the extent of their red meat eating – often radically underclaiming in group discussions what their food diaries showed they were actually eating. If actual eating moved in line with these attitudes, then red meat volume would decline even more dramatically in the future.

MLC FIVE-YEAR MARKETING OBJECTIVES 1994 TO 1998

We and the MLC had to be realistic. On an £8 million annual advertising budget, the strength of the forces acting against consumption of red meat at home meant that restoring the market to growth in the short term was unlikely.

Instead we set out to slow down the ongoing rate of decline in red meat in-home volume.[12]

Importantly, this decline was more of *frequency* than penetration – ie, red meat eaters were eating red meat less often at home, but the number of eaters remained relatively static (Figure 4).

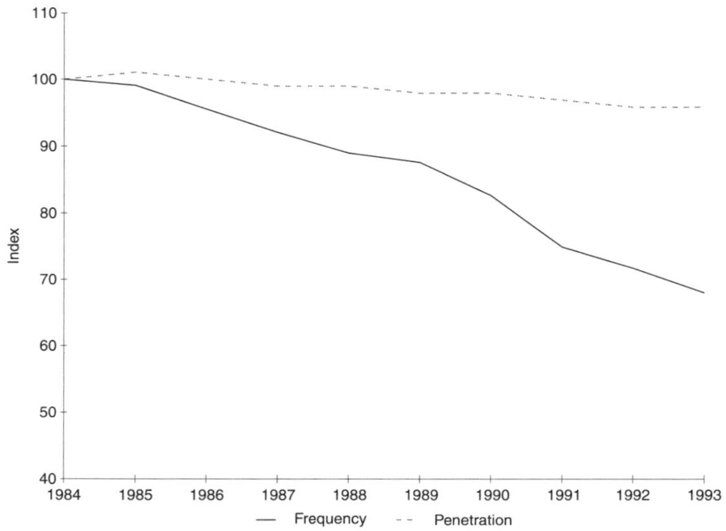

Figure 4: *Red meat – frequency of purchase vs. penetration indexed*
Source: AGB

ADVERTISING STRATEGY DEVELOPMENT 1993

For some years, MLC advertising had been split into four separate campaigns (beef, pork, lamb and red meat) and in fact it was handled by two different agencies.[13]

This resulted in two problems:

— Because of the fragmented spend, awareness of any red meat advertising was low.

— The focus on each species as competing 'brands' (for example, beef – the tasty one, lamb – the easy one, and so on), didn't match the way people thought about and bought red meat – as flavour variants, not separate brands.

'We rotate them – one Sunday we'll have roast pork, the next beef ...'

Source: BMP Qual 1993

We decided to pool the four individual ad budgets and refocus the advertising first and foremost on promoting red meat.

12. In a market worth over £2 billion, this could still have huge profit benefits for the farming and related industries.
13. Campaigns like 'Take a Fresh Look at Pork' (talking about pork versatility) and the 'Meat To Live' campaign featuring healthy-looking, active men (talking about the benefits of eating red meat).

People also felt that the previous ads were *tonally* wrong – slapstick humour and clichéd stories were not appropriate. Red meat was thought worthy of respect as it was usually the most expensive part of a meal.

'They're all just a bit naff.'

'You shouldn't really talk about meat like that – it's expensive – not like a bag of crisps.'

Source: BMP Qual, 1993

The Opportunity

Many people were not *actively* avoiding red meat – other meals were often just seen as more convenient.[14] However, research revealed unique rewards when red meat was cooked.

Home-cooked red meat meals were uniquely filling, warming and sustaining. They provided a sense of comfort and well-being – a feeling of being loved and valued. As someone said:

'You wouldn't welcome your long lost son back with a piece of quiche.'

Source: BMP Qual, 1993

Importantly, red meat meals were associated with pleasurable, convivial eating compared with chicken and fish meals (which research discovered were felt to be rather soulless and associated with single-person eating).

These findings helped us to define our advertising strategy.[15]

Advertising Objective

To stem the decline in frequency of people cooking meals with red meat at home.

Advertising Strategy

We believed that advertising could achieve this objective in two main ways.

1. We needed to develop much more popular and impactful advertising.

14. Many red meat meals do involve a little more effort in terms of preparation and cooking time (for example, red meat does not microwave well), as do many of the things that people like to eat with red meat (such as gravy and vegetables).

15. NB. At this time (1993) BSE had faded from the press after the initial flurry of media comment in 1990. There was still uncertainty as to the human significance, if any, of BSE and the public it seemed were becoming bored with it. It was therefore agreed that there was no role for advertising at this time regarding BSE.

Thus, advertising needed to be more relevant – we had to bring out the unique feelings that red meat meals provide – and so encourage people to make a little effort and cook them more frequently (instead of ready meals, chicken, and so on) in order to give and share in these rewards. If we could get this relevance right, we hoped to make people feel more comfortable about their red meat eating.

2. We needed to counter some of the mounting negative health misperceptions about red meat eating, with facts which challenged these views.

We had two strong stories based on the fact that red meat is higher in iron levels and lower fat levels than people thought.

Target Audience

We were talking to all buyers and cookers of red meat – no group was unaffected by the trends outlined earlier.

THE PLANNED NEW RED MEAT CAMPAIGN 1994 TO 1997

There were two elements planned in the creative work for red meat over the period 1994 to 1997.

Television: The Recipe For Love (RFL) Campaign

Eleven RFL ads have run over this period. Each features a different meal made with pork, beef or lamb, a different meal situation, and a different personal relationship. Each dramatises the unique pleasures of red meat meals.

Responses to the proposed TV campaign in pre-testing were very positive.[16]

> 'Overall this has the potential to be a very popular and noticeable campaign which could considerably raise the salience of red meat as a whole.'

Source: Ockwell Associates 1994

The RFL campaign had a total media spend of £28 million between 1994 and 1997. The ads have typically run almost continuously between September and May each year.[17]

---

16. Over the period of the TV campaign we have refined our understanding, and moved the ads away from what research suggested was too much of a focus on posh, dinner party scenarios and romantic situations, to more down-to-earth situations rooted in family relationships.
17. People cook far less red meat meals over the summer months when the weather is warmer and people are out and about.

RECIPE FOR LOVE 'AWKWARD AGE'

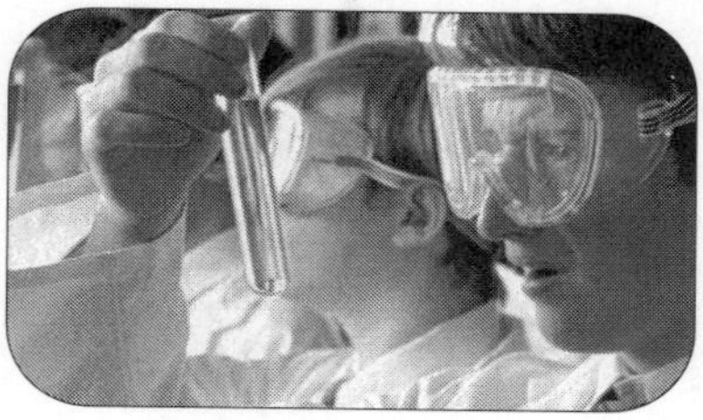

RECIPE FOR LOVE 'ANNIVERSARY'

The Nutritional Campaign

A series of press and poster campaigns, targeting people concerned about eating healthily have also been run.[18]

Research suggested that people were more likely to be receptive to these factual nutritional messages (which challenged their existing views of red meat quite aggressively) if they were already emotionally on the side of red meat. The nutritional campaign began in 1995 (a year after the new TV strategy).

Nutritional campaigns have been run in press and posters at a total media spend of £4.3 million between 1995 and 1997.

THE MODIFIED CAMPAIGN PLAN 1996 TO 1997 – BEEF REASSURANCE

After the March 1996 Commons bombshell (admitting the probable link between BSE and CJD), the headlines went wild.

Schools and McDonald's banned beef – respondents in groups told how they had cleared their freezers of beef and their cupboards of anything (stock cubes, biscuits, jelly babies) that was likely to contain beef by-products such as gelatin. Collective hysteria at school gates meant that confessing to letting a child eat beef was seen as akin to wilful poisoning. However, as the weeks passed, hysteria gave way to more balanced press coverage, and a further role for advertising emerged.

There were two main groups of people who had given up beef immediately following the 1996 BSE scare.

'Rejectors'

These people claimed they would only return to eating beef when a cast-iron guarantee that BSE had been eradicated could be given (a minority). There was little role for advertising for these people.

> 'I will never go back to beef until I see guaranteed BSE free on it.'
>
> 'They've betrayed my trust so why should I ever eat their beef.'

Source: BMP Qual 1996

'Worriers'

These people wanted to return to eating beef but were just looking for emotional reassurance (the majority).

18. In the first year (1995) these consisted of dramatic comparisons of the superior iron or low-fat nature of red meat compared with apparently more healthy alternatives (like cottage cheese or spinach). When we had exhausted relevant comparisons these were replaced with non-comparative facts about red meat.

NUTRITIONAL PRESS

BEEF REASSURANCE PRESS

'It's hard not being able to give them spaghetti bolognese – we love it – but you do worry about the children.'

'You just want to feel you are doing the right thing.'

Source: BMP Qual 1996

As a result, in 1996 and early 1997, the planned red meat campaign was supplemented by a Beef Reassurance campaign on posters, press and TV to communicate emerging facts, the measures put in place to prevent BSE from entering the human food chain and, in particular, to inform people of the new Minced Beef Quality Mark.[19] Total media spend on this Beef Reassurance campaign was £3.9 million over 1996 and 1997.

SUMMARY MEDIA PLAN 1994 to 1997

Total red meat advertising spend over the period 1994 to 1997 was £36.2 million (Figure 5).

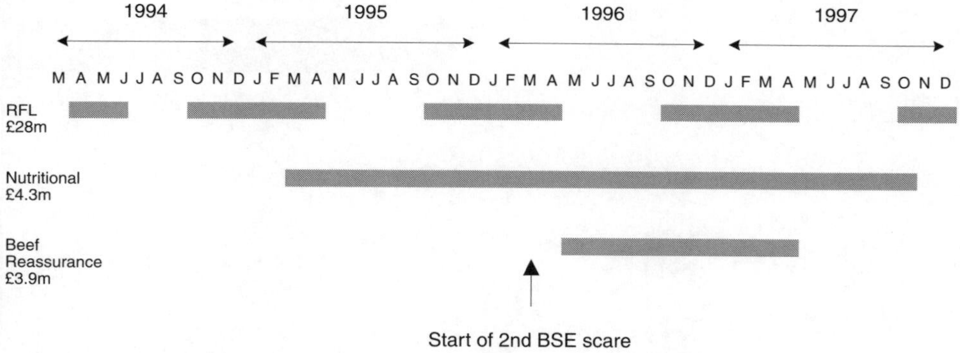

Figure 5: *Total red meat ad spend, 1994 to 1997*

EVALUATION 1994 to 1997

What happened to red meat sales from 1994 to 1997?

The rate of decline in red meat sales slowed as planned (Figure 6). Unexpectedly, in 1997, red meat sales actually grew year on year (Figure 7).

19. This mark was introduced on selected beef mince packs in June 1996 following research which showed that the main BSE-related volume loss for beef was focused on mince rather than on the more 'premium' cuts like roasts and steaks.

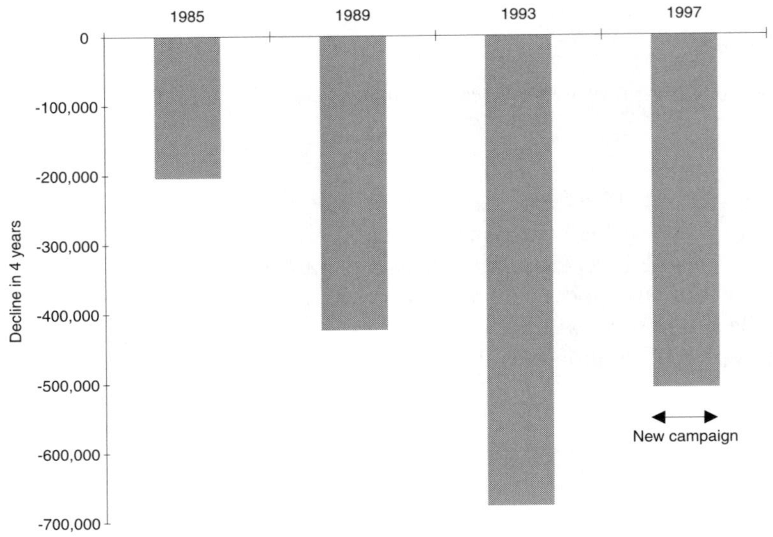

Figure 6: *Rate of decline in red meat sales*
Source: AGB

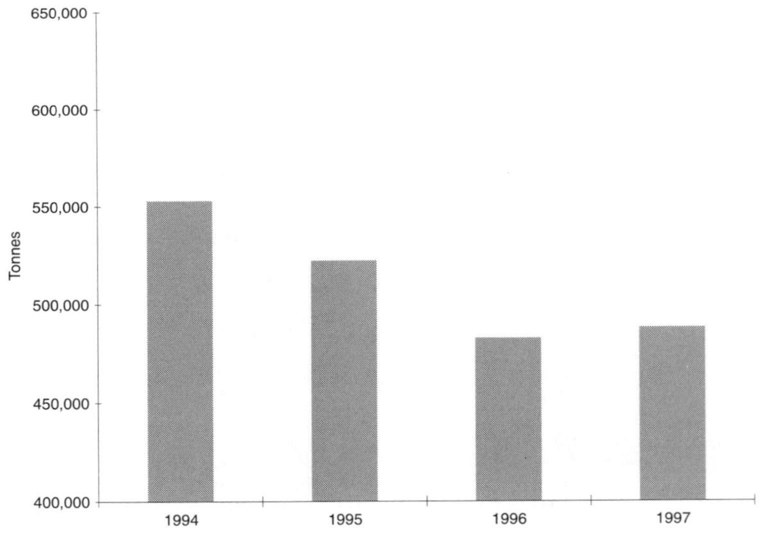

Figure 7: *Red meat volume sales*
Source: AGB

We will now prove the powerful role of advertising in this achievement by considering:

1. The effects of advertising on intermediate data.
2. The effects of advertising on sales.
3. Any other possible factors that could have caused this turnaround.

EFFECT OF ADVERTISING ON INTERMEDIATE DATA 1994 TO 1997

Tracking data and qualitative research show that the new campaign has worked in exactly the way we intended.

ATTITUDES TO ADVERTISING – THE 'RECIPE FOR LOVE' TV ADS

Our new advertising broke into people's consciousness.

TV advertising awareness of red meat (see Figure 8) which had been static for some years at around 20% grew over the period of the new campaign, to over 45% by 1997 (while in real terms advertising spend was constant).[20]

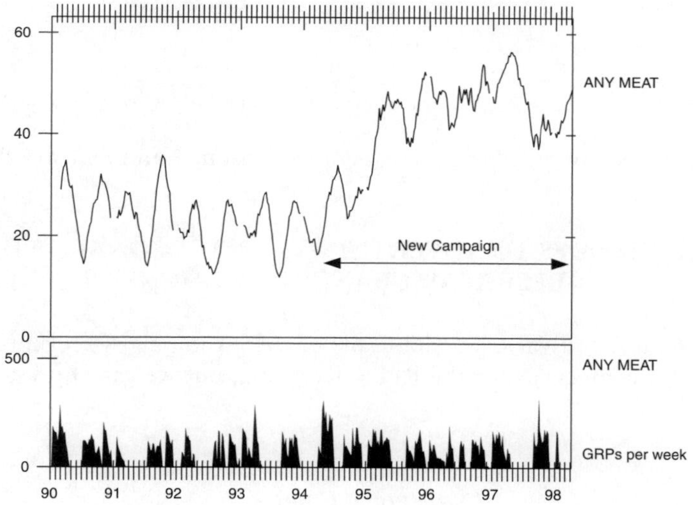

Figure 8: *Claimed TV ad awareness*
Source: Millward Brown

20. This is a result of the advertising budget deriving from a statutory levy on animals which changes only to reflect inflationary changes.
NB. There was a small change in the way this question was asked on the tracking study at the end of January 1995. When asked 'Which of these have you seen advertised on TV recently?' before the change, respondents were shown a list of prompts. After the change, the prompts were read out. However, this effect did not come through well in this data (eight week rolling) until the end of March 1995 and the trend was sharply upwards before this point.

In group discussions,[21] red meat TV advertising is often debated in the 'warm-up' discussion about favourite ads. This popularity is confirmed in tracking data (Table 2).

TABLE 2: PERCENTAGE OF PEAK MEASURES VS. BEST FROM PRECEDING CAMPAIGNS

	New meat ads	Old meat ads
Any positive	95	68
Enjoyed watching it	55	28
Liked the people in it	48	17
Sticks in the mind	51	29

Source: Millward Brown

Qualitatively, the ads are extremely well received and are seen to talk about red meat as planned.

'They're very true to life – life's like that.'

'Some of the best ads on TV.'

'I know it sounds silly but for love is right. That's a meal my gran always used to make for me. She knew it was my special dinner.'

'She shows her appreciation and love for her son by cooking him a proper meal. She loves him enough to take the time.'

'You think – mmm – haven't had a steak for ages.'

Sources: BMP Qual and Ockwell Associates 1994 to 1997

Finally, the ads have generated considerable consumer and industry PR.[22]

ATTITUDES TO ADVERTISING – NUTRITIONAL AND BEEF REASSURANCE CAMPAIGNS

The diverse nature and varied media usage of these campaigns prevents as detailed an analysis of the effects as for the RFL advertising, but we can show the following results:

Nutritional Campaign

The nutritional advertising campaign was challenging people's preconceptions about the healthiness of red meat as planned (Table 3).

21. For food and non-food sectors
22. Most recently for 'Anniversary', an *Evening Standard* article, a feature on London Tonight and The Richard and Judy show. ' House Husband' recently appeared in *Campaign* magazine's People's Jury as a favourite ad. The ads have also received considerable industry recognition – four British TV Advertising Awards in 1998 and four ads have been chosen as *Campaign* magazine's Pick of the Week.

TABLE 3: PROMPTED IMPRESSIONS OF NUTRITIONAL ADS 1995 TO 1996

I found them convincing	59%
The information was relevant to me	53%
They made red meat more appealing	46%

Base: Those aware of nutritional ads 1995–1996
Source: Millward Brown

'Well, to think that all these years on a diet I've been eating cottage cheese and I could have been tucking into pork.'

Source: BMP Qual 1995

Beef Reassurance Campaign

Our target, the 'worried' former beef eaters, reacted in the way intended to our advertising.

'Well, that makes me feel a lot better.'

'It's saying that you can feel reassured.'

Source: Ockwell Associates 1996

So people's attitudes to our advertising were as we had hoped they might be.

ATTITUDES TO RED MEAT

Image of Red Meat

Red meat's image on a number of 'nutritional' dimensions has shown a marked improvement (both absolutely, and relatively to chicken and fish) over the years since the start of the new campaign.[23]

The RFL and nutritional ads appear to have played interesting roles in this turnaround, ie, – the RFL ads, which began in 1994, seem to have helped to get people emotionally on the side of red meat, (so negative feelings about red meat started to decline in 1994)[24] (Figures 9 and 10).

23. Although it was the nutritional campaign which was specifically designed to address people's health concerns about red meat, qualitatively we have evidence that many of the RFL ads communicate that 'red meat is good for you' too.
For example, 'Awkward Age' (schoolboy coming home after disastrous day) 'She's giving him a good meal to build him up after that day.'
For example, 'Anniversary' (old couple celebrating their silver wedding anniversary with a steak) 'They've lived a long happy and healthy life eating their beef.'
24. NB. Gap in data in image charts in 1997 due to temporary replacing nutritional questions with BSE -related questions.

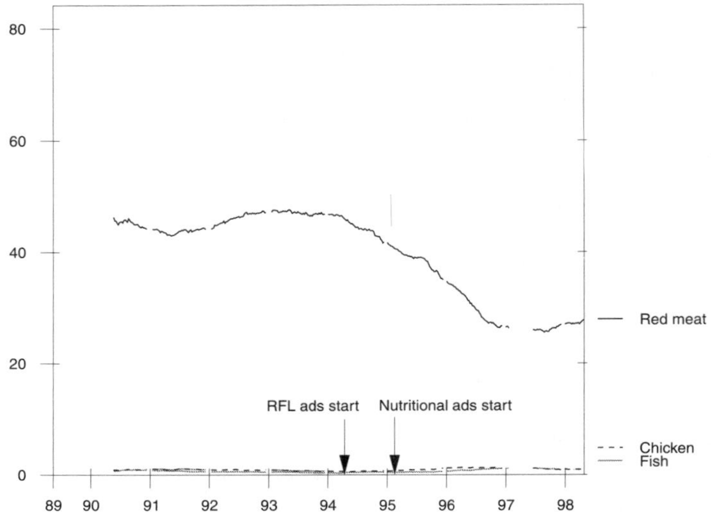

Figure 9: *Percentage agreeing – Not very good for you*
Source: Millward Brown

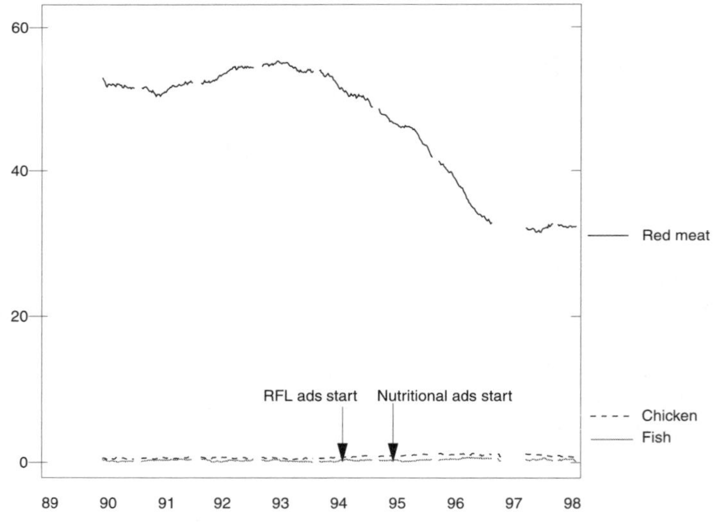

Figure 10: *Percentage agreeing – Can cause high blood pressure*
Source: Millward Brown

Once negative feelings about red meat had started to decline, the nutritional ads beginning in 1995, began to move people's *positive* beliefs (Figures 11 and 12).

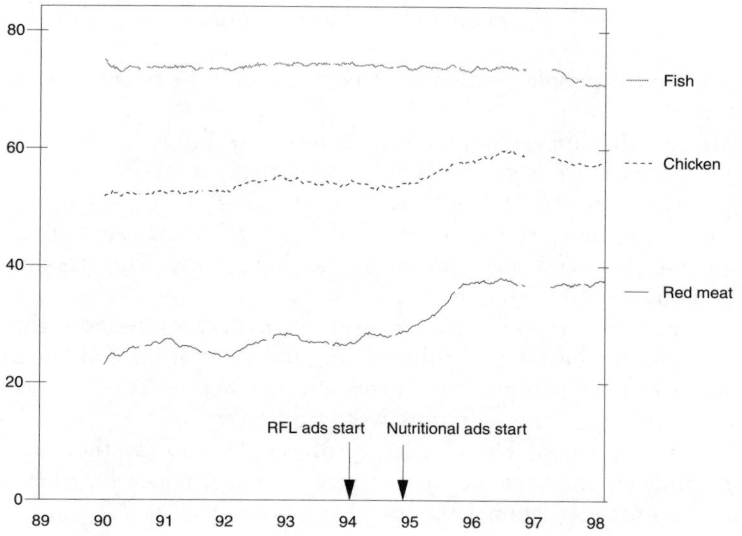

Figure 11: *Percentage agreeing – Important in healthy/balanced diet*
Source: Millward Brown

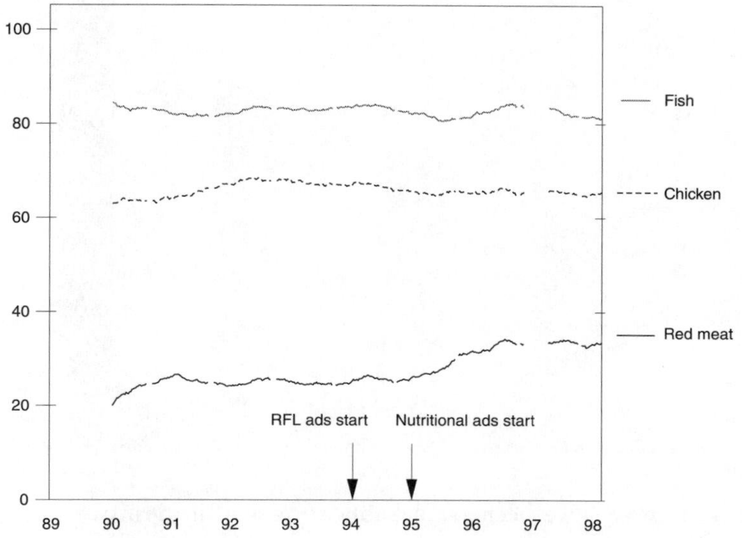

Figure 12: *Percentage agreeing – Good for you*
Source: Millward Brown

Image of Red Meat Eating

As we had planned, people seemed increasingly happy to be and to be seen to be red meat eaters!

Qualitatively, the image of red meat eaters was far more positive. The 'Les Dawson' image was waning and people increasingly described typical red meat eaters as 'people like them' or people like Gary Lineker!

This type of user imagery is difficult to measure *quantitatively* but we believe we can demonstrate this via a question on the tracking study. This asks people 'How often are you buying red meat compared to a year ago?'.

Now we know this is not a true measure of *behaviour* because this started to increase in 1994, but sales were still declining until 1996. Instead we would argue that any increases in this measure indicates improvement in people's *perceptions* of what red meat eating says about themselves.

And this has happened. The percentage of people who say they are buying red meat 'more often or the same compared to a year ago' since the start of the new campaign has *increased* (Figure 13).

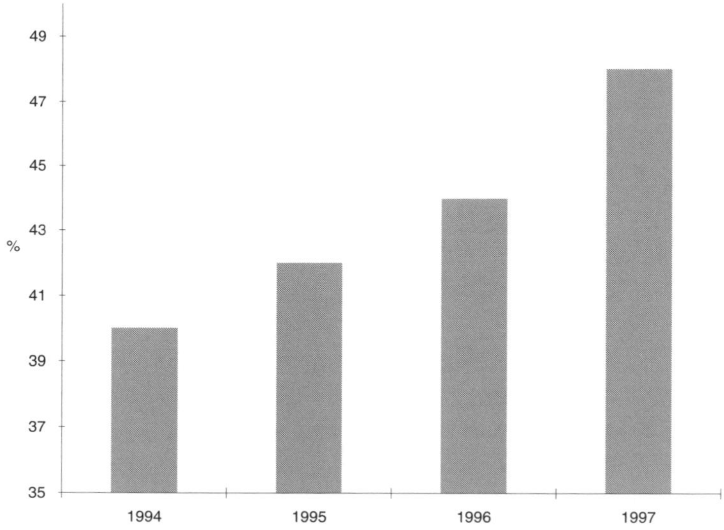

Figure 13: *Percentage claiming to be buying red meat more often or the same compared to a year ago*
Source: Millward Brown

The ads seem to have been remarkably successful in terms of their attitudinal effects.

We now go on to prove that these were translated into *sales* effects.

EFFECTS OF ADVERTISING ON SALES 1994 TO 1997

Before evaluating the effects of advertising on *total* red meat sales as planned, we first address beef separately.

The Effects of Beef Reassurance Advertising on Beef Sales 1994 to 1997

It would be ludicrous to have expected beef sales to have done fantastically well during the period in question. Beef sales were hammered by the publicity surrounding BSE in the immediate aftermath of the 1996 crisis.

Nevertheless we will argue that given the sheer *quantity* of bad publicity,[25]

— Beef sales following the 1996 BSE crisis did better than might have been expected;

— Beef Reassurance advertising played a crucial role in holding up this beef volume.

Beef sales did better than might be expected

To demonstrate this, we compare beef sales after the second BSE scare in 1996 (following which we started Beef Reassurance advertising) with sales after the first BSE scare in 1990 when there was no change to ongoing advertising.

This shows that contrary to expectations, the fall in beef sales during the second and most newsworthy BSE crisis was smaller than that during the first BSE crisis – despite higher levels of bad publicity (Figure 14).

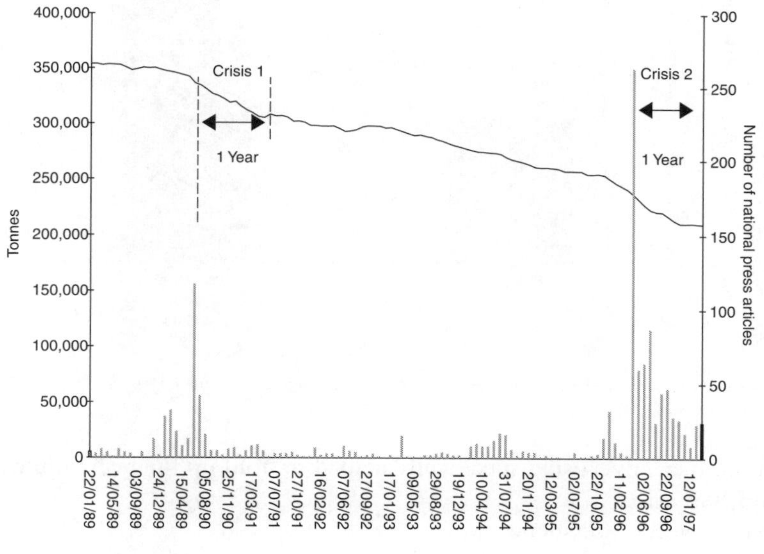

Figure 14: *BSE press mentions vs. beef volume MAT*
Source: AGB, MLC, MMD

25. Of course this publicity was far more alarming in 1996 (when the probable link between BSE and CJD was publicly announced) compared with the scare in 1990 which was essentially a more theoretical debate (and rigorously denied by all official bodies) about whether diseases like BSE could potentially jump species.

	BSE crisis 1	BSE crisis 2
Beef volume lost in year post crisis (Start of crisis defined from the week when the major outbreak of publicity occurred)	37,089 tonnes	30,868 tonnes
Number of national press articles in year post crisis	229	715
Beef volume decline per national press article	162 tonnes	43 tonnes

We also know from a special AGB panel analysis, 'pre' and 'post' the second BSE crisis, that by April 1997, 6% of former beef buyers were still not buying beef. But our target for the Beef Reassurance advertising ('the worriers') were buying *more* beef than they had before the second BSE scare (Figure 15).[26]

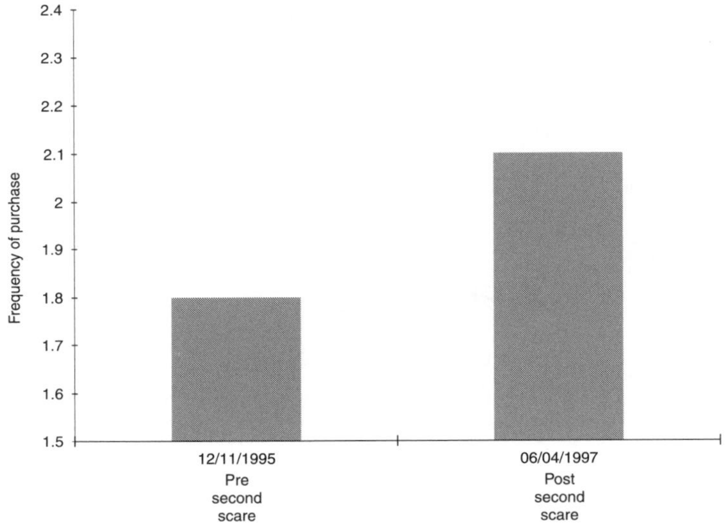

Figure 15: *Frequency of beef purchase of 'worriers' – four weeks ending 12 November 1995 vs. April 1997*
Source: AGB Special Analysis

Beef Reassurance advertising specifically helped to hold up the beef volume during the second BSE crisis

We have two pieces of evidence.

— Regional analysis[27] 1996/1997 (Figure 16).

26. NB Obviously, higher income and lower beef prices helped sales in the second BSE crisis but the beef econometric model and regional analysis (see next section) negates these effects.
    There is a seasonal difference between November and April red meat sales, but as November sales are higher, ie, without seasonality effects, this difference would be even more pronounced.
27. There was no planned regional 'test'. All regions received Beef Reassurance advertising but, due to media buying share deal arrangements, some regions received more advertising than others.

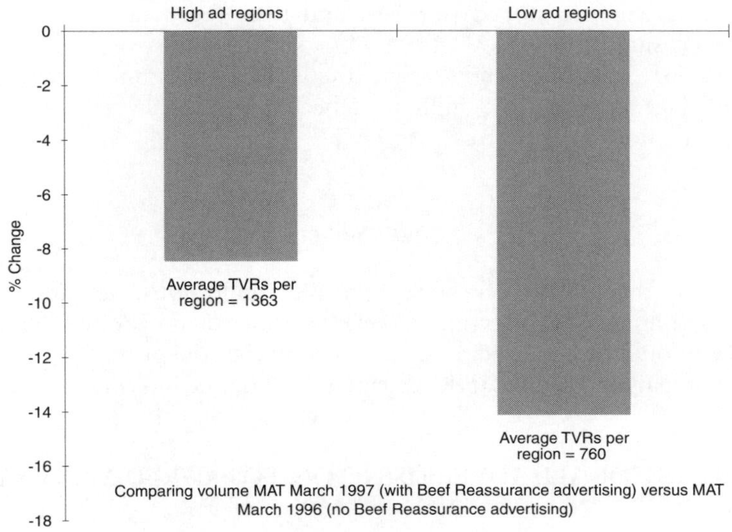

Figure 16: *Decline in annual beef volume during BSE crisis of 1996*
Source: AGB

A regional comparison of beef sales over the period of the second BSE crisis shows that regions with higher levels of Beef Reassurance TV advertising showed *lower* beef volume declines than did regions with less TV advertising.[28]

— A beef econometric model (Figure 17).

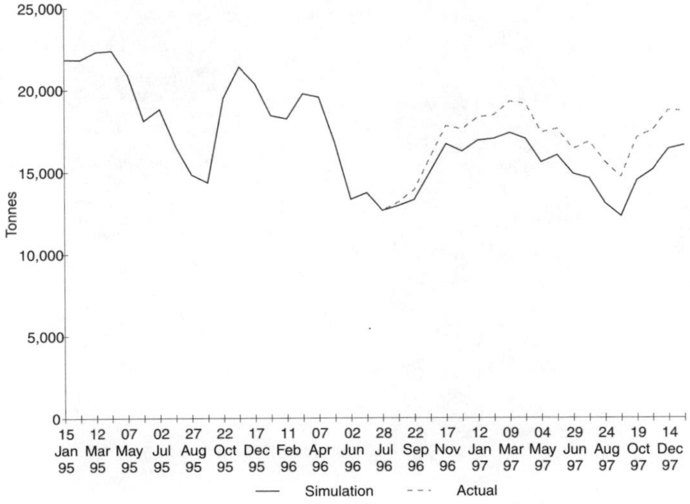

Figure 17: *Beef volume sales – actual vs. simulation: effect of Beef Reassurance advertising in 1996/1997*
Source: AGB, BMP, Model

28. TV advertising accounted for over 60% of the spend on the Beef Reassurance campaign.

Two models were developed (for beef and total red meat) to investigate the effects of advertising.

Modelling of beef sales shows that the Beef Reassurance advertising was responsible for generating £138 million of beef sales over 1996 and 1997 which would otherwise not have occurred.

Summary

There is no way that a scare on the scale of BSE could *not* have had a significant effect on beef volume. In this section however we have demonstrated that this effect was less than would be expected, and have proved the role of the Beef Reassurance advertising campaign in significantly lessening this volume impact.

THE EFFECT OF ALL ADVERTISING ON TOTAL RED MEAT SALES 1994 TO 1997

Now that we have looked at beef, we turn to total red meat sales.

As we have seen, the rate of decline in red meat consumption slowed as planned and was eventually reversed over the period under discussion. We have two pieces of evidence for the contribution of advertising to this:

1. Regions with higher levels of all advertising for red meat performed better than regions with lower levels of advertising over 1994 to 1997 (Figure 18).[29]

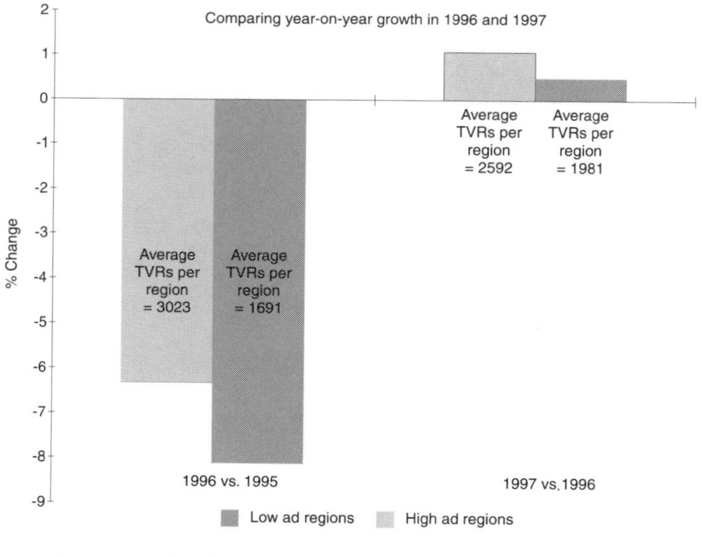

Figure 18: *Red meat volume – regional evidence*

29. Unfortunately we only have regional data for three years.

2. The econometric model of total red meat sales proves the direct effect of advertising (Figure 19).

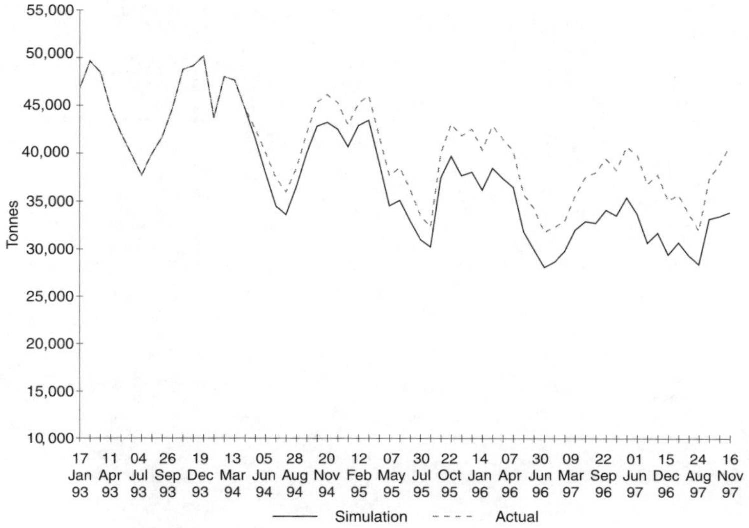

Figure 19: *Red meat volume sales – actual vs. simultation – effect of all MLC advertising*

The model shows that £739 million of red meat sales can be directly attributed to the new campaign over 1994 and 1997.

ELIMINATING OTHER POSSIBLE CONTRIBUTORS TO THIS TURNAROUND SINCE 1994

Red Meat Price Relative to Poultry

This is accounted for in the models but it is also worth noting that red meat prices *grew* relative to poultry over the advertised period 1994 to 1997 (Figure 20).

'Competitor' Advertising

Advertising spend on red meats' main 'competitors' has grown over this period, not declined (Figure 21).

New Zealand Lamb Advertising (NZL)

There has been no increase in the level and no change in the nature of NZL advertising over this period which could explain the effects seen (Figure 22).[30]

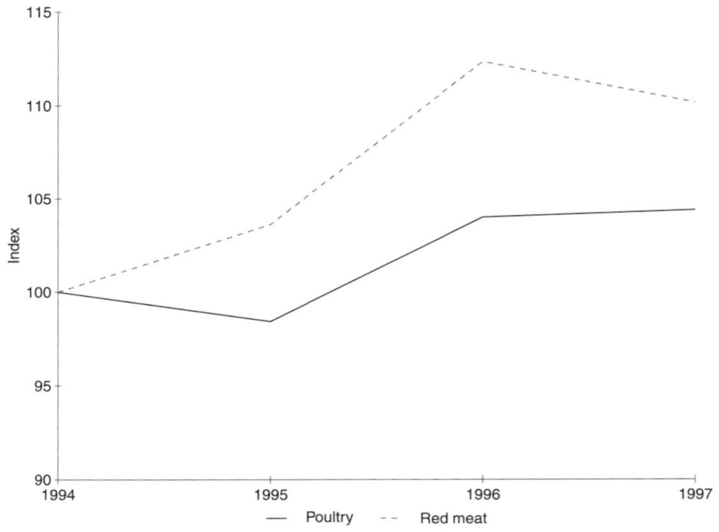

Figure 20: *Red meat and poultry prices – indexed*
Source: MLC, ONS

Expenditure on Promotions by the MLC

In addition to advertising, the MLC ran a promotions programme[31] over 1994 and 1997 – where possible themed and timed around the new campaign. However,

— There has been no change in real terms in the promotional spend over the past ten years.

— Very little change is attributed to promotional activity in the red meat model. What is more, any change that there has been in promotional effect over 1994 to 1997 is really a result of the new campaign, because promotions were themed around the new campaign from 1994.

Demographic Changes

There were no demographic changes over the period 1994 to 1997 which could explain the sales patterns seen.

30. On average over the period between 1994 and 1997, NZL adspend has been less than 6% of the total red meat adspend. In addition, advertising recall of New Zealand Lamb advertising was consistently low at around 5% (Millward Brown 1997).
31. Including trade advertising, recipe cards, on-pack promotional tie-ins with products like sauces and so on.

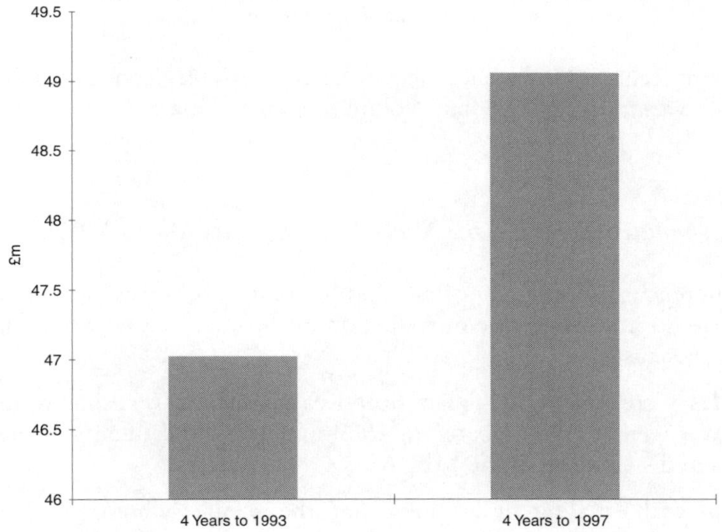

Figure 21: '*Competitor advertising*' – *average adspend per year*
Source: MEAL

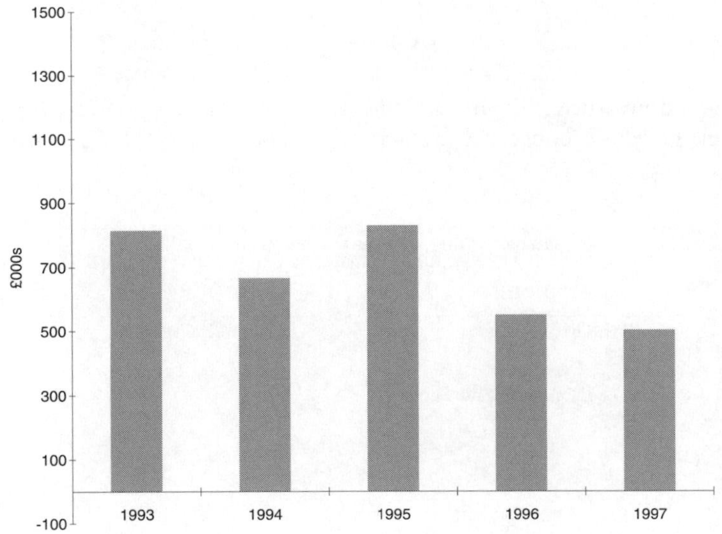

Figure 22: *New Zealand Lamb real adspend (1993 base)*
Source: MEAL

Regional Differences

There were no regional differences in any of the variables considered which could explain the variation in regional volumes seen – apart from regional media weight.[32]

The Introduction of the Minced Beef Quality Mark (MBQM)

A key difference between the first and second BSE crisis was the MBQM. However, we do not believe the introduction of this mark alone would have caused effects seen, because:

— Beef sales were higher in higher Beef Reassurance advertising weight regions than lower weight regions between 1994 and 1997 and there was no difference in regional distribution of the MBQM.

— This fits with qualitative findings that the people whom the MBQM was addressing (those who had temporarily given up beef or at least given up beef mince) were simply not going to the beef section of the meat counter – so they would not have found the new mark on-pack for themselves.

BSE 'Fatigue'

Beef volume did not suffer less in the 1996 crisis because people were less concerned by BSE then. Levels of concern were actually *higher* in 1996 (152%) than in 1990 (100%).[33]

Percentage saying 'very/quite concerned by BSE' Indexed on 1990	
1990	1996
(BSE Crisis 1)	(BSE Crisis 2)
100	152

Source: The National Health Survey

32. In fact, the regions making up the high and low advertised regions changed in each of the three years studied so it is even less likely that anything other than the advertising weight differences could explain the regional volume variations seen.
33. Indexed on 1990. As described, the 1990 scare was purely speculation about BSE type diseases crossing species barriers – the 1996 scare was completely different – caused by a government announcement confirming the probable link between BSE and CJD in humans.

PAYBACK

Extra Sales due to Advertising

The scale of return and the financial consequences of the turnaround in red meat sales were dramatic.

> 'The returns for red meat advertising are much higher than the returns typically found for commodity products of this type (indeed it would be high even for a branded product).'
>
> Source: MMD[34]

The model below shows that the total media spend of £36.2 million spent on red meat advertising between 1994 and 1997 resulted in additional red meat sales of £739 million at retail value, ie, a return of nearly 18:1. This compares with average figures of other generic advertising as follows:

Red meat	18:1
Milk	3.5 – 6.5
Cheese	2:1
Butter	4:1

Source: MMD

Profitability of the Extra Sales to Farmers 1994 to 1997

Farmers' profit margins have varied both by year and by species over the period 1994 to 1997.

To give some indication of advertising payback we therefore use the average gross margin (across the four years and three species). This is 59%.[35]

The extra £621 million retail value of British-produced red meat due to advertising (which includes income for the whole production chain) resulted in an additional revenue to farmers[36] of £155 million. Using the average gross margin of 59%, this resulted in an additional £91 million gross margin to farmers (£51 million after subtracting advertising media and production expenditure).

However, the longer-term profit implications of both the attitudinal improvements regarding red meat, and the damage limitation to beef sales brought about by advertising, are difficult to quantify but will be far, far greater.

---

34. MMD is a company with wide experience of econometric modelling of a range of generic campaigns.
35. Gross margin = farmers' revenue minus variable costs (veterinary/medical costs plus feed and forage costs).
36. Who funded the advertising with their levy payments.

Effects of the 1994 to 1997 Advertising on Other Stakeholders

We have analysed the benefits and profitability of advertising-generated sales for farmers. However, the red meat industry in total is a huge one. Apart from the farmers, there are large numbers of other stakeholders in the carcass red meat market – a chain from auction markets (240 markets) to abattoirs (15,000 employees) to meat processors (60,000 employees) to butchers (50,000) and multiple retailers.[37] All these businesses' fortunes are harnessed to the fortunes or otherwise of red meat retail sales.

All have faced the potentially crippling effects of BSE over the past two years. And all have benefited from the advocacy of the MLC's advertising – a lone voice of support, helping (on a very modest budget) to counter-balance the deluge of hysterical BSE-related media coverage on top of the ongoing long-term problems facing red meat. The following quotes illustrate these stakeholder's views regarding advertising's benefit to them.

> 'In very difficult times, the MLC's campaign provided a reassuring platform on which we can rebuild the market.'
>
> 'For a market to be hit by the scares we have, without the advertising over the past 4 years – well the effect would have been catastrophic.'
>
> 'When you're down you've got to fight back and nothing else was doing this on our behalf.'
>
> Meat Processor 1998

> 'What the MLC have done is excellent – without the advertising over the past 4 years the effects would have been catastrophic for butchers.'
>
> Family Butcher 1998

> 'The Beef Reassurance campaign dramatically improved sales and limited damage to red meat.'
>
> 'Supermarket displays are demand-led. Without the advertising, meat space in supermarkets would be much lower than now.'
>
> Multiple Retailer Meat Buyer 1998

Profitability of the Extra Sales 1994 to 1997 to These Other 'Stakeholders'

It is difficult to calculate precisely the financial contribution to the various elements of the chain but they would all benefit from £584 million of extra sales between 1994 and 1997 (£739 million advertising-generated extra retail sales minus £155 million extra farmer revenue).

Even at 10% gross margin (one-fifth of the level of the farmers' gross margin) this would result in an additional £58 million gross profit along the chain. In reality, the profit would probably well exceed this. And of course, beyond the retail

37. MLC 1998.

sales benefits of carcass red meat, there are knock-on profit benefits for other retail markets (ready meals, burgers and so on) as well as other sectors (catering, fast food) from the advertising effects shown.

CONCLUSIONS

Advertising succeeded in transforming attitudes to red meat. This in turn has resulted in a very profitable boost to sales over the four years studied. This increase in sales was beneficial not only to the farmers who directly funded the advertising that caused it but also to other numerous stakeholders in this vast food market. In addition, the effects of the advertising will deliver significant benefits to the industry into the future. We believe that three key conclusions which emerge from this case history are worth reiterating for advertisers contemplating the consequences of advertising investment in other markets.

1. Well-conceived and executed advertising can have tremendously powerful effects even at relatively low levels of expenditure (£8 million p.a. versus £2 billion p.a. market). Advertising can indeed move the seemingly immovable, such as huge long-term structural forces with an unprecedented short-term crisis on top.
2. Truly significant returns from advertising are often the result of 'thinking outside the box' – in this case by looking beyond competitive 'brand' activity (pork vs. beef vs. lamb) and focusing on the total category and its generic, yet powerful, benefits.
3. Effective advertising can not only directly generate large returns for those immediately involved in its funding, but can, and often does, have very significant effects on other stakeholders. These in turn can go on to generate additional benefits for the advertising funders. In this example, increases in profit all along the chain of stakeholders have improved the health and long-term viability of the whole industry, which must in turn protect farmers' long-term prospects.

Index